MIDDLEMEN OF MODERNITY

A Study of the Weatherhead East Asian Institute

MIDDLEMEN OF MODERNITY

Local Elites and Agricultural Development in Modern Japan

CHRISTOPHER CRAIG

University of Hawaiʻi Press
HONOLULU

Paperback edition 2022

Printed in the United States of America

Library of Congress Cataloging-in-Publication Data

Names: Craig, Christopher (College teacher), author.
Title: Middlemen of modernity : local elites and agricultural development in modern Japan / Christopher Craig.
Other titles: Studies of the Weatherhead East Asian Institute, Columbia University.
Description: Honolulu : University of Hawaiʻi Press, 2021. | Series: Studies of the Weatherhead East Asian Institute, Columbia University | Includes bibliographical references and index.
Identifiers: LCCN 2020055798 | ISBN 9780824886257 (hardcover) | ISBN 9780824889272 (adobe pdf) | ISBN 9780824889289 (epub) | ISBN 9780824889296 (kindle edition)
Subjects: LCSH: Agriculture and state—Japan—Miyagi-ken—History. | Rice farming—Japan—Miyagi-ken—History. | Elite (Social sciences)—Japan—Miyagi-ken—History. | Agricultural innovations—Japan—Miyagi-ken—History. | Miyagi-ken (Japan)—Economic conditions.
Classification: LCC HD2092 .C73 2021 | DDC 338.10952/115—dc23
LC record available at https://lccn.loc.gov/2020055798

ISBN: 9780824889395 (paperback)

Studies of the Weatherhead East Asian Institute, Columbia University

The Studies of the Weatherhead East Asian Institute were inaugurated in 1962 to bring to a wider public the results of significant new research on modern and contemporary East Asia.

University of Hawaiʻi Press books are printed on acid-free paper and meet the guidelines for permanence and durability of the Council on Library Resources.

Cover photo: Kamata Sannosuke traveling on foot to a speaking engagement in Hiroshima. Courtesy of Kamata Sannosuke Tenjishitu, Kamata Kinen Hōru, Ōsakishi Kyōiku Iinkai Kashimadai Shisho.

For Noriko and Cuchulainn

Contents

Acknowledgments

This work has been made possible by the generous help and support of the many scholars, teachers, classmates, organizations, and friends who have aided me in the fifteen years since I began work on the project. While any errors that may be found within are solely mine, very little else of what follows would exist if not for these people.

My interest in modern Japanese farming villages and rural society dates back to my years at the University of British Columbia, where William Wray encouraged my interest in local elites and supervised both my basic education in Japanese history and my earliest work on the subject in my master's thesis. I owe an enormous debt of gratitude also to many at UBC for the support I enjoyed during my four years at the school. In particular, I extend my thanks to Tim Brook, Nam-lin Hur, and Steven Lee, all of whom offered their support in improving and refining my early scholarly efforts.

The book took on much of its present form during my doctoral studies at Columbia University, and I benefited immensely from the support of faculty, staff, and students. I owe thanks first and foremost to Carol Gluck, who nurtured the project in its infancy and supervised my work at every stage of its development. Gregory Pflugfelder, David Lurie, and Eugenia Lean all provided formative advice in the early stages of planning my research. Kim Brandt, Elizabeth Blackmar, and Daniel Botsman all took active roles in shepherding my dissertation toward completion, and each of them improved the work with the insight they offered.

During my research in Sendai, Japan from 2009 to 2011, I was fortunate enough to receive assistance from an extraordinary collection of scholars and students. Okamoto Kōichi got me off to a running start by connecting me with historians and students in Japan who provided invaluable help in my early efforts to negotiate archival collections in Japan and become familiar with Japanese academia. In Sendai, Adachi Hiroaki invited me to become an unofficial participant in his modern Japan seminar at Tōhoku University, beginning a pattern of warmth and unrestricted support that continues to the present day. Teshima Yasunobu gave unsparingly of his time, introducing me to a wide range of local resources and helping me muddle through linguistic difficulties. Finally, I owe special thanks to Abiko Rin, whose enormous generosity with his encyclopedic knowledge, his decades of experience, and his friendship were pivotal in the progress of my research.

This work also owes its existence to the numerous organizations that have provided funding for my research. The graduate scholarship of the Social Science and Humanities Research Council enabled me to complete my master's degree in Vancouver. In New York, the Weatherhead Institute and the Donald Keene Center of Japanese Culture provided specialized training and travel grants for preliminary research. Language training was furnished by the Japan Foundation at the Japanese-Language Institute, Kansai. Funding for the two years of research upon which this book is built was provided by means of the Japan Foundation's Japan Studies Fellowship and the Shinchōsha Graduate Fellowship for Study in Japan. To all of these groups I offer my most sincere thanks.

The Association for Asian Studies, the Weatherhead Initiative on Global History at Harvard, the World History Association, the Hasekura League, the Centre for Japanese Research at the University of British Columbia, and Hallym University all provided venues for me to present my research at various stages of its completion and gave me access to invaluable comments and advice from top scholars.

This work has been made possible by the generous assistance of the staffs at a number of remarkable archives, libraries, and collections. The librarians at the Asian Library at the University of British Columbia and the Starr Library at Columbia University provided crucial aid during the earliest phases of my research. In Japan, I depended heavily upon the help I received from the employees at the Tōhoku University Library, the National Diet Library, the Miyagi Prefectural Library, the Fukushima Prefectural Library, and the National Archives. I owe special thanks to the wonderfully helpful and exceptionally generous staff at the Miyagi Prefectural Archives, who not only tolerated my weeklong occupations of their reading area, but also introduced me to source materials I would never have found on my own.

In the later stages of the work, the current study was much improved by close readings by Steven J. Ericson and Ann Waswo. Their kindness helped dispel the despair that had set in at the eleventh hour and their advice made this a much better book. Both Ross Yelsey at Columbia University's Weatherhead East Asian Institute and Masako Ikeda of the University of Hawai'i Press gave unsparingly of their time and expertise in helping to usher the manuscript to publication. Marina Nascimento contributed her formidable skills at the last moment to help make my maps suitable for publication.

I am also thankful for the classmates around the world with whom I have worked over the years. In Vancouver, New York, and Sendai I benefited immensely from my associations with Jeffrey Alexander, Oleg Benesch, Adam Bronson, Sayaka Chatani, Desmond Cheung, Chad Diehl, Clay Eaton, Arunabh Ghosh, Anne Giblin, Eric Han, Reto Hofmann, Colin Jaundrill, Abhishek Kaicker, Katō Satoshi, Tomoko Kitagawa, David Luesink, Weiwei Luo, Chelsea Szendi Schieder, Tim Sedo, Malcom Thompson, Tim Yang, and Jason Young.

Finally, for this and all things, I would like to thank Noriko Sugino for her infinite patience and invaluable support during the years of classes, research, and writing, and Cuchulainn Craig for coming along at just the right time.

Introduction

Agriculture is given short shrift in the story of Japanese modernity. Farming and modernization seem to exist at opposite ends of a spectrum. Factories, rifles, banks, ships—all connected with mechanization, centralized power, and urban environments—stand as the symbols of modernity, while agriculture, associated with human labor, traditional social relations, pre-capitalist economies, and underdeveloped rural land, represents the despised antithesis of the modern. The countryside of the historical imagination tends to exist only as the last refuge of superstitious, irrational premodernity, each farming village a citadel against the inexorable press of reason and progress.[1]

There are, of course, large and obvious problems with this formulation. The new political, economic, and ideological realities that signal the coming of modernity did nothing to free human populations from the need for food. Worse, the industrialization of the workforce and the concentration of populations in urban centers more often increased the need for agricultural production. To meet these needs, new pressures were placed on farmers, who received scorn, rather than support to help them navigate the stormy waters of the new age.

No area in Japan evokes more clearly this image of anti-modern agriculture than the prefecture of Miyagi and the larger Tōhoku region of which it is a part. Widely known for its "backwardness" (sympathetically by later scholars, less so by contemporary bureaucrats and ideologues) during the period of Japan's modernization, the prefecture is emblematic of regions whose underdeveloped economies, supposed hierarchical social structures, and dependence on agriculture marked

Tōhoku

them as anathema to central government planners and scholars of Japan's modernization alike.[2] It was a problem region, dotted with "distressed villages" (*nanson*), the stubbornness, stupidity, and laziness of whose residents combined with their dependence upon agriculture to prevent them from accepting the largesse of modernity.

Yet my own experiences in Miyagi stand at odds with these ideas of backwardness. Farming shaped my initial impressions in the prefecture. I first lived in Miyagi from late 1997 to early 1999, when I worked in Sendai as an English teacher. I arrived in the port city of Ishinomaki by overnight bus from Narita airport, after which I was taken south to Sendai by car through the rich agricultural lands of the Senboku (north of Sendai) region. Recently harvested rice patties stretched out from both sides of the road, bracketed in the rear by mountains that appeared to be draped in green velvet. The bounty of the harvest was attested to both by the breadth of the denuded swaths and the prodigious size of the farmhouses. My conversations with local residents over the next year reinforced this initial impression. Coworkers, friends, and host family members alike

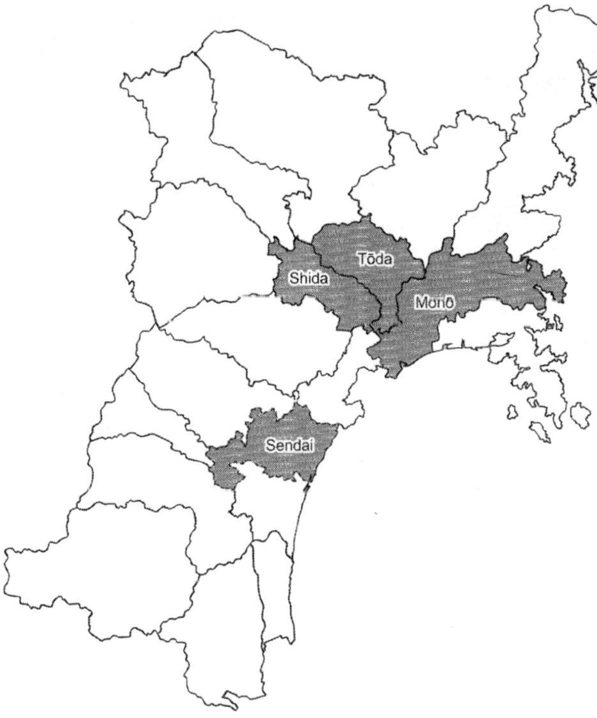

Senboku

described Miyagi as a rice prefecture, more often than not while apologizing for its cultural failings in comparison to Tokyo and other metropoles. Even among the expressions of hinterland shame, agriculture's success in Miyagi could not be suppressed.

While residents of two decades ago thought of Miyagi in terms of marginality and agriculture, today the prefecture is remembered more widely for two things. The first is the illustrious history of the region during the early modern period and its celebration in popular culture. The Date lords of Sendai, particularly the late-sixteenth-century patriarch Masamune, have enjoyed historical prominence for the house's importance and vigor, and rose to new fame in 1987 with a popular television drama series starring a young Watanabe Ken. Masamune has since been enshrined in video games, comic books, television cartoons, and products ranging from vending machine figurines to ornamental helmets used as decorations for Children's Day.

The Great Tōhoku Earthquake and Tsunami of 2011 is the second point of reference for Miyagi. With the event's seismic epicenter in the waters off the coast of the prefecture and the position of Ishinomaki (home to the prefecture's second largest urban population) as the site of the greatest damage in terms of human life and financial cost, the disaster has been linked to the prefecture since its occurrence. The attention the earthquake and tsunami attracted worldwide has helped to cement its association with Miyagi. When I traveled from Sendai to Honolulu in April of 2011, the staff at my hotel greeted me with expressions of sympathy and inquiries about the current state of the region. This outside attention has had a complementary effect within Japan, where Miyagi is now known for being linked internationally with the disaster.[3]

These two claims to fame seem to offer departures from the older image of backwardness and peripherality, but they in fact act more decisively to firm it up. Both faded feudal glory and natural disaster reinforce the idea of Miyagi as a region characterized by marginality and vulnerability. While the celebration of the Date house appears to point to strength and vitality, it more nearly emphasizes the opposite. Not only did Masamune move into the region after establishing his fortunes elsewhere, but his clan's power is associated with the Edo-era domain of Sendai, while the modern prefecture was built upon the ruins of his ancestors' disastrous alliance with the losing side in the Meiji Revolution. Miyagi's early modern history serves to highlight the distinction between a vibrant past as a regional power and a debased modernity as a marginal and defeated prefecture.

Contemporary weakness is also the theme of the earthquake and tsunami. The devastated coastal communities testify to the region's continuing vulnerability to natural forces and the outflow of former residents to larger urban centers raises questions about the viability of established settlements. At the same time, the resultant nuclear disaster in Fukushima and concerns about reactors in Miyagi point to the marginality of the region and the threats arising from that status. The flip side of Miyagi's celebrated feudal past and the admiration for its efforts to recover from disaster are its modern failures, helplessness, and second-class status.

More than just conflicting with my initial impressions of the region, these negative appraisals of Miyagi contain internal contradictions that raise questions about its past. Sendai urbanites of the 1990s may have been embarrassed about the prefecture's connections to rice farming, but these feelings of shame did nothing to mitigate the obvious agricultural prosperity that lay behind this image. How did Miyagi, emerging from the catastrophic failure of the Sendai domain, come to host such a productive and prosperous agricultural sector? The poverty and backwardness of Miyagi are persistent themes in historical works and popular memory, but how did many of the largest landlords in prewar Japan emerge in the prefecture under these circumstances? Natural disasters highlight well-known vulnerabilities in the region, but what enabled Miyagi to become a leader in producing rice, a crop known for its sensitivity to climate and other environmental factors? Clearly, there is a story of farming success central to the modern experience of Miyagi that needs to be told.

To find the answers to these questions, it is necessary to look past the usual suspects. The activity of the Meiji government in promoting the modernization of industry, the military, and society is well known, even if its efficacy is still subject to debate. Government leaders applied generous quantities of money and effort to promote the building of factories, banks, and transportation infrastructure in the quest to construct a nation strong enough to meet the European powers on their own terms. But this official push to modernize the country did not extend to farming in the same ways. While agriculture, as the means to feed the growing population and provide employment to the mostly rural population, was an integral part of the mission for national power, it did not enjoy the same material support from the government as the military and industrial sectors. The bulk of public funds was reserved for these more visible expressions of a modern state, and what little remained was largely dedicated to exhortations, chastisements, and criticism, along with limited and often misguided investigations into new crops and techniques, as the official means for promoting the modernization of agriculture and the increase in farm production.

The story of Meiji agricultural development is instead the story of the interactions, cooperations, competitions, and conflicts between three distinct groups composed of constantly shifting memberships. Looked at hierarchically, the top group existed closest to central authority and was peopled by politicians, bureaucrats, and other governmental functionaries concerned with agriculture, rural communities, and the planning and institution of policies relating to both. At the opposite end of the spectrum were farmers. Embedded in villages across the country, they were defined by their active involvement in agricultural production and the host of concerns and interests that this involvement gave rise to. A vast gulf, both geographic and administrative, separated these two groups, and the effective improvement of agriculture demanded a third type of figure to bridge the distance. The solution to the mystery of what made Miyagi's agricultural development possible lies with this last group, composed of a shifting cast of rural elites identified by the blanket term *chihō meibōka* (local notables).[4] Drawn predominantly from the same large landlords whose preponderance in Miyagi raises doubts about backwardness, *meibōka* played political, economic, and social roles that defined the ways in which local areas weathered the shocks and dislocations of the modern era. They were what I call "the middlemen of modernity," figures who served as the intermediaries between villages and the prefectural and national governments. With officials offering more rhetoric than concrete support, it was these local elites, not the national government, who assumed responsibility for managing change in rural areas. While their roles and their roster changed with the economic and political shifts of the late nineteenth century, *meibōka* set the course of agricultural improvement, determined its character, and linked farming in new ways to the interests of the central government.

Meibōka overlapped and intersected with a spectrum of elite types assigned to certain landowners and locally prominent residents, themselves in states of near-constant flux, in Meiji-era farming villages. Often coined by officials or outside observers and set in stone by scholars working after the fact, the terms describing these types were and are a useful means of highlighting the different activities upon which village elites focused their attention. They could be used to signal notability through farming accomplishments, as in *rōnō* (experienced farmer) whose long years and personal interest in agriculture enabled them to develop new techniques and equipment to increase harvests, moderate environmental threats, and reduce the labor needed to farm, or *gōnō* (wealthy farmer) whose material resources were connected to their success in farming. Other terms for elites highlighted social position and local reputation, most often built upon service to the community (often across generations within a family) and fame within and beyond the borders of the village. *Yūshisha* (willing/active person) denoted individuals who were notable for their activities in service of the community and their involvement in public life, while *meibōka* itself used the ideograms for "name" (or "fame") and "hope" to mark the motives that might propel individuals in this work.

While the broad categories of the three groups can be traced across the late nineteenth and early twentieth centuries, political, economic, and social pressures brought about significant changes in the populations that they denoted. Agricultural bureaucrats experienced a generational change over the Meiji period in which early modernization-minded technocrats connected with the victorious factions in the Meiji Revolution were replaced by younger professional bureaucrats who often found problems with the systems created by their predecessors. Economic dislocations in villages and ongoing challenges presented by climate and market fueled a steady change of status for Miyagi farmers from small landholders, to partial tenants, to full tenants, an especially prominent trend in the rice-producing north of the prefecture. These same economic shocks also brought changes to the roster of *meibōka,* precipitating the downfall of some older elite families while opening the doors to wealth, reputation, and local office to others.

In both Miyagi and the country as a whole, the Meiji period saw the development of *meibōka*-led agricultural development to its highest potential (or, perhaps, its logical conclusion) and its subsequent decline, collapse, and reconfiguration. The story began with independent action on the part of successful farmers and village leaders to improve the lots of village residents, expand agricultural production, and defend local communities in the amorphous rural order of the early period. As these efforts proved their effectiveness and became the basis for widespread networks of farmers, they drew the attention of the central authorities, who had already tied their hopes to various types of village elites as the means to modernize and rationalize agriculture and integrate far-flung farming villages into the national order. In response, government leaders laid down the framework that went on to define the state's approach to farming for the next generation and beyond. Identifying elites as *meibōka,* the philosophy guiding agricultural policy placed them at the heart of a system in which they would provide the information needed by central planners to craft developmental goals and then gather local resources and mobilize farming communities to achieve them.

When government officials identified *meibōka* as the lynchpin in their plans for agricultural development, they had their eyes on elite families long established in farming villages with reputations backed by generations of local leadership and more recent efforts to discover or disseminate new and improved methods of production. In the 1880s, however, economic shockwaves rattled villages everywhere and the foundation upon which this model was built shifted. Many older elite families experienced jarring reversals of fortune and were replaced by a new generation of landlords propelled to the apex of village economic status by their business acumen and ruthlessness. Government conceptions of the *meibōka* to whom they would entrust the development of agriculture were explicit in their reference to economic resources, and newly risen landlords automatically became the object of the designation originally created for those whom they had displaced.

The plans for agricultural development thus came to center on figures very different from those envisioned during their drafting, a situation that gave rise to three distinct phases in the relationships between central authorities, the new landlord *meibōka,* and village populations. In the first, bureaucrats in the capital remained at arm's distance as *meibōka* joined forces with disgruntled former officials in established organizations to press for support for landlord-led development in the form of public funds and legal change, while at the same time beginning tentative moves into local leadership and village administrations. The granting of these demands at the turn of the century marked the beginning of the second phase, providing landlords with increased government funding and mobilizing the power of the state to enforce their version of agricultural development, which placed increased demands on tenants as it reserved profits for landlords. The tensions caused by this order erupted into conflict in Senboku at the end of the decade as tenants rose up in union to successfully challenge the domination of their landlords in the third phase. At the same time, bureaucrats disappointed at the failure of landlord *meibōka* to bring about village prosperity enacted dramatic revisions to agricultural policy, assuming direct governmental control over key aspects of agricultural improvement and seeking out new local leaders to support the work on the ground.

In the years that followed, Senboku landlords abandoned completely the *meibōka* ideal, but the work that had been accomplished under their leadership at the beginning of the century left a longer, and more complicated, legacy. Paired with improvements to waterways and other large terraforming projects made possible by the new active involvement of the central government, *meibōka* efforts to consolidate farmland, reform cultivation techniques, introduce new crops, and promote the expanded use of fertilizer realized their full potential, and rice farming became more stable, productive, and profitable. This success, however, failed to produce the mid-Meiji leaders' visions of stable and prosperous villages. The concentration of land and local offices in the hands of landlords and the forcing of increasing numbers of smallholding farmers into tenancy had been the ends pursued by landlords in their quest for improved agriculture, and these goals were attained earlier and more fully than the improvements themselves. Villages continued to experience enormous and growing disparities in wealth, intra-village conflicts became more common and more desperate, and landlords maintained a monopoly over the profits of agriculture, even going so far as to roll back improvements when it served their interests. This rural order imposed limits on the potentials for both agricultural improvement and a solution to the endemic problem of rural poverty. It would take national mobilization during war and land reform after defeat to open the way to repair the holes left in prewar farming society.

The current study begins in northern Miyagi in the 1880s and continues through the Second World War and its aftermath, but the lion's share of the attention is given to the Meiji period (1868–1912). These were the years in which the most dramatic of the changes to Miyagi's agriculture took place and the period in which individual farmers and local communities wrought lasting transformations on the agricultural landscape. The chapters proceed thematically, often overlapping in time. I begin with a look at the most famous representative of Miyagi's *meibōka,* offering a biography of an individual who gave the appearance of an ideal notable as conceived of by the bureaucrats in charge of local government and agriculture (chapter 1). The story then moves to a dispute between neighboring Senboku communities over riparian improvement in the 1890s that illustrates both the changing character of notables and the problems associated with environment, technology, government policy, and administrative change at the end of the nineteenth century (chapter 2). The third chapter examines the growth of agricultural associations in Japan, following their roots in the experienced farmers of the early Meiji period forward to the consolidation of local associations under an officially recognized central organization peopled with recently risen landlords at the end of the nineteenth century. The press by this new centralized organization for legal and administrative change is the topic of the fourth chapter, which describes the processes that saw the national government pass a series of laws placing official support behind landlords and their visions for agricultural and village improvement. The fifth chapter explores the short-term consequences of this legal change in Miyagi and across the country, as the increased pressure placed on tenant farmers and the failure of landlords to create the orderly and prosperous villages sought by central bureaucrats resulted in a backlash against landlord-*meibōka* that saw Senboku tenants rise up and force the revision of tenancy contracts and the government take control of key aspects of farming improvement. The final chapter explores the legacy of *meibōka*-led development and the subsequent stewardship of farming improvement by the central government in Miyagi, charting the fortunes of both farmers and notables through the challenging decades of economic recession, advancing militarism, and war.

Decades of scholarship have produced a rich and complex picture of the processes of change and their effects on rural Japan in the late nineteenth and early twentieth centuries, but Senboku deepens the picture in four major ways. First, it introduces Miyagi to English language scholarship and integrates both the prefecture and the larger Tōhoku region into the tale of Meiji modernity. Tōhoku has not been wholly absent from the historiography, but it is most commonly presented as a region whose backwardness makes it an exception to social and economic trends elsewhere in the country.[5] Such interest as it has excited tends to arise from times at which this backwardness incited unrest in local populations.[6] The present study offers a different perspective on the north. A focus on agriculture illustrates some of the additional challenges faced by Tōhoku prefectures, but it also shows Miyagi to be bound to the rest of the country in the common quest for greater farm yields, better protection from the vicissitudes of weather and climate, and increased support from central government. More than simply swept along with the "more advanced" areas, Miyagi was a leader in this quest, its residents forming organizations and undertaking initiatives that government authorities held up as models for regions everywhere.

Senboku's second contribution to the understanding of Meiji modernity is to highlight the importance of agriculture to the central modernization project. Concrete images of ships, factories, and railways, together with more abstract institutions related to education, finance, and administration, comprise the common symbols of Japan's modernization. Researchers have explored the contested and contingent nature of these developments to great effect, providing a nuanced view of the plethora of actors in the modernization drama, as well as its context, costs, and consequences. Farming, however, has found little place in the story as it has been told.[7] The study of northern Miyagi offers a corrective. The experience of Senboku farmers demonstrates that agriculture was neither contrary nor ancillary to the larger project of modernization. It was in fact at the very heart of the Meiji government's quest for modernity and was a chief concern for both government leaders and modern-minded ideologues alike. While farming did not enjoy the same degree of generosity from the public purse as the more emblematic aspects of modernization, it nevertheless occupied a position of undeniable importance. Tokyo officials organized agricultural fairs, promoted the formation of regional organizations, established study groups, engaged in agricultural experimentation, and issued forth an unrelenting stream of advice, accolades, and admonitions aimed at farmers across the country. Passionate bureaucrats continued to promote agricultural improvement after their retirement from officialdom, successful farmers were sought out by the government and given positions of significance and responsibility, and central planners obsessed about the dangers of impoverished farming villages. Neither obstacle nor afterthought, agriculture was key to the national pursuit of modernity.

But the central government was not the chief actor in the move toward agricultural modernity. The third way in which this study modifies our understanding of modern Japanese history is by shining a light on the fact that it was local farmers, not official planners or bureaucrats in the capital, who played the largest role in bringing about the Meiji agricultural revolution. Historians have already exploded the myth that the Meiji government was the sole architect of Japan's rapid industrial and economic modernization. Despite the public funds that were committed to the construction of model factories and railways, much of what are seen as key successes in industrialization was accomplished through the activities of private businessmen and industrialists. As with these worthies, rural elites also stood behind the successful modernization of the agricultural sector. In place of the private capitalists who made Japan an industrial powerhouse, it was local landlords who, both individually and collectively, reformed the farming practices, planned and undertook limited terraforming projects, and introduced the new varieties of seed and fertilizer that transformed agriculture. As with their industrial cousins, success did not come from their efforts on the ground alone. Equally important was the work of notables in forging links with figures in the government and directing official attention and public funds to their home regions.

These efforts to push the central government to action hit upon the fourth theme arising from the study of Senboku: the multidirectional initiative that characterized state-society relations during the Meiji period. While the late nineteenth and early twentieth centuries saw a centralization of political authority and the extension of the Japanese state's power deeper into villages and the private lives of citizens, these represented only one aspect of the interaction between the government and the people. Agriculture and the widespread interest in its development during the Meiji period created the context for local farmers to influence, and even shape, policy decisions made in Tokyo. Begrudging acceptance of the success of local farmers in improving production without relying on government-backed Western models, official support for autonomously organized agricultural associations, the recognition and publicizing of the work of "model" village mayors, and the revision of laws in accordance with the demands of landlord organizations all demonstrated the capability of local residents to influence the actions of the national government.

The unraveling of the mystery of backward prosperity in northern Miyagi highlights many of the ambiguities that characterized modernity in the margins. Village social relations derided as "feudal" produced results that were celebrated as models of modernization. Farming at the geographic limits of rice production generated family fortunes to rival the most prosperous industrialists. The tenant farmers of the region, often ridiculed as a modern-day peasantry, joined together in the largest organized movement against landlords in a successful effort that presaged developments in more advanced regions decades later. In these ways and more, Senboku and its notables offer a new perspective on the history of modern Japan.

CHAPTER ONE

Mayor Straw Sandals

Kamata Sannosuke and the Meibōka *Ideal*

One day in 1907, Kamata Sannosuke, a landlord and farmer from northern Miyagi, received a telegram. It was a message forwarded to him by the Japanese diplomatic official in Mexico, where Kamata had been for a year planning the establishment of a Japanese farming colony, and it was as simple as it was urgent. "Trouble with the Shinainuma matter. Awaiting your mediation."[1] The appeal came directly from Kamei Eizaburō, the governor of Kamata's home prefecture. The drainage of Shinainuma, a wetlands area bordering Kamata's village of Kashimadai, had been an obsession of his family for three generations, and Kamata had set out for Mexico only when he was certain that the work had at last progressed to its final phase. Realizing the seriousness of the matter, he dropped what he was doing and headed for the Mexican coast, pausing only to get the envoy's agreement that the official would oversee the colony project in his absence. Arriving at the port to discover that he had missed the last passenger ship to Japan, Kamata boarded a Pacific mail carrier bound for Yokohama and settled in for a voyage made uncomfortable by Spartan conditions, bitter disappointment, and troubling uncertainty.

Three years later, he found himself in somber conversation with his mother in the family home in Kashimadai. Kamata's return accomplished what Governor Kamei hoped for. He smoothed the ruffled feathers of the various parties involved in the drainage of Shinainuma, restored local faith in the work and its goals, and set the project back on the path to completion. Convinced his work was finally finished, Kamata prepared to return to Mexico to complete the arrangements for the farming colony. Local matters, however, complicated these plans. The village council of

Kashimadai had met and unanimously chosen Kamata to fill the recently vacated post of mayor, displaying an almost unthinkable degree of accord for a group that had experienced a decade of acrimonious and seemingly intractable hostility. Kamata stood before his mother now, uncertain which path to take. On the one hand, he had worked since his youth in service of his home village, striving to improve local health and education and, most important, following in the footsteps of his father and grandfather in championing the drainage of the Shinainuma marshes. On the other hand, he had long dreamed of gaining wider fame as the architect of an overseas farming colony, which would deal with the national problems of impoverished agricultural villages, expanding population, and uncertain food supply. His mother broke the deadlock for him, saying simply, "Someone else could undertake the immigration plan, but only you can handle the rebuilding of the village."[2]

What both Governor Kamei and the Kashimadai village council needed was not so much the philanthropist who had formulated and led the Mexico colonization project with such vigor. As they and Kamata's mother recognized, any number of public-spirited individuals in Japan were capable of handling work of that nature, while Kashimadai and Shinainuma required a rarer sort of person. These demanded someone with an intimate knowledge of their problems and the local lay of the land. They demanded someone who could be a bridge, both among villagers and between the village and the prefectural and national governments. And they demanded someone with the will and resources to operate autonomously, drafting plans for local improvement on his own accord and undertaking work that furthered the interests of both local farmers and the planners of the central government.

Governor Kamei and the village of Kashimadai needed a figure known as a *chihō meibōka* (local notable). Kashimadai's problems, though extreme, were far from unusual in Meiji Japan. Towns and villages across the country faced overwhelming challenges in the late nineteenth and early twentieth centuries. Largely cut off from official support and facing new pressures from changes to the taxation system and encroaching capitalism, rural communities struggled to achieve prosperity and modernize agriculture in line with the industries that monopolized the attention of government officials and investors. Yet, as rhetoric issuing forth from Tokyo constantly reminded them, they served no less important a role in the national drive for power and modernity. Rural land taxes remained the primary source of national wealth, farms fed the country, and village youth provided the backbone of the imperial army. The health and development of villages were vital to the survival of the nation and its quest for a place among the "civilized nations" of the nineteenth-century world order. But assigned a low priority for scarce government funds, the localities required leaders who could marshal the resources necessary to improve farms and villages, build local support and unity behind development, and lead their communities to prosperity and modernity.

Meiji government leaders recognized these needs and provided an ideological construct to answer them: the *chihō meibōka.* Building on the roles wealthy farmers (*gōnō*) had played in autonomous Tokugawa villages, the architects of the Meiji local government system placed the *meibōka* at the center of the rural order they intended to forge. Much as their forebearers had done, these new figures would employ their social and economic resources to ensure the economic health and stability of their home villages and apply themselves fully to the oversight of local administration and the modernization of agriculture. They would ensure the survival and prosperity of villages, leaving scarce government funds for the national purposes of military and industrial development.

But while officials in the Home Ministry may have given a name to the figures they saw as essential to the survival and development of the countryside, they were not the only ones to recognize the need for them. Villagers and farmers faced directly the pressures that the planners of local government only understood as theoretical aspects of their calculations for a modern state. The local leaders that rural residents envisioned shared much in common with the conceptions of officials, but there were important differences. As was true for the government's idea of *meibōka,* these local elites would use their wealth and influence to organize and undertake public works and improvement projects to improve conditions in their home villages. The nature of their roles as middlemen, however, diverged significantly from Home Ministry plans. Rather than drawing upon untapped or wasted village resources—both human and otherwise—to accomplish their work, the leaders sought by villagers would act as a bridge between the village and the central government and would direct government funding and support to local development.

In his activities surrounding the drainage of Shinainuma and in accepting the office of mayor of Kashimadai, Kamata embodied the characteristics that defined the *meibōka,* matching the vision of local leaders that central bureaucrats had enshrined in the local government system while at the same time answering the new needs that had taken shape among village residents and advocating on their behalf to remote government authorities. Unquestionably effective as an intermediary, intensely focused on his village, and possessing the drive and the skill to take the lead in planning and directing developmental projects, Kamata exemplified the best hopes that both local farmers and government planners had for *meibōka*. His success in Kashimadai illustrated what these figures could accomplish. Kamata's early efforts supporting schools and doctors, his involvement in the Shinainuma drainage project, and his renunciation of wider glory to take up the post of mayor of Kashimadai laid the foundation for the transformation of the village—which had been called the poorest in Japan at the turn of the century—into one of the most affluent rural communities in Miyagi by 1927.[3] He stepped forward during a period of acute difficulty for agricultural villages, employing a range of assets—some of which he had inherited from the previous age and some that were newly available to him—to blunt the adversity that the village faced, to integrate it into the national administrative system, and to secure its prosperous future. While others did similar work, Kamata's success stands out as unusual. His example showed the realization of a *meibōka* as a middleman of modernity, brokering success in a modernizing environment hostile to agricultural villages.

The initial conception of the figure of the *meibōka* and the roots of the term itself emerged in the context of the planning for the local self-government system (*chihō jichi seido*) in the Home Ministry during the 1880s. Yamagata Aritomo, together with key allies in the Ministry and among the Meiji elder statesmen (*genrō*) as well as foreign experts brought in for the purpose, incorporated overlapping, and sometimes contradictory, goals in their vision for the system. Along with its prosaic function in establishing a legal order for town and village administration, local government was also seen as a means of advancing the agenda of Yamagata's Home Ministry. First, it was a mechanism by which to incorporate towns and villages across the country, which had been virtually autonomous only two decades earlier, into the national government structure and subject them to the power of the state.[4] In line with this goal, the second purpose of self-government was to insulate rural villages from national politics. Recent years had seen villages become the breeding grounds for Freedom and Popular Rights Movement (*Jiyū minken undō*) activism, producing steady streams of critique against the national leaders and expanding calls for representative government. The local government system offered a means to quiet restless villages by cutting them off from the disruptive potential of national politics. The final goal of the new local order was to establish a framework for local development accomplished by means of local resources. The true meaning of "self-government" was not "autonomy," rather it referred to a kind of atomized self-sufficiency made necessary by the central government's reluctance to assume financial responsibility for village prosperity and improvement. The local government system would push towns and villages to marshal their resources to plan and fund local improvements. The countryside was to pay for its own modernization.

The system assigned *meibōka* an important role in village administration and development, but it did so in a way that substituted informal expectations for formal structural integration. In the initial forms of the system, these expectations were largely couched in political terms and related to central government fears about the Freedom and Popular Rights Movement and the spread of activist politics in rural villages. Yamagata, the Home Minister at the time of the implementation of the new local government system, explained that it would be "people with local 'renown' (*meibō*)" who would take up local administrative offices and, in doing so, redirect both their own and their fellow villagers' attention away from politics on the national stage.[5] This explicitly political purpose was to be fulfilled in intentionally apolitical ways. Yamagata envisioned *meibōka* engaging in administrative and other expressly non-political activities in order to prevent the politicization of the villages. These *meibōka* were to distract themselves from politics by working for their communities, work that included distracting the other members of their community in the same way. The involvement of *meibōka* in agricultural improvement was to serve a similar purpose. Acting as a check on radicalism through the economic benefits it offered, the improvement of farming also promised to divert village elites from political activities by focusing their concentration on farming and village infrastructure. It was no coincidence that both the *meibōka* that officials envisioned and the village political activists they abhorred came from the landlord class, who had the most to gain through the rationalization and expansion of agricultural production.

Although isolating landlords and wealthy villagers from disruptive political activities and ensconcing them in local government offices preoccupied Yamagata and other Home Ministry planners, the need to maintain order among the wider village population soon made clear the greater importance of the economic and developmental roles that *meibōka* would have to play. The concern of the central government with imposing financial responsibility for village administration and development on the villages themselves was intended from the beginning to open a gap in local administration that Yamagata and his advisors predicted would draw local elites to employ their own resources and energies as leaders. At the same time, however, it left a space in the development of the local economy and the village as a whole that demanded to be filled. *Meibōka* would have to take up the slack and ensure that villages not only avoided falling into poverty, but also that they met the expectations of farmers looking excitedly toward the better future promised by the new age.

The needs that the system of local government had given rise to in villages ensured that village residents brought forth their own list of hopes and expectations that contributed to the evolving definition of *meibōka.* Cut off for the most part from funding from the central and prefectural governments, villages were forced to assume responsibility for their own upkeep and administration. Rural areas were already under pressure at this time; the shaky recovery from a decade of recession combined with the ongoing commercialization of farming and growing concerns about the food supply to create a period of intense demand for increased agricultural development. Both external market forces, which were wreaking havoc on the economic health of villages, and increasingly strident calls for expanded production from the Agriculture and Commerce Ministry impelled villages to improve agricultural infrastructure and methods of farming, to explore new crops and forms of cultivation, and to adapt agriculture to face the challenges that threatened village prosperity. Faced with these demands and driven by their own desires for stability and prosperity, villagers sought in *meibōka* intermediaries who could provide access to figures in the national government and who could overcome official injunctions against rural spending to pry loose public monies. While villages shared with central bureaucrats the expectation that *meibōka* would devote their own resources to the cause of village development, the promise they held for opening the public purse and bending the wealth and power of the state to serve the interests of the local community was at least as important in their eyes.

Caught between the overlapping, but often incongruous (if not utterly incompatible), expectations and demands of officials and villagers, *meibōka* were forced to develop a discrete set of definitive characteristics beyond the affluence that marked them for local service in the eyes of government planners. To Yamagata and other figures in the Home Ministry, money made the man. *Meibōka* needed wealth not just to fund the necessary work to build and improve village health care, education, infrastructure, and agriculture; they also required the time that their affluence freed up to plan such projects and build local consensus behind them. This spectrum of needs, combined with a desire verging on desperation to avoid spending public funds on villages, often led government bureaucrats to focus on the wealth of *meibōka* to the exclusion of any other defining characteristics. In practice, however, it quickly became apparent that financial resources, while a prerequisite for becoming a *meibōka,* was not sufficient, but required an additional set of rarer qualities to produce the leaders needed by both the planners of the local government system and village residents. In fact, it was the inconsistencies between these overlapping sets of needs that helped to shape these crucial qualities. Wealth alone was not enough to negotiate the space between the call for orderly and self-sufficient villages on the one hand and the dream of prosperous and stable communities enjoying the benefits of the new age on the other.

One characteristic needed for success as a *meibōka* was a tight connection with the village. As their full title of *chihō meibōka* suggests, the close identification of notables with their local areas was a key factor in fulfilling the roles assigned to them. Their function as the shepherds of village development required *meibōka* to be local figures. From the beginning, they were intended to provide a counterbalance to the expanding numbers of absentee landlords that were appearing in villages in the last decades of the nineteenth century. Officials were quick to cast the blame for rural poverty, social turmoil, moral decay, and a host of other village ills on the influence of non-resident landlords, whom they accused of extracting wealth and leaving nothing in return. Outside ownership of land and the ways it crossed geographic and administrative boundaries was incompatible with official visions of self-sufficient villages. While these visions often appeared unrealistically hopeful, they approached impossibility in cases where the profits of local farming were channeled into the hands of landowners residing in other areas. The spread of absenteeism from economically advanced to later developing regions gave this aspect of *meibōka* increasing importance in the 1890s and 1900s. They were to be the glue holding together villages, remaining in place as residents to fulfill their social role as elites and ensuring that local resources were used to promote local development.

The local character of *meibōka* was also a function of their position as individual and unofficial actors. They relied upon their own resources to support them in their work, using private funds to pay for travel expenses, public works in the village, and the myriad of other costs that they incurred. While nearly all came from locally wealthy families, this wealth had limits that made work beyond the village borders difficult, if not impossible. The social resources that were so important to *meibōka* were subject to similar limitations. The personal connections and influence that men like Kamata enjoyed on the local level were bound tightly to their places of residence and the communities of which they and their families had long been members. The shared interests that tied these communities together defined their shape and size and placed limits on the geographic scope of local action. At the same time, the attachment of *meibōka* to their villages was a matter of will and personal dedication, a key factor when their activities as intermediaries took them beyond the village into the worlds of national politics and business. They could act in larger arenas, but these actions were invariably connected to and in service of their home areas. Whether chasing down political and economic elites in Tokyo for support of local projects or addressing a national audience on issues related to rural communities, the locality always remained at the center of the activities and identity of the *meibōka.*

Their position between the village and the central government, two groups that both wanted things from each other while being reluctant to give up anything in return, gave rise to the second characteristic that defined *meibōka.* They were above all intermediaries: middlemen between the village and the prefectural and national governments. Employing a combination of their personal skills as bridge builders with extensive social resources, both local and further afield, a key function of *meibōka* was to negotiate the seemingly inimical interests of officials and villagers and manipulate both to promote local development. Their effectiveness in this role depended on the twin qualities of familiarity and influence. Personal connections with and stature among officials and villagers complemented an intimate knowledge of the landscapes—physical, social, and administrative—of the village community, on the one hand, and the labyrinthine structures of prefectural and national government on the other. This familiarity enabled *meibōka* to exercise influence in both directions, soliciting policy and funding from the government and pushing government-friendly reform in the village. At the same time, *meibōka* employed these qualities in making connections between groups and individuals in each of the two spheres in which they operated. They brokered cooperation and coordination between government agencies separated by administrative or jurisdictional distance and organized collective efforts and groups within the village and local area.

Voluntary work and personal initiative together represent the third defining characteristic of *meibōka.* In the dearth of central funding and explicit planning for development under the new local government system, there was an acute need for *meibōka* to be self-starting individuals who would proceed without direction or support. In fact, these active individuals were in a better position than distant officials to plan improvements for their villages. They had a direct understanding of local conditions, populations, and problems. To deal with the challenges facing the villages, *meibōka* could deepen their knowledge of local circumstances, craft strategies to deal with them, and implement plans on their own initiative and with support they provided themselves or personally solicited.

Their sense of mission and the forms that their efforts took demonstrated their internalization of the self-help brand of development put forth by government ministries. The work assigned to *meibōka* was presented as unified in intent and purpose, differing only according to local conditions and the verve of local leaders. With this clearly formed ideological basis for their activities and the need to involve their neighbors in order to ensure its continuing effectiveness, the *meibōka* worked to inculcate their ideology and ethics among the wider village population. In areas with the most successful *meibōka,* other villagers also internalized the rhetoric of the Home Ministry and other government ideologues and pursued goals in line with them. In these cases, the *meibōka* were able to spread their self-initiative among their neighbors, creating a cooperative and active ethos of development that accorded nicely with that promoted by the government.

Kamata Sannosuke was born in 1863 in the village of Kimazuka in north-central Sendai domain (later part of the amalgamated village of Kashimadai and currently a neighborhood in the city of Ōsaki, Miyagi). Like *meibōka* throughout the country, he came from the *gōnō* (wealthy farmer) class of affluent agriculturalists and his family enjoyed local prominence and respect as the largest landholders in the region.[6] The family name was also associated with local development. Both his grandfather, Genkō, and his father, Sanji, gained renown for their dedication to water control on Shinainuma, a lowland lake that was the source of perpetual flooding in the area. Genkō's efforts in this work and in other forms of agricultural improvement led to his enshrinement as a local farming deity after his death.[7]

Kamata's youth was marked by a focus on education and cultural development. He pursued Chinese studies as a child against the background of the new Meiji government's political centralization and his family's subsequent social transformation from rural samurai to landlord-farmers. After his grandfather's death in 1877, Kamata followed in the footsteps of many an elite son in early Meiji, walking the long road to Tokyo and a modern education. He geared his studies toward a career as an officer in the national army, but was forced to change his plans when illness prevented him from passing the entrance exam to officer training school. He turned instead to law and politics, enrolling in Meiji Law School (Meiji Hōritsu Daigaku, currently Meiji Daigaku).

Kamata's biographers place great dramatic stock in his time in Tokyo, weaving from it a beginning to his future character arc in a pattern that appears in countless memoirs of rural visitors to the capital in the late nineteenth century. Like many young villagers who come to the big city for the first time, so the story goes, Kamata quickly fell victim to the lures

Kashimadai

of urban life. He spent his nights in cafés and bars with a new clique of urban sophisticates, developing expensive tastes in liquor and women. Tottering on the brink of a pit of epicurean excess and on the point of forgetting his family's work in Shinainuma, Kamata experienced something akin to a divine intervention. At a talk on modern ideas of independence and self-respect by the celebrated public intellectual Fukuzawa Yukichi—as close a figure to a god of modernity as there was in Meiji Japan—his grandfather's dying words came flooding back into his mind: "Worry about draining Shinainuma even before you worry about your own food and clothing."[8] Kamata repented of his unfilial and wastrel ways and resolved to finish his studies and return to Kimazuka and Shinainuma to complete the task that his grandfather had assigned to him.[9]

Kamata's epiphany represents an early manifestation of the locally oriented character that helped to define *chihō meibōka.* While the population bleed of young males from the countryside into the thriving urban locales that went on to concern government and moral activists in the decades that followed had not yet reached its peak (particularly not in the late-developing northeast), the fact that Kamata left behind the glamour of Tokyo to dirty his boots once more in Shinainuma mud stood in contrast to the dominant spirit of the times. As he was a progressive young man looking toward the future, the bustling and rapidly transforming urban centers were realms of progress and possibility; far-off villages in regions like Tōhoku were despised as backward holdouts against the inevitable flow of history and modernity. Kamata, however, decided that his work was to be done in his native village. This was not a rejection of the forward-looking vision that had taken him to Tokyo in the first place; it was rather a reconfiguration of its particulars to be used to bring modernity to Kashimadai. This relocation of the object of his efforts may have related to sentimental feelings of home, disappointment at frustrated ambitions, or a reawakened sense of duty to his native place, but it also had concrete links to his family. The call of his grandfather from beyond the grave aside, Kamata's father had continued to serve as a village leader and work toward the drainage of Shinainuma while his son sampled the delights of the capital. The lure of Kashimadai included the family home and business, which added his father's current work in local administration to the family's history of pursuing local development. Fukuzawa's revelatory oration coincided nicely with the most rational choice for a young man from a well-to-do house in the northern countryside who had failed to achieve his dreams in the big city.

Moving from hazy urban mythology into the reliable concreteness of the countryside, Kamata returned to Kashimadai in 1883 at the age of twenty and began the work that defined the rest of his life. His father held the post of *kochō,* village head under the system of local government at the time, and Kamata joined him in his work in local administration.[10] While assisting with village business, he also took the initiative in planning and undertaking a number of village improvement projects that displayed the self-starting ethos that helped define *meibōka.* Likely influenced by what he had seen in the capital, much of Kamata's early efforts focused on improving the state of health care in the village. In 1885 smallpox struck an unprepared Kashimadai, and Kamata moved quickly to locate a source of vaccine outside of the village, purchase the needed quantities, and distribute it among affected villagers. To guard against the possibility of future crises, he sought out a doctor willing to relocate to Kashimadai and establish a practice, finding a suitable candidate in Tochigi the next year and furnishing him with a fully equipped clinic.[11] He showed similar initiative toward education in the village. The year 1885 also saw Kamata open a night school for village youth, an initiative he followed up on a decade later by hiring an agricultural technician to train farmers in advanced techniques.[12] He thus applied his time and resources to the betterment of the minds and bodies of his neighbors, but Kamata's true priority remained the family's generations-long dream of draining Shinainuma and freeing Kashimadai from the perennial threat of flooding.

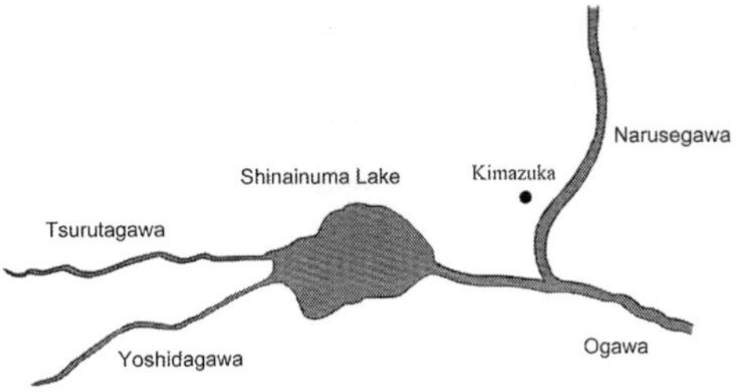

Shinainuma

Shinainuma was a wetlands area on Kashimadai's southern border roughly twenty kilometers northwest of the coastal town of Matsushima. A vast reservoir on the Naruse River system, it stretched from the inland mountains of central Miyagi to the edge of Matsushima and the Pacific Ocean. To human settlement, Shinainuma presented a dilemma. The lands surrounding the wetlands were richly fertile, with readily available irrigation and great promise for rice production, but Shinainuma itself was prone to destructive flooding. Despite this constant danger, residents cultivated lands all around the area and fell into a pattern of farming when they could and rehabilitating their lands after they were flooded.

Rulers and residents had long recognized the potential of improvements on Shinainuma for increasing agricultural production in the surrounding areas. In the late seventeenth century when the aggressive land reclamation of the first four lords of the Sendai domain exhausted the supply of land that could be easily developed in their territory, subsequent leaders turned to ambitious drainage projects that involved the mobilization of mass numbers of laborers under the supervision of domain authorities.[13] These efforts resulted in the construction of the Genroku tunnel (*Genroku senketsu*) in 1693, which drained the southern reaches of Shinainuma and reduced the size of the wetlands significantly, thus adding a measure of protection against flooding.[14]

On the freshly opened lands, the cultivation of new fields began in earnest. Even reduced, however, flood damage continued to be endemic on the now smaller Shinainuma, ruining two out of every three harvests. Still, the fertility of the newly opened paddyland was such that farmers could get by even under trying circumstances.[15] As time passed and the Genroku Tunnel fell into disrepair, conditions worsened. Spurred by the degradation of the drainage system and the suffering that he saw during the Tempō Famine from 1832 to 1836, Kamata's grandfather Genkō became an active proponent of further development and drainage of the wetlands.[16] He organized collective efforts among villagers to maintain and expand existing drainage channels and exhorted domain officials to dig new conduits. For these and other efforts, including emergency flood control, the provision of relief rice during poor harvest years, and the promotion of improved strains of rice, the local Moniwa lords rewarded him with monetary prizes and an increase in the family stipend.

The new central government established after the Imperial Restoration in 1868 brought about renewed official interest in the improvement of Shinainuma. While uncertainties in the immediate aftermath of the change in government led a group of nine worried residents of the area to sign an agreement to remain in solidarity for the purpose of improving Shinainuma in the face of whatever administrative chaos might come, their fears that the wetlands would be forgotten proved unjustified.[17] Miyagi governor Matsudaira Masanao became an early advocate of work on the wetlands in the 1870s and 1880s, and he remained in close communication with the Home and Finance Ministries about the potential for government-led drainage. His efforts proved fruitful, securing funding from the Finance Ministry for badly needed repairs and improvements to the Genroku tunnel and a government-funded survey of further drainage of Shinainuma. In 1879 the Home Ministry dispatched Cornelis Johannes van Doorn, a Dutch technician employed by the Meiji government, to conduct a series of examinations of the wetlands to investigate the possibility of draining it.[18] He concluded that this would require elaborate construction, elevating costs far beyond any benefits the project promised to yield.[19] Matsudaira petitioned the Home Ministry to offset the costs by using the forced labor of local prison inmates, but it was to no avail.[20] The project was written off as unfeasible and the Home Ministry washed its hands of the matter, ending the first period of the Meiji government's involvement in Shinainuma.

This was the context in which Kamata returned home from Tokyo to assist his father. Sanji had been carrying on his own father's work while promoting the development of Kashimadai as village head. In this capacity, he oversaw the construction of a succession of weirs and canals on the wetlands in continuing efforts to offer local farmers a modicum of protection against floods. He also provided a model for his son's later activities as a *meibōka*. His work for local development included supervision of the reclamation of new farmland, the planting of trees to provide village income for poor relief, and the construction of a new building for the Kimazuka Elementary School at his own expense after the village council was forced to abandon the project in the wake of destructive floods in 1879. For these and other works, the village council presented a total of seven awards to Sanji, even bestowing on him a village-owned building in a show of their appreciation.[21]

Kamata followed his father's example after his return from Tokyo, building upon his family's long history in the region and the reputation earned by his father to smooth over local opposition to the project and construct a broad base of support. Descriptions of his activities in concert with his father in the 1880s and early 1890s tell how he "went one day to a village to the west, the next to a village to the south with lunchbox in hand, using his own money to visit the concerned offices and *yūryokusha* (local power brokers) and strive to win them over."[22] These efforts were very personal in nature, with Kamata using his position as a fellow landlord and combining appeals to logic and long-term economic interest with his own passion and dedication for the drainage problem to win over the plan's opponents. His familiarity with and in Kashimadai and its neighboring villages enabled him to fulfill the *meibōka*'s role as local intermediary. He used his specific knowledge of his individual neighbors and their particular (and often conflicting) interests and his broad understanding of local circumstances to cajole, reassure, and convince. His efforts brought qualified success, building enough local support to carry the project forward in the 1890s and to sustain at least the hope of one day winning the official interest that the drainage would need in order to succeed.

With the amalgamation of Kimazuka and five other hamlets into the village of Kashimadai in 1889, a new mayor was elected and father and son focused their full energies on the Shinainuma problem. They worked both alone and in concert with the Association of Villages Surrounding Shinainuma (*Shinainuma enson kumiai,* hereafter SEK), which landowners from the villages of Kashimadai, Ōmatsuzawa, Ōtani, Kasukawa, and the town of Matsushima formed in 1889, attempting to build both local and official support for plans to drain Shinainuma. Kamata also began his political career at this time. He rose through local offices in the village and the district assembly, eventually becoming the youngest member of the Miyagi prefectural assembly in 1895. In both his organizational activities and his early political success, Kamata was able to transfigure his family's association with Shinainuma into a self-sustaining reaction powering his efforts to complete the drainage of the wetlands. The work of grandfather and father, as well as the connections and influence that this work had won for them, were the means by which Kamata achieved success building the SEK, climbing the rungs of village administrative offices, and earning a seat in the prefectural assembly. In a consistent pattern, family reputation brought increasing numbers of supporters behind Kamata, enabling him to win his way to ever more important and influential positions from which to continue his quest for drainage. These efforts earned wider and wider praise and new ranks of supporters, positioning Kamata to continue his political ascent. Typical of the sorts of friendships his work in the prefectural assembly earned him was that of Ichiriki Kenjirō, the founder and owner of Sendai's influential Kahoku shinpō (Kahoku Newspaper). Impressed by Kamata's dedication, Ichiriki followed Kamata's lead in advocating for the drainage project inside and outside the assembly chambers, becoming an important ally in the years that followed.[23] Kamata's political successes made the 1890s a decade of consistent progress for the Shinainuma project. By the time of Sanji's death in 1898, it appeared that it would not be long before the family dream would become reality.

The turn of the century brought with it a new spate of uncertainties. High projected costs again dissipated government support for the project, prompting the SEK to reform its membership in order to ensure full support for the project by excluding communities not directly affected by flood damage and to rename itself the Shinainuma Flood Prevention Association (*Shinainuma suigai yobō kumiai,* hereafter SSYK). Despite these efforts, constant personnel changes in the Miyagi governor's office impeded the search for allies in the prefectural administration and led to further delays and frustration.

Kamata's shifting relations with Miyagi's governors during this period point to the importance of his interpersonal connections, both inherited and self-forged, and highlight the limits of *meibōka* power and their vulnerabilities as informal actors facing a formal, and often unsympathetic, national government. A key ally at the turn of the century emerged in the form of Onoda Motohiro (1848–1919), appointed as Miyagi's tenth governor (the seventh in half a decade) in 1900. Onoda had experience with both Shinainuma and the Kamata family prior to his posting to the prefecture. One result of the efforts to lobby the national government in the 1880s had been an official survey into the establishment of a national penitentiary in northern Miyagi that would provide prisoner labor to complete the drainage work, a survey that Onoda, then a police superintendent attached to the Home Ministry, was assigned to lead. While the governor's role in this abortive venture undoubtedly contributed to his later interest in the project, Kamata's personal appeals and his family's long connection with the marshland were the key factors that won him over as an enthusiastic proponent.[24] From the governor's office Onoda joined forces with Kamata in efforts to mediate between Tokyo and Shinainuma on the project, assigning the younger man the task of bringing local residents and the mayors from villages on connected waterways into line and volunteering to use his own connections to appeal to the Home and Imperial Household Ministries. Before this arrangement could produce results, however, Onoda was transferred to Kagawa prefecture and a new governor who proved unsympathetic to the problem took his place in the prefectural office.

The outcome of Onoda's transfer and the subsequent development (or lack thereof) of the Shinainuma project demonstrated two things. First, it showed the idiosyncrasies that characterized governmental decision making and the importance of individual personalities in determining the directions government funding would take. The newly installed Governor Munakata Tadasu (1854–1921) illustrated this randomness when, distracted by growing international tensions with Russia and uninterested in the prosaic matter of land reclamation, he canceled Onoda's plans and gave no indication that he would do anything to move the drainage project forward. Second, it highlighted Kamata's ability to make impersonal and distant matters of administration personal and direct to officials who were involved with them. Onoda expressed his emotional investment in the project in the farewell letter he sent upon his transfer, declaring "I have moved away from my sentiments as an official and am giving my support, so please complete [the Shinainuma project] without fail."[25] The former governor's continuing interest in the project even when his official duties lay far away demonstrated the truth of his words. He remained in active correspondence with Kamata concerning the project right through to its conclusion, playing a part in brokering the transfer of loan money from Tokyo and offering his heartfelt congratulations to Kamata when construction finally got underway. Thus, Kamata as an individual and unofficial actor played at least as significant a role in the future course of government involvement in Shinainuma as the official and highly placed Munakata. The young man effectively countered the new governor's apathy, ensuring that the persistent and unchanging needs of Kashimadai would continue to draw government attention, no matter what passing crises might distract the attention of the prefectural government, while at the same time appealing to the personal sentiments of interested officials to ensure a commitment that went beyond the prosaic fulfillment of their duties.

Kamata entered national politics at this time in order to work from within the central government and was elected twice to the Imperial Diet as a member of the Friends of Constitutional Government Party (Rikken Seiyūkai) in 1903 and 1904. As had the Miyagi Prefectural Assembly, the Diet chamber proved a fruitful forum for Kamata's quest for influential allies. Fellow party members Ozaki Yukio and Katō Takaaki, both at early stages in their notable political careers, befriended Kamata in the capital and took personal interest in the Shinainuma project. Although Kamata's term in the Imperial Diet proved short-lived, the connections he forged there often proved enduring, as attested to by Katō's later involvement in both the drainage project and in plans for the Mexican farming colony.

As a Diet member, Kamata pushed for official support for the Shinainuma project while at the same time leveraging the connections he had made in less formal ways that built new bridges between Tokyo and Miyagi. His friendship with Onoda opened the door to a new field of opportunity in the capital when the governor suggested securing a loan from the Japan Hypothec Bank (Nihon Kangyō Ginkō) and mentioned that the elder statesman Matsukata Masayoshi (1835–1924) had appointed his son-in-law as the bank's head.[26] A confluence of factors that included the history of the Kamata family's involvement in Shinainuma, the relationship Sannosuke and his father had built with the prefectural government, and the limited size and tightly knit structure of the national government of the mid-Meiji period were the means that enabled Kamata to make an ally of such a powerful political elite and his family and to mobilize them in service of his goals in Miyagi.

Upon learning that it would be necessary to secure funds from the Japan Hypothec Bank to have any hope of completing the drainage project, Kamata recalled that his father had been introduced to Matsukata by the first governor of Miyagi, Matsudaira Masanao, in the 1880s and resolved to approach the elder statesman himself. His persistence won him a series of face-to-face meetings in Tokyo, where two fortunate developments ensued. First, Matsukata remembered the work of Kamata's father fondly and remained impressed and enthusiastic about the drainage of Shinainuma. Second, and more important, it happened that two of Matsukata's sons-in-law held positions of responsibility in the loan section of the Hypothec Bank. The appropriate wheels were soon greased, and one of the relations, Kawakami Naonosuke, became a close friend and enthusiastic proponent of Kamata's work. Impressed with Kamata's pestering of the venerable Matsukata—he expressed joyful amazement that Kamata had actually "hassled the old man" into action—Kawakami stayed at Kamata's house while surveying the area and pushed aggressively for the bank to approve the SSYK's loan application.[27] When the approval came through, Kawakami feted Kamata at no less a venue than the fabled Western-style hall, the Rokumeikan, where he gathered luminaries from Tokyo and told one and all of his own and his father-in-law's unabashed delight at having been able to assist in the project.[28]

The bank loan eased the immediate pressures surrounding funding, but new hurdles related to the ownership of parts of Shinainuma by the

Japan Railway Company and the Imperial House threatened further progress on the drainage. These two challenges, both of which had the potential to undo years of work and sink the drainage project altogether, and the actions that Kamata took to answer them again illustrate the characteristics required by *meibōka*. Kamata once more took a direct role in tackling these problems, engaging on a personal level with the parties that threatened the success of the project and using his name and the influential friends he had made to smooth out the path forward.

The railroad problem emerged first. As the plans for the drainage took on their final forms in 1905, it became clear that a stretch of track stood in the path of one of the channels that was to be dug out from Shinainuma. Kamata entered into direct negotiations with the management of the Japan Railway Company in pursuit of a solution. By midsummer, he had succeeded in winning not only the chairman's agreement to sell the land and move the track, but also his pledge to pay for half of the expenses of the move from company coffers.[29]

The difficulties with the Imperial House were a horse of a different color. Even as the potential conflict with the railroad was surfacing in 1905, Kamata and his compatriots learned that part of Shinainuma was in fact under the ownership of the Imperial Household. As the Imperial House, particularly as regarded its private landholdings, was entirely autonomous and outside the control of the central government, this presented a different kind of challenge.[30] Contacts within the prefectural government or the banking circles of Tokyo would be of little use.

Despite the personal intervention of the newly appointed Miyagi governor Tanabe Teruzane, whose efforts included traveling to Tokyo to plead for the land's sale directly, the Bureau of Imperial Lands refused to consider relinquishing it. Once again, the Kamata family's influential contacts proved more effective than appeals through official channels. As progress on the land deal ground to a halt, it was discovered that the former lords of the Kashimadai region, the Moniwa house of which the Kamata family had been retainers, had intimate ties with the Fujinami horse stewards within the Imperial Household.[31] Armed with this knowledge, Kamata secured a referral from the scion of the Moniwa family in the spring of 1905 and departed to meet with the Fujinami in Tokyo. He impressed the head of the house, Fujinami Kototada, with tales of his forefathers' ceaseless efforts to tame Shinainuma and won the man over as an ally to the drainage cause.[32] This success brought with it a double victory, clearing the way for the SSYK to purchase the imperial land on May 14, 1906, and creating in Fujinami a lasting ally to the project.

While Kamata's national political career ended in embarrassing defeat in his third campaign in 1904 after he resigned from his political party as part of a mass exodus over a political scandal, plans for the drainage of Shinainuma moved in more positive directions. The project had gained the full support of the Home and Finance Ministries by the end of the Russo-Japanese War in 1905 and the challenges of the Japan Railway Company and the Imperial House were overcome soon afterward. Armed with surveys from the prefecture and the Home Ministry and the loan from the Japan Hypothec Bank, the SSYK hired a contractor and prepared to start draining Shinainuma, a work that promised to reduce the wetlands to a fraction of its size and reclaim over 1,300 hectares of arable land in a transformation of the region and its agriculture.

With work underway, Kamata was free to turn to a matter that had long occupied his thoughts: a solution to what he and many others saw as a looming Malthusian crisis. A rapidly expanding population and increasing awareness of the limitations of domestic agriculture had long troubled mid-Meiji citizens and officials alike and focused their attention overseas. For Kamata, this became a personal mission. In the Diet, he had addressed problems surrounding agricultural production and food supplies in partnership with prominent politician (and future prime minister) Katō Takaaki, but outside of national politics and with the end of Shinainuma in sight, he cast his eyes farther afield. With the blessings of Katō and Governor Kamei, he created a limited partnership with like-minded individuals from Miyagi and other prefectures in mid-1906 and began work on his new project, a farming colony in southern Mexico.

Kamata and his group set off from Yokohama in October of 1906, making landfall in San Francisco (then still recovering from the devastating earthquake earlier in the year), before heading south by train.[33] Their target was the Escuintla region in the state of Chiapas on the southern Mexican border, the site of an earlier officially sponsored farming colony in 1897.[34] At their destination, Kamata discovered a land rich with agricultural and industrial potential, offering the promise of three harvests a year as well as secondary production in coffee and rubber.[35] He found an enthusiastic supporter in the chief Japanese diplomat stationed in Mexico, who offered his aid in negotiating with the Mexican government. A year of effort by Kamata's group and the envoy yielded extensive surveys and promising contacts with the Mexican government, but just when the arrangements seemed to be nearing completion, the telegram from Governor Kamei arrived and Kamata was forced to begin his uncomfortable ride home on the mail boat.

Kamata returned home in 1908 to find Shinainuma in virtually the same state as when he left. In his absence, the tenuous alignment of local support behind the project had collapsed, and conflict broke out between parties on all sides in the face of delays, accidents, and escalating costs. The SSYK fired the first contractor after a year had passed with no sign of the work starting. The awarding of a new contract failed to restart construction and now a personal enmity bordering on hatred divided the new foreman and the head of the SSYK. Worse, factions for and against the drainage project had formed among both residents and the members of the Shida district assembly.[36] Governor Kamei's attempts to intervene personally proved fruitless, leading him to conclude that only Kamata's return could break the deadlock and get construction back on track.

While Kamata was able to reconcile the various conflicting parties with relative ease, restoring the faith in the drainage project amongst the wider community proved more challenging. It had taken Kamata more than a decade of work traveling around the areas affected by flooding on Shinainuma and making personal entreaties to skeptical parties to build the level of support that he had upon his departure in 1906. The conflicts that arose during his Mexican adventure shattered this fragile latticework and left an atmosphere of bitterness and disillusionment that informed a renewed and strengthened opposition to the project. Flooding on the wetlands in the summer of 1908, far from impressing local residents with the need for drainage, drove up projected costs on the project and instead hardened animosity toward it. Officials in the central government now recognized the project as being of national importance, accepting the promise of future rents on reclaimed lands as collateral for an additional bond issue without complaint, but frustration at delays and skepticism over the project's viability again took hold among residents and put the future of the project in question.

For a final time, Kamata's successes as an intermediary and the network of influential contacts he had built over the course of his work became the decisive factor in overcoming seemingly intractable resistance. Reading in a newspaper that the Crown Prince (and future Taishō emperor) would be making a tour of historical sites in Tōhoku later in the year, Kamata saw an opportunity to shore up support for the project and usher it through to its completion. He again approached Fujinami in the Imperial House, who by this time was known as a devoted backer of the drainage project, and asked about the possibility of having a chamberlain attached to the tour make an official visit to the Shinainuma construction site in order to add imperial luster to the work and cement local faith in it.[37] Fujinami and Kamata continued to sketch out the arrangements for the visit even as the imperial train carrying the Crown Prince began to crisscross the northeastern prefectures. When the entourage arrived at Morioka in neighboring Iwate prefecture, Fujinami sent word to Kamata to come with all haste, as a "once-in-a-lifetime chance" was awaiting him.[38] Kamata caught up with the group to find that his lobbying had succeeded beyond his hopes, and he rushed back down to Kashimadai to spread the word that the train carrying the prince himself would be making a special stop to allow the young man to survey the drainage channel. At 3:40 in the afternoon on the third of October, 1908, the train paused on a bridge passing over the site of the drainage channels on Shinainuma's southern reaches and the future Taishō emperor spent a full minute admiring the construction from the window of his car. The purpose of the visit as a means to regain the support of the fickle villagers was made clear with the delivery of the prince's message to the people of the Shinainuma region: "This is a work for the whole country (*tenka*), so complete the construction without discouragement until it is done."[39] Awed by this unprecedented display of imperial approval for a project of local development and moved by the growing sense of nationalism taking root in villages across the country, local opposition to the drainage project evaporated. The last barriers to construction were removed and an additional 400,000 yen was raised locally to ensure its success.[40] Now at last with officials and locals united, the final construction on the wetlands could begin.

The two episodes with Fujinami are especially notable for the inconsistencies they reveal in both the role that government officials envisioned for *meibōka* on the one hand and that of village residents on the other. Kamata's intermediary activities were not limited to the binary choices of either forging connections to higher authorities in order to communicate the interests of the village or exercising his influence in his home community to transmit government policy and accomplish government goals. His orchestrations of the sale of imperial land and the princely visit present a more complicated alignment of motives and means. In the earlier episode, Kamata's efforts bridged a gap between separate parts of the central government. Governor Onoda, a prefectural official enjoying a lofty position in the bureaucracy of the central government, charged Kamata explicitly with this mission when his own efforts to secure the agreement of the Imperial House to sell its possessions in Shinainuma failed. It was Kamata, using familial connections that were artifacts of a governmental system four decades gone, who was able to prod the Imperial Household into movement, fulfilling the hopes of the now personally invested governor as much as those of himself and his community. The visit of the

Crown Prince displayed an even more arresting reversal of roles. Rather than exercising his local influence, gathering the support of villagers, and mobilizing it to fulfill plans of the prefectural or central governments, Kamata arranged for a personal visit by the future emperor, a figure near the pinnacle of the state structure, in order to consolidate local support behind a local project.

On December 26, 1910, a water release ceremony was held to mark formally the beginning of the drainage of Shinainuma through a northern drain, three tunnels, and a southern channel. Local and national luminaries, including the Home Minister and the heads of the various bureaus concerned with the construction, attended, attesting to the wider importance attached to the work that had been accomplished. Kamata Sannosuke, who had accepted both his mother's advice and the position of Kashimadai's mayor the previous year, arrived late after his failure to offer proper devotions at shrines to his father and grandfather earned him a lecture on filial piety.[41] Still, the ceremony played out without trouble and the draining of the wetlands proceeded as planned. In the first phase of reclamation, more than 800 *chō* (hectares) of farmland were opened for cultivation, with hundreds more coming from related improvements over the next few years.[42] While Kamata would go on to greater fame as Kashimadai's Mayor Straw Sandals (*waraji sonchō*) in the decades that followed, it was his work as a *meibōka* that proved critical in bringing about the draining of Shinainuma. As notable as the possibilities inherent in this role that his success suggests, however, are the paradoxes it exposes in a model of agricultural and village development depending upon such figures.

Looked at from the correct perspective, Kamata and his work on Shinainuma seemed to vindicate the thinking of Yamagata Aritomo and the other architects of the local government system. Acting on his own initiative and persevering in the face of multifarious opposition, he appeared to mobilize his own intimate knowledge of the local situation and of local populations to mediate the impossible distances between central planners and local villagers and usher a project of national significance to completion. His efforts laid bare the hidden wealth in fertile land that lay smothered beneath Shinainuma, unleashing the productive bounty trapped in the wetlands and harnessing it to work for Kashimadai and the nation. Just as significantly, he appeared to unearth similarly latent resources hidden in the village and its residents. His work as middleman brought together previously contentious segments of local society, concentrating their social and economic resources and directing them toward local development.[43] This accorded precisely with the logic that reserved the vast majority of public funds for political, military, and industrial modernization while entrusting agricultural development and village improvement to farming communities. Kashimadai and Shinainuma seemed to show that the brand of self-help made famous in Samuel Smiles' best-selling book existed in latent and collective form in villages across the country.[44] Local self-government, in the politically neutered sense it had been implemented, could lead the countryside to prosperity. *Meibōka* could be the middlemen of modernity.

But Kamata's activities as middleman went in directions that government planners could hardly have anticipated and whose role in his success stood in direct contrast to their vision of a self-sufficient countryside. Just as he had opened the hidden resources of Shinainuma and Kashimadai to be exploited for the developmental goals of officials, so too had he worked in the opposite direction to gain access to locked away government resources, freeing them to meet the needs of the village. In much the same way as Shinainuma hid rich farmland beneath its surface, the prefectural and national bureaucracies harbored material, organizational, and technical resources representing a potential means of transformation and development for villages everywhere. But the sheer number of hard-pressed agricultural communities and the remoteness of prefectural and national offices created barriers as daunting as any swampland. Here again it was Kamata's activities that delivered the resources of the government to Kashimadai. Using his family's name and contacts and the relationships developed through his political activities, he solicited support with a personal tenacity that was often the key to winning over his influential targets. The official planning, approval, and bank loans that flowed into Kashimadai as a result provided the fuel for the transformation of the village.

More disruptive to the government's conception of *meibōka* than the multidirectional nature of Kamata's work as an intermediary were the contingencies upon which his success depended. His example shines light on troubling ambiguities that lay at the heart of the idea of *meibōka* and its foundational place in plans to modernize rural Japan. Idiosyncratic elements in his family background and fleeting aspects of the historical moment in which he was active were as essential to his success as his skills or personal devotion. The Tokugawa order was not yet so remote a past during the quest to drain Shinainuma as it would soon become, and Kamata's connections to his family's former lords played a crucial role in opening doors to officials in higher positions. The house of Moniwa stood as the bridge between Kamata's and his father's relationships with several of the prefectural governors as well as between each of them and the Fujinami in the Imperial Household. The latter case in particular stands out as something that would have been impossible in later years, based on friendships across a great distance between a member of the court (Fujinami) and a former chief retainer of a defunct domain (Moniwa). At the same time, the relationship between the houses of Kamata and Moniwa was not something that was possible in many other places. Only in the handful of prefectures like Miyagi, where the preceding domain had featured an unusual integration of samurai in village society, could connections of this type evolve in a rural area. As the scion of a samurai house of high position serving under a local lord, Kamata was born into a web of connections that extended from the village to the highest levels of the central government. The specific form that the results of his efforts took were also particular to their time. It is difficult to imagine an event like the visit of the Crown Prince happening at a later date. The increasingly ritualized treatment of the imperial family and the remoteness at which they were kept from the Japanese populace in subsequent years would have made an unplanned stop at a local construction project impossible.[45]

Still, even if Kamata did not stand as the embodiment of the *meibōka* that featured in official plans and his success relied upon a set of qualities unlikely to be widely reproduced, the drainage of Shinainuma represented a type of work that was both needed and at least theoretically possible in other parts of Senboku and throughout the country. Flood control, irrigation, and associated matters of water management were of pressing concern in many villages and a necessary foundation for subsequent agricultural rationalization and modernization.[46] While Kamata's pedigree and influential contacts may have been irreproducible in most villages, riparian works by their nature required *meibōka* in order to find success. The financial remoteness of the central government, the contentious interests that overlapped on waterways, and the organization necessary to plan improvements demanded skilled intermediaries with local knowledge who were willing to devote themselves to the work. Other villages, however, often faced challenges in this work beyond those overcome by Kamata. Whereas Shinanuma lay comfortably within the administrative boundaries of Kashimadai and ranged in significance to most of its residents only from threatening to irrelevant, other villages lacked this geographic convenience. River systems, lakes, and wetlands by their very nature tended to transgress administrative boundaries, filling a need in one village while threatening the well-being of another. Drainage and other riparian works in these circumstances threw into question the nature of "improvement" and added to the difficulties concerning funding, organization, and local and official support faced in Kashimadai the additional challenge of asserting one community's interests in opposition to those of another.

We will turn now to water control efforts in other parts of Senboku and the outcomes of tackling them. As Kamata was beginning his rise in the local political sphere in the 1890s, other villages were also looking to solve their long-standing problems with waterways. Unfolding before the backdrop of transformations to village society, official policy, and local administrative systems, these efforts often proved to be the trigger for the development of new types of local leaders who stepped forward and took up roles resembling those of the idealized *meibōka.* Even as Kamata was learning the lay of the land from his father, events surrounding a reservoir in the area bordering Kashimadai to the east were taking a different turn, heading toward a conflict that would shake the social foundations of two villages and threaten order in the entire region.

CHAPTER TWO

The World Turned Upside Down

Hydrological Conflict and the Transformation of Local Leadership

An act of rebellion occurred on the 15th of June, 1893. Suzuki Suminosuke, the prefectural official in charge of the northern Miyagi district of Tōda, appeared at the station overseeing the Meiji sluice, a dam that controlled the flow of water outward from Lake Nabire. The officer overseeing the station, located in the neighboring district of Monō, must have greeted his visitor with some confusion. For over a year, water organizations in Monō and Tōda had been embroiled in an increasingly bitter conflict over the lake and the dam, conflict that had nearly exploded into violence only weeks before and left the two districts in a situation of tense hostility. Throughout the clash and in spite of the passions it aroused, Suzuki had proven himself a force for moderation, a fact that may have put the Monō custodian's mind at ease.

Today, however, the district chief was on a secret mission that belied his earlier equanimity. Under the cover of routine maintenance, he borrowed keys from the office and removed the locks securing the seven gates of the dam. Replacing them with a second set whose only key was in Tōda, he locked the gates in the open position and let the lake drain out through the sluice. The following day prefectural officials, alarmed that one of their colleagues would engage in such illegal and potentially disruptive activity, demanded that he turn the key over to Monō, but Suzuki refused. What his nonplussed superiors in the prefectural government did not know was that prior to his act of sabotage, a council of Tōda residents had called Suzuki to a meeting where they criticized him roundly for his lack of support for the district during the conflict. These local worthies demanded that their district chief prove his loyalties to his home region and bring the divisive dam under Tōda control once and for all. The admonition proved decisive. Local popular pressure trumped official responsibility, turning the administrative order upside down and bringing the situation to an impasse.[1]

Suzuki's act of rebellion marked the high point of the Entō Incident, a clash between Monō and Tōda over water rights that began in July of 1892 and continued for eighteen months before ending in a prefecture-brokered amelioration agreement in January of 1894.[2] At the heart of the dispute was the dam that had spurred Suzuki's insurrection and the lake that it protected. Lake Nabire and the Meiji sluice were the center of the region's water system and stood as the physical manifestation of the irreconcilable water interests that divided Tōda and Monō. Seeing opportunity in the social and political changes that swept across rural Japan at the end of the nineteenth century, Tōda residents sought to tear down the generations-old hydrological order that irrigated downstream regions in Monō at the cost of almost certain flooding for their upstream neighbors. Farmers in Monō rose in opposition, defending the system that provided unstable but vital supplies of irrigation water to farming communities in the dry interior of the district. On the cusp of a new era in local administration and with everything to lose, the two districts entered into a conflict whose increasingly audacious episodes captured the attention of Miyagi residents and officials and eventually forced a revision of the water order in the north of the prefecture.

The Entō conflict and its outcomes illustrate the early processes of *meibōka*-led agricultural development in a region that lacked many of the contextual advantages enjoyed by Kamata in his work on Shinainuma. As it had in Kashimadai, the institution of a new system of local government and a shift in the central government's policies toward water use and agriculture combined with ongoing technological development to open paths for new actors to pursue new modes of development. Like Kamata, they turned their attention to water control and riparian improvements as the first step in the direction of future advances in agricultural production. The drainage of wetlands and securing of riverbanks promised the expansion of arable land and protection against floods, while dams, sluice gates, and new channels offered the means to stabilize and expand irrigation.

Important differences in historical experience, village society, and geographical and geopolitical context, however, set the communities around Nabire Lake apart from their neighbors to the east in Kashimadai. The region lacked the unusual historical continuity embodied in the Kamata family, as well as the social and political advantages that this continuity gave to Kashimadai. In Monō and Tōda, and in other parts of

Senboku, economic turmoil in the 1880s had exacted a punishing toll on the economic and social elites surviving from the earlier Tokugawa period, leaving village institutions, official and otherwise, weakened and vulnerable. A new class of landlords emerged, making their fortunes in the same context of transformative instability. Social and economic capital were thus split in a way that inhibited the formation of *meibōka* like Kamata. Spurred by their increasing economic dominance and bitter at their exclusion from village leadership, the emerging stratum of newly wealthy landowners took the first steps to fill the spaces left vacant by fading early Meiji village elites and uncommitted government planners. Defined by their social ambitions, fierce localism, and contentious relationships with government officials, these landlords became the key figures in local agricultural development. The need for *meibōka* to lead this work combined with disruptions to the village order caused by administrative change in the local government system in the 1890s to present them with the means to achieve their goals.

Suzuki's rebellion at the Meiji sluice was one result of their efforts, a model of the subversion of official institutions that these new elites went on to expand and perfect over the course of the decade. These efforts helped win the support of prefectural officials and the ministries of the central government for landlords at the end of the century, setting the stage for the next phase in agricultural and local development. While the changes of the 1880s and 1890s provoked an explosion in Monō and Tōda, they produced quieter but similar developments throughout northern Miyagi. Other areas avoided open conflict, but the factors that set communities against one another in the Entō dispute were at work in villages across the prefecture: a central government that preferred to pay for improvement with official recognition rather than money; rising landlords hungry for both growth and authority; and an agricultural system desperately in need of fundamental improvement. This context gave the leaders who came forward in most areas of Senboku a character quite distinct from that of Kamata and the *meibōka* ideal that he embodied.

While the basic problems concerning unruly waterways were shared between the two areas, the physical and administrative geography of Lake Nabire and its environs introduced a host of complications that were unknown in Shinainuma. The Entō conflict was a product of the hydrological structure, both in its geographic and its administrative sense, of the Monō-Tōda region. The area had long played host to a local iteration of the timeless battle between humans and their environment, but here it divided the population and set people against one another. The two adjacent districts were located in north-central Miyagi roughly fifteen

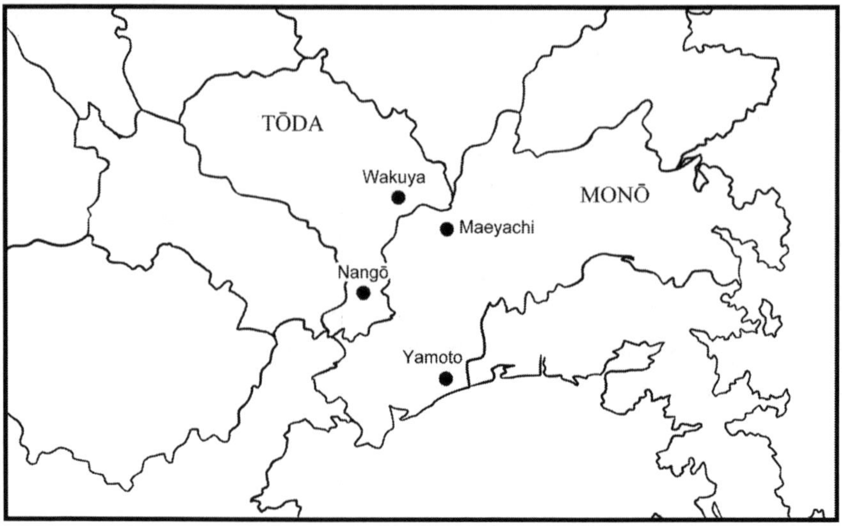

Tōda and Monō

kilometers inland from the port city of Ishinomaki. Lake Nabire lay just west of the district boundary in Tōda and unraveled into a series of waterways that extended eastward into Monō. The most important was the Uki River, which flowed northeast from the lake through the Meiji sluice on its way to drain into the Eai River. In the stretch between the lake and the sluice, the Uki branched off into canals delivering irrigation water directly to a number of Monō villages and feeding the Hirobuchi Reservoir, which supplied others. While this system provided vital water supplies in these areas, Lake Nabire was the object of intense resentment in Tōda. The sluice kept water levels on the lake dangerously high and created a constant threat of flooding, retarding development and devastating fields and homes in the Tōda villages of Nangō and Wakuya with vicious regularity. Farmers in these areas fixed their hopes for flood relief on the Aoki River, which ran through Nangō to feed the lake; the Jō River, which drained it to the southwest; and the sluice. They dreamed of linking the first two, destroying the last, and erasing Lake Nabire from the landscape.

Although the prominence of lakes and rivers gave a natural façade to the conflicting interests of the two districts, it was human intervention in the environment that made water use along the Monō-Tōda boundary so desperate a contest. Advantage flowed downstream like water along the northern Miyagi river systems, and the position of districts inland and upstream cast them in the role of sacrificial victims to the stability of communities in the lower reaches of the rivers during the Tokugawa period.

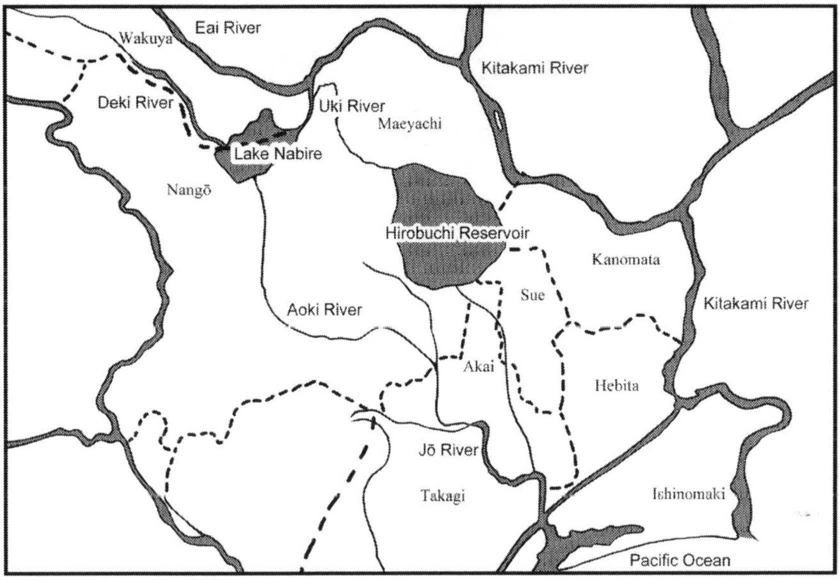

Tōda and Monō Waterways. Source: Sunaga Shigemitsu, ed., *Kindai Nihon no jinushi to nōmin: suitō tansaku nōgyō no keizaiteki kenkyū, Nangō-mura*. (Tokyo: Ochanomizu Shobō, 1966), 426.

In order to protect Sendai's chief rice port of Ishinomaki from flooding, domain officials in the seventeenth century ordered the construction of artificial narrows on the Kitakami River at Wabuchi in eastern Monō, an area just downstream of the point where the Eai River merged with its larger sibling and far upstream of the shipping hub. While this alteration caused some increased flooding around the Wabuchi area, it had a more pronounced effect farther upstream. Choking off the water flow, the Wabuchi narrows redirected high waters to the upstream regions of the Eai River in Tōda and the Hasama River in the northern district of Tome. Regularly inundating existing farmlands in these areas, the effect of the terraforming work at Wabuchi exercised a more pernicious influence in the longer term. It transformed vast areas in Tōda and Tome into floodplains, rendering acres of land that would otherwise have been forest commons unexploitable and depriving farmers of an important free source of fertilizer and other agricultural products while concentrating local power in the hands of wealthy residents.[3] This was not an unforeseen result. For domain planners, the flood protection that the narrows offered to Ishinomaki, as imperfect as it was, more than offset the opportunity costs that they consciously imposed on the upstream communities.

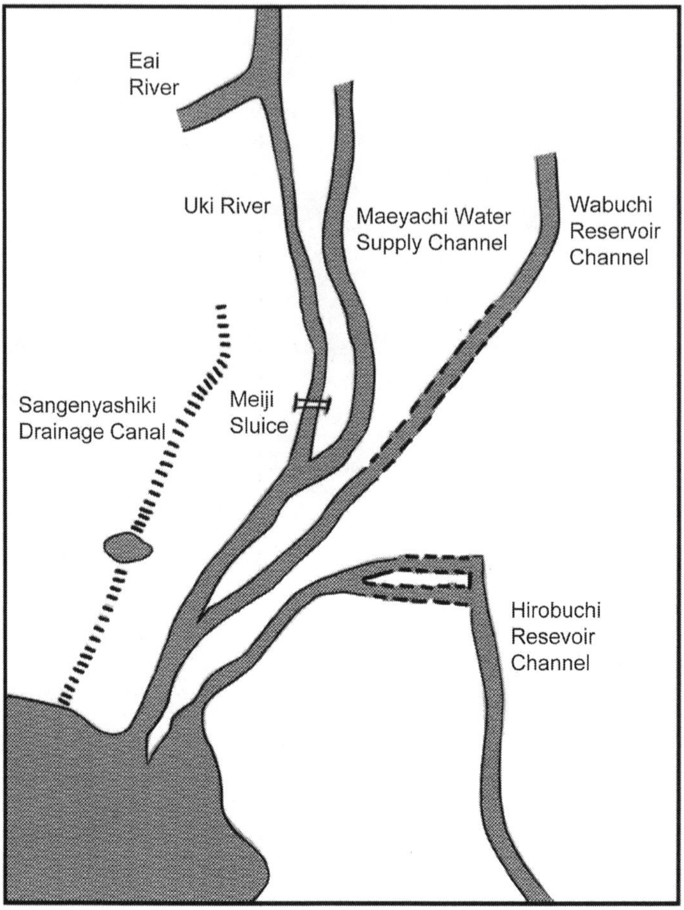

Lake Nabire Drainage. Source: Nangōchō, *Nangō chōshi*, vol. 1, 2 vols. (Nangō: Nangōchō, 1980), 700.

While both Tōda and Monō suffered in the quest to protect Ishinomaki (however unequal their suffering may have been), efforts to alter the waterways within the districts created further disparity and set the interests of each against the other. Again, it was riparian improvements under the Sendai domain that determined the balance of interests in the region. From 1662 to 1665, the two guardians of the young lord in Wakuya oversaw the creation of the Hirobuchi Reservoir (then called Ōzutsumi) as part of a plan to open over a thousand hectares of new farmland in northern Monō.[4] After the work was completed and the domain's offers of free farmland had begun to attract settlers, however, it became clear that the water supply was insufficient and technicians embarked on further work to link the reservoir to Lake Nabire and the plentiful waters of the Eai River. Domainal technicians dug the irrigation canals from the Uki River to the reservoir, installed a stone sluice, and established the hydrological order that defined agricultural life in the region for over two hundred years.

Both the narrowing of the Kitakami and the connection of Lake Nabire to the Hirobuchi Reservoir reflected the resignation that guided agricultural improvement in northern Miyagi during the Tokugawa period. At the heart of this way of thinking was the understanding that nature imposed fundamental limitations on the potential for agricultural production and that, while it could reposition disadvantage, human effort could do nothing to eliminate it. Accordingly, planners created a hierarchy of acceptable vulnerability that privileged Monō above Tōda and Ishinomaki above all other areas. In the mid-nineteenth century, domainal administrators demonstrated their continuing commitment to this scheme and acceptance of its costs. They first ruled against a Tōda request to dredge the Jō River (which would have lowered levels on Lake Nabire) as a means to protect newly reclaimed farmland around Nangō and then put an end to a prominent Tōda farmer's energetic campaign to carve a system of canals that would remove the lake's source entirely.[5] The former decision in particular, defeating a plan in which the Wakuya lord himself had a personal stake, demonstrated the guiding power of the belief among domain planners in the inevitability of disparity.[6]

In the context of this developmental ethic, their shared inferior status relative to Ishinomaki, and the irreconcilability of their interests, Tōda and Monō became competitors in a zero-sum game. Marginal prosperity in Monō equaled flooding in Tōda and an escape from bare self-sufficiency in Tōda meant drought in Monō. Prefectural officials, summarizing the issues later in the official report of the Entō conflict, described the relationship between the districts as defined by an "absolute conflict of interest (*mattaku rigai sōhan*)."[7] Farmers on both sides knew that the drainage of Lake Nabire and the reclamation of its land as arable could be accomplished just as clearly as they knew that the successful defense of one district's interests meant unavoidable damage to the other. The stakes could not be higher for either side and, if one were to win, the other must lose.

The unequal system of water use that surrounded Lake Nabire survived the dislocations of the end of the shogunate and the establishment of the Meiji government. Administrative instabilities arising from this transition, however, augured the shakeup that would come and lead directly to the Entō conflict. In the Tokugawa period, the lord in Wakuya had authority over the water control devices on the Uki River, which consisted of a moving wooden gate to prevent reverse flooding from the Eai River into Lake Nabire and a fixed stone sluice that stored irrigation water for Monō villages while allowing waters to flow over it in the event of flood. With the dismantling of the shogunal-domainal structure in the first years of the Meiji period, control over these installations devolved to the communities whose interests they served. Lacking the domainal finances needed for maintenance and suffering a series of costly floods in the 1870s and 1880s, the Tōda guardians of the reverse floodgate allowed it first to rot into disrepair and then to wash away completely in 1889.[8] Suzuki Suminosuke, the district head of Tōda and the man in charge of the wrecked gate, approached his Monō counterpart, Miyazawa Chikahiro, with a plan for the two districts to cooperate in financing the construction of a new sluice that would incorporate the functions of both the lost floodgate and the still-functioning stone sluice, which it would replace. After Suzuki agreed to pay for seventy percent of the work, a condition upon which an alliance of Monō villages insisted, Miyazawa gave his approval to the plan.[9] Suzuki agreed to the additional stipulations that his district would neither pursue projects to create new drainage channels on the lake nor allow the water levels on the lake to fall below their Tokugawa-era height. Prefectural technicians began surveying the waterways in preparation for construction in 1890.

With the results of the survey came the complication that would eventually push the two districts to open conflict. Prefectural technicians announced that the original plans for the amalgamated sluice, which detailed a simple reconstruction of the existing stone dam in brick with the addition of the reverse floodgate, were unfeasible and that fundamental changes would be necessary. The original design would lead to silting on the Uki River, a danger that could only be avoided, they claimed, by replacing the fixed gates of the earlier sluice with seven moving gates that could be opened and closed. Miyazawa balked at this development and Suzuki was only able to regain his committment by promising to give Monō complete control over the operation of the gates.[10] Together, the two district heads produced a set of guidelines stipulating the gates remain locked shut during the spring and summer and opened only in case of flooding, which would replicate the conditions that had prevailed in the past.[11] With rules in place and both districts seemingly in agreement, work began in earnest and the Meiji sluice was completed in mid-1890.

The motives of Suzuki in continuing to press for the construction of the dam after the change in its design and in agreeing to the terms that Miyazawa imposed are difficult to discern. The changes to the water order that came with the Meiji sluice seemed decidedly contrary to Tōda's interests. Having already given up any plans to carve new drainage channels from the lake, the control that Suzuki gave Monō over the new sluice guaranteed that even the unsatisfactory amount of drainage that the old dam allowed would worsen. The high waters that had flowed automatically through the fixed gates of the old dam now had to be released manually by a guardian from Monō whose undisguised interest was in keeping water levels in the lake high.[12] No one could expect him to be excessively diligent in the fulfillment of his duties. Predictably, tensions between the districts increased every time the gates had to be opened, with Tōda residents accusing the gatekeeper of dragging his heels and the resentment that Monō residents felt in response making them increasingly reluctant to open the gates at all.[13] Tōda's circumstances grew direr as animosity between the two districts worsened.

While it is possible that he was blindsided by the prefecture's changes to the design of the dam or simply caught in a momentary lapse in judgment, both the persistent attempts by Tōda leaders to get control over the sluice in previous years and Suzuki's own subsequent actions leading up to the Entō conflict suggest instead that the district head saw the new dam as an opportunity to change the status quo in the region. Tōda's efforts to monopolize the operation of the sluice on the Uki River got an early start in the late 1870s. Farmers in the areas that later became Nangō and Wakuya formed the laboriously named Babayachi and Lower Nine Villages Joint Alliance (Babayachimuraikakyūkamura Heigō Kumiai) and dedicated themselves to the twin goals of restoring the Aoki River and taking control of the dams at Lake Nabire and two other locations.[14] Although the group experienced little success in either endeavor, its successor organization, to which Suzuki was named head, took on these same objectives and continued to pursue them before and during the Entō conflict. In line with these efforts, Suzuki also moved to undermine the sluice agreement almost as soon as he signed it. He refused to hand over the gate keys to his Monō counterpart as he had pledged, forcing Miyazawa to file a formal complaint with the prefecture and leading to an atmosphere of distrust that saw both Monō and Tōda build watchtowers to keep the sluice under observation.[15] Whether his acceptance of the Meiji sluice agreement had been a miscalculation or a ruse, it was clear that Suzuki was going to be less than meticulous in observing its terms.

Transformations to the administrative, social, and technological contexts in which Monō and Tōda found themselves in the early 1890s played as significant a part as the new dam in the eruption of the Entō conflict and influenced the course and character of the dispute. The 1880s brought a broad spectrum of changes to rural areas, stacking reimaginings of local government on top of important developments in the economic and social realities of agricultural villages. Together, these transformations destabilized the upper echelons of village society, weakening structures of control and leadership and inviting new leaders to step forward and remake relations between and within communities and between local areas and governmental authorities. This created the crucible in which figures resembling, but exhibiting significant differences from, the *meibōka* forecast by Home Ministry officials were forged in the Entō region.

The end of the 1880s and beginning of the 1890s witnessed administrative changes in rural areas more revolutionary than any since the establishment of the Meiji state. At their center was the new system of local government established between 1888 and 1890. The "Three New Laws" (Sanshinpō) that defined this system wiped thousands of villages (*mura/sonraku*) from the administrative map, banishing them into shadowy half existence as hamlets (*buraku*) and subsuming them within the new, larger towns and villages (*chōson*). The communities that lined up against one another in the Entō conflict were the products of this system. The village of Nangō and town of Wakuya in Tōda and the Monō villages of Takagi, Akai, Kita, Hirobuchi, and Sue all came into existence in 1889, fusions of formerly distinct villages. In these new "administrative villages," former village assemblies and other village-based groups were demoted to unofficial organizations, hollowing out the bases for power and influence of many village elites in a concerted plan to bring local areas more tightly under the power of the Home Ministry.[16] Lacking local notables with the staying power of Kamata and his father, leadership in these new villages was up for grabs.

The administrative villages became the new organizational basis for local associations, particularly those formed for flood control and water use, giving shape to the groups of actors that faced off against one another in Monō and Tōda.[17] Following up on the Three New Laws, the Water Use Association Ordinance of June 1890 aimed at aligning irrigation organizations with the new system. While the law placed these groups under the authority of the new villages where possible, the nature and size of water systems often made this impractical, if not outright impossible. In some cases, river systems laced with smaller tributaries produced associations covering limited areas that were indistinguishable from the hamlets that the Three New Laws aimed at eradicating.[18] Here water groups provided an official means for the continuation of the hamlet organizations, preserving roles for dispossessed village elites and working contrary to the goals of the new system of local government. More commonly, and with a greater impact on rural society, a number of separate villages shared interests in a single river system. In these cases, cross-village water associations were created that included as members all landowners whose holdings were directly connected to the waterway in question.[19]

Two such water associations crossing village lines formed around Lake Nabire soon after the passage of the association ordinance. The first of these was the Monō-based Hirobuchi Reservoir General Irrigation Association (Hirobuchi Ōtameike Futsū Suiri Kumiai; hereafter HOFSK), approved in April of 1891, which represented the towns and villages that drew irrigation water through canals from Lake Nabire and the Uki River, including parts of Fukaya, Hirobuchi, Akai, Sue, Kita, Kamata, and Nakatsuyama in Monō and Hebita and Ishinomaki in the neighboring district of Oshika. Tōda residents followed soon after with the organization of the Meiji Sluice Flood Damage Protection Association (Meiji Suimon Suigai Yobō Kumiai; hereafter MSSYK), a group whose name proclaimed its confrontational goals.[20] Including the Tōda communities of Nangō and Wakuya, as well as parts of the Monō villages of Ono and Fukaya, the MSSYK covered a vast area that straddled the boundary between the two districts (*gun*).[21] As in similar groups everywhere, both the HOFSK and the MSSYK were nominally headed by their respective district heads; however, when the two associations soon took over the central roles in the Entō conflict, the empty nature of these new district positions and the autonomy of the landlords that made up the organizations' officers and their rank-and-file members quickly became apparent.

The revolutionary administrative changes that produced the new villages and water associations were imposed on top of socioeconomic developments that had transformed northern Miyagi villages in the preceding years. The 1880s and 1890s saw the rise of a new class of landlords who attained economic preeminence. The hardships that afflicted agricultural villages were the means of their ascent. The economic recession of the late 1870s and the Matsukata deflationary policies of the early 1880s and the trying economic conditions that followed exacted a fearsome toll on Miyagi farmers, dispossessing middling owner-cultivators of their lands and undercutting the bases of wealth and property that had supported village elites. Flooding and bad weather compounded these problems in northern Miyagi, imposing costs that hard-pressed farmers could ill afford. While many suffered disaster, others discovered opportunity. Some landowners were better able to weather the storms, both figurative and literal, of the 1870s and 1880s and found themselves in a position to profit from the misfortune of their neighbors. Buying up land that banks had repossessed, these farmers became the "great landlords" (*ōjinushi*) who went on to lead the charge for agricultural improvement that took place from the 1890s to the 1910s. Despite their gains, however, these new economic elites found themselves shut out of positions of social and administrative leadership in their villages, which remained occupied, at least initially, by the former elites, however impoverished they had become.

In dismantling the hamlets and creating a new platform for leadership in the administrative villages, the local government system presented new landlords with the opportunity to make the social gains that had thus far eluded them. For hamlet elites, most of whom based their local prominence on family wealth and reputation dating back to the Tokugawa period and modest gains in landholding in the early Meiji years, leadership positions in village administration and local organizations had been a way to maintain their status and prestige even as adverse conditions sapped their actual economic power. The imposition of the new villages eliminated these secure posts at the same time that they reduced the total number of official positions up for grabs. In newly formed villages like Nangō, where there had been six village assemblies, six mayors, and six sets of all the various offices that went along with them, only a single set of positions replaced what had been lost. This left little place for longstanding local families who had camouflaged their growing weakness with the sheen of local office.

The Kubo family of Neriushi provides an example of the difficulties that the 1880s and 1890s in general, and the new local government system in particular, presented to early Meiji village elites in Miyagi. Based on its status as counselor to the Wakuya lord in the Tokugawa period, the Kubo house carried its prosperity into the early years of Meiji and rose to the top of Neriushi's economic world as the largest landholding family in the village. The family head quickly translated this economic power into political and social capital, taking control of the mayor's office and creating and heading a high-profile local political society designed to defend village interests in the context of changing prefectural administration.[22]

The focus of the family on the local village, however, introduced weaknesses to both its economic and political positions and eventually proved the undoing of its fortunes. Where Kamata Sannosuke's father was able to parlay his family's links to the local lord into wider political authority, taking on the cross-hamlet office of *kochō,* the Kubo house never pushed beyond the boundaries of their home village. Kubo offices, landholdings, and moneylending were confined to Neriushi, tying economic transactions to the political and social responsibilities that the family bore in its community. As a result, it found itself compelled by its position in the village to continue to lend money at low interest rates to its tenants and neighbors, even as its own economic difficulties forced it to borrow at high interest in order to do so.[23] The family's land accumulation stagnated, as much a victim of the Kubo's limiting of their holdings to their home village as it was to the punishing economic environment of the 1880s, while the more widespread landholdings of other houses with less to lose socially matched and then surpassed them. The Kubo patriarch retained control over the administrative structure of Neriushi during this decline, but the folding of the village into Nangō in 1889 removed this remnant of his former power.[24] With the family's decline no longer hidden behind administrative positions, the fall of the Kubo house unfolded in the 1890s and 1900s for all to see. Barely weathering a legal challenge at the turn of the century that consumed the last of the family's dwindling social and economic resources, the patriarch pulled up stakes in the 1910s and moved the family to Hokkaidō to start anew.[25]

The Suzuki and Noda houses, both of whom rose to the top of economic and social life in Nangō at the beginning of the twentieth century, provide a revealing contrast to the Kubo family. Starting as poor farmers and minor samurai, respectively, both the Suzuki and the Noda families parlayed success as merchants and farmers into significant land accumulation in the 1880s and 1890s. Despite their economic flourishing, these rising landlords remained at the start of the Entō conflict as far removed from the offices of the new administrative village as they had been from those of the defunct hamlet. A lack of social capital accounted in part for this situation. Unprotected by the reputation and status that sheltered the occupants of village offices, Suzuki Naoji was formally ostracized from Neriushi for five years in 1888 after backing the wrong side in a dispute over fishing rights. Evidence of his low social position, Suzuki's penalty was the harshest suffered in the outcome of the conflict, in stark contrast with his more respected colleagues who were allowed to make a formal apology to Kubo Gengo and rejoin village life.[26]

Even when they successfully dodged the difficulties that afflicted Suzuki, newly risen landlords in the 1880s and 1890s often preferred to avoid service in village administration. Noda Saiji, who had continued his father's accumulation of land—and who eventually made his house the second largest landowners in the prefecture—shunned village service in Neriushi and concentrated on building the family's fortunes.[27] Although he became the second mayor of Nangō in 1893 (a position from which he played a role of some significance in the Entō conflict), he accepted the office only reluctantly, resigned in a matter of months, and held only minor village posts subsequently until the beginning of the twentieth century.[28]

He justified his avoidance of village service and his earlier non-participation in the Freedom and Popular Rights Movement (a virtual prerequisite for Nangō's mid-Meiji leaders, including Kubo Gengo and the village's first mayor, Abe Kumanosuke) on the grounds that he was an only son who bore sole responsibility for the family's fortunes.[29] While the lack of siblings may have been unusual among rising landlord families, the prioritization of interests was not. Though they went on to take control over village administrations at the beginning of the twentieth century, most chose to concentrate on private economic pursuits in the 1890s.

In contrast, these landlords found the new water associations to be more closely aligned with their interests than local government. The expansive memberships of these cross-village groups enabled the first official recognition of landlords outside the confines of their home villages. While the nature of village administration under both the old and new local government systems prevented landlords with dispersed holdings from participating in public life in villages other than the one in which they lived, the official recognition that the Water Use Association Ordinance gave water groups, as well as the landlords who belonged to them and elected their leaders, a formally acknowledged existence that granted them the legal right to fund themselves from local taxes.[30] They became *de facto* landlord unions, enjoying the full sanction of the government and invested with collective authority over water rights. Along with this new power and legitimation, water groups freed landlords from the social obstructions they had faced in their home villages. The associations were as divorced from the hamlets as they were from the new villages, shaking off the control of the older class of village elites over water and opening a field for rising landlords to make their mark independent of their social betters who had often held them back.[31] Finally, water associations were neatly aligned with the economic interests of landlords. Having few avenues for profit other than by increasing agricultural production on the lands they farmed themselves and those they let out to tenants, northern Miyagi landlords coveted tighter control over waterways. The associations and their authority over rivers provided a means for landowners to increase their profits through improvement. The Entō conflict was born of one such early improvement, presaging the two decades of concerted, and much more successful, agricultural improvement that Miyagi landlords went on to pursue.

Technological development and changing popular understandings of the relationships between nature, technology, and the state provided the context for the outbreak of hostilities between Monō and Tōda. Science and technology quickly became two of the most celebrated aspects of the new Meiji era. Trumpeted by Fukuzawa Yukichi and a cohort of new public intellectuals, rendered tangible by the first generation of successful industrialists, and embedded throughout the country in railway projects and military bases, the promise of modern technology seized the attention of people everywhere. With the new age came new ideas. The conception of natural limits to the potential of human endeavor weakened as faith in man's ability to direct and control nature took hold.[32] This philosophical shift instilled a new assertiveness in Miyagi farmers toward their interactions with the natural environment. For Tōda residents, the new potential for human control over nature invalidated the system of distributive disadvantage that demanded the sacrifice of their interests for those of Monō and Ishinomaki. They rejected the long-held stamp of inferiority, embracing instead a set of rising expectations that envisioned, if not a complete remaking of the water order in the two districts, at least a reworking of the system to meet their long-neglected needs.

The application of new technology to water control and riparian improvements in the first decades of the Meiji period stoked faith in its potential to reorder nature. The hydrologic expertise of northeastern Europe was especially prized, and Dutch technicians took on positions of leadership in a series of well-publicized, government-funded river improvement projects in the 1870s and 1880s. The high regard government planners held for Dutch technicians took concrete form in northern Miyagi in 1879 when celebrated engineer Cornelis Johannes van Doorn added to his efforts across the country a series of surveys on the waterways surrounding Shinainuma in the neighboring district of Shida. Inspired by this and a continuing faith in Dutch engineers on the part of the national government, Tōda resident Azumi Jintarō (who became a key player in the Entō conflict) solicited prefectural support for and used his own resources to fund Western science-based surveys in 1881 and 1882 on waterways in the area that would later become the new village of Nangō.[33] Although these investigations did not lead directly to improvement projects, it was clear from an early point that figures in Tōda saw in technological developments a potential solution to their age-old water problems.

While the new technology of the Meiji period offered a means of improvement in many areas, a technological fix that would satisfy all parties in Monō and Tōda was unlikely. While terraforming efforts could improve water supplies and help to resolve competing claims over a single water source, these were not the issues in the region.[34] The dispute between Monō and Tōda hinged on the question of whether or not a single water source should be allowed to continue to exist. It was a problem rooted in earlier human transformations of the natural environment and the political decisions that informed them. Despite the advances since the fall of the shogunate, the scale of the work that would be required to meet the needs of both districts placed it beyond the imaginations of the leaders of the conflict. Rising expectations based on new methods of water control and terraforming led Monō and Tōda residents to believe that they could improve the situations in their home areas, but they created no firm belief in a fix that would be beneficial for all. The construction of district-operated watchtowers on each side of the Meiji sluice after its construction in 1890 showed that, if Tōda and Monō residents had faith in the possibility of progress through technology, that same trust extended neither to the unlimited potential of that progress nor to the goodwill of their neighbors.

The hopes surrounding the promise of new technology were tied to evolving government policies on riparian works. Beginning in 1868 with the appointment of a chief national water use official given the explicit task of "bring(ing) happiness to the people," the Meiji government placed an early emphasis on water management.[35] Its approach to rivers in the first decades of its existence, however, took a one-sided view of the role of the state in riparian improvement. Eschewing calls across the country for flood control, the proto–Home Ministry of Ōkubo Toshimichi defined the government interest in rivers solely as their potential as a transportation network that would obviate the need for expensive rail.[36] National funding and planning went to so-called deep water improvements aimed at deepening major rivers to remake them as arteries in a system connecting markets across the country, while villages asking for help against flooding were told that dams, weirs, and other high water construction were the responsibility of localities.[37]

Changes in government leadership and policy goals brought with them tentative moves toward flood control in the years leading up to the Entō conflict. Ōkubo's assassination in 1878 took the riparian transportation network off the government agenda temporarily and introduced a new focus on rail.[38] This did not lead immediately to policies promising relief to flood-plagued communities. Recession and austerity measures inhibited government support of flood control projects, even worsening the prospects of such work in 1880 with a tax law revision that eliminated existing opportunities for villages to apply for funding from the central government, and conflicts between government ministries that helped neutralize attempts to change the tide.[39] New hope came only with Yamagata Aritomo's assumption of the office of Home Minister in 1883. Reviving the plans for the river transportation network, he also acknowledged the importance of flood control and inaugurated a new program through which prefectures could apply directly for central government support for their projects.[40] Additional pressure for national funding of flood control came with the opening of the Imperial Diet in 1890. The landlords from rural areas all over the country who took up Diet seats quickly made water management a key political issue, criticizing the focus on deepening projects and calling for the government to take responsibility for flood control.[41] Despite the promise of these developments, the situation remained uncertain for major river projects at the beginning of the Entō conflict, with flood control improvements still cast as "the problem of each region."[42] At the same time, the construction of the Meiji sluice as the third major national water infrastructure project since the fall of the shogunate built the hope in northern Miyagi that a new era in riparian improvement was at hand.[43]

The construction of the Meiji sluice, in concert with the social, economic, and administrative transformations that villages underwent during the 1870s and 1880s, thus left water usage in Monō and Tōda in a flammable state. A bold proposal from Tōda's MSSYK, however, put the spark to the tinder. Excited at the news that engineers had declared the draining of the lake possible and predicted it would result in improved flood protection and new lands for reclamation, the group quickly drafted concrete plans and announced a conference of influential parties (*yūshi no kyōgikai*) to be held in Sendai on July 14, 1892. Leading the meeting were the most prominent members of the MYSSK, including Tōda landlords, the mayors of Nangō and Wakuya, as well as Fukaya landlord and Monō prefectural assembly hopeful Yamoto Heidayū. The leaders of the MSSYK did not limit attendance to those likely to support their plans. In a significant miscalculation they also invited Fukaya mayor, Endō Imagorō, to the event and proposed that he not only accept the lake-draining project, but also pay for related improvements on the Jō River to ensure the smooth completion of the drainage.[44]

Endō's response was swift. After flatly refusing the proposal, he returned to Monō to organize resistance to Tōda's plans. The mayor proceeded methodically, first convening a "prominent people's congress" (*omodatte kaigi*) that called for a Fukaya assembly vote, then presiding over the village administrative body as it produced a resolution of "absolute opposition" (*danzen hantai*).[45] A wider anti-Tōda movement flared in Monō, fueling the victories of fiercely partisan Monō candidates in the Miyagi prefectural elections in the summer of 1892 and effectively ending the political ambitions of MSSYK member Yamoto. In August, a group of delegates selected by the Fukaya assembly went to Sendai, where they received the backing of Miyagi governor Funakoshi Mamoru and his pledge to protect the status quo on water use in the region.

These initial stages of the conflict were orderly, but they displayed the early leadership of the newly prominent landlords. The conference of influential parties that Tōda leaders held in Sendai illustrated the importance of unofficial and semi-official actors and hinted at the inaction that would characterize the involvement of prefectural officials in the later stages of the fight. The name of the gathering expressed its orientation, with the word "*yūshi*" pulling double duty in describing personal interest in the matter as the prerequisite for inclusion while at the same time making reference to "*yūshisha,*" a term for "men of influence" who worked in the interests of their communities. Both Tōda's *yūshi* and the "prominent people" gathered in Fukaya resembled the locally influential residents whose support was sought by Kamata Sannosuke for the Shinainuma project. There, as in Tōda and Monō, they were figures who existed at a distance from the prefectural government, whose officials avoided direct involvement in the brewing conflict. While mayors and village officeholders took their places in the Tōda meeting, Suzuki Suminosuke, district head and nominal chief of the MSSYK did not.

More tellingly, landlords who held minor or no official positions played important parts in this and subsequent meetings. Azumi Jinjirō, a Nangō landlord who held the minor office of ward head (*kuchō*), presented the drainage proposal to the surprised mayor of Fukaya at the concerned parties' conference, while Yamoto Heidayū, holding no official position in his home village, attempted to convince the mayor to go against the interests of the majority of his fellow villagers.[46] A similar group of landlords led Monō's response. Who precisely attended the Fukaya "Prominent People's Congress" cannot be known, but there is little doubt that both that group and the village assembly that met in its wake were composed of local landlords. Clearer are the identities of the leaders of the wider "anti-Tōda movement" that spread in Monō in the fall of 1892. Bolstered by the governor's promise of support and the success of anti-Tōda candidates Endō Imagorō (Fukaya) and Itō Taizō (Kanomata) in the prefectural assembly election, Monō landlords Endō Ryōkichi and Saitō Jintarō began their significant involvement in the conflict by holding mass meetings in September to select a committee to visit the prefectural office in Sendai a second time and request a formal injunction against Tōda's plans.[47]

The motivating forces in the various groups further illustrated the dominance of unofficial over official leadership. The Fukaya Congress, an ad hoc meeting of residents in an unofficial capacity, was the first response in Monō to the announcement of the MSSYK's plans for Lake Nabire, and its resolution to elicit a condemnation of the scheme by the village assembly testifies to the role of unofficial action in provoking a response from the men in office. Both the mission of the representatives chosen by the Fukaya assembly and that of the group selected at the September meeting of Endō and Saitō to solicit the governor's explicit condemnation of the Tōda plan followed a similar pattern. Village-based groups of various levels of official status prodded the top bureaucrat in the prefectural government into action. Suzuki's later act of insubordination with the locks on the Meiji sluice in response to the demands of Tōda residents was simply a logical progression from these early activities.

In many ways, the actions taken and leadership roles assumed by these local officials and landlords hewed more closely to the Home Ministry's conception of *chihō meibōka* than even Kamata himself. Like him, they were local leaders who moved on their own, employing their influence in their home villages to accomplish work designed to increase agricultural production and ensure local prosperity. Lacking the connections with national political elites that Kamata enjoyed, their actions necessarily took on a more local character. The village meetings convened by both sides in the conflict and the leaders' relentless canvassing for local support appeared to be the embodiment of the atomized self-sufficiency dreamed of by Home officials. Although their trips to Sendai to woo the prefectural governor may have deviated from the official *meibōka* script, as attempts to draw upon public resources they were milder than Kamata's similar efforts by several orders of magnitude. The Entō leaders devoted the bulk of their energies to mobilizing local people and local resources. When they looked to higher officials, it was to secure either commitments to maintaining the current order or permission to make changes to it on their own. The plans for the sluice and the maintenance of the various channels feeding into or drawing from Lake Nabire all proposed using village resources and such official support as was already provided for under existing laws and policies. They presented a much clearer picture of local self-sufficiency than Kamata's troublesome efforts to free up additional public funds and solicit an active role from the central government in the drainage of Shinainuma.

The irreconcilability of interests surrounding Lake Nabire and the actions taken by *meibōka* during the Entō conflict offer a new perspective on localism in the Meiji period. Kären Wigen has shone light upon the ways in which the quest for support from the central government among village elites diverted the potential for conflict away from the prefecture-capital axis and redirected it toward the relations between neighboring villages in what she calls "the benign character of Meiji regionalism."[48] What appeared benign to central authorities, however, could assume a much more disruptive character in the context of natural scarcity and conflicting interests. While elsewhere the absence of government involvement in local development could "channel . . . local sentiments everywhere into forms conducive to national goals," in Monō and Tōda it approximated the opposite effect.[49] Local need and local passions achieved such force that the conflict infected first district politics, then reached up to the prefectural assembly itself. Rather than acting as a moderating influence due to its function of connecting local lobbyists with a conduit to state resources, the assembly became another site in a conflict that threatened to destabilize the prefectural administration. The prefectural government remained aloof at this stage of the dispute, but its growth to the point where it could shape the results of a prefectural election must have raised concerns among administrators and likely played a role in prompting the later direct involvement of prefectural officials.

While adhering to the letter of the law regarding local self-government and *meibōka,* the path followed and the decisions made by the leaders in the Entō conflict led to consequences that Yamagata Aritomo and other Home Ministry officials had not foreseen. In the final months of 1892, battles lines were drawn between the two sides and the irreconcilability of their respective positions became increasingly clear. The lobbying and organizing efforts of the spring and summer had failed to produce either a firm agreement between the two sides or a clear decision on the part of the prefectural authorities. For Monō leaders, this meant a satisfying continuation of the status quo that favored them, but the untenability of their own position drove Tōda leaders to new extremes. Stymied in their appeal to Fukaya's leaders and facing the danger of a hostile prefectural administration, Tōda actors turned to direct and illegal action in the autumn of 1892. Two weeks after Governor Funakoshi's declaration of his support for Monō in the brewing conflict and two days after Endō's and Saitō's mass meeting, the MSSYK held a general assembly to formulate their strategy for the rest of the year. Ignoring the lack of official sanction and the danger of legal backlash, the meeting produced resolutions to deepen the Aoki River and seize control of the Meiji sluice.[50] Suzuki Suminosuke, as both district head and nominal leader of the water group, registered his firm opposition to the plans, urging moderation and respect for legal processes. While it eventually accepted his entreaties to abandon plans to steal the key to the dam's sluice gates, the MSSYK membership roundly voted down his motion to forestall the river improvements. A meeting of the Wakuya town assembly soon followed, cementing the rejection of the district chief's line and resolving to dig a new drainage canal from the northern banks of Lake Nabire at Sangenyashiki. Tōda would respond to official condemnation with unofficial and direct action, the complaints of Suzuki be damned.

The MSSYK's dismissal of Suzuki's advice, which in the context of his position as leader of the organization might better be read as orders, reveals his marginal place in the organization he was supposed to head. But if he was not in charge of the group or of the other actors on the Tōda side of the conflict, who was? It was not the elites of the early Meiji period who had been displaced by the new local government system. The hamlet-based elite houses of Nangō played limited parts in the conflict or stood to the side as it progressed. In contrast, those who had managed to secure places for themselves in the new administrative villages took on important leadership roles. The mayors of Nangō and Wakuya each championed direct action that defied the orders of the district chief, destabilizing the local order and pushing the conflict toward violence.

While, despite their degree of autonomy, mayors could be considered tied to the larger administrative structure, the same was not true of the many important figures in the Entō conflict who occupied only minor village offices or held no official position at all. In Monō, mayors and prefectural assemblymen may have taken the lead against Tōda's drainage scheme, but it was landlords and others holding positions as village clerks, ward heads, postal officials, and teachers who provided the most energetic leadership in the active phases of the conflict.[51] In part, the prominence of people of this type as leaders related to the need for action that went beyond the boundaries of the strictly legal. Officially mandated organizations like water associations could hardly lead the charge in illegal activities. Landlords with local prestige but little or no official authority instead took on this role on both sides of the conflict, successfully mobilizing their neighbors and pushing forward the interests of their districts with force. In so doing, they also made themselves vulnerable to legal retribution. It was leaders from the rising landlord class with minor or no official positions in the village administration who went on to face arrest and prosecution for their roles in unsanctioned river works.[52]

Tōda farmers proceeded with their plans for the Aoki River and the Sangenyashiki Canal in the fall and winter of 1892. After inclement weather forced delays in October and November, Nangō's mayor led workers in damming the Deki River upstream of Lake Nabire in order to begin excavations to connect it directly to the Aoki River draining from the lake. Startled Monō observers, hurriedly dispatched at the first indications of activity, reported a massive workforce who had rendered the source of the lake "as dry as a road."[53] Both sides petitioned the prefectural governor to intervene on their behalf in the weeks that followed, citing the damage promised by either the destruction of the lake or its continued existence as demanding official action. In response the prefecture offered silence, effectively backing the Monō-friendly status quo, but doing nothing explicitly to deter the aggressive moves of the Tōda side.

The lack of official response invited direct and illegal action from both Tōda and Monō, leading to a series of incidents and arrests in the winter of 1892 and the spring of 1893. To surreptitious Tōda attempts to dig out new drainage channels from Nabire Lake, Monō responded with legal gambits and sabotage campaigns that resulted in the arrests of leaders Endō Ryōkichi and Saitō Jintarō.[54] A flurry of lawsuits between officials in the two districts followed in the spring of 1893. As of the beginning of April, both district heads, the water associations, village officials, and the leaders of the unauthorized dredging and refilling were all embroiled in legal wrangling. As the first blossoms of spring brought color to the landscape, enraged residents on both sides of the district line waited in states of nervous tension for legal resolution.

In Tōda, the tension broke on the third of May, when the Sendai local court acquitted Monō leaders Saitō and Endō of all charges. While the local officials leading the MSSYK filed formal appeals, Tōda residents rejected legal means of resolution and took to direct action en masse. Farmers from Wakuya and Nangō gathered at the Meiji sluice, ignoring police demands to disperse and threatening violence. While cooler heads eventually prevailed, leading to the peaceful dispersal of the assembled farmers, a small group led by a minor Wakuya official struck at the Monō watchtower, seizing the keys to the flood gates and claiming a Tōda victory. The beleaguered Tōda district chief Suzuki was able to prevail upon the raiders to return the keys, but the next day the mayor of Nangō defied his orders and led another group to complete the work cutting off the water supply to Lake Nabire.[55] In the face of legal paralysis and government inaction, the threat of violence between the two districts grew increasingly likely.

The ineffectiveness of the legal response to the worsening conflict and the inability of the court system to hand down verdicts that did anything but reaffirm an amorphous commitment to the failing status quo provided both the impetus and the means for landlords and minor officials to take roles of leadership in the increasingly radicalized conflict. In settling the cases surrounding the dispute, Miyagi judges based their decisions entirely on customary use and precedent. Actions like the excavation of the canal at Sangenyashiki were condemned as being against "customary practice" (*jūrai no kankō*), making it impossible for Tōda to effect any legal change in a system whose entire purpose was to preserve the order in its current form.[56] Where legal and official means failed, however, Tōda actors found that illegal and unofficial actions could paradoxically succeed. In the face of illegally undertaken works presented as *faits accomplis,* courts accepted the status quo as a moving target and scrambled to hand down verdicts that exonerated the people who conducted the work and left the transformations they had accomplished as they were. The stable order that courts were dedicated to defending amounted to whatever conditions existed at the time of trial. This flexible conservatism encouraged leaders on both sides to take direct action to force the changes that they wanted, confident that the courts would back them up in the end. In this context, the only rational response for actors in Tōda or Monō was to escalate the conflict and aggressively pursue their interests before their opponents could. By the spring of 1893, empty threats of legal penalties no longer acted as an effective deterrent and the situation veered dangerously toward anarchy.

It was with the region in this state that Suzuki found himself forced into the key-stealing gambit that opened this chapter, finally provoking the prefectural authorities to mediate a resolution between the two districts. Dissatisfaction ran high in Tōda after the earlier standoff at the sluice and the forced return of the keys to the floodgates. Frustrated farmers organized a conference of Tōda residents (*Tōda gunmin kyōgi*) at the beginning of June, where they demanded that Suzuki seize the key to the sluice gates. This confrontation completed the pattern of the inversion of leadership that began with the mayors of Nangō and Wakuya flouting the district chief's calls for moderation and continued in the taking of center stage by non- and minor officials like the Tōda key thief and the Monō saboteurs. It also proved the means finally to bring the prefecture into the conflict in search of a solution. More surprising than simple insubordination, the fact that Suzuki had followed the will of the assembled residents rather than his duty as an administrator put the lie to the notion that he was a bureaucrat who would put service to the prefecture (and hence to the central government) ahead of local interests, a revelation underlined by his refusal to return the key to the officials sent out to admonish him after his crime.

The long road to resolution and reconciliation began with Miyagi governor Funakoshi castigating the district heads of both Monō and Tōda and convening a special meeting in Sendai of the district officials, mayors, and prefectural assembly members involved in the conflict. The ineffectiveness of this gathering, in which the governor stressed the need for the two districts to work together to formulate a solution that would work for both, became clear almost immediately. Only days after the meeting, new lawsuits were filed by both sides, killing the promise of a quick end to the legal struggles. When Suzuki, bound for a meeting with the governor in Sendai, was forced to turn back to his home district to deal with reports of another group of farmers again threatening violence, the prefecture finally decided to adopt a new approach.[57]

The governor organized a second series of meetings for July 20–23 aimed at restoring order and resolving the fundamental problems that afflicted the region. Unlike the first meeting, the guest list this time included all the concerned parties from the two districts, whether they held official positions or not, and featured four respected prefectural mediators to hear their cases and resolve their differences.[58] Mediator Hayakawa Tomohiro summarized the conclusions at the end of the conference, noting that "what is at the root of the conflict between the two districts are the problems caused by the fact that Tōda is worried about the drainage of damaging water and Monō is concerned about the lack of a water supply. These alone are the roots of the current situation."[59] The problems were declared to be purely geographic in nature, unrelated to failings in administration and governance, and could only be solved by more concerted human intervention in the natural environment.

Accordingly, a follow-up meeting in mid-August marked the first move down the path toward a concrete proposal that pledged the use of the prefecture's resources to end the disparities preventing harmony in the region. After abortive suggestions of a return to the status quo, quickly shouted down by Tōda representatives, the prefectural mediators agreed to deliberate about a Tōda-produced plan calling for the draining of Lake Nabire and the opening of a new water source for Monō. By the end of autumn 1893, the last of the lawsuits had been thrown out, the prefecture had taken direct control of the Meiji sluice, and technicians had completed extensive surveys of the region. From December 3 to 5, representatives of the affected towns and villages were assembled at a meeting in Sendai and given the prefecture's draft resolution agreement outlining the plans for a prefecture-led remodeling of the local water system.

Proposal in hand, the representatives at the December conference returned home to have their town and village assemblies vote on it. Governor Funakoshi followed hard on their tail, conducting a two-day goodwill tour in mid-December that included an evening with the mayor of Wakuya, who remained deeply unsatisfied with the new proposal, and meetings with the influential citizens (*yūshi*) on each side.[60] Villages across Monō signed off on the agreement over the course of December, but its treatment of the Sangenyashiki canal and omission of the Aoki River issue made their Tōda counterparts leery. Finally, at a special session on January 13, the MSSYK withdrew its opposition to the agreement and abandoned all plans for a legal challenge. A large group of representatives from Tōda, Monō, and Oshika met in Sendai on January 17 and signed a conciliation document (*chōtei riyūsho*) and a treaty (*jōyakusho*), ending the two-year conflict.[61]

While the inclusion of the team of prefectural mediators at the second round of summer meetings in Sendai has been credited as the key to a solution to the Entō conflict, equally important was the invitation of the various unofficial and semi-official actors who had taken roles of leadership during the recent months of radicalization.[62] Alongside mediators and mayors, the July meetings included prefectural assemblymen, minor local officials, and men with no official positions at all.[63] The August meetings opened the rosters still further, adding more minor officials from Tōda. In the face of a failure of local administration, the prefecture had little choice but to include all those who exercised practical influence if it were to have any hope of resolving the conflict and restoring order.

The agreement that terminated the Entō conflict promised to put an end to the disparities that made the interests of the districts irreconcilable. It presented concrete plans to recreate the waterways around the Monō-Tōda boundary, introducing improvements that would benefit all connected areas. Its stipulations included: prefectural planning and funds for a new irrigation canal to Monō from a water source in the northwest of the prefecture within the next two years, with provisional rules in place to ensure the water supply in the meantime; the preservation of the Sangenyashiki canal in its buried state; the continuation of prefectural control over the Meiji sluice until the time came to drain Lake Nabire (at which point the dam would no longer be necessary); and a promise that the prefecture would commit to such construction as would prove necessary to solve any further water problems as they arose.[64] Tōda's objections concerning the Aoki River and the Sangenyashiki canal aside, the resolution promised benefits to all and seemed to herald a sea change in the prefecture's involvement in local development.

The long-term significance of the conflict and its resolution were twofold. First, it signaled a new course for future agricultural improvement in Miyagi. This course was not, however, the one outlined so carefully in the reconciliation agreement that restored order to the region. The ink on the documents signed in January 1894 was scarcely dry when Governor Funakoshi handed his office over to Katsumata Minoru, late of Ehime prefecture. Technicians began preliminary survey work on the waterways, but, foreshadowing Kamata's experience in the following decade, the new prefectural head had little interest in the project and rising tensions on the

Asian continent diverted what waning attention it might still have drawn from him.[65] With the outbreak of war with China in the summer of 1894 and the tremendous costs associated with it, water infrastructure in northern Miyagi seemed a minor issue indeed. Improvement plans were shelved and by the time peace was concluded the following year, it had become clear that the prefecture would not be making good on its promises.

While the plan detailed in the mediated settlement would have transformed the water order in the region, the actual outcome augured changes that were considerably wider in their significance. The failure of the agreement was not the mechanism that brought these changes; it served rather as a compass pointing to the site of action in agricultural improvement and suggesting the direction of its development in the years to follow. If bureaucrats in the prefectural administration (and by extension, their superiors in the Home Ministry) had demonstrated a new interest in improving farming and a willingness to consider fundamental changes to age-old systems of land and water use, they had also revealed that they could not be counted upon to be the agents of these transformations. Figures within the villages would have to step forward and lead any efforts that were to find form in reality. This reaffirmation of local responsibility also had implications for the size of any potential projects. While a multi-tiered drainage operation that involved the construction of a canal stretching dozens of kilometers through mountainous terrain was at least theoretically possible when backed by government funding, it was far beyond the means of any village, particularly one that would require such extensive work.[66] Improvement would have to be homegrown and modest in scale. Piecemeal work would be the rule.

The Entō conflict did not clearly identify the village figures who would lead these stunted improvement efforts, but it provided significant hints, at least of who they would not be. Their power waning and their positions under siege in the new local government system, the elites of the early and mid-Meiji periods were of limited significance during the conflict and there was little cause to believe that they would prove any more important to local development from that time forward. Other candidates appeared more promising. Distinguishing themselves during the dispute were local officials, advocating for their villages' interests from mayoral offices, and the new class of recently risen landlords, generally holding positions no higher than the lower reaches of village officialdom. In the course of the conflict, they had assumed the roles of *meibōka* leading the drive for local development.

The second significance of the conflict and its outcome lies in its confirmation of the official recognition of landlords outside the context of the formal local administrative system and demonstration of the importance that the prefectural government (and by extension, the national government) attached to them. The inclusion of so many individuals from the edges, or completely outside, of village government in the mediation conferences and as signers of the final settlement documents conferred a formal role on people without formal positions. It represented an extension of the wider official recognition that had come with the water association law, showing clear connections between the memberships of the Monō and Tōda associations and the signatories, who were identified as belonging to one group or another in the documents. These people did not, however, take part in the resolution process only as members of water associations. Conducting surveys in September of 1893, a prefectural official noted his official meetings with "Entō committee members" (*Entō jiken iin*) in both districts, making no reference to the MSSYK or the HOFSK.[67]

Government officials also gave implicit approval to the unofficial, and even illegal, actions taken during the conflict. The contracts declared a general amnesty, forgiving all improprieties done during the strife even as they promised to fulfill the goals in the service of which they had been committed. Not stopping at simply excusing illegal activities, the prefecture went on to endorse them. The mediation document noted the incompatibility of legal guidelines and water disputes, stating "conflicts over water use are not something that can be satisfied simply by the sole means of applying legal restraints and demanding the rights of oneself and one's allies while putting aside the suffering of others."[68] This was at once an appeal for cooperation in place of narrow parochialism and an admonition to local areas to resolve their problems themselves without relying upon, or even turning to, law or formal government.

The anonymous official advocating a better way forward for Miyagi farming communities inadvertently hit on the basic inconsistency upon which government policy (or non-policy) toward the development of farming villages was constructed. Despite its apparent incompatibility with the vision held by the architects of the Meiji rural order, the Entō conflict remained consistent with the principles undergirding the conceptions of local development and administration. Far from deviations from the local self-government system that arose from exceptional circumstances, these developments were a direct and logical result of that system. They exposed the flaw at the heart of village self-sufficiency and the place of rural villages in the larger project of modernization pursued by the Meiji government. Villages were to identify and pursue their own interests, providing a decentralized engine for a national rural development formed as an aggregate of infrastructural and other improvements on the village level. While this mobilization of self-interest held the promise of increases in agricultural production and the rationalization of village administration without reliance on state funding, the atomization of local interests produced its own set of problems. The natural world upon which agriculture depended did not divide itself according to the boundaries drawn around human settlements. In situations like that of Tōda and Monō, the pursuit of one village's interests could and often did mean threatening or damaging those of a neighboring village. To the increasing pressures imposed by the ongoing integration of farming villages into national and international markets, this added the additional stress of regional intrigue and competition and worked in opposition to the goals of local self-government. The rising tensions between villages increasingly monopolized the attentions of village leaders, both established and emergent, and drew effort away from village maintenance and improvement. The enmity broke free of the local area, moving on to infect district assemblies and other administrative bodies and threatening to take on a political character that central planners would have found horrifying.

In the end, the drainage of Nabire Lake, the carving of a new irrigation canal to Monō, and the fundamental transformation of the water use system in the region would have to wait for more than thirty years until a new government commitment to development emerged in the 1920s. In the meantime, it was up to local figures to lead more modest, if more realistic, efforts. Sporadic minor conflicts flared up in the region during the 1890s, never threatening to approach the Entō incident's level of seriousness, but serving as a constant reminder of local dissatisfaction. A spate of intense flooding in 1897 inflicted heavy damage in Monō, Tōda, and Oshika, prompting a series of meetings between the three districts aimed at solving their water problems. Stalled for months over the usual conflicts, the district representatives eventually agreed to shelve any plans for fundamental alterations to the current order and instead to focus on what improvements were possible within their own district boundaries. Pledging to avoid inter-district strife, the region began the twentieth century in atomized self-reliance.

While the Entō conflict failed to bring about the infrastructural improvements that farmers in Monō and Tōda sought, it marked social changes with important implications for the development of agriculture and farming villages in the years that followed. In both its extension of official recognition to unofficial actors and its revelation of potentially destructive competition between villages cut off from government support, the Entō conflict highlighted the dynamics of local development under the mid-Meiji ethics of local self-government and augured the future of *meibōka*-centered agricultural policy. The increasing recognition given to the role of unofficial actors, the rise to prominence and local power of newly risen landlords, and the necessarily parochial character of village development all took on a local coloring in Monō and Tōda, but similar phenomena were playing out everywhere. The forces exerted by government agricultural policy, ongoing change in agricultural markets, and social evolution in villages made similar developments in farming and farming villages systematic. New landowning elites stepped into the places of their former social betters and took on the roles of leadership sketched out for *meibōka*, demanding and receiving increasing levels of official recognition.

The resolution of the Entō conflict left behind compelling questions that demanded answers. Agricultural development was clearly both needed and possible, but who would lead it? Rumblings from within the Home and Agriculture and Commerce Ministries betrayed government interest in increasing agricultural production and enriching poor villages, but what would they do to promote these goals? New technologies were emerging that offered the means to solve age-old problems of farming and production, but how would they come to the villages and in whose interests would they be used? Northern Miyagi found itself in a liminal moment, faced with clear evidence of the ending of the old order, but only vague suggestions of the shape of the new. These suggestions began to take concrete form in the late 1890s with the growth and maturation of farming associations, and with the links that they forged with the prefectural and national governments.

CHAPTER THREE

A Harvest of Knowledge and Ambition

Rōnō *and the Rise of Agricultural Associations*

In January of 1897, members of local farming groups (*nōkai*) from all over Japan gathered at the Yayoi Hall in Tokyo's Shiba Park for the fourth general meeting of the Zenkoku Nōjikai (National Agricultural Association).[1] Over two hundred representatives in total had been elected by local members to attend the event, and they spent the next three days discussing the resolutions passed at local industrial meetings over the previous year, lamenting the deplorable state of villages, and planning for the future of their organization. The Zenkoku Nōjikai was of relatively recent pedigree, having broken off from the Dai Nihon Nōkai (Greater Japan Agricultural Association) two years earlier in a split that was less than amicable. The 1897 meeting highlighted the differences of the new group from the old. On the one hand, the assembled representatives revisited concerns about the failures of wealthy farmers to promote agricultural development that had long been as common a topic in the Dai Nihon Nōkai as among Home Ministry bureaucrats in the central government. Alongside old chestnuts like this, however, were features pointing to the new directions taken by the Zenkoku Nōjikai and its affiliated local groups. The composition of the association was one such departure. Here the growing influence of the newly risen landlords was apparent, as they formed the majority of the assembled ranks of regional *nōkai* branch representatives, elected and dispatched by their home organizations, and represented a change from the mass of self-selected local *yūshisha* (concerned individuals) and *rōnō* (farming experts) who had peopled the meetings before the split.[2]

More important than the meeting's roster, however, was its vision of a new role for the central government in promoting the development of agriculture. Picking up on the relatively modest proposal at the previous year's meeting that the central government begin providing funding for the prizes at local *nōkai* agricultural product exhibitions, the 1897 assembly presented an expanded roster of proposals for official support of farming improvement. Resolutions called for direct government funding for the establishment and maintenance of local agricultural lecture halls and experimentation stations and indirect support for improvement through an immediate reduction of the registration tax for new paddyland.[3] Alongside financial commitments, the assembled members also demonstrated a keen interest in legal change. Joining the perennial push for the passage of an Agricultural Association Law (Nōkaihō), which the Dai Nihon Nōkai had been promoting since the beginning of the decade, was a proposal for an Farmland Consolidation Law (Kōchi Seirihō). This law would provide an official apparatus to structure and support the ongoing efforts of landlords to consolidate scattered paddies, open up new farmland, and seize and develop the commons that had been the collective property of villages rendered defunct by the local government system of 1890.

Produced by a group that, whatever its ambitions, lay outside the lines of official patronage and advocating changes that appeared to be no more than modest alterations to the existing order, the 1897 Zenkoku Nōjikai resolutions might seem unlikely harbingers of revolutionary transformation. The government funding sought by the members was limited in scope and appeared neither unreasonable nor unexpected in the context of the vocal support for local agricultural improvement regularly proclaimed by the Home and Agriculture and Commerce Ministries. The legal proposals similarly resonated with the professed goals and activities of the central government. Official promotion of agricultural associations had been a policy since the late 1880s and the government had also made efforts to encourage reordering of farmland to allow improved cultivation techniques and eliminate the last vestiges of the old village land tenure system.

Yet, for all their seeming innocuousness, the Zenkoku Nōjikai resolutions carried implications that went far beyond publicly funded experimentation stations or government prizes at farming exhibitions. In fact, they proposed a fundamental rewriting of the relationship between the central government and farming populations and the roles of each in agriculture and its 'development.' The preponderance of new attendees at the meeting pointed to the roots of this systemic challenge. The landlords making up the local agricultural organizations whose coordination was a primary goal of the Zenkoku Nōjikai were drawn from the same ranks as the leaders of the Entō conflict of a half decade earlier: the recently risen village elites displacing their earlier social betters in the new administrative villages. The 1897 general meeting resolutions reflected their increasing confidence in their assumption of the roles of *meibōka* and their success in promoting their interests as an economic class. Having gained limited official recognition and improved their positions on the local stage, they now sought to reorder their relations with the national government.

The government's policy toward agriculture and rural areas in the late nineteenth century was nothing if not consistent. Issuing a steady stream of praise for the virtues of self-sufficiency, early Meiji officials largely limited their direct involvement in the countryside to the maintenance of order, the conscription of soldiers, the enforcement of compulsory education, and the extraction of taxes for military and industrial development. Rural populations were all but cut off from direct government support, left to the motivation provided by their straitened circumstances to produce the agricultural growth that both they and the state needed. The 1897 resolutions struck at the central pillars of this structure, proposing an extension of government protection over a portion of the farming population and the direct involvement of government in agriculture. The landlord-farmers that government officials had designated *meibōka* and to whom they had entrusted rural administration and development were to be the beneficiaries of this expanded embrace. No longer local figures upon whose financial and social resources central planners relied in their plans to promote the development of rural areas and agricultural improvement on the cheap, these *meibōka* aimed at becoming the object of government funding, which they would employ to oversee the development of their villages.

Yet the supposed *meibōka* who sought the support of the central government were not the same rural figures around whom officials had built their plans for local self-government (*chihō jichi*) in the 1880s. The new direction outlined by the Zenkoku Nōjikai represented the culmination of two decades of concerted efforts toward agricultural improvement, but it also reflected the evolution of the figures that led this charge. Two distinct types of farmers, each serving as middlemen of modernity, were instrumental in bringing about the changes to agriculture, farming organizations, and official involvement in rural villages that set the stage for the group's proposal. In the first stage of these developments, the veteran farmers known as *rōnō* were the key players. Coming from the ranks of the earlier village elites and linked with farming experts from an earlier era, *rōnō* represented both continuity with Tokugawa-period agricultural villages and consistency with official visions for village leadership.[4]

The collapse of the Tokugawa polity removed the restraints on their activities, allowing them to spread the "backlog of indigenous technology" they had built up to areas across the country.[5] During the 1880s, these farmers advanced the development of agriculture by means of this backlog, providing an alternative to misguided government plans for the modernization of farming, building confidence among officials that rural elites held the knowledge for successful improvement, and laying the foundation for future agricultural development.

The second type of farmer shaping the changes leading to the 1897 proposal were the landlords who rose to new positions of wealth and local prominence in the 1880s and took up membership in the local agricultural associations (*nōkai*) that spread across the country in the 1890s. As was seen in the events surrounding the Entō conflict, they had supplanted the village elites of the 1880s economically, but still lacked their social status and administrative authority. In much the same way that water use and control associations had in northern Miyagi, agricultural associations served the related functions of bringing together these landowning farmers into effective lobby groups, attracting the attention of key officials in the Home and Agricultural and Commerce Ministries, and providing them with the means to organize and assert themselves on the local and national stages as *meibōka.* To officials, they were islands of stability in villages unbalanced by the very social, economic, and administrative disruptions that had enabled their ascent in local society.

The 1897 resolutions of the Zenkoku Nōjikai came to naught, but the transformation that the organization sought was not long in coming. A burst of legislation at the close of the nineteenth century saw changes to agricultural and rural policy that confirmed landlords as *meibōka* in new positions of singular advantage in their home villages and shaped the course of agricultural development for the next decade. The contours of the shift were traced in a series of laws, a raft of officially recognized organizations, and a spectrum of government financial support, but it represented an even more significant departure from the status quo than these expansive measures indicate. It brought an end to the government's pronounced neglect of the financial needs of the countryside. No longer would officials treat the rural population as a single mass, left on its own to negotiate the treacherous ground of expanding capitalism and the withering challenges of the natural environment. Village elites stood poised to enter the new century backed by new sources of government funding and authority born of legal change.[6]

This change marked the beginning of an extension of government influence into villages, but in the indirect form of increasingly formalized support mechanisms for the *meibōka* and their organizations, rather than the exercise of direct control over the economic fortunes of the villages. At the same time, in leaving village administration and the planning of agricultural development and all types of improvement efforts to resident elites, the government also allowed for a kind of autonomous self-government. This, however, is best understood as a compromised continuation of the cost-free approach to local government that had informed central visions of village administration since the beginning of the Meiji period. What was new at this point was the use of government resources to strengthen one group within villages, who government planners hoped would use their power to improve villages and agriculture in particular ways. This empowerment weakened the rest of the rural population, cementing the local supremacy of the landlords-cum-*meibōka* and opening for them a new period of opportunity.

Official policy toward rural Japan in the early Meiji period provided little in the way of concrete benefits to agricultural villages. As Penelope Francks describes,

> Despite the still overwhelming importance of the rural sector in the economy as a whole, agriculture and rural industry clearly did not receive top priority in the Meiji government's economic policy agenda . . . it was railways, shipyards, large-scale, state-of-the-art textile mills, mines and metal foundries that figured in government-sponsored technology-transfer schemes and public investment programmes.[7]

While rural communities as the soul of the nation and font of morality occupied a central place in the ideological pronouncements of the Home Ministry, in practice the central government maintained a mostly extractive relationship with villages, seeing them as a source of tax money, a locus of compulsory education, and a supply of bodies to be drafted into military service.[8] To the extent that rural populations and agricultural development figured into official plans, they did so at the nexus of government interest in domestic stability and national security. Economic development was the key to both of these goals, but the situation the country faced, its limited resources, and the nature of the social dislocations that resulted from the changes after the Restoration focused efforts at it in particular directions.

A chief concern of the early Meiji government, and one that intersected with agriculture and rural Japan, was the problem of the samurai. The abolition of the Tokugawa domains, feudal stipends, and samurai status in the first decade of the new order left tens of thousands of former warriors unemployed. Officials looked to farming as a means of finding livelihoods for ex-samurai, but the plans they enacted consumed scarce resources and produced mixed results. Before the establishment of the Agriculture and Commerce Ministry in 1881, a key aspect of agriculture policy was the promotion of large-scale farms that could provide relief work for samurai.[9] When these plans proved abortive, officials turned to the cultivation of undeveloped lands, again with qualified success. The freshly established ministry's efforts to promote the opening of new farmland in Tōhoku and Hokkaidō in the 1880s struggled to find an audience among the dispossessed class the project was intended to aid, and those who did show interest often found the opportunity to cut and run with a quick profit more appealing than life as a farmer.[10]

Samurai relief programs did not represent the only official interest in agricultural development in the 1870s and 1880s, but other government programs often offered only limited benefits to farmers. Silk and other textiles, as Japan's most valuable exports in the late nineteenth century, figured large in the plans for rural areas. Government funds provided for the famous Tomioka Silk Mill, as well as more modest efforts that offered machinery to privately owned textile plants in Miyagi and other regions.[11] Less emblematically modern plans were also enacted in the textile sector. One such project designed to spur native wool production and protect domestic industry ended in failure when the sheep imported by the central government succumbed as a group to a deadly parasite.[12]

The second type of early Meiji official initiative aimed directly at the improvement of agriculture and the promotion of textiles, but it did so at a physical distance from the villages. Far from the rural areas in whose name they were purportedly undertaken, government plans for agricultural development centered on the testing of foreign crops and tools at facilities in Tokyo and other urban centers. The inspiration for these plans was also remote from rural Japan, coming, like the models for factories, mines, and military forces, from Western Europe and North America. Much as the future of industry was thought to lie in turbine-driven machinery, the future of farming, according to Home Minister Ōkubo Toshimichi (1830–1878), the central figure in the early Meiji government, lay in large-scale farms plowed by draft animals and planted with crops developed and proven outside of Japan. Model farms and agricultural testing centers were established at Komaba and other places in the greater Tokyo region in the 1870s and began investigations into the suitability of foreign products and techniques for Japanese farms in pursuit of Ōkubo's decree to "draw upon the best in the farming methods of the countries of the West" (*taisei shoshū no hō o sanshakushi*).[13] Rice was brought in for testing from Southeast Asia, Europe, and the United States; European and

American draft animals and tools were examined; and technicians were dispatched overseas to study foreign farming *in situ*.[14]

The Japanese farmers who were to put into practice the new modes of agriculture figured into government plans as the passive recipients of the knowledge generated by officials and the technicians they sponsored. The practical agricultural knowledge that villagers had acquired over generations was considered a dead end and the adoption of foreign methods of farming an essential means of achieving the modernization of agriculture. Teachers of Western techniques were dispatched from Tokyo across the country in the early 1880s, holding lectures and offering demonstrations to farmers in their home villages.[15] The government also loaned out equipment and draft animals to prefectural planners, who used them to establish model farms and made them available to local groups of farmers proposing major land reclamation projects.[16]

The provision of equipment did not, however, represent a solid financial commitment on the part of the government for the support of either villages or agriculture; in fact, it was more nearly the opposite. Tamari Kizō, a teacher at the Komaba Agricultural School and a researcher dispatched to America at the time of the programs, later remembered them as having been designed "to bring forth an enterprising spirit" among the local populations who made use of them.[17] The central government was in effect declaring the directions in which it wished to see agriculture progress and leaving its realization on the ground to local hands and local resources.

While officials attempted to carve a new path for Japanese agriculture, efforts on the parts of independent farmers, autonomously organized agricultural associations, and local governments continued seamlessly from the Edo period and offered a counterpoint to the largely ineffectual plans of the government. As they did around Shinainuma and Lake Nabire in Miyagi prefecture, early Meiji farmers across the country showed a keen interest in expanding their productive capacities and the profitability of their agricultural activities. The same sense of new possibility that drove the quests for industrial and urban modernization also permeated the countryside, combining with the new pressures and opportunities that came with the commercialization of agriculture to spur a flurry of improvement activities.

Efforts by farmers to improve agriculture in early Meiji differed from government programs in three chief respects: they were undertaken on individual or local community bases without wider organization; they sought to build on existing practices, rather than emulating foreign farming; and they often proved effective in stabilizing production and raising yields. It was in this context that the figure of the *rōnō* rose to prominence. Possessed of detailed local knowledge where central officials chased after the universal and the foreign; embedded in farming communities, rather than handing down directives from central offices; and building on techniques with proven effectiveness, *rōnō* offered a distinct contrast to the high-handed official planners of the new agriculture. Their efforts in the 1870s and 1880s laid the foundation for the transformation of agriculture at the end of the nineteenth century and made the figure of the experienced, self-motivated, and locally renowned promoter of best practices central to official schemes of agricultural modernization in the decades that followed.

In a number of regions, *rōnō* attacked the problem of agricultural improvement with a canniness and vigor that successfully expanded farming production. Such enduring advances in agriculture as were experienced in the first decades of the Meiji period came for the most part from the work of these *rōnō* and their compatriots in villages across the country who implemented and spread their ideas. Drawing on lifetimes of experience as farmers, *rōnō* approached the improvement of agriculture practically, seeking out means of increasing production that did not impose onerous new demands on financial resources or labor. Success in this quest brought them nationwide attention. In the 1870s, Gunma *rōnō* Funatsu Denjibē (1832–1898) sought out the best means of cultivating rice and potatoes and the most effective uses of fertilizers in his native prefecture, publishing these in pamphlets along with advice on storage and sericulture.[18] These efforts won him fame among farmers who adopted his techniques, and an invitation to enter officialdom as an educator. Nakamura Naozō (1819–1882) in Nara prefecture, Ishikawa Rikinosuke (1845–1915) in Akita prefecture, and Nara Senji (1822–1892) in Kagawa prefecture all pursued practical improvements to farming techniques and gained similar renown for their work educating farmers all over the country.

Supporting these figures was a network of local farmers who, if they lacked the technical knowledge or the financial wherewithal to commit time and fields to experimentation, played a crucial role in providing the social infrastructure that made possible the circulation of the ideas of the more famous *rōnō*. These men organized agricultural discussion meetings, purchased and shared farming pamphlets, promoted the implementation of improved cultivation methods, and invited their celebrated cousins to present lectures and answer questions. Outside government oversight and with no formal coordinating body, these webs of farming innovators, promoters, and students spread agricultural best practices across the country, helping local farming populations adjust to the changing market realities of the new era and laying the foundation for the flurry of organization and centralization that came at the end of the century.

The successes of early Meiji *rōnō,* both in practical agricultural research and in the dissemination of improved techniques, drew the attention of officials. The attraction of these figures and their agricultural work was obvious. Self-motivated and self-funded, they embodied the virtues that hopeful planners in the central government associated with *meibōka* and seemed to point the way to the self-sufficient countryside envisioned by the perpetually cash-strapped government. The autonomous nature of their activities also allowed officials, accused of excessive interference by Freedom and Popular Rights activists, to remain at a healthy distance from villages even as the increases in farming yields and improvement of village finances they sought came to fruition. Most important, *rōnō*-led improvement offered concrete results. Even the chief architect of the foundering program of agricultural Westernization, Ōkubo Toshimichi, expressed frustration with the shortcomings of the book-educated and theory-spouting agricultural specialists heading up the government's initiatives, pleading in exasperation to Tomioka Silk Mill chief Hayami Kensō in 1877, "I want to improve national agriculture further. Is there no one skilled in practical farming?"[19]

There were in fact practically skilled farmers available, and Hayami's answer pointed Ōkubo toward the *rōnō.* Hayami endorsed fellow Gunma resident Funatsu Denjibē, whose pamphlets and speeches, which often put advice about farming, fertilizing, and harvesting in the forms of easy-to-understand songs, had already earned him fame in his native region and were starting to spread beyond the prefecture's borders.[20] This recommendation served as the first step in a decade of increasing official interaction with and dependence upon *rōnō* as the central and prefectural governments integrated their teachings, methods, and persons into agricultural policy. A decade before Yamagata Aritomo named *meibōka* explicitly in his plans for the system of local government, their experience, knowledge, and renown placed *rōnō* in the roles of middlemen between farming villages and government, building bridges to modernity for farming communities.

Agricultural policy shifted to integrate *rōnō* and their work in the 1880s, beginning with the publication of their names and addresses to encourage sharing and network building and quickly moving on to more direct means.[21] Their discoveries and refined techniques became the most obvious and immediate target for the attentions of central and prefectural planners, and officially backed tests of these innovations were conducted on the national and prefectural levels. Prefectural governments in

Ishikawa and Fukushima, with no small degree of condescension, each conducted a series of tests in the 1880s designed to shine the light of "scientific principles of the wider world" (*seken no gakuri*) on the rice selection methods discovered by Hayashi Enri (1831–1906), a former samurai official from Fukuoka prefecture who first took up farming and agricultural experimentation in his forties.[22] If the tone of the goals sounded dismissive of local farmers and native development, the results were not. The tests in both prefectures found Hayashi's techniques to yield results superior to other methods, prompting prefectural governments in Tochigi prefecture and elsewhere to conduct their own tests.

To help ensure that *rōnō* continued their productive activities in research, officials also offered rewards. Kagawa's Nara Senji, a pioneer in the improvement of rice seeds and cultivation, filled both the display space of his small home and his wallet with a litany of honors that ran the gamut from minor awards from local exhibitions in the prefectures of Chiba and Akita through more prestigious laurels at the newly inaugurated nationwide meetings of the Dai Nihon Nōkai in Tokyo, culminating in his receiving the Imperial Medal with Green Ribbon in 1892.[23] The plaudits accompanying the medal, which celebrated Nara's personal funding of his improvement work, suggest that the awards were still based on the government's hopes for self-motivated and financially independent local elites, but the not-insignificant monetary prizes that were attached to it and the other awards hinted at a new recognition of the necessity of providing additional motivation through public funds.

Government officials also sought to integrate *rōnō* and their work more directly into agricultural policy and official initiatives. Disquiet at government interference in local matters was on the rise in the 1880s, however, and concerned authorities were anxious to avoid heavy-handed intrusions into agriculture.[24] Instead, they pursued ways of either bringing successful *rōnō* into the government as advisors to agricultural offices and as educators or by making use of the name *rōnō* had made for themselves. The earliest move in the former direction came from the Nara prefectural government, which gave their official support in 1872 to Nakamura Naozō's continuing efforts at training local farmers and experimenting with new crops. Officials redoubled their efforts two years later and placed Nakamura in charge of the prefectural agricultural experimentation office, where he conducted tests on the Western crops promoted by the Home Ministry.[25] The national government took a direct hand in 1878, when Ōkubo took Hayami's advice and convinced Funatsu Denjibē to take a position as a technician and a teacher at the Home Ministry's Komaba Agricultural Research Station. The agricultural pioneer spent eight years at the facility, proving his techniques superior to the German farming methods that the school had concentrated on up to that time and contributing to the development of official policy both materially and by means of his reputation among farmers.[26] Fully integrated into official agricultural posts, he moved on to the Agriculture and Commerce Ministry after leaving Komaba and worked there until his death in 1898. The Home Ministry's opening of its Second Industrial Exhibition in 1881 marked the beginning of more active employment of *rōnō,* who through both the exhibition and the spread of agricultural associations were reaching new levels of fame. Hayashi Enri was the most prominent of the figures thus employed in the early 1880s, hired to lead government-administrated agricultural research in 1881 before returning to his native Fukuoka in the summer of the following year to take up a similar position in the newly organized prefectural branch of the Dai Nihon Nōkai.[27]

Further government effort went into promoting the work of *rōnō* as traveling educators. In a program based on systems of traveling farming instruction in France and Germany, government officials gave their encouragement and limited degrees of financial support to *rōnō* to continue their tours of the countryside and the dissemination of their improvements.[28] Prefectural administrations went their national counterparts one better, moving to put the practical skills and experience of *rōnō* to work directly for local development. The Chiba prefectural government invited Nara Senji to act as a traveling instructor to help villagers improve rice quality, and Akita officials had Ishikawa Rikinosuke continue his earlier work as a touring educator after he was brought into the prefectural administration.[29] Authorities in Miyagi and Akita demonstrated the local interest in proven native methods by seeking out former central official Hida Rōichi, not for the research in Western agricultural methods he conducted in the Home Ministry, but for his experience with advanced Kyūshū farming techniques in his earlier life as a farmer and village headman in Ōita prefecture.[30]

While there remained, at the very least, pockets of resistance to movements away from early plans for Western-style, science-based modernization of agriculture, calls for the abandoning of these plans in favor of small-scale farms and practical improvement began to come from central officials in the 1880s.[31] The most important and energetic early advocate for fundamental change in agricultural policy was Maeda Masana (1850–1921). A colorful figure influential both within and outside of the government, Maeda traced a circuitous path through the intersection of agricultural development and official policy in the late nineteenth and early twentieth centuries. As a director in the Agriculture and Commerce

Ministry, Maeda echoed Ōkubo's late-career concerns about the impracticality of an agricultural policy based on the imitation of European and North American farming techniques. He expressed his frustration with the meager efforts and poor results of the promotion of Western-style farming in 1884, declaring "Now the necessary testing is not trivial work like the cultivation of foreign fruit trees or the production of tin cans. In the future, the purpose [of industrial policy] can be nothing other than devising a new form of Japanese agriculture."[32] While at first glance his call for a "new form" of agriculture might not seem all that far from the sentiments behind the push for large-scale foreign farming, the fact that Maeda was seeking a new form of specifically Japanese agriculture was important. He had seen the effectiveness of the improved *rōnō* techniques that moved northeast across the country via agricultural discussion societies, whose virtues became all the more apparent when contrasted with the disappointing results of the "trivial work" that Maeda lamented.[33]

Maeda laid out his vision for the government role in agricultural development in his 1884 *Kōgyō iken* (Advice for the Encouragement of Industry).[34] Comprised of thirty volumes, this series outlined a plan for economic development that emphasized native agriculture and existing modes of traditional production as the means of creating a firm basis for future industrial development and raising the national standard of living. Lamenting the debased condition of the countryside and the scant hope for its improvement under present policies, Maeda singled out for blame the financial austerity of the Matsukata Deflation and what he characterized as a wrongheaded and tunnel-visioned focus on modern industry.[35] To counteract the baleful influence of these factors, Maeda called for a new focus on native forms of agricultural production for the market and a more active role for the government in promoting it.

While representing a change in approach in its concern for farmers and its focus on Japanese farming, *Kōgyō iken* is inconsistent and noncommittal in advocating any concrete fundamental change to official policy. Even were it not for the fact that, like Matsukata Masayoshi himself, Maeda held the reestablishment of fiscal stability as a prerequisite that had to be met before government funds could be applied directly to industrial promotion, he continued to see the problems with agricultural production and rural prosperity as coming from failings in the work ethic of farmers.[36] A chief concern was finding the means to cultivate the "willingness" (*kokoro*, also translatable as "spirit") of farmers to use their labor to shore up the economic basis of the government in the rural regions—what *Kōgyō iken* characterized as improving villages and developing agriculture.[37] This willingness held a privileged place over the other ingredients of economic production, contributing 50 percent to its effectiveness, while relevant laws and capital provided only 40 percent and 10 percent, respectively.[38] The ethos of self-sufficiency and independent motivation that made *rōnō* and other *meibōka* key to government plans remained central to Maeda's new direction.

Kōgyō iken's author attached the same importance to independent improvement efforts as did other policy makers, but Maeda had less faith in the capacity of natural forces to foster villagers who would undertake them. Early Meiji statesman Iwakura Tomomi described the processes that were supposed to produce local leaders in 1882, laying out the basic elements that Yamagata would incorporate in his local government system at the end of the decade:

> People who have resources and renown (*meibō*) in agriculture and business will, by means of accepting government orders and undertaking public business, be respected as honorable by the people of their villages. Most of the people with resources and renown in agriculture and business that appear in villages, if they are not district heads (*kochō*) or health committee members (*eisei iin*), are post office managers. Positions like district heads, health committee members, and post office managers are all low-paying, and what they receive of course does not match their labor. Further, they enjoy occupying themselves with this business and, in the case of district heads, they want by all means to be chosen when the time comes for reelection, whether they have to bribe the villagers or secretly buy their votes. . . . They satisfy the three needs of clothing, food, and shelter for themselves; the only need that is not satisfied is for honor (*eiyo*), so there is absolutely no difference between the way they want honor and the way a thirsty man wants drink or the way a cold man wants clothing.[39]

The pervasive village poverty that Maeda saw, however, convinced him that, not only was a hunger for honor failing to drive wealthy villagers to local service, more corporal forms of need were not even pushing middling and poorer farmers to act rationally. "If we examine the condition of the people closely," Maeda explained,

> those who live by the old traditions of frugality are still in a safe position today but very many have turned to luxury and outward show. Now, with mountains of debt, they are mortgaging or selling off the real estate, etc., handed down by their ancestors with the result that they can no longer maintain even the standard of living they once had. In extreme cases, we see the pitiful spectacle of people gathering grass and roots for food. Apparently, this is the result of people not advancing their individual standard of living in line with their real capacities but putting on an empty show of following the latest fashion.[40]

A lack of sense and an unnatural hunger for luxury not only accounted for the desperate straits in which marginal farmers found themselves, it also dispossessed landowning farmers who might otherwise have risen to become village leaders. These problems lay behind the novel aspects of Maeda's idea of willingness. While it was an innate trait of farmers, willingness nonetheless required cultivation and activation. The self-motivation that Iwakura and other planners counted on to fill local offices and spur village development would neither appear on its own, nor could it accomplish its purpose without laws to support it. The assistance of government was necessary.

Ultimately, *Kōgyō iken* failed to become the guiding document for a new phase in Japanese industrial policy. It faced an implacable adversary in the person of Matsukata Masayoshi, who, in addition to taking offense at its criticisms of his deflationary measures, had plans to establish an industrial promotion bank attached to his own Finance Ministry. As a similar bank run by the Agriculture and Commerce Ministry was central to Maeda's proposal, the rewrites that Matsukata forced upon the proposal removed much of the purpose of *Kōgyō iken* and left it without clear conclusions.[41] But while it failed to dictate the course of policy, it did provide hints of what was to come. The 1880s and 1890s saw government planners move toward closer coordination with *rōnō* and the village leaders who followed their examples, creating a favorable legal context for their efforts and cultivating their willingness through increasingly substantial offers of material aid. Central to both of these initiatives were the agricultural associations (*nōkai*) and other farmers' groups that were instrumental in the transmission of the knowledge of *rōnō*.

While *rōnō* stood out for their knowledge and practical innovation in improving farming, they relied on wider networks of interested farmers to spread the word about their techniques, purchase and share their publications, and host them on their speaking and educational tours. Over the last decades of the nineteenth century, both farmers' groups and their memberships underwent transformative changes. Beginning as independent local organizations peopled by older elite farmers connected to one another through personal bonds, farming organizations evolved into nationally organized and officially recognized associations gathering newly risen landlords-cum-*meibōka* and presenting them with the means to achieve their political and economic objectives.

The earliest roots of the farming groups that worked with *rōnō* to spread improved agricultural practices lay in the first years after the establishment of the Meiji government. Much as they had led residents in Shinainuma and Babayachi to organize, the power vacuums left by the collapse of the Tokugawa bakufu provided both space and impetus for farmers to form cooperative bonds. Both autonomously and with the encouragement of the new central government, farmers assembled on a regional basis to exchange seeds and discuss agricultural matters. Appearing first in Kansai in 1875, gatherings of this type quickly became common across the country, reaching Miyagi and other far-flung regions by the decade's end.[42] As figures who brought together landowning farmers spurred by their own initiative to pursue the development of agriculture, the organizers of these meetings represented local iterations of the *rōnō* type who made up in enthusiasm and energy what they lacked in advanced technical knowledge.

The success of these early meetings and their evolution into local agricultural associations were marked from the beginning by the cooperation between *rōnō* and the local elites surviving from the Tokugawa era. The first *nōkai* (agricultural association) is said to have been established by an Aichi district head and *rōnō* named Furuhashi Genrokurō.[43] Son of a man ranked among the "three exceptional farmers" (*santokunō*) of the Edo period, Furuhashi organized meetings of the *rōnō* in his district every spring and fall to share and spread their accumulated agricultural wisdom. He moved toward more concrete efforts at organization in the 1880s, taking advantage of changes in local administrative structure to establish agricultural discussion groups in each village of the district. His successes in these efforts earned him the attention of prefectural authorities, who seized on his model and encouraged the formation of similar groups in each of Aichi's districts.[44] A similar pattern marked the efforts of Hayashi Enri. Finding it impossible on his own to spread the techniques he had pioneered to farming communities across the country, Hayashi moved to organization in search of a solution. He established the "*Kannōsha*" (Agricultural Encouragement Society) in Fukuoka prefecture in 1883 as a group to train the next generation of agricultural leaders and farming pioneers.[45] In patterns similar to Furuhashi and Hayashi, *rōnō* across Japan leveraged their positions in local government to promote meetings of farmers and lay down the foundations for lasting agricultural organizations.[46]

These meetings and groups of local farmers proved more interesting to officials than even the *rōnō* who organized them and who were becoming integral to agricultural policy by the mid-1880s. Aiming at the cultivation of willingness in much the same way as Maeda had suggested, central officials took early note of *rōnō* organizational success and attempted to replicate their efforts on a larger scale. As Aichi officials had done with Furuhashi's groups, the national government often piggybacked on such autonomous organizing. In the 1880s, agricultural officials followed a policy of promoting the establishment of local agricultural discussion meetings, competitive fairs, and similar events in order to demonstrate to farmers the benefits of the Western agricultural techniques upon which they hung their hopes.[47] These efforts often found receptive audiences. A group known locally as "industrious farmers" (*seinō*) formed in Shizuoka prefecture in the 1880s to promote farming based on Euro-American models in their home district.[48] The cooperative activities of officials and *rōnō* derived in part from the concerns shared by both groups. They each saw village poverty as a dire threat and held a common interest in minimizing the local difficulties arising from the commercialization of agriculture, which included the spread of absentee landlordism in economically advanced regions. At this stage, the confluence between landowners and officials moved toward the same goal of the well-being of rural society writ large. This unity fell apart, however, in the particular means that each envisioned for the goal, as well as in the specifics of what "well-being" meant.

The commercialization of farming and the expansion of agricultural capitalism created challenges that attracted the attention of officials and *rōnō* alike and demonstrated the interests shared by the two groups. The change to the cash payment of land taxes tied producers to markets more profoundly than ever before and combined with the disintegration of systemic controls on rice production to deleterious effect.[49] The maximization of production became the governing preoccupation of rice farmers everywhere. The new tax laws were nakedly exploitative, but the freshly opened markets served the purpose of firing the ambitions of the most economically marginalized elements of society and sending them rushing off to work in pursuit of an imagined windfall. The exclusive focus on increasing production that resulted took an immediate toll on quality. In Miyagi, perennial difficulties with the drying and storage of rice worsened the downward trend, and by 1877 grain from the prefecture had fallen to the lowest grading on the Tokyo Rice Exchange. Quality continued to fall thereafter, and Miyagi farmers soon faced the very real possibility that their rice would be dropped from the exchange altogether.

The response to the looming rice crisis in Miyagi exposed both the shared interests of the prefectural government and landowning farmers, and the gulf that separated the practical concerns of prefectural officials from the grand plans of their counterparts in Tokyo. Matsudaira Masanao, then at the beginning of what would be remembered as an assertive and effective term as Miyagi's governor, issued a set of compulsory regulations for the threshing and grading of rice in 1878. Ostensibly targeting "gangs of dishonest merchants" (*kanshō furyō no to*) who soaked rice in water or added chaff to filled sacks to increase their weight, the rules represented the first direct application of punitive legal force to the production of rice.[50] They required that all rice shipments leaving the prefecture be subject to official inspection and imposed legal penalties for non-compliance, stipulating that police reports be immediately filed and legal action proceed with haste.[51] The measures quickly proved effective. The quality of rice leaving the prefecture improved, securing its place on the Tokyo exchange. In spite of its explicit condemnation of the practices of rice merchants (a role that many a landlord-farmer still filled at this point), the lack of protest or resistance to the regulations attested to the harmony between government goals and landlord interests.

Government stewardship over the quality of rice in Miyagi was short-lived. Pointing to clauses in the regulations that referred to farmers as "peasants" (*hyakushōdomo*), central officials condemned the regulations as "feudal" and in 1881 ordered the prefecture to rescind them and return to the earlier system of unregulated rice.[52] The charge of "feudalism" seems suspect (or at least ironic) in the face of both the Meiji government's exploitation of the countryside for tax income and the directions that agricultural policy went on to take at the end of the century. The ministry's refusal of a proposal from a Tokyo rice producers' union to establish similar regulations the same year suggests that the reason was instead a general unwillingness to risk the public ire that direct government involvement in private production might provoke.[53] As it was, the abolition of the regulations ended the brief recovery of Miyagi rice. The collapse of rice prices in the early 1880s joined the ongoing pressures generated by encroaching market forces in encouraging Miyagi farmers to again turn a blind eye to quality as they struggled for their livelihood. The progress made while the regulations were in effect and the universality of the difficulties facing rice farmers nationwide ensured that Miyagi grain held on to its place on the Tokyo exchange, but the quality problems persisted and cast a shadow that stretched into the new century.

While central bureaucrats argued over the course of agricultural policy and local officials struggled with the practical promotion of agriculture, a new push for consolidation and centralization was transforming farming organizations nationwide. Figures on the fringes of government in Tokyo reached out to the networks of *rōnō* and local farmers that agricultural policy centered on and built the bases for nationwide organizations of farmers. This was the context in which the Dai Nihon Nōkai was formed.

The founding of the Dai Nihon Nōkai marked a transition point in the development of agricultural organizations in the Meiji period and pointed to the course of relations between official institutions and private groups for the rest of the century. The society's roots lay in two earlier organizations that crossed the boundaries between public and private in convoluted ways. The Tōyō Nōkai (Oriental Agricultural Society) emerged in Chiba prefecture in 1879 around the government-run Shimofusa Sheep Ranch (Shimafusa Bokuyōjō) founded in the same year. Organized by the first class of graduates from the facility's educational program, the society was led by ranch head Iwayama Keigi and counted central agricultural bureaucrats, local officials, and farmer-advisors attached to the ranch among its members.[54] As the Toyo Nokai was meeting in Chiba, the Tōkyō Dannōkai (Tokyo Agricultural Discussion Association) brought agriculturalists together in the capital. In a pattern closely reflecting that of the Chiba organization, the Dannōkai was centered on the semi-official Mita Crop Nursery and drew on figures associated with the facility, as well as other bureaucrats, for the bulk of its membership.[55]

Both the Tōyō Nōkai and the Tōkyō Dannōkai were products of their time, but in their structure and membership, they pointed to a new direction in agricultural organization. Attached to officially sponsored agricultural testing centers, the groups shared links to the Western agricultural methods that formed the basis for government policy at the time. It was the ways in which they diverged from the official philosophy, however, that aligned them with the emerging thought of progressive bureaucrats like Maeda Masana and set them upon the path toward the foundation of the Dai Nihon Nōkai.

While central bureaucrats held prominent positions in both the Tokyo and Chiba groups, a striking common feature was the organizations' inclusion of *rōnō* and other farmers in their ranks. In addition to the notable farmers who had been employed as educators at the Shimofusa ranch, the Tōyō Nōkai's membership also included ranchers and farmers from the surrounding area.[56] Private farmers had an even more foundational place in the Tōkyō Dannōkai. The group had evolved from weekly discussion meetings of local farmers held at the home of seed dealer and agriculture booster Ozawa Kihei and the periodic seed exchange meetings and *rōnō* conferences that grew from these.[57] By including farmers who had no formal affiliation with the central government and existing as voluntary groups divorced from official business, both organizations established a model for membership based on practical experience and set a precedent for meaningful cooperation between officials and non-officials in agricultural development.[58] These ideas formed a cornerstone of Maeda Masana's thought in *Kōgyō iken* and played a key role in the efforts that Maeda later put into the formation and development of a central agricultural organization that would coordinate the efforts of similar local groups throughout the country.

The Second National Industrial Promotion Exposition (Dai-2 Kai Naikoku Kangyō Hakurankai) (March 1–June 30, 1881) in Tokyo provided the setting for the transformation of the two smaller groups into the Dai Nihon Nōkai. The immediate stimulus for the formation of the new organization was a discussion meeting set up by the Agriculture and Commerce Ministry Agricultural Bureau head Nagaoka Shōsuke to which he had invited up to three *rōnō* from each prefecture.[59] The purpose of the event, according to Nagaoka, was "to discuss (*kenron*) the practices of each region and hear the opinions of each attendant, to investigate (*kōkyū*) their advantages and disadvantages, and to foster a spirit of competitiveness and progress (*kyōshin no kisei*)."[60] Apparently impressed with the meeting, the official interest it demonstrated, and the opportunity it offered, leaders from the Tōyō Nōkai and Tōkyō Dannōkai held discussions of their own at the Exposition and agreed to merge their groups. They moved quickly, laying out the new association's regulations, electing its officers, soliciting members far and wide, and setting up its headquarters at the Mita Crop Nursery before the Exposition had closed its gates.[61]

The circumstances surrounding the foundation of the Dai Nihon Nōkai highlight the key features of the group at its inception. Continuing along the developmental paths of its progenitor groups, it represented an evolutionary progression in agricultural thought that retained many of the features of the conservative philosophies of bureaucrats even as it set out in new directions. From its formation, the association displayed the familiar veneer of official endorsement applied to self-motivated and privately funded developmental activities. Its establishment by means of a private donation by Agricultural Bureau head Nagaoka Shōsuke embodies the group's melding of the public with the private.[62] The extensive list of government bureaucrats that held membership outside their official capacities ensured that the group remained closely tied to government administration, while the ostensibly private nature of the group obviated any claim on official funding. It duplicated official policy toward agriculture and rural administration in miniature.

The informal ties that bound the Dai Nihon Nōkai to the government ensured that, at least in the first decade of its existence, it cleaved closely to the thought guiding government officials. The 1880s saw a continuous stream of interactions between the organization and the central government. While the group retained responsibility for its own operating costs, it found limited access to public monies through contract work. The Agriculture and Commerce, Finance, Home, and Imperial Household

Ministries paid the group to undertake a range of testing activities, publish official reports, and take over operations at official agricultural facilities, bestowing upon it commendations, monetary awards, and even a headquarters building.[63] The potential for radical innovation in the organization's goals and methods was accordingly muted. The Dai Nihon Nōkai's new focus on the useful knowledge among the larger mass of the farming population did not at this point signal as great a break with policy makers' top-down approach to farming villages as would come later. For all the appreciative words that its organizers spoke about local *rōnō* and their experience-based knowledge, the association was initially intended primarily as an instrument to transmit the plans and goals of the Agriculture and Commerce Ministry down to local farmers, experienced and otherwise, that comprised its membership on the local level.[64] Ensconced in government facilities and undertaking official commissions, the Dai Nihon Nōkai poured much of its efforts into the program of Western-style modernization whose failings were drawing the ire of Maeda and other forward-looking bureaucrats.

The organization hinted at a new direction in public-private relations concerning agriculture through the meaningful autonomy that non-official members of the group exercised. This autonomy was evident from the association's earliest roots in the officially sponsored meeting of *rōnō* from all prefectures. The participants were not celebrity innovators like Funatsu or Hayashi, whose proselytizing efforts were even then being coopted by officials. They were rather landowning farmers whose fame, if it ever existed, was limited to their local area and likely had more to do with the economic success of their farms than any wider efforts to develop and disseminate improved techniques. The representatives from Miyagi, two landowners from the Tōda district who left behind no evidence of remarkable agricultural achievement, were typical of the attendees.[65] Still, it was the economic success of these local farmers that made them attractive to agricultural officials. The *rōnō* congress was intended to distill their experiences into a formula that could be applied far and wide, a goal enshrined even more clearly in the Agriculture and Commerce Ministry's abortive plans the following year to create an official clone to the Dai Nihon Nōkai in an Industrial Promotion Council (Kangyōin) enlisting "wealthy merchants" (*gōshō*) and "rich farmers" (*funō*).[66] Irrespective of the Nōkai's subsequent efforts to toe the government line in reproducing foreign agricultural techniques, the importance of *rōnō* to organizers both official and otherwise was in the association of prosperity with practical expertise in farming.

The local *rōnō* who attended the 1881 congress and went on to make up the wider membership of the Dai Nihon nōkai had reasons of their own for participating. While they may not have been the brilliant and selfless agricultural innovators with which the term was popularly associated, they did represent a distinctive slice of rural society and shared a particular set of interests. From the beginnings of their involvement with the *nōkai*, these landowning farmers inserted their interests into their agricultural discussions. Along with the more prosaic answers the assembled *rōnō* offered to the scripted questions put to them by the organizers of the 1881 congress, they emphasized their acute concern about the negative impact of the inroads of capitalist markets on the quality of rice. Echoing the justifications presented earlier by Miyagi in defense of its quality regulations, they called for official support for a course of corrective treatment that included agricultural discussion groups, production promotion organizations, product exhibitions, agricultural unions, and the improvement of landlord-tenant relations.[67] Officials may have seen them as a resource for the betterment of agriculture and Nagaoka could talk of fostering their spirit of competitiveness to excite an Iwakura-esque hunger for honor, but the landlords cast as *rōnō* in the meeting saw rich opportunities of their own in the Dai Nihon Nōkai and its official connections.

Government attention to, recognition of, and eventually active support for agricultural groups of rural landlords gave these figures an increasingly effective means of exploiting these opportunities. Two additional changes instituted by the central government fostered the growing intimacy between government offices and the Dai Nihon Nōkai to strengthen the position of landlords in the 1880s. The first was a May 1884 ordinance abolishing elections for the leadership of districts, towns, and villages (*ku, ko, chō, son*) and making them appointed positions. Undeniably a step backward for meaningful local autonomy, the tightness with which it bound the landlords appointed to these offices to prefectural and national officials presented them with a new avenue through which to interact with higher levels of administration. Further official recognition and political opportunity for landlords and rice merchants came in the form of the Industrial Association Standards (Dōgyō Kumiai Junsoku) and the Rice Dealer Association Regulation Standards (Beishō Kumiai Kisoku Junsoku) passed in 1884 and 1885. Providing official recognition for groups that landlords had begun to organize on their own, they opened a doorway for the kind of intervention in market conditions that the central government had objected to so strongly when undertaken by the Miyagi prefectural government. Only three years after the Agriculture and Commerce Ministry dismantled Governor Matsudaira's rice quality regulations, the Neighboring Village League Rice Dealer Association (Moyori Chōson Rengō Beishō Kumiai), a Miyagi organization formed under the provisions of the new laws, imposed their own system of rice inspections. Establishing inspection stations at exit points around the prefecture, they enforced quality standards on rice bound for outside domestic markets in a pattern that differed from the earlier prefectural system only in its official, but indirect, endorsement by the national government.[68]

In subcontracting the enforcement of quality to landlords, the officials in Tokyo were doing more than skirting charges of overly intrusive involvement in local affairs. They were making use of the informal, but coercive, power that landlords naturally held over their tenants, relying upon them (with a confidence arising from the knowledge that landlords shared the government's interest in improving rice quality) to bring about the ends desired by central officials. The bureaucrats involved demonstrated no concern over the resemblance between this direct authority of landlords over tenants and the verboten feudalism that was the justification for the erasure of Miyagi government's rice regulations. The new style of decentralized regulations was as attractive to government officials as they were to the landlords who created and enforced them. The national government was able to avoid charges of onerous interference in local matters by leaving the regulation of quality up to independent but officially recognized local groups whose members derived immediate benefits from their enforcement.

Under these favorable administrative conditions, the middle years of the 1880s saw an explosion of landlord-led and landlord-staffed agricultural organizations. Dai Nihon Nōkai branches opened in dozens of prefectures, adding to the scores of existing landlord and merchant groups. The first appeared in Akita only months after the formation of the central group in December of 1881, followed by branches in Kyōto, Yamanashi, Gifu, Tokushima, and Gunma the following year.[69] At first organized independently, the groups soon found themselves the objects of insistent attention from local governments. The Miyagi government locked the rapidly expanding agricultural associations in the prefecture under its authority in 1883, assigning responsibility for the establishment and supervision of agricultural promotion associations to each district, city, town, and village in the prefecture.[70] The form that the authorities imposed at that time anticipated the later shape of the fully realized Dai Nihon Nōkai of the 1890s, with a cell-like arrangement of two or three representatives of each village group collectively comprising the membership of the district group, each of which then contributed similar numbers to make up the prefectural version of the organization.[71]

Despite their initially rapid spread, fortunes soon turned for the new crop of agricultural associations. The most obvious challenge was economic. The fiscal austerity policies of the Matsukata Deflation and their devastating effects on rice prices drove rural communities deeper into poverty, and support for *nōkai*, production unions, and similar organizations faded as members no longer had the money to pay their dues. In the case of the Dai Nihon Nōkai, the group's continuing commitment to the officially promoted but unimplementable techniques and technologies of Western European and North American farming and its failure to follow through on its early promise to refocus agricultural development on practical, native agriculture compounded the difficulties presented by the recession.[72] The success that the group's early organizing efforts enjoyed quickly dissipated in the latter half of the 1880s as branch after local branch suspended operations. The year 1886 alone saw the collapse of five regional *nōkai* and the withdrawal of the central group's commission to run the operations at the Mita Nursery, the crest of similar developments that greatly limited the local penetration of the organization by the decade's end.[73] By 1891 (when, in fact, the worst was over and the associations were beginning to come back into prominence) former Finance Ministry official Shibusawa Kisaku bemoaned the state of agricultural associations and their experimental stations in five prefectures. "In all these places, even though the experimental stations and *kumiai* management offices seemed to have had some effect when they were first set up, for one reason or another as days passed they eventually took on a degraded form. Today, it has come to the point where their effectiveness has all but disappeared."[74] Tamari Kizō, reminiscing a decade later, issued an even broader damnation. The deterioration by the close of the 1880s, he claimed, was such that "the efforts of bureaucrats and the people ended in failure and it became a time when the idea of agricultural improvement was completely abandoned."[75]

The hardships that agricultural organization and general improvement efforts suffered proved short-lived. The new decade brought with it an end to recession and a resurgence in rice prices that galvanized the hard-nosed group of landlords who had survived the bloodletting of the 1880s with their landholdings intact and the newly risen landlords who had found opportunity in adversity. The return to prosperity brought new life to agricultural associations, but not through a simple return to the fold of delinquent members. The new landlords emerged as leaders shaping what was, for all intents and purposes, a new movement for agricultural organization. Their economic strength bolstered, they turned to dispense with two threats that had come to the fore as landlord power waned under the trying conditions of the late 1880s.[76] The first of these came from the implications of the market economy for the place of tenant farmers in rural society. The commercialization of rice imposed stresses on villages and tied the price of grain to distant market forces, but this could also be an opportunity for tenants, who could respond to price jumps faster than their rents could be raised. In this context, the growing rates of tenancy in Miyagi, normally evidence of the success of landlords, became a potential threat.[77] Producers' associations represented means both of opposing the empowerment of tenants by market opportunities and of organizing landlords in preemptive opposition to potential tenant conflicts and the development of tenants' movements.[78]

The second threat felt by landlords came from grain merchants. Before the shocks of the Matsukata Deflation, agricultural associations brought together producers and marketers of grain, two strata with overlapping but not necessarily complementary interests. The hierarchical structure of these groups reflected the monopoly over rice sales that dealers gained with the rise of the speculative rice markets.[79] Merchants assumed positions of power in the associations, forcing landlords to acquiesce when conflicts arose and consigning the interests of smallholders and tenants to a distant third place.[80] The newly formed groups of the 1890s aimed to redress the imbalances of their predecessors. Landlords provided aggressive leadership, creating producer-centered groups that aimed for increased production (rather than increased prices) and pushed to the periphery the merchants who were even then completing their wresting of control over grain marketing from landlords.

The first indications of this new kind of organization in Miyagi appeared in 1890. A coalition of large landlords (defined by landholdings of over 50 hectares (*chō*), a class newly born in Miyagi but growing at a notable rate) crafted plans for a prefecture-wide Agricultural Improvement Union (Nōji Kairyō Kumiai) to be composed of farmers owning twenty or more hectares of land as compulsory members and open to willing participants holding five or more hectares.[81] The group experienced rapid success in rehabilitating the prefecture's poor reputation, its formation leading to an increase in confidence in Miyagi grain on the Tokyo Rice Exchange and earning praise from the Agriculture and Commerce Ministry as a unique and effective organization.[82] Similar groups soon formed in other regions. The first of a new brand of hierarchically structured *nōkai* (*keitō nōkai*) appeared in Kyoto in 1891. Closely resembling the Miyagi government's consolidation of agricultural associations in the 1880s, the Kyoto group installed *nōkai* in villages across the prefecture, subordinated them to district *nōkai,* and set a prefectural *nōkai* at the top of the entire structure.[83] Farmers in other regions took Kyoto's organization as their model and hierarchies of local, district, and prefectural associations began to appear across the country.

Initially, the new landlord-led associations surged past the lethargic Dai Nihon Nōkai, but the older organization soon took note of their success and reoriented itself to work in tandem with them. Until 1892, the activities of the Dai Nihon Nōkai were limited to the publication of its monthly journal and the holding of semi-annual product fairs.[84] Recognizing the direction the new *nōkai* were taking, the association became cognizant of the need for fundamental restructuring in order to become the centrally coordinating group for the rapidly spreading local organizations. To accomplish this transformation, the Dai Nihon Nōkai appointed as its secretary-general Maeda Masana, who had retired from official service in frustration to become a "private Nōshōmushō" (Ministry of Agriculture and Commerce), and assigned him the task of heading up an aggressive campaign for the nationwide establishment of hierarchically structured *nōkai* linked to itself at the apex.[85] By 1893, the Dai Nihon Nōkai had made up the ground lost during its period of decline and inactivity and stood at the top of a structure incorporating 26 prefectural, 212 district, and 1,824 village *nōkai*.[86] It built on this early success, developing an aggressive program to promote the establishment of affiliate organizations in every region. From 1893 to 1894, association councilors Ikeda Kenzō, Tamari Kizō, Yokoi Toshiyoshi, and Sawano Jun, member Hida Rōichi, and special advisor (and celebrated *rōnō*) Ishikawa Rikinosuke traveled around the entire country to aid in the formation and linking of groups to the Dai Nihon Nōkai and in the dissemination of agricultural knowledge and advanced techniques.[87] Meeting with success, the organization created guidelines for attaching existing associations to itself and distributed them across the country in the summer of 1894. By the middle of the decade, its reach extended into every corner of Japan and *nōkai*, like many other mid-Meiji local organizations, were becoming locked into a nationwide hierarchical organization.

Reaching out and bringing together regional agricultural organizations under its central leadership was only one aspect of the reinvigorated Dai Nihon Nōkai's activities in the 1890s. As important was a parallel thrust to gain recognition, funding, and sympathetic legislation from the central government. This represented a reversal in the location of initiative. In contrast to the pattern of the 1880s in which Maeda and other officials organized events and helped plan for the formation of agricultural groups, in the 1890s the leaders of the Dai Nihon Nōkai (many of whom had been officials during the prior phase) embarked on an aggressive program of lobbying the government for legal changes and recognition. They were aided in this quest by the newly created Imperial Diet. Filled with the same rural landlords and independent farmers who were the backbone of the *nōkai* movement, the Lower House played host to the debates and conflicts that surrounded the annual submission of proposals for an Agricultural Association Law (Nōkaihō). The contents of these proposals remained relatively consistent and reflected the key interests of the Dai Nihon Nōkai. As outlined in the first proposal of 1891, they included official support for local agricultural events, official mediation in the sharing and exchange of key farm inputs like seeds and fertilizer, official support for agricultural testing stations, government publication and dissemination of *nōkai* farming reports, and regular communications between officials and *nōkai* leaders.[88] Although success eluded these efforts until 1899, some figures in the central government quickly proved receptive to the appeals for recognition and support. Agriculture and Commerce official Sakō Tsuneaki took issue with the condemnation of agricultural organizations by others and voiced his own opinion in 1891 that the Dai Nihon Nōkai and its affiliated local groups served an important purpose and that the government should support them and enact laws to aid in their work, stating that "the important points now are that we must organize *nōkai,* agricultural schools, and research stations big and small across the entire country in a form like a spider's web or telegraph lines and thereby link them in a mutual connection, then plan for the development and improvement of agriculture."[89]

In advocating official support for the Dai Nihon Nōkai and its local affiliates, officials were responding to the changing political circumstances of the times and continuing the strategy that had guided the central administration of the countryside since the abolition of the Tokugawa-era domains. At the heart of both aims were rural landlords and their involvement in *nōkai.* Landlords formed the core of the new agricultural organizations, taking positions that promised both to contribute to the ongoing government mission of agricultural improvement on the cheap and to replace their political combativeness—on clear and disturbing display in the Freedom and Popular Rights Movement of the 1870s and 1880s—with the central concern of profiting from agricultural development.[90] Revisions to the land tax and the convening of the Imperial Diet had worked toward the latter goal, purchasing a degree of political quietude by the early 1890s. In pursuit of the former goal, officials extended new consideration for the concerns of landlords and support for their organizations. An early nod toward the interests informing the new associations came with the 1890 National Industrial Promotion Exposition, which signaled a change in official policy away from the heavily criticized drive to impose technologically advanced models of Western farming toward the fostering and dissemination of native techniques.[91] Officials also busied themselves with promoting the further spread and organization of the farmers groups that popped up autonomously in the early 1890s. Along with the commendations offered by the Agriculture and Commerce Ministry for the organizational efforts of landlords in Miyagi and elsewhere, prefectural governments threw their weight behind *nōkai*. As had the administrations of Kyoto and Miyagi, the governor of Niigata began an official push in 1892 to encourage the formation of groups of large landlords and induce them to apply their substantial resources toward the establishment of a prefectural *keitō nōkai* in a move that became increasingly common.[92]

Nōkai also attracted the attentions of officials with their promise as a means of depoliticizing rural areas. The political activism that had characterized the Freedom and Popular Rights Movement in the previous decades prompted an extensive course of government countermeasures to quell the political passions of rural landlords and ensure that they would not boil over again. Reform of the land tax and land registry systems and the promulgation of the Meiji constitution, with its qualified nod to the suffrage of rural landlords, all represented successful attempts by government leaders to drain energy from disruptive political opposition. Less directed, but equally effective in dissipating resistance, was the economic devastation of the 1880s, which purged landlord ranks of all but the most hard-nosed, business-focused farmers. The *nōkai* presented another means to deal with the new forms of political contrariness that arose with the convening of the Diet. For the leaders of the government-backed "bureaucratic parties" (*ritō*) in the Lower House, a centrally administered agricultural association could be an effective tool for binding the assertive landlords who challenged them as members of the so-called people's parties (*mintō*) to an organization tied in various ways to the national government.[93] The Dai Nihon Nōkai seemed to be just what many were looking for.

Evolving to keep pace with the changes unfolding below it in local areas and above it in the halls of the central government, Maeda's active leadership took the group in a new direction in 1894 that fractured it in two and expelled its conservative elements in a press for dramatic changes in the pervading order. The first turning point came in the summer. At a special assembly on the 15th of June, the disposition of sixteen key issues concerning agriculture was identified as the overriding mission of the Dai Nihon Nōkai. Reiterating earlier calls for solutions to rural debt; institutions to facilitate the purchase and exchange of seeds, tools, and fertilizer; and means of encouraging farmers to save their earnings, this new program added items that reflected the centrality of the new landlords-cum-*meibōka* in the organization and represented an aggressive defense of their interests. Among the goals that the group now dedicated itself to were the domestic replacement of imported secondary agricultural products like cotton, soybeans, and sugar (as well as the encouragement of underemployed tenants and smallholders to take up this secondary production), incentives for wealthy farmers to undertake agricultural improvements, and unspecified mechanisms to compel smaller farmers and tenants to move from over- to underpopulated regions "without complaint" (*naigai o ronzezu*).[94] These initiatives highlighted the new concerns that directed the Dai Nihon Nōkai. Alongside a nationalistic, and potentially profitable, opposition to the importation of foreign agricultural products were calls for laws compelling economically vulnerable farmers to adopt methods of production favored by the group, and for official funds and other benefits to encourage landlords to pursue improvement. In its 1894 meeting, the Dai Nihon Nōkai announced its position as the advocate of landlord interests and its mission to lobby for official support for them.

The course change of the summer led to a rupture at the year's end. Not everyone in the association stood behind Maeda's new direction and dissatisfaction deepened through the autumn in those who resented the abandonment of the organization's original goals and methods. Tensions between the discontented and the authors of their unhappiness came to a head during the All-Japan Agricultural Conference (Zenkoku Nōji Taikai) in Tokyo in 1894. Seeing close cooperation with the government in the creation of centrally coordinated hierarchical *keitō nōkai* as a sign of the devolution of the Dai Nihon Nōkai into a tool of central bureaucrats, a faction in the leadership council around Yokoi Tokiyoshi claimed the group's name and remade themselves as a research-oriented organization tied to the Komaba Agricultural School.[95] Maeda and the other leaders retained leadership over the remaining members, who comprised the greater part of the association, and continued with the plans they had crafted for a nationwide network of *nōkai.* At a general meeting in April of 1894, their group adopted the name of Zenkoku Nōji Shokai Chūō Honbu (National Headquarters of Agricultural Associations), simplified in 1900 to the enduring Zenkoku Nōjikai (National Agricultural Association).

Geopolitical conflict and the shattering of the long-standing Sinocentric Asian international order by Japan's victory in the Sino-Japanese War of 1894–1895 provided the opportunity for the new organization to advance its agenda. The costs that the war imposed on villages and the heightened sense of crisis and responsibility that officials felt in its wake strengthened the attention paid to the Zenkoku Nōjikai and made its plans more attractive to central planners. Lamentations concerning "distressed villages" (*nanson*) became a common refrain in the halls of government, the troubled communities presenting a spectrum of potential threats ranging from the stalling of economic development to the incubation of rebellion. The sources of these difficulties exposed the flaws in the thinking at the basis of government policy and gave new credence to the ideas that Maeda Masana had first voiced over a decade earlier. The connection of food production to markets both national and international and the ties of the rural economy to financial centers in Tokyo and other capitals around the world demonstrated the impossibility of the self-sufficient and depoliticized villages dreamed of by officials. Market forces affected by war and exploitative tax expropriations drove farmers who had been producing enough to feed themselves into poverty and starvation.

Not all the challenges to village prosperity after the war grew out of macroeconomic forces. Rates of absentee landlordism jumped in the late 1890s as older elites were replaced by the canny new actors who had profited from the economic dislocations of the previous decade, adding urgency to a problem that had long been lamented by officials.[96] Non-resident landlords presented a dual threat to village prosperity and development. Their relations to the villages in which they owned land were limited to the extraction of rent rice, relocating scarce resources needed for local farming improvement and administration to be held or spent in the urban centers the landlords called home. To this direct economic toll, they added further opportunity costs. As non-residents, they took on none of the social, administrative, or developmental responsibilities that officials attached to *meibōka* and that villages required to achieve self-sufficiency. Absentee landlords were in effect anti-*meibōka,* and their spread turned the attention of government to the resident landlords in the Zenkoku Nōjikai and the local *nōkai* with which it was affiliated.

With eyes in the capital focused on agricultural villages and official coffers flush with reparations from the defeated Qing rulers of China, the Zenkoku Nōjikai intensified its efforts to reform agricultural policy. It continued upon the course that had led to the rupture in the Dai Nihon Nōkai and, informed by the increasingly important influence of the landlords that made up its membership base, pushed off in new directions. The resolutions passed at the 1896 All-Japan Agricultural Conference picked up the themes voiced two years earlier and added to them a call for the central government to fund the agricultural awards that had been a defining feature of the Dai Nihon Nōkai since the 1880s.[97] A minor concession requesting little more than the coverage of the minimal financial costs associated with the product shows and awards that were becoming popular among *nōkai,* this demand in fact represented an attempt to abdicate financial responsibility for what was then a central aspect of agricultural improvement and a defining function of the earlier incarnation of the association. The list of attendees of the meeting at which this new call was made exposed the roots of the change. Breaking from the trend shown in previous conferences, the 1896 event saw landlord representatives from local *nōkai,* a group defined by their economic interests and one that was reluctant to direct private resources to village development in the abstract, replace the random collection of agriculturally minded individuals that had peopled the earlier meetings.[98]

The general meeting of the following year stated even more explicitly the commitment of the Zenkoku Nōjikai to this new direction. The pursuit of government funding for local agricultural lecture halls and experimentation stations and a reduction in the tax for registering paddyland took precedence over matters of actual farming improvement, clear hallmarks of the influence of local landlords.[99] Calls for legal change also came to the fore. Along with the constant push for an Agricultural Association Law, the meeting produced a resolution to pursue a Farmland Consolidation Law. These twin aims of official support for landlord-led improvement in the forms of government funding and legislation defined the Zenkoku Nōjikai's activities for the rest of the decade.

Organizationally, the Zenkoku Nōjikai tightened its links with local branches and firmed up the hierarchical structure linking them together. It redrew the administrative map of Japan in 1895, dividing the country into eight major agricultural districts (*nōku*). Meetings of the groups heading up the new districts followed soon after, with Tōhoku's Coastal Agricultural District Association (Riku Nōku Nōkai) gathering for the first time in Yamagata in September of 1895, while prefectural *nōkai* continued their work testing new tools and methods, establishing model farms, and spreading information downward through district and village *nōkai.*[100] Vigorous efforts to install *nōkai* in every corner of the country were also ongoing. Noted *rōnō* and Dai Nihon Nōkai/Zenkoku Nōjikai spokesman Ishikawa Rikinosuke proselytized for the organization in his native Akita, extolling the benefits that *nōkai* offered farmers and nation alike with a utopian formula: "when we connect the house and the village to the district and the prefecture, we will enrich the state and it won't be difficult to bring our spirits close to paradise."[101] The image was one that harkened back to Maeda's time as an official and illustrated the Zenkoku Nōjikai's vision of its place as a bridge connecting the central and the local. In his original critique of industrial policy in the 1880s, Maeda had declared, "if [we] don't build village strength, there will not be enough strength in the district. If there is not enough strength in the district, there will not be enough strength in the prefecture. If there is not enough strength in the prefecture, national power cannot possibly reach its full fruition."[102] Much as Maeda himself had done, the source of this call had moved outside of official corridors. As the century drew to a close, the Zenkoku Nōjikai was poised to take up its position at the podium, conducting the orchestra of hierarchic *nōkai* in a symphony that aimed to improve farming and remake the agricultural order in Japan.

While the Zenkoku Nōjikai lobbied for support from above and below, the national government was embarking on a new program of reaching out to landlords and local villages. The depressed economic conditions in the countryside following the war and concerns about newly formed tenants' organizations drove the agencies of the government to take a more active stance on village prosperity.[103] At the same time, officials were loath to give up their particular vision of local autonomy with its ideals of hands-off rural governance and self-powered agricultural improvement. They found a means to negotiate between these conflicting concerns in the concerted promotion of *gunze* and *chōsonze* (district, town, and village plans). The plans were another idea prominent in the recommendations of Maeda a decade earlier. Foreseeing a time in the near future when Japan's development would crash headlong into barriers of overpopulation and insufficient food supply, he presented town and village plans as the means to "bring forth the strength of the village" and to ensure that the countryside and the nation it fed would survive the coming Malthusian challenges.[104] By the end of the century, officials were prepared to embrace this aspect of Maeda's thought. Encouraging the formation of autonomous local groups to draft the policy plans for their towns and villages, Home Ministry bureaucrats identified a set of goals that included ending tax defaults, shoring up village and school assets, promoting thrift and savings among farmers, improving agriculture, spreading social education, and organizing youths and women.[105] In addition to these stated goals, officials also hoped that involvement in planning the policies would cultivate a self-starting spirit (*jihatsusei*) and a new sense of identification with the villages created by the local government system less than a decade earlier.[106] While the particular form of the plans was new, they were in fact little more than a novel iteration of the tried and true guiding philosophy of ideological promotion in place of direct government aid or support. The active protection and cultivation of village life remained outside the concerns of the state, and the resources and work required to meet the government goals of restoring prosperity and increasing production largely continued to be the responsibility of villagers and farmers.

While treading a familiar path with the promotion of town and village plans, government officials were also embarking on new forms of direct and substantive interaction with local communities. Their programs, however, showed a marked predilection for the wants and needs of landlords. In 1898, the Miyagi Agricultural and Industrial Bank (Miyagi Nōkō Ginkō) was established in Sendai as a prefectural subsidiary of the Japan Hypothec Bank and the Japan Agricultural and Industrial Bank, founded the previous year. Ostensibly intended to ease farmer access to the capital needed to pursue improvements, the Miyagi bank displayed a distinctive focus on the interests of landlords. It offered loans at lower than half the interest rates charged by Miyagi landlord-moneylenders, but the conditions it attached to these disqualified many applicants and worked directly for the benefit of large landlords. Loans required the staking of significant landholdings as collateral, which were packaged with the debt and sold to large landlords in the case of default, concentrating lands in the hands of the wealthiest members of rural society and consigning debtors to punishing tenancy terms. Any role for the bank as an engine for driving agricultural improvement was eclipsed by its actual function of providing landlords a means of expanding their holdings at a cost far below going rates.[107]

The national government made a full expression of its new commitment to the support of landlords and their work as *meibōka* for the development of farming in a series of laws at the turn of the century that marked a fundamental shift in the nature of agriculture in Japan. Described collectively as measures for the "protection of the middle class of industrial and agricultural producers" (*kōnō chūsan hōgō*), this legal shift reflected the success of the Zenkoku Nōjikai in achieving its goals under the leadership of Maeda and the increasingly strong influence of its landlord constituents. The major components of the legislative blitz were laws granting government funding to farmland consolidation (*kōchi seiri*) and agricultural experimentation stations in 1899; the Agricultural Association Law (Nōkaihō) in 1899, which granted both official recognition and a degree of authority to local *nōkai;* and the Industrial Cooperative Law (Sangyō Kumiaihō) in 1900. The Civil Code of 1897, though not the result of landlord lobbying, provided a complementary backdrop for the new legal order, firming up property rights and strengthening the positions of landlords relative to their tenants.

In one sense, the new laws followed a familiar pattern, entrusting the solution of rural problems to the upper echelon of village society.

Changed, however, was the degree of government involvement in this process. Decades of failure and ceaseless rural difficulties had made the inadequacy of the idea of truly self-sufficient villages clear to even the most unreceptive of officials and the ascent of landlords-cum-*meibōka* drove the point home. Just as basic physical needs had not proven capable of ensuring that farmers would be productive and prosperous, government leaders now knew that a hunger for honor could not be counted on to drive *meibōka* to improve their communities and foster the development of farming. The new laws were designed to compensate for this second failing by shoring up village landlords to enable them to fulfill the roles of *meibōka* and see to the rehabilitation of their distressed communities.[108] They provided for the first time a formal basis for the amorphous position of *meibōka,* giving a legally concrete reality to a concept that had, for all its centrality to agricultural and rural policy over the previous two decades, been little more than a rhetorical abstraction. Bolstered by public funds and secure in their officially recognized organizations, *meibōka* had forced government officials to abandon their vision of self-directed and self-supporting stewards of farming villages.

Along with this enshrining of ideals into law came a refinement in the vision of the *meibōka* who would receive government support in their newly supported roles as intermediaries and local leaders. While Kamata Sannosuke and other notable figures like him continued to be appreciated for performing their functions as envisioned in the original conception of decentralized and self-powered village development, these exemplary individuals stood out as much for their rarity as for their successes. If *meibōka*-led development were to power village development nationwide, it would have to be carried out among the ranks of general landlords, against the backdrop of whom the accomplishments of Kamata and his ilk shone so brightly. These people were the "agricultural middle class" that the *chūsan hōgō* laws aimed to protect. Not a middle class in an economic sense, those referred to in the law were instead a stratum defined by their relationship to agricultural production and their function as a cushioning agent between the two more problematic strata of absentee landlords and tenant farmers. They were resident rural landlords who made at least token attempts to farm some part of their landholdings. As such, they maintained the connections to agriculture and tenant farmers that their non-resident cousins had lost, while retaining the deep personal interest in improvement derived from their land ownership that their tenants lacked. Their direct connection to farming was not the only feature of the middle class that attracted the interest of lawmakers, nor was it what brought wider support from an Imperial Diet staffed with no shortage of absentee landlords. Bureaucrats and absentee landlords alike understood this "middle class" to offer a means of ensuring social harmony in villages as a "border wall class" (*hanpeisō*) standing between tenants and non-resident landlords (or rather standing in the empty spaces the latter group left in villages) and stifling the unrest that might otherwise arise.[109]

The legal changes at the end of the century fortifying this class with direct government support only succeeded after overcoming concerted and entrenched opposition. Many of the new laws had legacies stretching back a decade or more with records of continuous defeat. In the early years of the Diet, they often became casualties of party politics. Draft proposals for the Agricultural Association Law and for funding for agricultural experimentation stations and rural credit unions were defeated in the clashes between the government and the popular political parties in the wake of the contentious second general election in 1891.[110] Success at the end of the decade was not, however, simply a matter of hammering through these same laws. The influence of the rising landlords who became increasingly important in the Zenkoku Nōjikai at mid-decade and increasingly assertive in the Diet is clear in the refinements to the proposals and the expanding support they enjoyed. Plans to limit local *nōkai* significance and chain them to the operations of agricultural experimentation stations were abandoned, doing much to win over recalcitrant Diet members.[111] Even as the Zenkoku Nōjikai broke free of the constraints of the conservative wing of the Dai Nihon Nōkai who had authored the abandoned plans, concentrating landlord members in an effective organization and moderating opposition from that quarter, the Sino-Japanese War and the village problems that followed it muted official opponents. The positive need to address rural poverty in the wake of the conflict coincided with the temporary solving of the chronic shortage of funds that had long precluded active government commitment to agricultural development. The financial windfall of the war probably also played a role in aligning reluctant landlords with the cause. Landlords had been burned by the failure of government to follow through on its promises to fund development, as seen in the Entō affair in Miyagi, but newly flush official coffers likely convinced many that there might be some truth to the official commitment promised in the new laws.

The new willingness of landlord-politicians in the Diet and their counterparts in the Zenkoku Nōjikai to consider legal change did not signal passive acceptance of the plans of the organization's leaders and their government allies. The issue of precisely who the laws were to benefit brought forth challenge and conflict in the final run-up to the seminal legal change. Participants at the sixth All-Japan Agricultural Conference in 1898 attacked the provisions of the *nōkai* bill that mandated compulsory membership for all landlords, arguing that this would ensconce the growing numbers of absentee landlords in the organization and undo its mission of improving agriculture.[112] Assurances that the residential requirement included in the bill would exclude anyone not present in the village placated these fears, but the fact that the landlord members raised them at all demonstrated their awareness of the empowerment inherent in the legislation.

While the residency requirement reflected the fact that officials and Zenkoku Nōjikai leaders alike shared concerns about the deleterious effects of absenteeism, the potential incompatibilities between the interests of landlords as landlords, resident or otherwise, and the brand of agricultural improvement envisioned by officials that gave rise to these concerns went unexamined. This lack of attention was especially important to regions like northern Miyagi, where landlords had not retreated into absenteeism, but nevertheless moved away from farming in ways not entirely unlike their non-resident counterparts. In these areas, the largest landlords remained planted in their communities, but put ever-increasing distance between themselves and direct participation in agriculture. They were, in effect, pursuing the same divorce from agriculture as their absentee counterparts, the difference being that they kept the family home in the settlement. Although this problem escaped attention at the turn of the century, it would return to influence the course of agricultural policy in the decade that followed.

In the end, opposition to the laws from all quarters was overcome and their passage inaugurated a new era in agriculture and a period of unprecedented opportunity for the landlords in the agricultural associations. New legislation protected their property, reducing potential threats to prosperity from tenants and providing official recognition of the economic power that they had relied upon to that point. The costs of key aspects of agricultural improvement had been passed to the central government, and local leaders and organizations could now apply their funds in potentially more profitable ways. The Land Reorganization Law provided just such an opportunity, offering official support and legal authority to efforts to consolidate and expand landholdings. And the passage of the Agricultural Association Law provided the landlord-*meibōka* that led local *nōkai* a set of powerful tools to ensure that their interests would be the standard that defined the qualitative aspect of agricultural improvement and, in mandating universal membership for farmers, yoked their less affluent neighbors to their will.

The designation of landlords as *meibōka* and the beneficiaries of government support and the coercive power given them over the remainder of the farming population marked the triumph of the provincial landlord membership of the Zenkoku Nōjikai over its Tokyo leadership. Although in many ways the culmination of nearly a decade of Dai Nihon Nōkai/ Zenkoku Nōjikai efforts, the *nōkai* law created power inequalities in farming villages of precisely the type that leaders of the central organization had opposed. In contrast to the Zenkoku Nōjikai's proposal that membership in the hierarchy of agricultural associations be limited to people paying at least two yen in annual tax (those granted suffrage in national elections) or owning at least four *tan* (roughly 1 acre) of land, the law in its final form dictated membership in the organization to all heads of household resident in its area. The groups that resulted took on what has been described as the character of a military hierarchy, with landlords as the commanders, self-cultivating smallholders as a class of noncommissioned officers, and tenants as foot soldiers.[113] The victory of landlord interests also appeared in the financial plans laid out in the new laws. Whereas the leaders of the central organization had proposed that local *nōkai* fund their activities completely through mandatory dues from member landowners, the final form of the Agricultural Association Law drew funding from the budget of the government to moderate these costs. Initially pegged at the relatively modest sum of 150,000 yen annually, the measure nonetheless freed landlords from the full expense of membership dues and the threat of increased local taxation.[114]

Local landlords thus stood empowered with unprecedented promise at the turn of the new century. By 1900, the ground rules of agriculture had been rewritten and the game was now more fully rigged in their favor than ever before. A new system of productive relations had been imposed on the countryside that presented landlords, in their roles as development-leading *meibōku,* with greatly expanded powers over farming villages. The rest of the rural population did not fare so well. Remaining outside the protection of government, middling farmers, smallholders, and tenants found themselves in positions of heightened vulnerability. Drafted into landlord-led organizations and subject to their rules, the unprotected majority of farmers faced the opening of an uncertain new era promising change, but little relief. The gulf separating the expectations of *meibōka,* smallholder, landlord, and tenant was a reflection of the contradictions that lay at the heart of the new agricultural order. The public good had been entrusted to private hands and the force of the state stood ready to back landlord-*meibōka* as they prepared to impose their vision of prosperity and agricultural development on the countryside.

CHAPTER FOUR

Fighting the Farmers for National Wealth

Landlord Meibōka *and the New Agricultural Order*

The February 1, 1907 issue of the *Heimin shinbun*, a socialist newspaper published in Tokyo, featured an alarming story about the difficulties faced by Miyagi farmers.[1] Entitled "Landlords and tenant farmers" (*Jinushi to kosakunin*), it reported the ongoing exodus of tenant farmers from Miyagi to Hokkaidō in the face of the worst crop failures to hit the region in nearly a century. The brief article was divided into three parts, "Flood of Emigrants" (*Ijūsha zokushutsu*), "Decay of Arable Land" (*Kōchi kōhai*), and "Nighttime Flight of Tenants" (*Kosakunin no yonige*), each focusing on conditions in a different part of the prefecture. Readers of the newssheet learned how tenants in the district of Kami, faced with impossibly high rents, abandoned the disabled, the elderly, and even their own children in their desperate flight to the north. They read of landlords in Kurokawa villages, long unused to farming, forced to take up plows in an attempt to cultivate fields left empty by fleeing tenants. And they were told about tenants in Iwanuma, forced to sell everything they owned before using the cover of night to steal past sentries posted by landlords to prevent the abandonment of their fields. These were tales of misery and desperation, painting a portrait of tenant farmers crushed between unsympathetic landlords on one side and merciless nature on the other.

While the article clothed it in the breathless prose of proletarian proselytism, the reality of the situation in Miyagi was indeed dire. Described as the worst food crisis since the Great Tempō Famine of the 1830s, the devastation that the crop failures of 1905 and 1906 wrought upon villages across the prefecture reduced thousands of farming families to poverty and hunger.[2] The scope of the damage left the continued viability of even the most basic of rural institutions in doubt. The toll that the collapse of rural incomes took on tax collection prompted the chief of the General Education Office in the Ministry of Education to publish an editorial in the journal of the Miyagi Education Association reassuring readers that elementary schools would stay open and reasserting the importance of elementary education.[3] The progress that agriculture was supposed to have made over the course of decades of modernization had amounted to nothing in the face of the vicissitudes of nature.

Yet underdeveloped crops, untended fields, and unfed farmers aside, the middle years of the first decade of the twentieth century were, by all other accounts, a period of triumph for agricultural improvement in Japan. The alliance between central bureaucrats and landlord-*meibōka* forged at the end of the 1890s led to stabilized and expanded agricultural production and increased profits across the country, making tangible progress toward the improvement goals of both planners in the capital and *meibōka* on the ground. Using the trust and interest of the government in their work, landlord-*meibōka* had taken the first steps toward revolutionizing agriculture. They began to sweep away old ways of farming, bringing in new and more efficient technology and techniques, and altered the very layout of the land. Their efforts moved farming toward the concrete improvements that officials had envisioned at the turn of the century. Agricultural yields were up, and the groundwork was being laid for further increases in the future. Wasteful practices of the past were under attack by the legal system, with punishments designed to force their abandonment. And increased productivity was married to a bolstering of the local government system, as the consolidation of paddyland removed the final remnants of the administratively defunct, but socially persistent, hamlets.

The ambitions of the authors of this improvement were not limited to the rationalization and expansion of agricultural production. Landlords found in the privileged status accorded them as the agents of agricultural development the means to monopolize the profits of farming, to absolve themselves of its costs, and to mobilize the coercive power of the established authorities in the tightening of their economic control over the countryside. From within the agricultural associations that had experienced such dramatic growth over the previous decade, landlord-*meibōka* exploited the interest of prefectural and national government officials to remake the rural order. They forged a system presaging the colonial orders that would soon prevail in Japan's overseas territories, one in which the property, labor, and even the persons of tenants and smallholders were left vulnerable to the predations of landlords. This internal colonization saw sword-wielding police dispatched to force the lower classes of village society to adopt the agricultural methods dictated by landlord-*meibōka,* to assume the costs of agricultural improvement, and to devote ever-increasing amounts of effort and money to farming. This exploitation completed the equation for improvement of which technology and rationalization were only a part. Agriculture was pushed into a process of imposed involution, in which tenants and smallholding farmers were compelled to intensify the use of their own economic and physical resources to complete improvements and increase production. This was the reverse face of the agricultural revolution, which, for all its lack of a technological sheen, remained as essential to the transformation of farming as official visions of rationalization and modernization.

The first years of the twentieth century marked the triumph of landlord-*meibōka* and their vision of agricultural development. Securely ensconced at the top of village society, they profited from the fruits of agricultural labor and enjoyed an unprecedented period of prosperity. Their efforts were transforming not just agriculture, but the balance of forces that lay behind its development. The government now stood more firmly behind agricultural improvement and rural development than ever before. The original conception of *meibōka* development had been stood on its head. Government money underwrote the efforts of *meibōka,* funding a remaking of agriculture designed to further the interests of rural landlords while meeting the production goals of officials in the Home and Agriculture and Commerce Ministries. But the Tōhoku crop failures and famine at mid-decade introduced a disturbing element to the triumph of landlords, revealing the tenuous nature of the system they had created and hinting at the troubles to come.

The new century opened in an atmosphere of hope for the future of agriculture, as landlord-*meibōka* stood poised to use the legal powers and government support that they had earned to solve problems of agricultural development and village poverty. They dedicated their first efforts to firming up their local organizations. A new day had dawned for *nōkai* (agricultural associations), now officially recognized and bolstered by government funds, and the *meibōka* who led them moved quickly to consolidate their control and steer the groups toward particular kinds of agricultural improvement. From their beginnings, local *nōkai* mirrored the political administration of villages and offered the means to extend the entrenched power of landlords. At both the district and village levels, the rosters of association offices reflected the membership of the local elected assemblies, reinforcing the power wielded by landlords and extending their authority in new directions.[4] The crossover between *nōkai* leadership and local government was open and obvious. Village mayors held the headships of local *nōkai,* as provided for in the 1899 national law, village assemblymen monopolized *nōkai* offices, and most associations established their headquarters in village administrative offices.[5] Power reinforced power on the village level, placing control over the decision making concerning village administration and that concerning agriculture in the same group of elites.

Further embodying the break between landowning elites and poorer farmers were landlord associations (*jinushikai*), groups dedicated to the interests of landlords that spread rapidly at the beginning of the century. Landlord associations had roots going back into the previous century, but the newly accommodating legal context of the early 1900s prompted landlords and officials alike to apply new energies to their formation and development. While bureaucrats saw the groups as another means of promoting the improvement of farming, for landlord-*meibōka* the associations offered the opportunity to drop the pretense of pan-agricultural community inherent in the *nōkai* and focus on their particular interests as economic elites. Freed from the need to couch their goals in terms of universal benefits to the farming community as a whole, landlord association members could forge a united front against the masses of tenant farmers and smaller landowners. Rather than working at cross purposes with the *nōkai,* however, landlord associations lobbied to cement the *nōkai* initiatives that best served their interests. By 1906, landlord associations in all parts of Miyagi had thrown their weight behind *nōkai* calls for the prohibition of fallow land and regulations for the drying of rice.[6] That the same individuals were often making the calls from both groups presumably didn't detract from the added weight given by the more exclusive landlord organizations' enthusiastic support.

Landlord associations appeared earliest and most prominently in the northern prefectures where the largest landlords dominated. The first groups were organized on the prefectural level. In 1891, an Agriculture and Commerce Ministry report on the improvement of rice commended Miyagi for having the only *ōjinushikai* (association of large landlords) of the six prefectures it had examined.[7] According to the impressed officials, the association met regularly and discussed means of improving agriculture, activities that they suggested were linked to the successful raising of rice yields in the prefecture. Seeing the same promise in the groups as central officials, prefectural administrators also began to promote *ōjinushikai* as a means of improving farming in the 1890s. The governor of Niigata prefecture, home to the densest concentration of large landlords, called the landholding elite to a meeting in the prefectural capital in 1892 and gave them explicit instructions to form an association.[8]

The organizations became ubiquitous at the start of the twentieth century, stacked in a hierarchical architecture mirroring that of *nōkai.* Beginning with northeastern Kurihara district in 1902, landlord associations formed in all Miyagi districts by 1906, where they offered active support to *nōkai* and their improvement initiatives.[9]

Just as the landlords had their own motives in organizing themselves into landlord associations, so too did officials see potential in organizing landlords that went beyond their role in farming. Early proposals for the *nōkai* bill called for membership qualifications that would exclude all farmers with land worth less than 400 yen. The purpose of the group they sketched out was not limited to farming improvement and the empowerment of local elites. Among the chief motivations of the drafters of the early proposal was the desire to concentrate quarrelsome landlords into a centrally administered organization as a means of smothering their political disruptiveness.[10] But landlords were not the foremost threat to social order; landlord associations were also envisioned as a means of suppressing the perennial threat of rebellious tenant farmers. In a 1900 editorial in the official journal of the Chūō (central) Nōkai, former Home Ministry agricultural official Hida Rōichi outlined the safeguarding function of the organizations.[11] Alluding to vague historical precedents for tendencies of peasants (*hyakushō*) to abandon rented lands (which Hida apparently believed put landlords in a position of weakness) and to vandalize landlord property, Hida argued for the need for landlord associations to break these destructive cycles. Peasant protests had roots going back hundreds of years, explained Hida, meaning they were free from dangerous associations with the modern evils of socialism and labor organization, but they did represent an insidious threat to the countryside.[12] Landlord associations would serve as an ideal mechanism to mediate between landlords and tenants, defusing the destructive habits of hotheaded tenant farmers before they exploded. Untroubled by the implications of assigning responsibility for mediation to one of the two contesting sides, Hida predicted benefits ranging from economic growth to the elimination of wasteful habits. Making peace between landlords and tenants, landlord associations would both encourage compliance with *nōkai* plans for improvement and reform the debased morals of farming populations.

While Hida and others saw promise in the *meibōka* leaders of the landlord associations and *nōkai,* some among the central leaders who had fought so hard to promote the groups ten years earlier were developing doubts. While they had overcome the reluctance of bureaucrats and lawmakers to provide official support and recognition to *nōkai* by presenting them as units composed of local agriculturalists sharing an interest in y imposed artificial limits on production levels that were often already lerline, preventing efficient means of planting and spacing and wast- fertile land with their geometric eccentricity. They played havoc with gation and water control, thwarting efforts to improve waterways, pre- ting the shift from wet paddy to the more stable and productive dry ldy production, and exacerbating the sort of intra- and intercommu- y tensions that led to the Monō-Tōda conflict of the early 1890s. They evented the use of draft animals, limiting the depth to which fields uld be plowed, and increasing the physical demands put upon farmers. nd they hampered the rational application of labor in agriculture, scat- ring the holdings worked by individual farmers into irregular sets of idely spaced plots.

What ages of erratic settlement, sporadic reclamation, periodic div- ion, and chaotic swings in economic fortunes had wrought, however, uman industry could now set right. The first *nōkai* had placed the reor- lering of arable land at the forefront of their goals. It was the first order of business for Miyagi's prefectural *nōkai* after its formation in 1895, and the group's publication of guides to consolidating land in 1900 and 1905 attest to its continuing importance to the organization.[14] The early interest in Miyagi reflected similar concerns across the country. In one sense, land consolidation represented a continuation, or at least a relic, of the vaguely outlined and ultimately impractical early Meiji vision of a Westernization of Japanese agriculture. Concerns about amalgamating scattered plots of land into large farms were central to this proposed transformation, which paired the work with short-lived ideas of the abandonment of rice cultivation and the massive expansion of livestock.[15] Where the less practicable elements of early agricultural plans were abandoned, however, land consolidation itself survived the changing trends in agricultural thought. Its persistence was due, in part, to the continuing influence of foreign agricultural scientists on central planners in Japan. First disseminated by the foreigners who taught at the Komaba Agricultural School, the idea of the consolidation of arable land in Japan found fresh purchase in the 1890s with the Japanese translation of German agronomist and Tokyo University professor Udo Eggert's volume *Land Reform in Japan* in 1891.[16] The goal, however, was no longer the recreation of Euro-American farming in Japan. Now land consolidation was part of an integrated program to improve native modes of Japanese agriculture.

The legal changes that marked the institution of the new agricultural order at the end of the nineteenth century cemented the importance of land consolidation. The Farmland Consolidation Law (Kōchi Seirihō) of March 1899 declared its purpose in its first article as being to increase the improving farming, Tamari Kizō and other leaders c soon voiced their concerns about the gulf between Speaking at the 1901 general meeting of the Chūō sented a pointed call for attendees to increase the rea ciation's journal (*Chūō nōkaihō*) in their local areas. H of a farming focus among large landlords (*ōjinushi*), st ganization's top priorities at the moment were to "ma and others familiar with the current trends in agricult somehow to awaken within them a "passion for agricul to a group defined by their estrangement from the core c ment, the objectivity of the criticism may be in question, echoes in the concerns of central *nōkai* leaders and gove with less ambiguous connections to *nōkai* and agricultura

At the turn of the century, discordant voices like drowned out by a general enthusiasm among officials ar leaders for the *meibōka*-led agricultural order. Hopes for th tive potential of the national network of *nōkai* and the nev around them were high. Alongside their imagined functio valves for social discord, boosters envisioned agricultural as the key to three major aspects of agricultural improvemen would be the means to accomplish the long sought-after m consolidation of farmland (*kōchi seiri*), using the direct ties be lords in the local organizations to build the necessary conse the work that officials had found impossible to do. Next, t introduce fundamental improvements to the practices of a eliminating outdated and wasteful modes of farming and repla with modern techniques. Finally, they would regulate the qualit ing output, leveraging the social position of their members t standards that the compromised market forces at work at the leve cultural production could not. Behind these explicit goals, howe less-publicized agenda. Planners and officials envisioned a more political purpose in the work of *meibōka* and the *nōkai* they led. drawing of the agricultural map, expansion of agricultural prod and raising of the quality of farming products were also the tool which central authority could be extended into the local area, finally ing the persistent bases of hamlet autonomy and completing the proj local government begun in the late 1880s.

The problem of landholding patterns and their implications for cultural improvement had been foremost amongst the concerns of n from their earliest incarnations. Miniscule and irregularly shaped p dies and fields had long been a bane to everyone concerned with farmi improving farming, Tamari Kizō and other leaders of the *nōkai* movement soon voiced their concerns about the gulf between the ideal and reality. Speaking at the 1901 general meeting of the Chūō Nōkai, Tamari presented a pointed call for attendees to increase the readership of the association's journal (*Chūō nōkaihō*) in their local areas. He lamented the lack of a farming focus among large landlords (*ōjinushi*), stressing that the organization's top priorities at the moment were to "make large landlords and others familiar with the current trends in agricultural thought" and somehow to awaken within them a "passion for agriculture."[13] Presented to a group defined by their estrangement from the core of the *nōkai* movement, the objectivity of the criticism may be in question, but it soon found echoes in the concerns of central *nōkai* leaders and government officials with less ambiguous connections to *nōkai* and agricultural policy.

At the turn of the century, discordant voices like Tamari's were drowned out by a general enthusiasm among officials and agricultural leaders for the *meibōka*-led agricultural order. Hopes for the transformative potential of the national network of *nōkai* and the new system built around them were high. Alongside their imagined function as pressure valves for social discord, boosters envisioned agricultural associations as the key to three major aspects of agricultural improvement. First, they would be the means to accomplish the long sought-after mission of the consolidation of farmland (*kōchi seiri*), using the direct ties between landlords in the local organizations to build the necessary consensus about the work that officials had found impossible to do. Next, they would introduce fundamental improvements to the practices of agriculture, eliminating outdated and wasteful modes of farming and replacing them with modern techniques. Finally, they would regulate the quality of farming output, leveraging the social position of their members to enforce standards that the compromised market forces at work at the level of agricultural production could not. Behind these explicit goals, however, lay a less-publicized agenda. Planners and officials envisioned a more nakedly political purpose in the work of *meibōka* and the *nōkai* they led. The redrawing of the agricultural map, expansion of agricultural production, and raising of the quality of farming products were also the tools with which central authority could be extended into the local area, finally erasing the persistent bases of hamlet autonomy and completing the project of local government begun in the late 1880s.

The problem of landholding patterns and their implications for agricultural improvement had been foremost amongst the concerns of *nōkai* from their earliest incarnations. Miniscule and irregularly shaped paddies and fields had long been a bane to everyone concerned with farming.

They imposed artificial limits on production levels that were often already borderline, preventing efficient means of planting and spacing and wasting fertile land with their geometric eccentricity. They played havoc with irrigation and water control, thwarting efforts to improve waterways, preventing the shift from wet paddy to the more stable and productive dry paddy production, and exacerbating the sort of intra- and intercommunity tensions that led to the Monō-Tōda conflict of the early 1890s. They prevented the use of draft animals, limiting the depth to which fields could be plowed, and increasing the physical demands put upon farmers. And they hampered the rational application of labor in agriculture, scattering the holdings worked by individual farmers into irregular sets of widely spaced plots.

What ages of erratic settlement, sporadic reclamation, periodic division, and chaotic swings in economic fortunes had wrought, however, human industry could now set right. The first *nōkai* had placed the reordering of arable land at the forefront of their goals. It was the first order of business for Miyagi's prefectural *nōkai* after its formation in 1895, and the group's publication of guides to consolidating land in 1900 and 1905 attest to its continuing importance to the organization.[14] The early interest in Miyagi reflected similar concerns across the country. In one sense, land consolidation represented a continuation, or at least a relic, of the vaguely outlined and ultimately impractical early Meiji vision of a Westernization of Japanese agriculture. Concerns about amalgamating scattered plots of land into large farms were central to this proposed transformation, which paired the work with short-lived ideas of the abandonment of rice cultivation and the massive expansion of livestock.[15] Where the less practicable elements of early agricultural plans were abandoned, however, land consolidation itself survived the changing trends in agricultural thought. Its persistence was due, in part, to the continuing influence of foreign agricultural scientists on central planners in Japan. First disseminated by the foreigners who taught at the Komaba Agricultural School, the idea of the consolidation of arable land in Japan found fresh purchase in the 1890s with the Japanese translation of German agronomist and Tokyo University professor Udo Eggert's volume *Land Reform in Japan* in 1891.[16] The goal, however, was no longer the recreation of Euro-American farming in Japan. Now land consolidation was part of an integrated program to improve native modes of Japanese agriculture.

The legal changes that marked the institution of the new agricultural order at the end of the nineteenth century cemented the importance of land consolidation. The Farmland Consolidation Law (Kōchi Seirihō) of March 1899 declared its purpose in its first article as being to increase the productivity of land through facilitating "the exchange of land or its reshaping by amalgamation or division (*bungō kukaku*) and the alteration or removal of roads, paddy ridges, or ditches."[17] While providing official recognition and limited compensation for privately undertaken consolidation, the law focused as much of its attention on ensuring that such undertakings actually got done. The Farmland Consolidation Law and the official bodies that stood behind it took aim at obstructionist elements in rural society. Article 20 dictated forced cooperation with consolidation work by all residents in areas where two-thirds of landowners (by number, size of holdings, and value of holdings) had agreed to undertake it.[18] Other official pressures added their force to the text of the law. Beginning in 1900, the Home Ministry issued directives to local *nōkai* to begin work on *kōchi seiri,* prompting the Zenkoku Nōjikai to issue their own orders along the same lines. Prefectural governments also directed their attention to the promotion of land consolidation, offering various forms of official and semi-official support for the work. In Miyagi, the prefectural *nōkai* served as the conduit for government direction and support. It collected funds from the prefectural government, funneling the money to land surveys and the drafting of detailed reordering plans and maintaining a staff of planners and technicians to advise when needed.[19] Behind the prefectural commitment to the work lay the same doubts concerning the reliability of local landlords seen in the legal provision compelling holdouts to cooperate. Miyagi officials believed landlords to be a naturally disunited group, crippled by short-sightedness and parochial self-interest, a viewpoint displayed clearly in prefectural *kōchi seiri* guidelines including instructions to farmers to plan for the long term so as to prevent early work from impeding later efforts and to owners of scattered plots to arrange amicable trades with one another.[20]

Official promotion of *kōchi seiri* grew in intensity over the first decade of the new century. War once again provided the impetus for government interest in agricultural improvement. Just as the promotion of *nōkai* had become a vogue among officials after the Sino-Japanese War a decade earlier, the conclusion of the Russo-Japanese War in 1905 prompted bureaucrats to strengthen their commitment to the reordering of farmland.[21] At the request of the Home Ministry, the Dai Nihon Nōkai began offering annual land consolidation training sessions at its agricultural college in 1905, attracting 1,534 participants and laying the foundation for an event that continued for two decades.[22] The following year, the Home Ministry made an even stronger commitment to the work in the form of direct funding. Paying out 300,000 yen in 1906 and 400,000 the next year, the ministry's annual investment in *kōchi seiri* stabilized at over half a million yen in 1908 and remained there for the rest of the decade.[23] This largesse was not simply the work of progressive-minded officials. The Zenkoku Nōjikai transferred the passion with which it had pursued official recognition and support for *nōkai* in the 1890s to the pursuit of funding for land consolidation in the new century. Money from the Home Ministry marked a degree of success for the organization, but it did not put an end to their efforts. At its general assembly in 1911, the commitment of the Zenkoku Nōjikai to strengthening official support for the work was still fervent enough to produce resolutions for proposals to both the Upper and Lower Houses of the Diet to increase government funding for model consolidated paddyland.[24]

Bolstered by legal and financial stimuli, land consolidation progressed widely in the first decade of the twentieth century. Northern Miyagi led the nation, giving the prefecture for the first time the reputation of an "advanced region."[25] By 1913, the 30,000 *chō* that had been reordered in Miyagi placed it comfortably in first place nationally and gained it widespread attention as a model for the work.[26] While the pace of consolidation slackened after that point, in 1935 Miyagi still enjoyed the third most extensive proportion of reordered farmland in the country at 43.7 percent of its total arable land, an accomplishment surpassed only by Tokyo and Kanagawa, whose farming acreages amounted to only a fraction of Miyagi's.[27] The success in consolidation had a profound impact on the nature of agriculture in the prefecture. It eventually made possible both animal plowing and a shift from wet field to dry field rice farming, allowing for the cultivation of higher quality seeds, increasing yields, and bringing the prefecture into conformity with the methods of farming known as "Meiji agriculture" (Meiji *nōhō*) in the 1920s and 1930s.[28] In the first decade of the twentieth century, however, this development was still in its infancy and the advantages of land consolidation remained an abstract conception floating above the concrete daily concerns of farmers.

Despite the benefits it bestowed over the long term, the early progress of *kōchi seiri* in Miyagi failed to progress in the autonomous and self-funded way that the drafters of the Farmland Consolidation Law envisioned. The prefecture often stepped up to provide early energy to projects that excited no more than lukewarm responses from landowners. The Miyagi Agricultural Improvement Union (Miyagiken Nōji Kairyō Kumiai) led the initial charge, establishing a handful of model fields in 1901 and bringing an agricultural technician from Shizuoka to demonstrate the viability of consolidation to local farmers who were skeptical about the revolutionary nature and expense of the work.[29] These official efforts continued throughout the decade. In 1905, the number of model fields doubled to ten, all of which were funded by the prefecture through the Miyagi *nōkai,* and regulations were put in place providing for two fully funded model fields for each district whose residents paid over 50,000 yen in total land tax and one in all others.[30] These endeavors suggest a notable absence of the "personal initiative" (*jihassei*) that remained at the heart of the philosophy guiding official agricultural policy.

The northern Miyagi village of Nangō became the showcase area for land consolidation in Miyagi. Between 1903 and 1909 (when the Land Consolidation Law was revised), farmers in Nangō reordered over 2,000 hectares of farmland.[31] The means by which this work was accomplished illustrates the pattern that consolidation assumed in the north of the prefecture. As the planners of model fields hoped, landlords followed up on official efforts and set themselves to the task of reordering. The largest landholders in the village took the lead, bringing residents together, laying the plans for consolidation, and putting forward the funds to make it possible. The extensive reordering accomplished in the Watadanuma area of the village beginning in 1905 was funded by the three largest landlord families of Itō, Ueno, and Azumi, the last the same house that had played a central role in the Entō conflict. In a cash-poor region beset by chronic water problems, it was loans of up to 10,000 yen from these families that enabled less affluent families to take part and make wider consolidation successful.[32]

The characteristics of Miyagi's natural and human environments exacerbated the problems of disunity and atomization among its landlord-*meibōka.* Problematic hydrological systems combined with perennial drainage problems and irregularly shaped and undersized farm plots to present an array of challenges. At the most basic level, topographic irregularities produced small and misshapen fields, making the government-mandated minimum of a 1,000 square meter (1 *tanbu*) rectangle impossible for many minor landowners to meet.[33] The unruly waterways of the north presented more serious challenges. The poor early progress of land consolidation in northern Miyagi attests to the savagery of the Kitakami River and the obstacle it presented to human efforts to tame it. Such progress as consolidation enjoyed was limited to those areas at a comfortable remove from the river, where farmers whose profits were not drained regularly by violent flooding could undertake work with reasonable confidence that it would not be washed away. Accordingly, while the districts of Toda and Shida accounted for much of the success with consolidation in the prefecture, Monō, through which the lower reaches of the river cut, took much longer to make any progress.[34] The destructiveness of the Kitakami reinforced the inherent difficulties of consolidation in the prefecture and highlighted the gulf separating the ideals of central planners and conditions on the ground. The river eliminated even the limited potential for landlord unity and cooperation that existed in neighboring regions. The threat of flooding and problems with the water supply had imposed increased costs on farmers for generations, setting survival above ideals of cooperation and community even as it undercut financial stability and limited the funds available for improvement works. Landowners bordering the river became exaggerated caricatures demonstrating the traits that impeded farmland consolidation elsewhere in the region and across the country. Preoccupied with the chronic struggles to keep their paddies dry and lacking the wherewithal to think beyond the next harvest, any surplus money and energy went into petty attempts to increase profitability by buying up tiny parcels of land.[35] Land consolidation was for those with reliable water control measures and stable incomes, and it would not enjoy significant progress in the Kitakami area until massive public works projects began to tame the river in the 1920s.[36]

But in regions free from the threat of the Kitakami, the reliance upon local initiative to drive land reordering still impeded its accomplishment. This was true even in Nangō, known nationwide for its success. While the work of Nangō landlords displayed hints of the initiative that central planners sought, the precise manner in which they undertook land consolidation failed to demonstrate the wider cooperative spirit called for by the Land Consolidation Law. Expressions of unity appeared in the landlord leagues (*jinushi rengō*) that brought neighboring landowners together and, along with numerous individual efforts, reordered nearly all of the farmland in the village. Yet the modest geographic extent of these cooperative efforts fell short of official hopes. The hamlets officially rendered defunct by the local government system could still impose strict limits on landlord collaboration and cooperation. In Nangō consolidation projects never extended beyond hamlet borders, making the farmland consolidation in the village more a collection of neighboring hamlet works.[37] While efforts within these limits accomplished the consolidation goals in Nangō, they had negative implications for more ambitious projects. Neither hamlet cooperatives nor individual efforts were sufficient to complete consolidation on a larger scale; nor could they tackle projects whose links to problematic waterways crossed village boundaries. These shortcomings left holes that only increased investment and involvement from the prefectural and central governments could fill.

While problems with cooperation among landlords tempered success in Nangō, their influence was more deleterious in less well-known areas of Miyagi. The concentration of land ownership in the north of the prefecture partly accounted for this failure. In the Monō villages of Ōshio and Akai, both of which were free from the threat of the Kitakami River, high tenancy rates and apathetic landlords resident in outside villages delayed consolidation efforts until the 1910s and limited them even then to a fraction of what had been accomplished in Nangō.[38] The same conflicting water interests that had ignited the Entō conflict a decade earlier continued to set landowners at odds with one another, exacting a further toll on the progress of consolidation. The land reclamation and drainage of wetlands that were part of consolidation in Nangō reduced water levels in Monō and caused land to subside, destabilizing water supplies to already thirsty villages.[39] Even in areas free of these problems, where landlords engaged in at least limited cooperative work, geography and topography conspired against them. Consolidated plots rarely exceeded 50 hectares, making the hoped-for improvements to irrigation and water control difficult and greatly limiting their efficacy.[40] These problems reflected the predominance of small-scale landlords in the north of the prefecture, whose numbers themselves complicated consolidation efforts. A 1910 consolidation attempt planned in response to damaging floods in Nangō required organizers to obtain the agreement of 226 separate landowners to undertake work on a mere 416 hectares of arable land.[41]

Nangō's success, and the gulf that separated it from other Senboku regions that lagged behind, exposed the fallacy of central planners' belief in landlord-*meibōka* as the engines driving farmland consolidation. Government investment, not the private initiative of landlords, brought progress. Where consolidation was completed, it began after model areas established and run by officials demonstrated the promise of the work and government funding lightened or eliminated costs. Official enthusiasm for consolidation went beyond simply demonstration, even funneling resources in directions that had been anathema in earlier years. The Miyagi government financed four new sluices for Nangō between 1899 and 1907, reducing the costs and difficulties associated with consolidation even as they eased the responsibility for waterways that had been borne by local landlords after the end of the Entō conflict.[42] It was this unusual level of official support that made possible Nangō's rapid progress in consolidating its farms, and the absence of comparable developments elsewhere can be explained by the lack of similar government aid. Even with its advantages, Nangō residents found it impossible to fund the fraction of the costs that remained to them. The initial loans to their fellow villages by the handful of leading large landlords in the village made the work possible, but the nature of these funds as private debt set them apart from the more ostensibly charitable work of Kamata Sannosuke in neighboring

Shida at the same time.[43] The government again found it necessary to assume part of these costs and the collective debtors of the village were only able to repay their wealthy neighbors when the Hypothec Bank (Kangyō Ginkō) granted them a low-interest loan in 1908.[44] Both before and after the work was completed, government funds were the primary resource behind the efforts with money generated by sales of new lands opened up by consolidation in a secondary role, and the private resources of landlords being drawn upon only when costs exceeded what these two sources offered.[45]

In stepping forward to direct public funds to land consolidation, the prefectural and national governments were responding to both natural and governmental pressure. Yet here again the stimuli exposed the gulf that separated the ideal of personal initiative and actual conditions on the ground. Crop failures were the single most powerful force driving the progress of consolidation in Miyagi. Officials identified the work as a means of relief for the poor, incorporating aid in the works they oversaw directly and arranging systems of compensation for village-level and private projects. Harvest difficulties plagued Miyagi in the first decade of the twentieth century and it was in the years of most extreme dearth—1902, 1905, and 1910—that the prefecture made the gains in consolidation that put it in the position of leading the nation.[46] The prefectural government, reaching upward to solicit aid from the Home and Finance Ministries, made its boldest and most direct moves to promote and aid land consolidation during these years. These efforts had the mutually reinforcing effects of expanding the work at the time official funds were released and laying the foundation for increasing government involvement in the future. As the years passed, consolidation came to be tinted with an official hue, a situation far removed from the self-initiative-powered enterprise enshrined in law at the turn of the century.

The report produced by the Miyagi government report detailing the responses to the 1902 crop failures in villages across the prefecture is replete with accounts of landlords quickly drafting plans for land consolidation in order to hire their impoverished neighbors as laborers and prevent their families from falling victim to hunger. Here again the prefectural government took the lead, revising its plans for the development of model consolidated fields to employ those affected by the disaster.[47] Villages throughout the prefecture followed the government's lead, giving consolidation work a place of honor in their listings of aid provision. The southern village of Funaoka proudly recorded the extensive plan of seven local landlords for consolidation and reclamation that offered paid employment to almost two thousand local residents left nearly destitute from the poor harvest.[48] Similar forms of relief were common in many southern villages, but the northern district of Kurihara reported the most extensive plans. The projects in Kurihara villages stand out not only for their scale, employing over fifteen thousand laborers in some cases, but also because of their conspicuous designation as "private relief work" (*kojin kyūsai jigyō*).[49] The section of the government report devoted to the district gives the impression of village after village rescued from the brink of disaster by individuals whose quick-wittedness and altruism were matched only by the formidable personal resources they were able to apply to farmland consolidation projects designed to aid their neighbors. The landlords of Kurihara appeared the very embodiment of the vision behind the *meibōka*-led agricultural order, their individual initiative so ubiquitous as to make their work appear systematic in its character.

In fact, the work in Kurihara reflected the efforts of personally motivated landlords only in a limited sense. As it did elsewhere, the real initiative came from the district-level government and the higher agencies and bodies with which it coordinated its efforts. As soon as the distress caused by the crop failures of 1902 became clear, the Kurihara district administration assembled the rank and file of the district *nōkai,* laying out broad plans for land consolidation as part of a relief program that included calls for donations of money and goods, the distribution of seeds purchased with the public purse, and a pedagogical program warning against luxury and waste.[50] The support offered by the district did not end with logistics. It applied for a loan from the Agricultural and Industrial Bank, receiving 21,800 yen of the 40,000 requested to be used for relief work. The private element of this work came in only after the plans had been laid and the money received, when district officials gathered 56 local large landlords and instructed them to initiate farmland consolidation projects as a means of distributing these funds among the tens of thousands of residents whom the crop failures had thrown into poverty.[51] In comparison with extraordinary individuals like Ogata Yasuhei of the southern village of Ōgawara, who donated 100 yen of his personal funds to 180 households in need, these versions of personal initiative and private work seemed limited indeed.

When famine struck again in 1905, the Miyagi government held the earlier relief work in Kurihara up as a model for villages across the prefecture. Noting the important role land consolidation had played in ameliorating the effects of crop failures in the district, as well as the longer-term benefits of reordered farm fields, the prefecture declared the work to be among the "most important" (*mottomo omoki*) countermeasures for

Kurihara Poor Relief Land Consolidation, 1902–1903

Village	*Laborers*	*Labor Cost (¥/day)*	*Cost/Laborer (¥)*
Nagaoka	10,520	2,104.00	0.20
Kiyotaki	3,606	721.29	0.20
Tamasawa	3,867	912.00	0.24
Tsukidate	7,043	1,281.94	0.18
Shiwahime	4,651	837.00	0.18
Tsukumo	6,872	1,374.43	0.20
Kannari	1,500	375.00	0.25
Monji	11,223	2,805.71	0.25
Himematsu	15,300	3,060.70	0.20
Nagasaki	7,549	1,358.86	0.18
Kurikoma	6,900	1,242.38	0.18
Tomino	5,000	1,000.00	0.20
Ichihasama	12,500	2,250.11	0.18
Hanayama	15,830	2,849.50	0.18
Omatsu	7,450	1,516.00	0.20
Miyano	8,239	1,483.00	0.18
Average	8,003	1,573.25	0.20
Total	128,050	25,171.92	

Source: Miyagiken, *Meiji sanjūgonen Miyagiken kyōkanshi* (Sendai: Miyagiken, 1904), 198–238.

the crisis.[52] In issuing calls for a general spread of *kōchi seiri* in the face of the famine, however, the Miyagi government highlighted a continuing lack of the personal initiative that was supposed to drive farmland consolidation. Even if skepticism about its efficacy could excuse the reluctance of landlords to engage in the work before 1902, the records of that disaster resound with claims that impressive results of consolidation in 1902 and 1903—both for short-term relief and longer-term production gains—convinced holdout villagers that the work could be beneficial.[53] Yet in 1905 the prefectural government again had to take the lead, declaring that all its relief efforts would be directed at consolidation and arranging funding from the Home and Finance Ministries and the Hypothec Bank to be passed down through district governments to local villages.[54] Support payments of 5 yen per hectare of consolidated land were offered to all undertakings that employed the local poor, prompting landlords to draw up plans for 12,000 hectares of work specifically designated as relief.[55]

The landlords who answered these calls gained the multiple benefits of preventing the flight of their tenants, improving their fields, and maintaining their economic and social position, even as the aid bestowed upon desperate villagers earned them reknown as "philanthropists" (*jizenka*).[56] More problematic for central agricultural planners than the initial reluctance of these landowners, however, were the individuals who remained unmoved by the official calls. The "philanthropists" came overwhelmingly from the middle echelon of the landowning class. These were the landlord-*meibōka* of the *nōkai,* landlords who both continued to cultivate part of their own lands and remained resident in the same villages as their tenants. Larger landlords, who even at this point had progressed in economically advanced regions well along the course of displacing their more public-spirited neighbors, did not share their enthusiasm for relief work. Remote from the social responsibilities that pressured their resident counterparts and with limited knowledge and interest in farming, they chose not to answer the call to initiate land consolidation projects as poor relief.[57]

The lackluster response of larger landlords to the call for consolidation as a relief measure did not indicate a complete lack of interest in the enterprise or its profitability. The interest in improving farming that bureaucrats and landlords had shared since at least the last quarter of the nineteenth century made the consolidation of farmland attractive to both, with benefits to landowners that were obvious. It provided a means for raising farming yields and land values, opening up new lands, reducing costs, and raising rents.[58] In a single stroke, it satisfied a checklist of landlord interests. Government funds to encourage consolidation projects and the opportunities for additional support that came with crop failures and famine nudged risk-averse or cash-poor landlords forward, but they convinced the more cynical larger landlords that a greater official fiscal commitment was coming. It appeared worth waiting for.

Although they often failed to usher reordering projects to completion, the pronounced interest that government officials had in consolidation and the direct benefits that it offered to rural landowners highlight the shared interests of the two groups. It was this confluence, after all, that formed the very basis of the *meibōka*-led system of agricultural development and colored all aspects of agricultural improvement under this system. While government interest in the work was often abstract, relating to explicit plans to stabilize the national food supply and improve conditions in "distressed villages" or more indirect schemes to tighten central control over local offices and foster nationalism in villages, landlords derived benefits that were both concrete and immediate. Despite these differences in orientation, the two groups found themselves aligned regarding the particular forms of improvement they sought.

Primary among these shared aims between government officials and landlords was the elimination of old, wasteful forms of farming and their replacement with modern techniques maximizing production and minimizing waste. The two groups displayed an impressive unity of purpose in their efforts to reform practices like plowing, planting, seed selection, field use, and fertilization. The consolidation of farmland represented one step in this direction, an attempt to eliminate the waste due to customary patterns of landholding. Other customs were similarly designated as wasteful and became the targets of reform. Campaigns enjoying firm support from both landlords and agricultural officials took aim at seedling nurseries, which established practice planted in inefficient configurations and left fallow for the growing season; plowing, which remained a manpowered exercise in areas with customary injunctions against draft animals; and the reliance on "green manure" (*ryokuhi,* decaying plant life used as fertilizer) and other natural fertilizers, which could not sustain newly developed strains of rice seeds.[59] It was partly in these conflicts with custom that tenants and smallholders, themselves holding solid, if somewhat more limited, interests in increasing crop yields and improving the efficiency of agricultural labor, found themselves at odds with plans for improvement. To poorer farmers, expensive and untested new modes of production that often demanded more work represented a form of progress that was doubtful at best. For those aligned against them, however, their resistance to change served only to cement the commitment of officials and rural elites to cooperation in the imposition of advanced agriculture. The image of the superstitious and stubborn farmer, almost indistinguishable from caricatures of the blockheaded peasants of the earlier era, became the enemy against whom officials and landlords united. Only through the forceful reform of obstinate farmers, both agreed, could farming be dragged from the shadowy wasteland of age-old custom into the light of agricultural modernity.

The shape of villages themselves and the type of communities with which rural residents identified presented another arena in which landlords and officials could advance their common goals in the early twentieth century. Even at the opening of the new century, the new villages (*chōson*) established as a part of the local government system between 1888 and 1890 had not yet completely displaced and eradicated the early "organic" villages, now called "hamlets" (*sonraku, buraku*), that preceded them. The defunct sociopolitical units survived in collectively owned property, in shrines that were strongly linked to the families and life cycles of hamlet residents, and in a range of local organizations. These survivals proved problematic to both central government officials and landlord-*meibōka,* who attacked them in ways that were, if not quite co-ordinated, certainly complementary.

Prominent in the criticisms of both groups were the common lands (*iriaichi*) held by the hamlets. An example of continuity with the Tokugawa era, village common lands assumed their modern form after surviving the challenges mounted against them by the first Land Tax Revision of 1873, when hamlets struggled to lay claim to reduced local holdings and reserve them for the use of residents.[60] Their survival reflected the vital role that common lands played for farmers in Miyagi and elsewhere in providing an array of supplies for the field and the household, from wood to charcoal to green manure, without taxing the fiscal capacities of cash-poor residents. Designers of agricultural improvement, however, portrayed them as the embodiment of the threats to development that lurked in the backward countryside. Commons were seen as a waste of land that could otherwise be producing food and wealth. This waste was particularly egregious in Tōhoku, where extensive reliance upon commons combined with regular crop failures to paint a clear picture of unmodern remnants in the eyes of government planners. In 1904, *nōkai* leader Tamari Kizō included these lands in the 620,000 hectares that he estimated were unused in Tōhoku, costing the region 60 million yen in lost production.[61]

Landlords saw opportunity in this waste. It was in their interests to portray the common lands as non-productive and similar to the undeveloped "wastelands" (*arechi, kōbuchi*) that absorbed so much of the blame for Tōhoku's backwardness. The critique of common lands opened the opportunity for landlords to add them to their holdings, often as a part of larger consolidation projects. Landlords in the southern Miyagi village of Kayatani, where the consolidation of land reached a notable level of completeness, were able to lay claim to the village commons in a pattern that repeated itself in villages across the prefecture.[62]

The wealth that the seizure of commons bestowed upon landlords was drawn directly from the tenant farmers and smallholders who relied upon hamlet holdings as sources of fertilizer and other resources. Forcing both types of farmers to rely upon commercially produced fertilizers, landlord development of "wastelands" had a similar effect to the enclosure of the commons in Britain, which narrowed the "possibilities of gaining a livelihood."[63] In the latter case this promoted the proletarianization of farming populations, but in northern Miyagi it intensified tenant reliance upon landlords and drove smallholders toward tenancy. Thus, the seizure of hamlet lands increased both the landholdings of landlords and their control over their tenants and neighbors.

While some degree of sincerity may have informed the criticisms leveled against the wastefulness of village commons, political motivations were at least as important to officials and landlords. These interests shaped the character of reform efforts. The Home Ministry launched a period of concerted assaults on the hamlets in the 1900s as part of a program that included the shoring up of town and village finances, the tightening of control over local officials, and the elimination of corruption in local administration.[64] The year 1901 saw the beginning of aggressive official promotion of town and village policy plans (*chōsonze*) that were designed to foster identification with the administrative unit as a part of a larger effort to excite nationalist fervor on the local level. In that year, the ministry solicited reports on local conditions and plans for village development, specifically calling upon elected village officials to take the leadership.[65] The nationalistic sentiments that suffuse the introductions of many of the plans drafted at this time have been taken as evidence of the Home Ministry's success in inculcating the values they sought to spread, but this was not necessarily the case. Where the officials behind the plan of a Miyazaki village may describe their work as "peacetime economic warfare," the preface of a similar document from the Miyagi village of Oide focuses entirely on the legacy of its legendary mayor Nagao Shichirōemon and makes no mention of a national mission.[66] In the case of Oide, it appears that the fact that the Home Ministry had celebrated the work of Nagao obviated the need to appeal to central officials with patriotic sentiments, casting doubt on the sincerity of similar exclamations in other village plans. Regardless, the initiative served to undercut the hamlets, rendering them subject to plans drafted by the landlord-*meibōka* in town and village offices and encouraging measures such as the consolidation of hamlet assets under the ownership of the administrative town or village.

Shrines were another bastion of the hamlets targeted by Home Ministry officials. Functioning as a basis for village communities since time immemorial, local shrines came in a range of shapes and conditions and served populations of widely varying sizes. In 1906, Home Ministry bureaucrats launched the shrine merger movement, portraying local shrines alternatively as decrepit wrecks that sheltered immoral activities and sullied the imperial honor or wasteful extravagances for tiny groups of devotees. Rural shrines were abolished by the hundreds and merged into single shrines with jurisdictions coterminous with the borders of the administrative villages.[67] Much the same as the elimination of the common lands through land consolidation had done, shrine mergers damaged hamlets in multiple ways. Apart from erasing a key symbol and point of identification for residents, the loss of shrines also removed one of the few remaining bases for the status of hamlet elites. The provision of support for shrines, the associations they had with prominent family names, and the roles that hamlet elites played in events centered on them had all contributed to the social prominence of leading families. Without them, these elites, many of whom had numbered among the frontline *meibōka* in the early agricultural association movement, moved further down the path to obscurity.

The dispossession of hamlet elites was closely related to the political goals pursued by the landlord-*meibōka* in their drive against the defunct villages. Older prominent houses derived much of their local reputation and influence from their leadership of mutual aid societies, credit unions, and irrigation organizations. Their monopoly of hamlet offices, as well as their connections to the local shrines, was a magnet for official ire. Rich in land but lacking in social capital, the landlords who had risen during the economic dislocations of the mid-Meiji period and become neophyte *meibōka* during the 1890s found in the administrative towns and villages (*chōson*) a space for translating their economic success into local prestige and political authority. Abandoning the minor positions some of them had held in hamlet organizations, they shifted their support to the *chōson* at the turn of the century and took aim at their top offices.[68] The attacks launched by landlords and officials against hamlet assets enhanced the significance of these offices and weakened the older elites. Hamlet lands and property had most often represented donations from prominent local families, and it was these that were consolidated under the administration of the the new towns and villages. Elimination and incorporation into the *chōson* removed a basis for the status of these earlier elites and worked against the wealthier hamlets by redistributing the resources evenly across the new village while raising the names of the new local leaders who spread the wealth.[69] Just as the Home Ministry's crusade against hamlets created political and social opportunities for ambitious landlord-*meibōka,* so too did the work of these local figures enable the realization of official plans and accomplish the work of finally eliminating the defunct villages. This was not an exercise of teamwork between parties with shared ideals and goals, however. It was, at best, a coincidence of overlapping interests that complemented each other for a time

While the larger mission of improving agriculture involved a more explicit degree of cooperation between landlords and officials than did the attack on the hamlets, here too disharmony lurked below the surface.

The quests for increased yields, rationalized production, enhanced quality, and greater integration in the market bound officials and landlords together and defined agricultural policy and its legal context from the 1890s. For all the common talk of improvement between Tokyo-based administrators and wealthy villagers, however, there were profound differences in the reasons the work appealed to each and the purpose each was pursuing in the bid to transform agriculture. Government planners in the Home and Agricultural Ministries aimed at strengthening the nation. Securing the food supply, improving the health of the rural economy, and spreading prosperity in farming villages promised the connected but distinct rewards of reducing the country's reliance upon foreign imports and ensuring the maintenance of order in rural areas. The goals of landlords in their pursuit of agricultural improvement were considerably less broad. The stabilization of farm production and expansion of agricultural yields promised increased profits, and they intended to reap its rewards. In order to do so, they had first to further cement their control over tenant farmers and secure places of leadership in local administration.

The gulf that separated the goals of landlord-*meibōka* and officials in the work of agricultural improvement demonstrated more than different shadings on shared interests; it revealed a dissonance about the basic nature of the work. Agricultural improvement meant one thing to government officials and something different to the *meibōka* charged with carrying it out. A veneer of agreement concerning seeds, planting styles, and paddyland use obscured the cracks in the purportedly shared interests between landlords and officials, but the irreconcilability between a vision of farming villages that maximized the exploitation of tenant farmers on the one hand and that of a stable countryside populated with generally content and loyal producers on the other lay below the surface. During the early years of the twentieth century, the pseudo-synergy that saw each of the two groups accomplishing their immediate goals in the betterment of farming hid the deeper incongruity. Tensions were building, though, and it was becoming increasingly clear that something would give before too long.

Tenants were the group that threatened to break the apparent unity of officials and landlords. The latter two groups agreed superficially on the function and importance of tenant farmers to agricultural production. They were the engines driving farming and its improvement. They provided essential labor, performing the role of the muscles to the brains of planners both local and central. This understanding of the place of tenant farmers made their exploitation central to the plans of both groups; what differed was the degree to which this exploitation would be pursued and the specific ends to which it would be applied. The interest of officials in maintaining order limited the extent to which they were willing to squeeze the productive classes. Some portion of the benefits from improved production, even if only a small fraction of the total, would have to be shared with those whose efforts had brought it about if social stability and a sense of membership in the nation were to continue. Landlords were not bound by such concerns. They pursued the expansion of profit with single-mindedness, locked in what they saw as a zero-sum struggle with tenant farmers hungry for a bigger slice of the pie.

Despite the support for land consolidation, central authorities still preferred to remain aloof from direct intervention in the villages at the beginning of the twentieth century. They continued to believe that the profits from farming improvements would work their way down to every level of village society. The laws for the protection of the rural middle class passed in the late 1890s reflected this faith even as they represented a necessary compromise of the previous hands-off policies. Still, the shape of the laws ensured that government contact would be limited to the elites who had been the chief focus of government agricultural policy since the 1880s and who, after all, were the group that stood to gain most from the legislation. The legal change displayed an acceptance of the fact that landlord-*meibōka* had proven unable, if not unwilling, to meet the government's expectations for the improvement of farming. They were designed to tighten up the links between officials and landlords, opening a direct channel through which the government could transmit its wishes to the *meibōka* as its local agents, who would proceed to translate them into reality in their home regions. Official recognition of agricultural associations and land reordering unions were means to this end, offsetting the increased provision of public funding with the promise of a greater degree of official control over local improvement efforts.

Landlord-*meibōka* saw their reformulated relationship with central authorities in a different light. Working in their newly recognized organizations, they reversed the direction of effort envisioned in official plans. Rather than acting as conduits transmitting government policies to local farmers, *nōkai* instead became the means of communicating landlord interests upward. Central officials, still reliant upon the local and agricultural expertise of *meibōka,* repeatedly deferred to the advice they received from *nōkai* leaders, shaping legislation to match. In the same way that the lobbying of the Zenkoku Nōjikai in the 1890s had driven the passage of the middle-class protection laws, continuing pressures from the central group and its local affiliates pushed for and won laws enforcing landlords' visions of improved farming villages. The eleventh general meeting of the Zenkoku Nōjikai in November of 1903 was explicit in its call for legal force to ensure that agricultural societies be formed in corners of the country that continued to hold out and to compel the payment of membership dues from those participants whose enthusiasm for the groups did not extend to their wallets.[70] The lobbying of *nōkai* members found sympathetic ears among bureaucrats and informed the expansion of increasingly punitive laws concerning agriculture. Chief Secretary Tamari Kizō of the Zenkoku Nōjikai emphasized the importance of *nōkai* to legal change at a gathering of Tōhoku farmers in Morioka in 1904, explaining how recent laws banning charcoal fertilizers in Kagoshima had not originated among prefectural officials, but rather came from local *nōkai* members who had lobbied tirelessly for their passage.[71] Prefectural administrations across the country faced similar pressures, responding with new laws that were reproduced widely across administrative boundaries. These laws positioned the coercive power of government behind the improvement initiatives of landlords, opening the central policy to a range of abuses and undercutting the philosophy of bureaucratic disengagement upon which central guidance of agriculture was supposed to be based.

The first forays of the national government into regulating farming practice came prior to its rewriting of the legal order at the end of the nineteenth century. Though lacking the explicitly punitive nature of later laws, they laid out a template for which techniques would be encouraged and which condemned in the new legislation that followed it. The laws passed at the time, which targeted inefficient land use, improper planting techniques, and other chronic concerns of the Zenkoku Nōjikai, functioned more as guidelines than proscriptions, providing the raw materials from which more forceful prefectural regulations were soon crafted. Beginning in 1898, the Agricultural Ministry issued directives that criticized the practice of leaving farmlands fallow and provided instructions for proper planting techniques, instructions that prefectural administrations picked up quickly and cast in firmer legal form.[72] The constant reiterations of these directions in Miyagi, issued by the central government and repeated no fewer than three times by the prefectural authorities between 1899 and 1903, attest to the resistance they aroused in local farmers.[73] Despite the fact that the instructions from the Agricultural Ministry were addressed to prefectural *nōkai,* the landlord-*meibōka* in these groups were not the holdouts against the plans for rationalization. On the contrary, they were often the original source for these improved methods, which offered the greater yields and higher quality that always appealed to landlords.

Those resisting new agricultural techniques, causing landlords to push the central and prefectural governments toward legal compulsion, were the tenants and smallholders who would be called upon to actually employ them. The non-elite segments of the farming population had good reason to oppose the improvement measures, which demanded more work and increased expenditures and often offered only limited benefits to productivity. The "narrow-strip" (*tanzaku*) method of seedbed planting that was favored by landlords demanded rigorous discipline and required spacious and level paddies of a type not common in northern Miyagi.[74] These limitations applied equally to the "regular-line" (*seijō*) planting prescribed for the growing season, to which were added demands for laborious additional weeding.[75] Particularly objectionable to smallholders and tenant farmers in Miyagi were injunctions against fallow lands. The common practice in northern Miyagi and rice-producing regions throughout Tōhoku was to reserve sunny paddylands that were protected from the cold for exclusive use as early spring seedbeds, which were left flooded and unused for the months following the transfer of seedlings to the summer paddies.[76] The roughly 4 percent of paddyland that this practice left idle in Miyagi during the summer months enraged landlords and agricultural officials alike, who condemned it as a wasteful extravagance of irrational premodern custom.[77] Reason, however, lay behind the reluctance of the working farmers to abandon fallow land, as any replanting of the seedbeds during the growing season made costly fertilizers and insecticides necessary for successful cultivation the following year.[78] Promising increased stress on limited financial resources, heightened demand for labor, and faint promise of success, the programs formulated by *nōkai* and handed down through officials looked to poorer farmers less like improvements than means of setting a precedent for more intense exploitation.

Adding weight to tenants' and smallholders' resistance to the landlord-*meibōka* vision of improved agriculture was the doubtful nature of its efficacy. While articles appearing in the journal of the Central Nōkai and speakers at the various meetings held by the Zenkoku Nōjikai consistently cited the positive results of lab testing of improved techniques, these successes often proved difficult to reproduce in the field. Many of the practices that landlord-*meibōka* pressed on lawmakers required improvements to related agricultural infrastructure that, for reasons of cost or technical difficulty, had not been accomplished. Effective and reliable water control systems were needed for the maintenance of dry paddies through the fall and winter seasons, a prerequisite that was unrealized and impossible around the lower reaches of the unruly Kitakami River. Even areas free from the scourge of savage waterways had difficulties attaining the degree of water control necessary to make improvements effective. This was the reason why the remarkable gains in agricultural production in Kashimadai were delayed until after the expensive work of draining the flood-prone Shinainuma marshland was completed by Kamata Sannosuke and his allies. Where new methods of agriculture were possible, there existed some question as to whether they truly represented improvements. Landlords and prefectural officials in Miyagi sought to end the cultivation of high-yield Honkokumei rice, arguing that the poor reputation of the grain made it unprofitable to cultivators and landlords alike. In western Japan, tenant farmers had resisted similar pressures against the local Shinriki rice, instead increasing the cultivation of the strain and successfully driving up its price on the national market.[79]

In Miyagi, particular aspects of the local experience presented compelling arguments against adopting the agricultural techniques advertised as improved. In some cases, testing done *in situ* cast doubt upon the rosy statistics produced in the testing labs of Tokyo. Experiments in deep plowing and dry fields conducted in Miyagi and other northeastern prefectures produced results suggesting that the practices were in fact damaging to production in these less fertile regions.[80] Official sanctions against fallow land encountered similar difficulties. In the adverse topographic and climactic conditions of Miyagi, itself close to the northern limit of the area in which rice cultivation was possible, soil fertility was a constant challenge. Despite the laws that passed and the violence with which they were enforced over the early decades of the twentieth century, resistance to the forced use of seedbed nurseries as paddyland for mature production (which amounted to as close an imitation of double-cropping as was possible in the harsh north) never disappeared. In the end it was prefectural authorities who eventually gave in, leaving farmers to re-adopt the practice of leaving seedbeds fallow as though it had never been discontinued.[81]

The resolve of landlords to force tenants to adopt improvements combined with official frustration at the disappointing progress of development to alter the terms of production and impose a new system of agricultural administration on the local level. While landlords denounced tenants who refused to adopt improvements that demanded more labor and money while offering minimal benefits, officials saw a simplified picture of tradition-bound peasants hostile to any hint of progress or modernization. Agricultural Directive 14 in 1901 was clear in its assignment of blame for the lack of progress, stating, "It is extremely regrettable that, despite the fact that agricultural testing centers and related agencies are making steady progress and there is no lack of results that should be adopted, there are not many in the country who are actually enacting these measures and demonstrating their effectiveness."[82] Prefectural lawmakers built upon directives handed down from the Agricultural Ministry, translating instructions to adopt improvements into orders backed by punitive force. The Miyagi government introduced its Nursery Management Regulations in 1902, dictating fines or prison sentences for cultivators who did not adhere to rules for seedbed widths, shapes, and spacing.[83] These regulations were not aimed at an obstructionist few who were short-circuiting the efforts of the larger body of cooperative farmers. Bureaucrats envisioned the legal sanctions as targeting the larger mass of rural society, stating their purpose to be "fighting the farmers and executing the objectives for the sake of advancing the national wealth" (*kokufuku zōshin no tame ni wa nōmin to tatakatte suikō*).[84]

The Nursery Management Regulations and similar legal measures in Miyagi and elsewhere instituted a mode of agricultural production that came to be known as the "saber farming system" (*saaberu nōsei*). Named for the swords carried by prefectural police dispatched on regular patrols in farming areas, the system saw state violence mobilized directly against farmers in the service of agricultural improvement. A 1904 extension to the regulations of two years earlier required all cultivators in Miyagi to post signboards in their fields displaying their names clearly.[85] This enabled police, on the lookout for infractions against planting restrictions and other heterodox practices, to quickly identify miscreants, even among the scattered farm plots and byzantine networks of ownership and tenancy characteristic of northern Miyagi. Armed with legislative authority, prefectural police in Miyagi instituted a reign of terror in the rice paddies of the north, forcing non-compliant farmers to rip up and replant seedbeds and paddies at sword point.[86] The dramatic break that the saber system marked from earlier philosophies of non-intervention did not pass without comment. Yet even the Dai Nihon Nōkai's Yokoi Tokiyoshi, whose animosity toward government involvement in agriculture had led to the splitting off of the Zenkoku Nōjikai in the 1890s, seemed to acknowledge the system as necessary, declaring in 1905, "I look at this situation and regret the weakness of the people, at the same time I lament the revival of the ideology of government intervention."[87]

For all the talk of "fighting the farmers," it was clear that the saber system set its sights on a significantly narrower target. The paddy signboard system was aimed squarely at cultivating farmers, the majority of whom were tenants or partial tenants. In fact, the demand for the posting of cultivator names, being a tacit acknowledgment that the individuals listed as landowners were very often not the actual cultivators of the land, put the lie to the continuing celebration in official statements of the resident landlord as the firm core of farming society. The shape of the laws further demonstrated that they targeted tenants in a way evocative of the improvements that landlords and *nōkai* had been promoting for years and that they were instituted in response to landlord demands.[88] From planting styles for nurseries and fields to seed types and methods of seed selection and injunctions against fallow lands, the saber system cast landlord-style improvement as law.

As jarring as the sight of police on horseback ordering farmers to rip up their seedlings must have been, it paled next to the change to productive relations that the saber system marked. Prefectural governments had taken over the role of landlords in enforcing the exploitative conditions formerly consigned to tenancy contracts. However unbalanced it may have been, standard landlord-tenant relations had been based on a negotiated (but often implicit) agreement between the two parties, in which each pursued its own interests and adopted an economic strategy in a system of mutual influence. Where landlords raised rents, tenants could respond by lowering the costs, both financial and otherwise, of their production. Should the landlord desire rent rice of a higher quality that demanded increased labor or costly inputs, it became necessary for him to lower rents or otherwise alter the terms of production and tenancy in order to make it both possible and desirable for tenants to meet their expectations. The saber system removed the reciprocal aspect of this relationship. Cold and unresponsive laws replaced negotiated settlements in dictating the mode of agricultural production, leaving landlords secure to collect the profits from intensified labor and higher costs while consigning tenant farmers to a state resembling unfree labor.[89]

The gap between official rhetoric and actual conditions should not be taken as a reflection of ignorance or blindness among bureaucrats and policy makers. Laudatory comments about virtuous landlords aside, officials in the central and prefectural governments were aware that there were parasitic members of the landlord class who were, through their uncompromising pursuit of self-interest, obviating the work of agricultural testing centers.[90] Tenants and smallholders, however, were both closer to the actual work of farming and more vulnerable to the exercise of legal and government power, making them a better object for bureaucratic encouragement. In this way, the saber system marked the completion of the official movement away from the fears of overly intrusive government interference that had shaped policy in the 1880s. The exercise of official power over the less vulnerable and potentially combative landlord class remained taboo, but the ongoing impoverishment of the countryside and development of an agricultural underclass had opened the path to direct interference. For officials, the saber system was a pragmatic solution to a frustrating problem.

In 1904, events unfolding in the capital showed that the threat of legal and physical force had not brought about the desired results in Miyagi. The directors of the Tokyo Rice Exchange (Tōkyō Beikoku Torihikijo) sent official word that it would soon drop the prefecture's signature Honkokumai rice from its product listing, sending landlords and local officials alike into a panic. At issue was the quality of the rice, which had fallen continuously over recent years. Though enjoying a reputation as a fine product during the Edo period, Honkokumai had not fared well in the transition to modernity. The pressures of market forces on cash-poor Miyagi had forced down the quality of the crop, earning it a listing of "inferior product" on the Tokyo Exchange in 1877. While this may have hurt the pride of some farmers, it did not spell disaster. Honkokumai found a comfortable place in the national market during the last years of the nineteenth century as a low-priced grain for the urban working classes and as an ingredient for cheap *saké* and other secondary products.[91] A continuing descent in quality, combined with the arrival of rice from Korea, compromised the suitability of the rice for even these uses, bringing the situation to a head in 1904 and presenting Miyagi marketers with the ultimatum of improve or be removed.[92]

The response in Miyagi to the threat of being cut out of the Tokyo Exchange was to institute quality standards for rice and back them with the force of law. Following vigorous lobbying by landlords, the prefectural government passed the Rules for Testing Export Rice (*Yushutsu kome kensa kisoku*) in 1905, designed to ensure that any rice leaving the prefecture meet a strict set of quality standards. The regulations marked a dramatic change to rice production in Miyagi, but they were not the first time that the prefectural government had made attempts along these lines. After the newly opened Agriculture and Commerce Ministry shut down the prefecture's first attempt at quality regulations in 1881, Miyagi officials devised another quality testing system in 1897, but the absence of immediate pressure for change led to apathy and it was shelved without being implemented. In 1905, however, the context had changed and landlords and officials alike stood in solidarity behind the new regulations.[93]

The details of the quality regulations revealed the landlord interests that had shaped them. In their weeding out of inferior rice damaged by improper drying or packaging or harvested before reaching full maturity, the new rules echoed the earlier regulations, but they applied responsibility for meeting the standards in a new way. The use of the word "export rice" (*yushutsu kome*) in the title of the regulations was doubly deceptive. First, it did not refer to grain that was destined for trading abroad; rather it targeted any rice leaving the prefecture. More important, landlord pressure had ensured that the need to pass quality standards was moved as close to the point of production as possible, making them closer to regulations on rent rice than rules for export rice.[94] The original plans for the system stipulated that quality tests would be conducted at a central facility, to which landlords and others seeking to send their rice outside the prefecture were required to bring the rice they had collected through harvests or rents. A failure to meet the official standards would then require the individual who brought the grain in to assume the costs for its rebagging, weight adjustments, retransportation, or whatever other measures were necessary. Landlord petitions resulted in extensive revisions to this plan, reorienting the system to work in favor of their interests. Testing under the final form of the regulations was to be conducted at the level of the village, with landlords themselves overseeing the tests on rice that now had to be packaged and transported by tenants, who were also assigned responsibility for the costs associated with failure to meet the standards.[95] All rice proffered as rent was required to pass the quality tests, which were revised to stipulate improved storage bags and drying styles designed to make Miyagi rice more attractive to consumers in the capital.[96] The system was designed to give landlords and officials the improvements they sought and have tenants and independent farmers pay for them.

The factors driving down the quality of Miyagi rice, which included the penetration of market forces and the changes in the productive relations in farming villages, suggest that government administration was both appropriate and necessary. While the expansion of the money economy and the pressures of market forces in the last quarter of the nineteenth century pushed rice farmers to minimize their own costs in order to maintain a degree of profitability, the position of landlords between tenants and the market prevented those same forces from exerting a positive influence to reward quality.[97] Tenancy contracts syphoned off profits to landlords, leaving producers with little incentive to improve quality for higher profits they would never see. Instead, they applied their efforts to producing the largest yields for the lowest costs in inputs and labor, ensuring that they could pay rent and taxes and supply their own needs.[98] They were, in effect, trapped in the survival-based economic system described by Iwakura Tomomi, rather than the comparatively complex model of Maeda Masana.

The abortive 1878 rice quality regulations and the efforts of the *rōnō meibōka* in the 1880s to promote agricultural discussion societies, product fairs, and producers' associations were attempts to reverse the trend toward production of higher quantities of lower-quality rice, but they were unable to rectify the problems caused by the disconnect between tenant producers and the market. The application of law in both the saber system and the second set of rice quality regulations were more aggressive means of plastering over this gap and introducing artificial coercive forces to fulfill the function that the market was prevented from performing. The new quality rules eliminated the ambiguity of the earlier regulations and took careful aim at tenant farmers (and, to a lesser extent, smallholders), the segment of the agricultural economy isolated from market forces. They created a kind of hothouse capitalism, where artificial legal compulsion took the place of market forces to incubate higher-quality agricultural products.

The measures produced the results for which they were designed, but problems lurked not far beneath the surface. While landlords sat comfortably secure in national markets, tenant farmers continued to be isolated from the potential for profit inherent in improved rice and were now forced to abandon their strategies to limit their own costs in labor and money. The problems inherent in this arrangement found form in a series of emblematic images from contemporary farming that stood in contrast to the claims of successful modernization. The saber system projected visions of armed policemen forcing desperate farmers to work at sword point. Rice quality systems presented scenes of tenants forced to subsist on inferior grains and marginal foodstuffs while they reserved what quality rice they could produce for landlords. These images seemed far removed from the national narrative of progress and modernity that enlightened government and capital market forces were supposed to have brought about. Rather, they drew easy associations with the Tokugawa period, revealing farming populations who in their quality of life and economic relations bore a strong resemblance to the "feudal" peasants whose mere mention had been taboo in official language only a few years before. As disturbing as the contrasts between ideals and actual conditions were the inequalities in rural society that accompanied them. The deepening poverty of tenant farmers and smallholders was thrown into stark relief by the growing wealth and luxury of the landlords who had forced this system upon them. As Miyagi landlords geared up at mid-decade for the institution of the rice inspection system, they rested easy in anticipation of the new age of comfort and profit that lay before them. It was, however, not a vision that would be realized in fact.

As it happened, both the implementation of the rice inspection system and its effects were delayed by crop failures and famine in 1905 and 1906. Nature's answer to the efforts of bureaucrats and landlord-*meibōka* to modernize agriculture and stabilize production at the turn of the century was years of recurrently punishing weather. The first fifteen years of the twentieth century saw a losing war against the elements for Miyagi farmers. Cold and damp summers brought about crop failures in 1902, 1905, 1906, 1910, and 1913. The worst of these struck just as landlords presided over the institution of the legal order that established their dominance over agricultural production. Summer began with fine weather in 1905, promising a growing season in Miyagi to suit the celebrations of victory in the Russo-Japanese War that were sweeping across the prefecture. But temperatures dropped at midsummer, and the cold weather continued through August, stunting the growth of the rice plants at a critical moment in their maturation. Unusual degrees of insect damage worsened conditions and, when unrelenting cold weather was joined by damaging rains in September, it was clear that the losses would be extreme. Autumn yields reached no higher than 12.5 percent of average prefecture-wide, recovering to only 76.7 percent the following year as sequential seasons of depressed production led to an exponential expansion of the damage to farming villages.[99] With little to no production, desperation struck farmers across Miyagi, leading to official designation of fully 52 percent of agricultural families at poverty level (*kyūmin*).[100] The situation became so dire that Miyagi officials arranged for the import of rice from Southeast Asia, which they distributed to a third of the prefecture's farmers with instructions to garnish the grain with boiled radish leaves.[101]

The severity of the crop failures exposed serious weaknesses in the agricultural development that had taken place. The improvements that landlords and officials introduced over the previous decade seemed to have even exacerbated the difficulties caused by weather. Fields fully treated with expensive fertilizers produced crops that appeared not to have been fertilized at all, giving rise to the belief that they worsened the problem.[102] Although officials characterized this as a "mistaken belief" (*goshin*), it contained more truth than fiction. Landlords had been halfhearted in their adoption of improved strains of rice that could better withstand inclement conditions, failing to provide for the deep plowing and extensive application of chemical fertilizers required by the advanced seeds they forced on their tenants.[103] Without the conditions they needed, these rice strains displayed increased, rather than decreased, vulnerability to weather and water. To tenants already bruised by the saber system and facing further distress in the upcoming quality regulations, the crop failures suggested that their experiences with agricultural improvement were not just painful, but futile.

As reported in the *Heimin shinbun,* many tenant farmers responded to the disaster by fleeing the prefecture for Hokkaidō and other regions of the country. The experiences of Kami, Kurokawa, and Iwanuma related at the start of this chapter were part of a larger pattern of migration that saw 13,312 farmers leave for Hokkaidō in 1906 and 16,211 the following year.[104] Outbound tenants would first apply to their landlords for permission to quit their paddies, then would most often leave surreptitiously when their requests were denied. In an effort to stem the abandonment of their lands, some landlords offered rent remissions and forgiveness. The Azumi family in the Tōda village of Nangō cancelled 71.4 percent of the rents they were owed in 1905 and 25.9 percent in 1906, sacrificing claims on short-term profits in a tried-and-true traditional form.[105] The same family also employed destitute tenant farmers as labor and paid them with imported rice, an activity in which other Nangō landlords also engaged.[106] Others took similar measures, providing enough relief to enable farmers and landlords alike to withstand pressures until harvests returned to normalcy in 1907.

While pragmatism forced concessions like rent remissions in some cases, the general landlord response to tenant difficulties in northern Miyagi was less than sympathetic. Rents across the region had been on the rise for over a decade, a trend that the crop failures did not halt. Nangō rents were representative of the wider region and continued to climb throughout the crisis to a high point in 1907, when other factors acted to check the upward momentum.[107]

Rather than considering a reduction in the profits they derived from their tenants, Miyagi landlords instead organized themselves to squeeze them harder. The landlord response to tenant hardship in Monō and Oshika was to form a landlord association (*jinushikai*) in February of 1906 and devise plans to promote tenant compliance with the upcoming rice quality regulations.[108] The prefectural *jinushikai,* which had been formed under the auspices of the Miyagi government to deal with tensions between landlords and tenants after the Russo-Japanese War, adopted similar priorities. Displaying either an ignorance of both the sources of the problems and the basic principles of economics or an impressive callousness, especially in the context of plans ostensibly designed to ease suffering, the organization proposed in its 1907 policy statement the strategy of staying the course.[109]

Nor was the elite response in general much more sympathetic than that of landlord associations. Lamenting in the December 1905 issue of the Miyagi Education Association journal that the crop failures and famine threatened the plans to spread general education after the Russo-Japanese War, Ōshō Shigeru of the northern district of Kurihara went on to suggest that the situation had a silver lining.[110] Despite their baleful influence on formal education, the crop failures provided children with valuable experience with hunger and poverty that would make them better prepared for the next famine than their parents had been for this one.

While landlords panicked in the face of tenant flights to Hokkaidō and the thought of having to resume cultivation themselves, the crop failures of 1905 and 1906 also provided some with unusual opportunities. The crisis served as a means to mobilize official power behind reforms and improvements that landlords had long pursued. *Nōkai* had been pushing to replace Honkokumai rice with Kame no O, an early harvest strain produced in Yamagata prefecture and tested in Akita prefecture that served as a lower-yield but more reliable producer. The crop failures brought the support of Miyagi officials to the plan, and provoked legal imperatives to force the changeover in the years that followed.[111] The crop failures also provided a means for some landlord families to advance their personal fortunes. The Noda family of Nangō, then in the middle of its rise to supremacy among local landlords, took advantage of its relative financial stability during the crisis to borrow money from a local credit association in order to lend it out at higher rates of interest to poorer farmers in need.[112]

Even discounting some of the crasser forms of opportunism, the situation at mid-decade did not cast landlord-*meibōka* in the best light. The crop failures of 1905 and 1906 and the punishing conditions they brought about for farmers stood as an unanswerable indictment of the results of *meibōka*-led agricultural development. The levels of hardship in rural Miyagi drew easy and damning comparisons with the Great Tenmei and Great Tenpō Famines of the Tokugawa period.[113] The lauded technological development spearheaded by landlords and government officials had failed to make farming more stable and productive than it had been in the times of their grandparents and great-grandparents. The thin veneer of modernity that improvement efforts had applied to agriculture and rural villages was stripped bare. Tenant farmers, now the majority of cultivators in northern Miyagi, were indistinguishable from the "feudal" peasants who were supposed to have disappeared in the newly modern countryside. Powerless against the lords of the land and state and the vagaries of nature alike, tenant farmers stood in mute contradiction to the progress claimed by *meibōka*, officials, and the nation as a whole.

Despite the severity of the famine and its implications for the success of their stewardship of agricultural development, landlord-*meibōka* did not feel a sense of crisis in the middle of the first decade of the twentieth century. In fact, they had a great deal to feel happy about. The first years of the new century had seen remarkable developments in the control of Miyagi landlords over the countryside. Laws now backed up their interests as the owners of arable land, ensuring that the tenants who rented the land would maximize profits for them and assigning government the responsibility for enforcing the terms of exploitative contracts. Also comforting was the imminent institution of rice quality regulations, which promised to end once and for all the uncertainty of Miyagi rice on the national market. Secure in their economic positions, progressing in their political control over the villages, and backed by a government that appeared committed to advancing their interests, *meibōka* had cause for satisfaction. Regrettable crop failures aside, the decade had clearly gone their way.

But things were not going as smoothly as they liked to believe. Miyagi landlords may have weathered the crop failures and famine with their fortunes intact, in some ways even strengthening their economic and political positions in villages, but they exposed troubling contradictions in the process. The danger to them was not in the families who stole past the guards to abandon their rented plots, it was in the tenant farmers that remained in place when harvests returned to normal. The alignment of law behind the landlord conception of improvement in the saber system and the rice quality regulations was advancing the landlords' vision of the modernization of agriculture, but the pressures they applied were pushing tenants to their limits. Concern with the situation was also growing among officials in the capital. The gulf between their ideals of a developing and stable countryside and the actuality of vulnerable and dependent villages emerging from the agricultural leadership of landlords disturbed many, and their vocal displeasure would soon make itself evident. Landlord-*meibōka* stood confident at the middle of the first decade of the twentieth century, but the twin forces of tenants below and bureaucrats above were converging behind the scenes in a pattern that threatened to change the nature of agricultural development in Japan.

CHAPTER FIVE

The Spirit of the Times Has Changed

A New Vision for Agricultural Development

In early March of 1908, the largest landowner in Miyagi was furious. Saitō Zen'uemon, whose extensive landholdings were second in Japan only to those of the Honma family of neighboring Yamagata prefecture, had been driven to distraction by developments in an ongoing dispute between landlords and tenant farmers in northern Miyagi. Recent weeks had seen public opinion rally behind the tenant organization that initiated the conflict, and in the last few days one landlord after another gave in and agreed to the group's demands. Saitō's exasperated response to these capitulations appeared in an article in the March 10 issue of the regional newspaper, the *Kahoku shinpō*.[1] He entreated his fellow landlords to persevere, telling them, "There is no need to go recklessly changing contracts; we can only wait until tenants everywhere realize that their labor is their own profit." He went on to vent his spleen at the editors and readers of the newspaper, whom he accused of naively falling victim to the manipulations of wily and media-savvy tenants. He accused his opponents of cynically trading on their public image as the unlettered and victimized peasants of the feudal past. In fact, he explained, the recent spate of anti-landlord editorials in the newspaper stood as proof of their adroitness in shaping an unfair public campaign against landlords, whose treatment of tenants was only rational and natural. "Landlords," he explained, "have no duty to tenants beyond what is written in the mutually agreed upon contracts" (*jinushi ni ha sōgo keiyaku ijō no gimu nashi*). Tenant claims of hardship were exaggerated—"making a mountain out of a molehill" (*shinshō bōdai*)—and their charges of injustice paradoxically threatened to revive the feudalistic practices of the backward past.

Saitō's frustration reflected the dramatically transformed situation of landlords in northern Miyagi. Only two years earlier, landlords had been secure in their positions and on the cusp of unprecedented prosperity. Laws were oriented firmly in their favor; profits from agriculture were on the rise, with tenancy contracts ensuring they flowed directly to landlords; and government policy on both the prefectural and national levels was committed to maintaining and advancing these realities. In Miyagi the potential of the period appeared bright. The return to stable yields after the crop failures of 1905 and 1906 not only brought the local economy back to normality, it also meant that the long-delayed rice quality inspection system could finally be implemented, promising to open a new period of landlord profitability and control over village society.

Now, however, Saitō and his fellow landlords were facing defeat at the hands of formerly powerless tenant farmers. Only months after the announcement that the rice quality inspection system was back on the agenda, tenants made preemptive moves against landlords in advance of its implementation. Beginning early in 1907, they formed organizations across the prefecture, pressing for revisions to tenancy contracts and threatening to abandon cultivation. The end of the year brought new cooperation and coordination between groups in the rice-producing north, where Saitō made his home, and the reversals that drove the landlord to voice his anger to reporters and the news-reading public.

As disturbing as the weakness of his compatriots was the absence of support for Saitō and his fellow landlords from the government. Saitō could be forgiven for his exasperation at the failure of Miyagi's administrative elite to intervene. The same officials had, after all, spent the better part of the decade transforming the terms of landlord-written tenancy contracts into the law of the land. The saber system that sent sword-wielding police to enforce tenant compliance and the rice quality inspections stood as evidence of the solidarity of both the Miyagi and the national government with landlords and their vision of agricultural improvement. Now, however, those same authorities stood to the side and allowed tenants to force contract revisions. While the justice of Saitō's claims regarding proper relations between producer and landowner was open to debate, his shock was not unreasonable in the face of what appeared to be profound change in the official approach to the management of rural society and agricultural development.

The defeat of northern Miyagi landlords in the spring of 1908 was a hint of the transformations to come. The victory of tenants was only partly due to the canniness and confidence they displayed in the conflict. As Saitō lamented, an equally important factor was the evaporation of the official support for landlords that he and his peers had expected to resolve the conflict in their favor. As tenants celebrated their victories, a more unsettling threat to the landlord-*meibōka* system of agricultural development had taken shape in the ministries of the national government. The dissonance between the official understanding of improvement and that of landlords had grown too disruptive for government leaders. The Home and Agriculture and Commerce Ministries launched new initiatives in the last years of the decade, attacking the positions of landlords in village leadership and reasserting control over agricultural development in a sea change to the approach of government to rural Japan. The new course that these leaders charted recast the idea of *meibōka,* challenging the direction taken over the previous decade by landlords, and instituted a new period in agricultural development.

As harvests returned to normal after the damage of the mid-decade crop failures, these dramatic changes still lay in the future. Landlords in Miyagi were confident of growing fortune. Among the first orders of prefectural business when the worst of the crop failures had passed was the delayed implementation of the rice quality inspection system. The Tokyo Rice Exchange made allowances for the climatic difficulties in Miyagi, but the return to normalcy brought with it the renewed threat of the exclusion of Miyagi rice from the national market. Fortunately for landlords, the basics of the new system had already been established before the crisis, and it stood ready to be launched. In January of 1907, the prefecture reaffirmed its commitment to the quality inspection initiative and announced plans to open testing stations throughout Miyagi.[2] Thus assured both that Miyagi rice would continue to have a place in the national market and that tenant farmers would bear the costs of making it so, landlords stood in a good position. The return of crops to normal yields and the ongoing production increases from gradually effective improvement efforts promised greater prosperity in the future.

Yet, official criticism of landlords and their involvement in agricultural development was growing. Concern among bureaucrats in the central government about the costs and benefits of landlord-led development was intensifying and some began to question fundamental aspects of the rural order. Although a minority had voiced similar doubts in the past, the economic and social problems that followed the Russo-Japanese War (1904–1905) prompted a reworking of priorities. Official fears of pervasive village poverty and disquiet that had failed to materialize in the wake of the Sino-Japanese War of 1894–1895 became fact. The Home and Agriculture and Commerce Ministries scrambled to find ways to repair the economic and ideological damage wrought by the war. Attention turned to the health of rural society and the effects landlord leadership had wrought upon it.

The earliest criticisms of landlord-led agricultural development stretched back to the 1890s, appearing among the same leaders who were urging government support for landlords and their activities. Speaking at the 1900 annual meeting of the Zenkoku Nōjikai, Tamari Kizō castigated landlords for abandoning their focus on agriculture to concentrate on personal profits.[3] To correct their failures, he prescribed a dual program that combined the creation of training programs to point landlords back toward farming and the formation of village economic cooperatives that would balance their power on a local scale. The following year, Tamari laid out a range of charges suggesting that the disconnect between landlords and farming had been a motivation in the original organization of *nōkai*. While expressing his hopes that the journal of the Central Nōkai could reform dissolute landlords, he voiced a withering litany of their failings. "Today's *ōjinushi* (large landlords)," he explained,

> put on the airs of a lord and give no thought toward agriculture. On the contrary, they consider agriculture beneath their station. Taking on these lordly pretenses, they focus in other directions and only a small number of them are thinking about farming. They think extracting large rents from tenant farmers is agricultural thinking. They pay attention only to other matters, even selling their land for high prices and buying stock certificates. You could say that the business of *ōjinushi* today is commerce . . . *ōjinushi gōnō* (large landlords/wealthy farmers) think this way and really cannot be trusted . . . when [*nōkai*] were established, I thought the next important work to undertake was to make *ōjinushi gōnō* subscribe to the ideology of agriculture (*nōgyō no shisō*).[4]

The crafters of village plans at the turn of the century echoed Tamari's concerns. The plans often included indictments of both absentee and resident landlords, condemning the predatory activities of the former and the inequality and conflict resulting from the latter.[5] If allowed to continue, these groups threatened the very survival of farming villages and the future viability of agriculture. Along with worries of these types came efforts to reform landlords and correct their excesses. A 1901 meeting of prefectural industry promotion chiefs sponsored by the Ministry of Agriculture included a panel on "how to get large landlords (*ōjinushi*) to apply their energies to the improvement of agriculture" and the annual meeting of the Zenkoku Nōjikai the following year raised the topic of "means to cultivate a spirit of agricultural improvement in *ōjinushi*."[6] To awaken this public spirit, the latter meeting proposed compulsory classes, new organizations, and the promotion of landlord participation in fairs and exhibitions in a curious inversion of the solutions landlords normally offered to correct the failings of tenant farmers.[7]

Officials in the central government also saw problems with landlord leadership over agricultural improvement in the early 1900s, but they identified it explicitly with the evils of absenteeism. A year before Tamari issued his indictment of landlords, Yamagata Aritomo, the chief architect of the local government system and an early proponent of *meibōka*-led development, looked back on the decade since the enactment of the system and counted absentee landlords among the causes of its shortcomings. While continuing to believe that local notables were necessary as the principal engines of agricultural development and local administration, he noted that "as the spirit of the time has changed, it is not necessarily true that *ōjinushi* are what we call *meibōka*."[8] The official focus of blame upon absentee landlords allowed faith in their resident counterparts as the stewards of farming to persist, preventing deeper criticism of the fundamentals of the *meibōka*-led system of agricultural development. Celebrated folklorist, Yanagita Kunio, an official in the Ministry of Agriculture in 1902, saw in the "middle class" of resident landlords a potential replacement for their delinquent cousins, lauding them as

> Landowning families who have lived in their villages for hundreds of years with land passed down from one generation to the next and who, past, present, and future, do and will continue to make up the backbone of the people . . . tax-paying landowners who, even as they gather bags of rent rice in their storehouses and use it to feed their families, watch over the house, are constantly active in service of the country or the prefecture, and still never forget their task of advancing agriculture.[9]

Although his adulation of resident landlords would soon change, as would similar sentiments among other officials, the idea at the heart of it continued to shape official policy for years to come. The solid middle core of village landowners (*chūnō* or *chūken jinbutsu*), characterized like Kamata Sannosuke both by residence in the villages in which they held land and by their initiative in pursuing agricultural improvement, continued to be the key element to rural development and to hold a corresponding place in official plans to promote it. Yanagita and others were restating the functional definition for *meibōka* that Yamagata had built into his system of local government requiring those designated as such to display initiative and an interest in the active pursuit of farming improvement. This functional definition, and the concerns that prompted it, laid open the contradictions inherent to the official approach to agricultural villages and explained the continuing reliance upon the consistently disappointing landlords in the first years of the century. Attacks on landlords, inevitably couched as a response to their failure of duty to tenants and community, had at least as much to do with agricultural improvement as with neglected social responsibilities. Absentee landlords disappointed bureaucrats because they failed to impose the improved forms of farming that their resident colleagues did. The fact that forcing tenants to employ these farming techniques, which invariably imposed greater labor and costs on them, was a major source of the village disharmony lamented by officials was irrelevant. Agricultural development was what was important, and the failure to accomplish it is what exposed non-resident landlords to criticism.

The realities of rural Miyagi were different from the village situations that raised the ire of Yanagita and other officials. Absenteeism, as the bureaucrats of the Home and Agriculture Ministries understood it, was in fact a phenomenon largely limited to the economically advanced areas of the country. There, landlords had leveraged multiple opportunities for profit to diversify their interests, moving to local cities or national centers to manage their businesses. Landholding and tenant management were only one source of their income and not one that required excessive attention or additional investment. This was not the case in northern Miyagi. In the early twentieth century, the prefecture, along with the Tōhoku region as a whole, retained a well-deserved reputation for economic backwardness. Facing an incompletely developed money economy and with landowning as the sole industry with a potential for profit, Miyagi landlords stayed in the countryside. Cut off from other opportunities, the successful among them devoted themselves to the acquisition of land, assembling extensive holdings that put them in the class of large landlords.[10] They were not absentee in the sense that drew official criticism.[11]

The most common means by which Miyagi landlords accumulated land had important implications for social and economic relations. Farmland in northern Miyagi was most often forfeited, rather than sold. Landlords tended to be moneylenders, whose control over land grew when they seized the lands of delinquent debtors. In this context, the annual payments made to them by the farming families who remained on forfeited lands took the form, not of actual rent, but of maintenance of their debt. This situation left tenants in a more precarious situation than elsewhere, without customary protections and vulnerable to eviction at any time.[12] The landlords that held this threat over their heads had not left their native places, thus avoiding the label of absentee, but it was not always true that they lived in the villages or regions where they owned land. As individual landholdings grew, more tenant farmers found control of their fields in the hands of landlords in other villages or districts. Entire villages could be owned by remote landlords, leaving these communities without the economic resources that provided for the emergence of local leaders or the improvement of agriculture seen elsewhere. This situation was a reflection both of the growing wealth of successful landowners and the extreme lack of capital in the north of the prefecture. Loans from wealthy landlords, wherever they might make their homes, were often the only source of funds for fertilizer, seeds, and improvements to farmland, a circumstance that placed even independent landowning farmers under the control of landlords.[13]

Saitō Zen'uemon stood as the consummate example of a northern Miyagi landlord. A moneylender first, he was nonetheless celebrated as the second largest landlord in the country, a role in which he served as a model for others in the region with ambition, wealth, and land. Although he came from a background of rural privilege, his rise to great wealth was a recent development. A legendary deal to buy the land owned by the failed Kawasaki Bank in 1890 more than doubled the total holdings of his house and propelled him to the forefront of landowners nationally.[14] By the turn of the century, the Saitō house controlled over 1,100 hectares of farmland, and it was said to be possible to travel all the way from Iwate prefecture in the north to Fukushima prefecture in the south without leaving Saitō's property.

It was the collapse of rice prices in the 1880s that made the Kawasaki land purchase possible, but Saitō had taken measures early on to insulate himself against the vagaries of nature and agriculture. In a pattern that was later reproduced among landlords across Tōhoku, Saitō moved his house out of direct involvement in farming. In 1879, just one year after taking over management of the family's business from his father, Saitō abandoned self-cultivation, devoting his attentions to the house's sake-brewing concerns and especially the moneylending business he shaped out of the family's pawn shop. By the time of the Kawasaki purchase, sake too had gone by the boards, abandoned like many independent brewing operations in the face of strict new laws and taxes levied on the industry. The Saitō house completed its movement into pure land ownership and moneylending, the roles that would define it through the next half century.

Saitō was also ahead of his time in his approach to managing tenant farmers. The sentiments that he expressed in the *Kahoku shinpō* article touched on the philosophy guiding this approach and reiterated ideas he had first committed to writing nearly two decades earlier. In his Land

Management Manual (*Jisho kanri kokoresho*) of 1892, Saitō laid out rational business administration as he understood it.[15] Relations between landlords and tenants were like those between capital and industrial labor. Both groups entered into business with each other in perfect freedom and in rational pursuit of their own interests. If tenants found reason to become unhappy with their arrangements with the landlord, they were welcome to leave and find another type of employment that served them better.[16] This rational arrangement of economic interests was not, he complained in 1892 in much the same way as he would in 1908, properly appreciated by the well-meaning but misinformed public:

> The public misunderstands this arrangement and claims that tenants are mistreated. Then, as a form of relief, they have the opinion that landlords should love their tenants like family, while tenants should respect their landlords like the heads of their houses and depend upon them. Thus, they make arguments that treat today's landlords and tenants the same as lords (*daimyō*) and peasants (*hyakushō*) in the olden days. But the old lords followed the principles of despotism (*sensei*), while today's landlords reject this in favor of the principles of democracy (*minshusei*), which is collaborative in all things.[17]

In line with this logic, the only reasonable response to conflict from the landlord's point of view was to adhere to the terms of the contract and iron out any disagreements through legal means. Saitō advocated the immediate seizure of land in the case of default and advised that any disputes should be resolved in court.

While Saitō's philosophy of landlordism might be considered fair in a ruthless way, his particular instructions for day-to-day business operations highlighted the hypocrisies that undergirded his view of "rational" landlord-tenant relations. Advising his future successors on the daily management of tenant-farmed holdings, he outlined a series of conditions as "the only circumstances" in which it was acceptable to raise rents beyond what was recorded in the tenancy contracts. These situations numbered six and included: changes to transport costs, changes to product prices, improvements to land and/or irrigation, rises in farmer income relative to labor in other industries, increases in the farming population, and rises in the cost of living in villages that prompted tenants to ask for more land to rent in order to meet their costs.[18] If the contract-based nature of Saitō's general approach could be forgiven as a classic conservative understanding of labor and capital, all pretense to fairness fell apart with these guidelines. From their positions of power, he averred, landlords could and should take advantage of any change in circumstances to increase their profits while shifting expenses to tenants, who would then have to fight them in court if they objected.

Saitō was the first major Miyagi landlord to abandon direct involvement in cultivation to concentrate on the business of tenant administration and moneylending, but it was not long before other *ōjinushi* began to follow his model. Faced with the same backward economic circumstances, they found their avenues for profitable investment limited. The same tax pressures that drove Saitō and others out of sake brewing killed the small-scale soy sauce industry, wiping out two of the industries formerly run by wealthy farmers and driving them instead toward investment in land. Also pushing this trend was the alienation of landlords from the rice market. By the first decade of the twentieth century, dedicated rice merchants took control over the increasingly complicated futures market for grains, cutting off the landlords who collected rent rice from active participation in the terms of its sale. While Saitō answered these circumstances with his uncompromisingly (and selectively) rational approach to tenant management, other Miyagi landlords responded with greater subtlety. The Sasaki family of Nangō followed a typical path, abandoning soy sauce production in 1897 and reducing the amount of land that family members farmed themselves gradually from 3.6 hectares in 1899 to 0.2 hectares in 1917.[19] Whether early and fast or later and gradually, large landlords in Miyagi increasingly distanced themselves from direct involvement in farming from the 1890s on. This separation made them nearly as remote from agriculture as their non-resident analogues in other regions, undermining official understandings of the differences between absentee and resident landlords.

The outbreak of the Russo-Japanese War in 1904 and the difficulties it left in its wake changed the nature and intensity of official criticisms of the landlord-led system of agricultural development. The ending of hostilities in 1905 pushed two overarching goals to the forefront of national policy.[20] The first of these was the establishment of a stable social order befitting Japan's place among the great powers. Victory had earned international recognition for Japan, but policy makers were keenly aware of the precariousness of the country's position in world geopolitics and hypersensitive to troubled domestic realities that cast doubt on Japan's qualifications as a world power. Countering the conditions that might give rise to these doubts required a renewed effort at national self-strengthening that went beyond what had been accomplished since the fall of the Tokugawa Shogunate in 1868. Yamaguchi prefectural bureaucrat Nishimura Yasukichi outlined the basic shape of the new imperative in national policy in a series of lectures he gave between February and April of 1906. Victory had placed Japan in a period of unprecedented challenges and did not mark an end to international conflict. "A declaration of the restoration of peace is," he explained, "on the one hand the announcement of the end of a military conflict, but, speaking from the perspective of a 'peace war' (*heiwa sensō*), it is in fact a declaration of war. . . . The Russo-Japanese War was simply a war between the two countries, but in the coming 'peace war' every single country in the world will be our enemy."[21] In order to survive this battle royale, Japan would have to stabilize and strengthen its society and economy by all means possible.

The second goal, closely related to the first, was to deal with the fallout of poverty and discontent that the war had brought to cities and rural areas alike. This dealt more directly with landlords and agricultural improvement. Symptoms of social disintegration during and after the war included the rural poor flooding into urban ghettoes and signs of ideological subversion in the mocking replacement of the national slogans of "*fukoku kyōhei*" (rich country, strong military) and "*kyokoku itchi*" (unity of the whole nation) with "*hinkoku kyōhei*" (poor country, strong military) and "*hinpuku kakuzetsu*" (division of rich and poor).[22] Tenancy rates across the country passed 40 percent during the war, and officials feared that the economic distress responsible for this increase was also the reason for the growing dissatisfaction among rural residents that threatened to evolve into open discord.[23] The search for the causes of these rural difficulties once again focused eyes on landlords and their leadership of agricultural villages. Just as they had been forced to recognize that the pursuit of economic development at the turn of the century meant that the countryside could no longer be ignored, officials now had to acknowledge that conditions inside villages were as important as their outward signs of collective prosperity.[24]

As we have seen, Saitō Zen'uemon's disappointment in officialdom in the wake of the tenant union action in 1908 was more than matched by the disillusionment among officials and central agricultural leaders toward landlords. Paradoxically, despite this disillusionment, some aspects of the new government commitment to national strength and rural prosperity resembled a strengthening of support for the landlord vision of rural improvement. In 1905, the Imperial Diet passed measures relating to a general program for "cultivating the foundation of the nation" (*kokuhon baiyō*).[25] This cultivation involved a torrent of new national funding for agriculture that included outlays for such landlord favorites as seed improvement, animal plowing, and land consolidation. Behind these public gestures, however, criticism was continuing to build. New doubts were emerging concerning even the resident landlords who stood so high in the estimations of Yanagita and others critical of absentee landlords.

A part of these doubts concerned political activities. One of the avowed purposes of the system of local government introduced in the late 1880s was the creation and maintenance of depoliticized villages that would be insulated from the political intrigues and conflicts that plagued Tokyo and other political centers. The actual conditions in villages demonstrated a failure to meet these expectations. Yokoi Tokiyoshi, a key figure in the Chūō (Central) Nōkai, depicted the evils of political activities in his 1907 novel *Mohan chōson* (Model Village), a dramatic portrait of an idealized rural community.[26] In the story, the father of the main character leaves his home village in the vain pursuit of a political career that ends in backstabbing and failure. He is presented in contrast with the selfless and diligent mayor of the village, next to whom he is a contemptible figure who "worked unceasingly and diligently chasing fame and fortune [, but] did not contribute a single thing to society."[27] Criticisms of the exploitative and unproductive nature of landlords of this type had long been a theme in Yokoi's thought and writing, appearing unfiltered in his statement nearly a decade earlier that the times "have reached the point where there is no small number of so-called economic parasites (*keizaikai no aburamushi*) among today's landlords."[28]

Prominent *meibōka* from northern Miyagi had a long history of involvement in precisely the sort of party politics that central planners like Yokoi held in such contempt. After calls for people's parties resulted in a broad reordering of the landlords elected to the prefectural assembly, Endō Ryōkichi, a major figure in the Entō conflict, and Kamata Sannosuke, in the middle of his crusade to drain Shinainuma, were among the party-affiliated landlords in northern Miyagi involved in disruptive political activities at the turn of the century. The political discord grew so heated that landlords launched no-confidence movements against the Miyagi governor and dispatched repeated missions to the Home Ministry to request support for their battles with the prefectural administration.[29] This was a far cry from the depoliticized and self-administering countryside that had been the object of the local government system. The embroilment of key members of the feuding factions in high-profile corruption cases at the same time only served to highlight the gap between vision and reality. Endō stood out as a particularly damning example, drawing concurrent accusations of misconduct relating to the disposal of funds for a dysentery outbreak and fraud in connection with the sale of a forest owned by an elementary school.[30]

Alongside the doubts raised by political misadventures were growing concerns about the separation of resident landlords from farming. Again, questions relating to the problem had received limited voice much earlier. As far back as 1894, Tamari Kizō remarked on the growing disconnect, observing that "most people with large landholdings are already, not farmers, but pure merchants. Rather than working with farmers, they are a species that works with merchants."[31] He singled out landlord-farmers in Tōhoku, a region notably lacking in absentee landlords, in 1904, declaring that they were "quick to find fault, but are, when compared to the people of other regions, extremely lacking in the spirit to get things done. It could be that the reason that the Tōhoku region doesn't bloom, doesn't rise, doesn't prosper, and maybe even why it is insignificant in the worlds of politics and business, is in the end that they lack a sense of inward motivation, the drive to move forward, and a spirit of daring and resolve."[32]

In the postwar environment of uncertainty, active officials joined agricultural activists in condemning resident and non-resident landlords alike. Now the positions of economic and political dominance that resident landlords had carved out for themselves in villages drew fresh criticism. In 1909, Home Ministry secretary Nakagawa Nozomu castigated the members of rural elected assemblies for raising local taxes to pay for administration and development and ensuring that the burden of paying them fell on the less-affluent segments of village society.[33] Other officials leveled similar charges against resident landlords. Home Ministry local office head Tokonomi Takejirō excoriated the "power brokers" (*yūryokusha*) holding honorary local offices as incompetents who harmed their villages far more than they helped them, while Oshio Shigenosuke, another Home Ministry bureaucrat, claimed that landlords abused their local offices and fostered disorder through the neglecting of their duties.[34]

Most strident in his postwar criticisms of the failings of landlords was Yanagita Kunio. By 1906 the scales had fallen from his eyes and little evidence remained of his former idealization of virtuous landlords or his belief in the potential for self-directed agricultural development. Disillusioned by endemic postwar poverty, he came to recognize that the masses of landless tenants populating villages were not a transitory phenomenon and that landlords did not match the portraits of benevolence he had celebrated. Predicting that a lack of government support would force independent farmers to launch their own, potentially destabilizing, movement for village prosperity and economic security, he grew critical of the government administration of villages under the local government system.[35] He lamented the outflow of rural residents to the cities and the costs it imposed on farming villages. The monopoly cities held over capital drew rural men of ability from their home communities, robbing villages of the potential for improvement or development. Expounding that "there is no means of accumulating capital in the countryside," he identified the problem as one "of policy, not of agriculture or economics" and declared that without active official policy "proper distribution to the countryside is impossible."[36]

The official recognition of the exploitative nature of landlord-tenant relations brought about a curious reversal of the criticisms that central bureaucrats had leveled at Miyagi's first attempts at a rice inspection system in the 1880s. Instead of local officials imposing a feudal order on the lower levels of village society, as the central government charged that Miyagi administrators had done with their use of the word "peasants" (*hyakushō*) to describe farmers, it was now the lower classes themselves that were recreating the debased social system. This system also now offered the only hope for rescuing village society. Home secretary Nakagawa Nozomu summed up the situation, discussing the continuing existence of "a custom among local tenant farmers to treat their landlords as lords (*tonosama*)." This tendency had to be exploited to quell any potential for discontent among tenants and to ensure that the two classes "do not cause hardship" to one another.[37] Here again, officials were recommending a paradoxical retreat from modernity in the countryside as a solution to economic and social woes.

Despite their increasing displeasure with landlords and their failings in agricultural villages, however, policy makers could not revoke their positions of local leadership. The fact was that the government still needed landlords to lead the ongoing improvement of farming. Their combination of assets, both financial and otherwise, and persistent assumptions concerning their social character made landlords infinitely more capable of agricultural improvement than tenants. Yokoi Tokiyoshi agreed with those criticizing the failures of landlords as *meibōka,* but continued to believe that they represented the only choice for local leaders and stewards of development, "as things like the improvement of agriculture and farmland [could] not possibly be entrusted to tenants."[38] This was not a matter of tenants simply lacking the economic means for the work. Against the failings of landlords, who took advantage of the trust that had been placed in them and enriched themselves at the expense of their villages, tenants were criticized for pseudo-biological immorality and character deficiencies. Influential social reformer and advocate of the Local Improvement Campaign (Chihō Kairyō Undō) Tomeoka Kōsuke presented a characteristic understanding of the social basis for failing villages. The laziness and immorality of smaller farmers destroyed village unity, while the selfishness and greed of landlords made them derelict in their duty to promote development.[39] Both exercised a negative influence, but the former was a fundamental and inalterable aspect of the makeup of the poor, while the latter was a choice among a group that was otherwise in sole possession of the moral and other assets needed to rebuild shattered villages.

While bureaucrats and improvement advocates attempted to salvage the ideal of the landlord-*meibōka,* matters were taking their own course in Miyagi. The crop failures at mid-decade had exacted a toll on tenant farmers in the prefecture, the seriousness of which was apparent in the flood of migration to Hokkaidō. It was the institution of the rice regulations, however, that threatened to be the more damaging development. Apart from the absolute increase in rents that it represented—demanding rent payments in grains of higher value, both in terms of their market value and the labor that went into their production—the quality standards also posed a danger in their lack of provision for relaxation in the event of future crop failures. Despite the return to plentiful harvests in 1907, the looming regulation system created an atmosphere of dread in the north in what Tokyo journalist Nishikawa Tadashi called "the sadness of a year of plenty" (*hōnen no kanashimi*).[40] The moves of Miyagi's landlords after the return to normal harvests did little to assuage tenant fears. They worked with rice merchants throughout 1907 and into the following year to lobby the prefectural government for the right to conduct the quality inspections at the point of rent payment in the villages. Success in spring of 1908 ensured that all costs for meeting the standards, including rebagging and adjustments, would be borne by tenants. At the same time, the leaders of the Miyagi Landlord Association (Miyagiken Jinushikai) publicly addressed the troubles of tenants. In the May 1907 issue of the journal of the Dai Nihon Nōkai, they expressed their sympathies for the difficulties facing poorer villagers and introduced a number of resolutions notable for their failure to address any of them. In answer to the suffering of tenants, the landlords offered a renewed commitment to raising the quality of rice, holding product exhibition fairs, reordering farmland, and organizing more landlord associations.[41] These measures indeed hit at the heart of the problems of tenants, but they promised to strengthen the causes of the difficulties and increase the pressure they exerted.

In response to the adversity they faced, Miyagi tenants fired the first shots against landlords in 1907. Their progress toward success was swift. Nishikawa, writing for the *Shūkan shakai shinbun* in December of 1907, reported that the tenant union (*kosakunin kumiai*) in the village of Tagajō had pressed the local large landlord family of Kitsukawa into a corner and that the landlord would have to give in to the group's demands or face the threat of violence.[42] From that beginning, the movement spread and landlords across the prefecture soon found themselves assailed. By the beginning of summer in 1908, socialist reporter Hirata Ichirō was able to proclaim with confidence, "in all of Japan, the prefecture with the most tenant disturbances (*sōdō*) must be Miyagi."[43]

In fact, the Miyagi tenant unions of the post-disaster period were building on organizational roots that reached back before the Russo-Japanese War. As they would do in 1908, tenant groups had formed early in the north of the prefecture, where landlord domination of the local money supply was most concentrated. The first two such organizations, reflecting the difficulties caused by this domination, were a credit union and a collective purchasing and marketing union, which established the precedent of smallholder leadership over a membership of tenant farmers.[44] *Kosaku dōmei* (tenant alliance) had first appeared as a term as assertiveness grew in tenant organizations in the wake of crop failures in 1902. A more aggressive form of tenant organization, and one that presaged later developments, the groups presented landlords with the choice between remitting and reducing rents or seeing the abandonment of their lands by tenants.[45] A new spate of organizations appeared with the return of crop failures in 1905.[46] While the difficulties of two seasons of dearth bled strength from the movement, the foundation was in place for the explosion of 1907 and 1908.

The tenant union movement revived itself in the wake of the disaster and approached critical mass in 1907. Beginning in the centrally located villages of Rifu and Iwakiri early in the year, tenants formed unions along hamlet lines in order to press demands for changes in their land use contracts. Over the months that followed, similar organizations spread through the north of the prefecture, reaching a total of twenty-three similar groups by the end of December.[47] Enraged by the return of heavy-handed landlordism after the crop failures and emboldened by newfound collective strength, tenant unions throughout Miyagi launched protests. The years 1907 and 1908 saw significant showdowns in each of the rice-producing Senboku districts and the prefecture as a whole hosted nearly 20 percent of the seventy-three landlord tenant conflicts experienced in Japan between 1907 and 1911.[48] While poor harvests provided the immediate backdrop for tenant activism, it was not the main motivating force. As Nishikawa's article made clear, the clashes that the unions initiated were linked to long-standing pressures from high rents, imposed improvements, and the new threat of the rice quality inspection laws. The actions of the Toyosato union in the northern district of Tome in 1908 illustrated the forces moving tenants to action. Pressing for the lowering of rents to make up for the loss of common lands and citing the impossibility of deriving profits or even maintaining subsistence from farming under current conditions, the groups' demands directly addressed the hardships brought about by landlord improvement and the hothouse capitalism that saw legal compulsion replace profits in encouraging more intensive production.[49]

Building on the precedent of earlier organizations, the tenant unions in Miyagi at this time relied upon the participation of independent farmers and minor resident landlords. Though composed chiefly of tenants and pursuing ends ostensibly in their interests, the unions placed the middling classes of villagers who constituted the hamlet elites in roles of leadership. The unity of these minor elites and tenant farmers was a characteristic peculiar to Tōhoku groups and emerged from the patterns of landholding in the region. The outsized holdings of Tōhoku large landlords created villages populated by tenants (often farming fields owned by landlords from other hamlets) and their minor landlord and smallholder neighbors. Pressed in similar, if not equal, ways by the increasingly onerous legal force behind the landlord vision of improved agriculture, these groups found themselves natural allies and banded together to resist those improvements that most threatened their interests. In his 1904 diatribe against Tōhoku backwardness, Tamari Kizō lamented this alliance and its deleterious influence on his vision of agricultural progress. "[Unlike places like Kagoshima,] in Tōhoku even simple things like narrow-strip planting and salt water (seed) selection are not done, and if one tries to force them, men of influence (*yūshisha*) together with foolish people (*gujin*) raise a stink (*guzuguzu iu*) or they pass on evil ideas (*akuchie*) to the ignorant people (*gumin*)."[50] Cooperation between the two groups made it possible to resist "improvements" that were not in their collective interests.

The decisive showdown in the Miyagi landlord tenant conflicts came in 1908 and centered on the cross-district Monō-Oshika Allied Tenant League (Monō-Oshika Rengō Kosakunin Dōmeikai). Unfolding over the first half of the year, the clash pitted tenants from fourteen villages in both districts in a collective body against two assemblies of large local landlords. The league was born of meetings held in a string of villages to the north and west of the port of Ishinomaki during the New Year's holidays of 1908. Initially composed of eight Monō villages, the group grew across district lines with tenants joining from a village in neighboring Oshika when landlords called in the rents for the previous year, and again expanded by a further five villages in February after the league resolved to press demands against landlords.

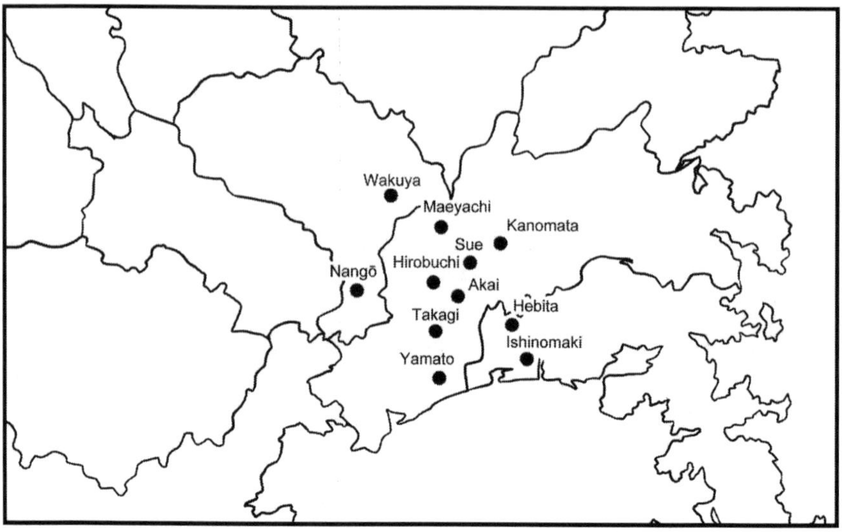

Monō-Oshika Allied Tenants League Villages

The Monō-Oshika League, and the hamlet and village groups comprising it, again displayed the influence of Miyagi landholding styles in their pluralistic composition. Village mayors were among the most prominent leaders of the groups, with officeholders from the Monō villages of Sue, Takagi, and Hirobuchi stepping forward to represent their fellow villagers. Fulfilling a crucial organizational role by means of their webs of contacts beyond village boundaries, these mayors and the petty landowners that joined them in leadership were not acting out of love for their neighbors. When large landlords enshrined their exploitative vision of improvement into law and passed the responsibility for its enforcement on to the prefecture, farming populations of all varieties found themselves under new pressures. The combination of crop failures and the new system of rice quality testing drove both resident elites and tenant farmers to assertive action and victory offered both a similar promise of relief.

Economic interests were not the only factor prompting independent landowners to cooperate with tenant farmers. The positions minor landlords held in village administration imparted a sense of responsibility for their communities. In part, this was a function of feelings of duty associated with the offices, but it also reflected the practical need for local support required for success in these positions. The active involvement of figures like Kaga Unosuke, mayor of Hirobuchi and a landless moneylender with no direct interest in agriculture, pointed to a sense of community responsibility, a suggestion enhanced by the fact that the most active elite leaders came from villages without resident large landlords of the type who had advocated for the new rice regulations. The absence of these figures left holes in local finances, administration, and more general leadership that helped push residents in these communities to action.[51] These leaders were continuing to perform a function that was associated with their offices in the past. In previous spontaneous conflicts between landlords and tenants, resident elites would act as intermediaries, relating the tenant demands to landlords and then stepping back to let district heads or *nōkai* officials begin the mediation process. Now, however, faced with the intransigence of the large landlords, these elites took on a more active part, casting their lot with tenants and aiming to break the control of non-resident landlords over their villages.[52]

Under the leadership of hamlet elites, the Monō-Oshika Tenant Union League went on the offensive in the first months of 1908. In response to the convening of an emergency meeting at the end of January by landlords in Oshika to discuss strategies of opposing the organization, the league held a planning session on the 13th of February. Drawing in the unions of five additional villages, it dispatched representatives to meet with the landlord associations of Monō and Oshika. The demands they presented reflected the pressures landlord improvements placed on tenants, as well as the difficulties experienced during the recent famine. They called for relief money for impoverished families; rent remissions when circumstances warranted, even if they were not provided for in tenancy contracts; an immediate and permanent 10 percent rent reduction; and the provision of interest-free loans for the purchase of fertilizer.[53] Behind the outward deference of the league representatives lay the threat of the abandonment of tenanted lands.[54]

The landlords of Monō and Oshika responded to the measured demands of the tenant league by rejecting them roundly. Landlord associations in both districts organized meetings immediately after receiving the ultimatum, producing counterproposals that disregarded the concerns of the Tenant League. In place of rent reductions and assistance in improving crops, the landlord-crafted plans called for stricter guidelines for the grading of rice quality and a system of rewards for excellence in production.[55] They presented their own demand for a resurveying of all tenanted land in the region, a measure they suggested would eliminate unfairly high rents but that tenants feared would have the opposite effect.[56] The proposal received a promising response from the prefectural government, which endorsed its basic elements and raised landlord hopes of official intervention on their side.

The Tenant League responded to the rejection of their demands by attacking the economic interests of landlords and exploiting their fear and disunity. Behind the apparent confidence of the landlords' refusals was a weakness born of their memories of absconding tenants during the crop failures and the threat a recurrence of such flights presented to their profits. Their two-district coalition was held together by nothing more than a determination to resist demands for rent reductions and a broad desire to resurvey their tenant lands.[57] In response to the refusal of their initial demands, the Tenant League sent out smaller groups the next day to approach landlords individually. In addition to announcing the immediate suspension of farming on tenanted lands, league members were instructed to express the organization's commitment to the type of morality that landlords and officials alike had accused tenants of lacking. Members were to explain their devotion to diligence and frugality (*kinben ken'yaku*) and the Tenant League's prohibition of unproductive leisure activities, tobacco, and alcohol.[58]

A deadlock followed this second delivery of tenant demands but the brittleness of landlord solidarity soon proved decisive. On February 25th, landlords in Oshika, fearing that the dispute would prevent planting and destroy an entire year of production, acquiesced and agreed en masse to accept the demand for support money and supplies to meet the rice quality standards. In the days that followed, Oshika landlords reached agreements individually with all tenant members of the League that reduced rents by 10–15 percent.[59] Shaken by the defeat of their neighbors, landlords in Monō followed suit in early March. This was the context in which Saitō Zen'uemon, incensed at the weakness of his fellow landlords, incredulous at the lack of support from the prefecture, and intent on giving no ground to tenants, took to the press.[60] In the end, his public outburst brought no results, and he was left to join the last landlord holdouts in signing revised tenancy contracts in early April.

Yet, Saitō's outrage at the failure of the prefecture to act was not entirely without basis. Article 17 of the 1900 Public Order and Police Law (Chian Keisatsuhō) gave specific attention to issues relating to tenants, laying out fines and imprisonment for the employment of violence, coercion, and slander to negotiate rents on farmland. Although the Monō-Oshika union didn't engage explicitly in any of these activities, it was hardly unknown for the authorities of the time to engage in eyebrow-raising distortions of the law in service of the establishment. Yet neither the national nor the Miyagi government made any move to come to the defense of Saitō and his compatriots. The closest the government came to intervention on behalf of landlords was historical revision after the fact.

The Ministry of Agriculture's 1909 report on the conflict absolved landlords of responsibility for its outbreak, casting it as a result of crop failures, and applied a rewritten ending, which, if it did not grant landlords victory in the conflict, at least spared them from defeat. What occurred in the spring and summer of 1908 was depicted as nothing more than a return to "normalcy" in landlord-tenant relations that left "nothing that would give rise to conflict" (*jūrai aete kattō o shōjitaru koto nakari*).[61]

This lack of official backing for landlords in the Monō-Oshika dispute was the key reason for the victory of tenants. The economic power that large landlords wielded was not in fact the basis for their dominant position over tenants, as the illegal flights of tenants during the 1905–1906 famine had revealed. The agricultural order that landlords throughout the country had created, and that Miyagi landlords were attempting to develop further with the rice quality inspection system, depended upon the commitment of the government to apply laws and coercive force to maintain it. When the prefecture refrained from intervening in 1908, it removed this commitment and eliminated the basis for the unassailable position of landlords. Without the support of laws and the threat of violence or punishment, landlords could not respond to tenant pledges to abandon cultivation with anything but acquiescence to their demands.

Regardless of the possible justifications for Saitō's indignation, the tenants of the Monō-Oshika Tenant Union League won the contract revisions they sought with all their demands met in full. Landlords pledged to contribute to the costs of farming improvement and production and, in doing so, to share the profits that the accomplished improvements were driving up yearly. The triumph set off a wave of similar victories across the prefecture. New tenant groups formed in the neighboring districts of Shida, Tōda, and Tōme and rode the successes of the League to extract contract revisions of their own from landlords made newly aware of their own vulnerability. Other unions already embroiled in conflicts found their landlord opponents more tractable in the wake of their peers' defeat. Disputes in the towns and villages of Matsushima, Takasago, Kitaura, Wakuya, and Furukawa all ended in tenant victory in the spring of 1908. The specific terms of the new contracts varied and conflicts could stretch on for longer periods (four years in one case), but the struggles of 1907 and 1908 produced a new order in tenant farming in Miyagi. Tenancy contracts in virtually every corner of the prefecture now dictated that landlords share in the costs of agricultural improvement and tenants receive a more significant share of its rewards.[62] Tenant farmers seized upon their own economic importance to landlords and successfully ended nearly a decade of unrestrained landlord dominance.

If some ambiguity existed as to the significance of government inaction during the Miyagi conflict in 1908, events set in motion by the Home Ministry later that year left little doubt that official views of landlords as *meibōka* had changed. The sporadic official criticisms of landlord excess, persistent village poverty, and rural social discord had grown louder over the course of the decade, prompting changes in the policies of agricultural development. Revisions to laws and government policy came one after another in the late 1900s. They began with the Home Ministry's Local Improvement Campaign in the fall of 1908, which took aim at the local leadership of rural villages in an attempt to improve economic circumstances and impose social stability. The Ministry of Agriculture followed soon afterward with the revision of the turn-of-the-century laws that had set the framework for landlord-*meibōka* leadership over agricultural development, assigning the central government a new active role in the improvement of farming. Together, these initiatives helped to bring about a fundamental transformation in the way forward for agriculture and rural villages.

The first part of the attack on the prevailing rural order was launched even as Miyagi landlords were coming to terms with their loss in the tenant union conflict. On October 13, 1908, the central government issued the Boshin Rescript. With a message promoting the cultivation of the triple virtues of sincerity, thrift, and diligence, the text of the document appeared anything but novel. This official repetition of long-repeated exhortations to the rural public, however, marked the launch of the policies, programs, and initiatives that comprised the Local Improvement Campaign. Designed to produce an enduring solution to the problems that had long troubled villages, the campaign took aim at many of the bases for the landlord leadership of agricultural development.

The first rumblings of the Local Improvement Campaign dated back to the Saionji cabinet of 1906. Policy makers drafted instructions dealing with the problems afflicting villages and passed them down to local administrators, signaling a more direct intervention of central officials into rural villages. Among the actions they dictated were the merger of shrines and hamlet assets under the administrative towns and villages, the formation of new village organizations, punishments for debt and tax default, and the reordering of police services and health administration.[63] These measures were a direct response to conditions after the Russo-Japanese War. The stability of the villages was now central, drawing official policy into a collision course with the brand of improvement that landlords had crafted with government support.

The official Local Improvement Campaign began after the incoming Katsura cabinet strengthened its commitment to these goals with the Boshin rescript in 1908 and the dispatch of personnel to train local officials in the summer of the following year. There were three main objectives. First, it was necessary for the government to take direct action to raise the Japanese economy and society up to a level commensurate with its status as a world power. Next, it was necessary to employ local resources in order to exploit the productive potential of a harmonious citizenry while avoiding the depletion of scarce government assets. Finally, it was necessary to establish the emperor as the central ideological force to accomplish the other goals.[64] Behind these aims lay fears based on the experiences of other countries. Government leaders were dedicated to avoiding the negative consequences of rapid industrialization and the spread of socialism that had caused and was continuing to cause discord in the countries of Europe and North America.[65]

As it related to farming villages and agricultural improvement, the Local Improvement Campaign rejected the narrowness of the approach taken by landlords and sought to correct the damage it had caused rural society. It aimed at reframing the notion of village improvement in order to expand it past the limited focus on production increases and the generation of private wealth. Yokoi Tokiyoshi's introduction to *Mohan chōson* articulated the new vision and its criticism of what it was replacing:

> Because their evil customs and vulgarity persist as of old, in towns and villages today, however much production grows and whatever utility this has, it will mean nothing more than increases in production and will only be subject to wasteful extravagance. The results that people have worked so hard to achieve will either scatter like the mist or become seasonal fodder for insects. If that is the case, the social improvement of towns and villages should be the most urgent problem today, but the world does not yet seem to have taken notice. Are these not deplorable circumstances?[66]

What was needed now, Yokoi explained, was the cultivation of "civilized farmers" (*bunmeiteki nōmin*) with the attributes of "economic security, morality, and aesthetic appreciation."[67]

The policies of the Local Improvement Campaign were shaped by the characteristic thrift of the Meiji government's approach to the countryside, but they were nonetheless ambitious in their aims. In line with government policy toward villages up to that point, the commitment of official finances to the programs of the campaign was limited. In 1909, its total budget languished at a paltry 43,000 yen for the year, fully 35,000 yen of which was earmarked to promote the postal savings system.[68]

Whatever the campaign's goals for ending rural poverty, it would appear the villages themselves would be responsible for paying for the remedy. For the means to accomplish its goals without increasing its costs, the Home Ministry turned to the earlier tools of town and village plans and model villages, as well as the central Hōtokukai (Hōtoku Association), an umbrella organization bringing together the local agrarian societies (Hōtokusha) dedicated to the memory of legendary Tokugawa agricultural ideologue Ninomiya Sontoku.[69] The aims of the village plans meshed nicely with those informing the new initiative. Combining the strengthening of national and local administration finances (preventing tax defaults, shoring up village assets), ending economic distress in villages (thrift and savings organizations, productive associations), the development of agriculture (agricultural associations, plans for agricultural improvement), and the firming up of ideological bases (moral education and reform), the prescriptions presented by the policy plans offered up a laundry list of locally funded means to achieve the Home Ministry's goals.[70]

Also informed by the tight-fistedness of the Home Ministry was the revival of its "model village" (*mohanson*) program. Begun in 1901, the original form of the initiative awarded three agricultural villages, one being the Miyagi village of Oide, the title of "model village" and publicized their mayors as ideal local leaders. The work of these leaders had been accomplished in the context of an epidemic of "distressed villages" after the Sino-Japanese War, a situation sharing much in common with the difficulties facing the countryside in 1908. With an emphasis on the importance of virtuous local leaders and presenting the "superb accomplishments of [their] administration" (*yūryō no jiseki*), model villages fit nicely with the goals of the Local Improvement Campaign, and the program was revived and expanded.[71]

In fact, the liberties that the Home Ministry took with Tamura Matayoshi of Inatori, Shizuoka, the first of the three original model village mayors, illustrated in miniature the incongruities that ran through both the *meibōka*-led system of agricultural development and the Home Ministry's new approach to villages in the early twentieth century. The concentration of praise and symbolic value given to model mayors in the truth-stretching pedagogic narratives of the model villages introduced problems for the Home Ministry that limited the effectiveness of the program. While accomplishing the economic and institutional goals that Home Ministry officials held dear through the means of tax payment associations, secondary occupations, and the promotion of frugality and diligence—all beloved by bureaucrats and central ideologues—Mayor Tamura deviated from the script in two major ways. First, he did not conform to the administrative narrative that was assigned to him. By resigning his post as mayor to take up the task of saving his village, he demonstrated the self-motivation (*jihatsu*) that officials were promoting but undermined their message of loyalty to the village in his tacit message that formal offices and village improvement were incompatible. Second, his conception of what was needed to make a village prosperous stood at odds with the Home Ministry's pursuit of national unity and social harmony. In a distorted mirror image of Nishimura Yasukichi's "peace war," Tamura saw villages coexisting under the modern capitalist order as being in a state of constant and ruthless economic warfare in which only the organization of the village as an "agricultural army" (*nōgun*) could fend off the predatory instincts of landlords and others in outside communities.[72] Connected to this vision of self-sufficiency were criticisms of class structure and capitalism that could not have sat well with Home Ministry officials. While his blaming of village ills on the predations of absentee landlords was in accord with the new direction that policy makers were taking in the Local Improvement Campaign, the solution he offered did not fit so comfortably. His answer to the problems of absenteeism was the elimination of economic inequality and the raising of the entire village population to an egalitarian state of farmers with significant landholdings (*dainō*).[73]

This radical egalitarianism was in direct conflict with the hopes of the Local Improvement Campaign to either rehabilitate landlords or find similarly atypical individuals to carry out their plans. A major thrust of the movement was a restatement of the need for *meibōka*-like figures to rescue villages. The problem, thought Home Ministry planners, was that the real meaning of the word (which their forebears had laid out three decades earlier) had been forgotten. The corruption of the landlords and village officials who monopolized the title had deviated from the true spirit of the term *meibōka* and divorced it from its roots as a marker of selfless public service. Ministry officials leveled constant charges of misconduct at local officials generally, contributing to a broad picture of the landlords who held local offices as impeding improvement by preventing more capable and public-spirited villagers from taking up the positions for which they were better suited.

To remind people of the meaning that had been lost, Home officials and supporters of the Local Improvement Campaign took up the task of remaking *meibōka* as *tokushika* (self-sacrificing volunteers). A relatively unknown term before the Russo-Japanese War, it took on a central role in the Home Ministry's push for model accomplishments during the war.[74] It represented a change in direction from the earlier terms used to describe the roles that officials hoped landlords would fill. In response to the failure of landlords to act as true *meibōka* and provide the leadership needed for local development, *tokushika* were defined by the desire to engage in public service. Unlike their *meibōka* predecessors, *tokushika* required neither wealth, nor special skill, nor reputation. In 1915 *Chihō kairyō no hanashi* (A Discussion of the Local Improvement Campaign) highlighted the sole prerequisite of willingness, noting that "with no qualifications, one cannot become a schoolteacher and with no qualifications, one cannot become a temple monk or a Shintō priest. Without qualifications, it is possible to become *tokushika*. . . . *Tokushika* are those who do great and amazing works (*erai osoroshii shigoto*)."[75] These figures were to come from the economically ambiguous strong middle core of villages (*chūken jinbutsu*) to whom the legal changes between 1897 and 1901 were purported to be dedicated, each one of whom was defined by Kenneth Pyle in "The Technology of Japanese Nationalism" as someone

> who, by the strength of his personality and resources and by the sincerity of his devotion to the good of the village, was capable of giving patriarchal leadership to the youth groups, industrial cooperatives, and soldiers' associations. They were men who because of their local responsibilities had risen only halfway up the educational ladder of success. They were free of the cosmopolitanism and cultural uncertainties of those who had attained the higher reaches of education.[76]

Meibōka were recast as *tokushika* in an explicit call to replace the self-interested landlords whose interest in improvement ended at the limits of easy profits with figures more like Kamata Sannosuke. The implicit criticism of those who had failed to live up to the earlier ideal was articulated in 1909 by Yamazaki Enkichi, the head of the Aichi College of Agriculture and Forestry. In a speech on Local Improvement, he presented examples of local *tokushika* and their works in Aichi.[77] Focusing on dedicated educators who built schools and promoted agriculture, youth organizations (*seinendan*) that placed as much emphasis on morality as farming improvement, and landlords who remained committed to agriculture and awarded good farming with their own funds, his speech presented an image of *tokushika* that combined lingering traces of an idealized class of resident landlords with the new hopes for non-elite men of ability and dedication concerned with moral development. Yamazaki's tale also touched on the more general trend of relabeling that came along with *tokushika*. In the new language of local leadership, now purged of economic references, terms like *gōnō* (wealthy farmer) and *rōnō* (experienced farmer) were replaced by *seinō* (hardworking farmer), defined by neither wealth nor special skill. This came with a commensurate widening of application, as in an Aichi *seinendan*'s ambition to transform all local farmers into *seinō*.[78]

The Local Improvement Campaign also opened new space and new roles for *tokushika* with the creation and imposition of new semi-governmental village organizations. These groups included *seinendan, hōtokukai, hahanokai* (mothers' associations), and *zaigō gunjinkai* (military reservist associations), and were designed to more tightly connect local leaders to the central government and provide a reliable conduit for government aid and guidance.[79] They also represented the most direct attack on the failures of landlord-*meibōka* to achieve officials' goals of stable and prosperous villages. An integral part of these groups was the call for *tokushika* to take up positions of leadership that were, in many ways, defined by their difference from those who had been entrusted with overseeing village development for the last decade. What qualified them for leadership was the *tokushi* (voluntary spirit) that both defined them and distinguished them from the earlier failures.

In the Miyagi of 1908, the site of recent and expensive natural disasters, the Local Improvement Campaign's emphasis on ideas of village self-sufficiency and the local financing of development made it attractive to prefectural officials. From the prefecture-organized meeting of mayors hastily convened two months after the promulgation of the Boshin Rescript, through the directives from the prefectural government, and down to programs implemented on the village level, the Miyagi iterations of local improvement focused on lowering costs and increasing tax revenue. Reflecting these priorities, the December 1908 mayors' meeting identified its goals as the increase and consolidation of local assets and the ending of tax defaults.[80] Government goals for villages remained the same, even if their vision of the figures who would accomplish them did not. Directives issued from the prefecture to the villages soon thereafter built on these basic aims and called for specific means to end farmer idleness and build local funds to finance local administration and disaster relief, sentiments upon which the government placed renewed emphasis when severe flooding in 1910 ruined fields and spread misery.[81] Unsurprisingly, given the recent changes in fortune for local economic elites, local organizations in Miyagi followed the national trend against the use of landlord status as a qualification for leadership in agricultural improvement. In Shida, district planners returned to older ways of fostering improvement and established an association of *rōnō* to oversee the creation of their district plan (*gunze*). The charter of the resultant organization listed its purposes as: the management of agriculture and the promotion of agricultural improvement, the advising of the district head, and the creation of proposals for policy, all functions formerly reserved for landlords.[82]

The Home Ministry's assault on the failings of landlords in the Local Improvement Campaign was followed up by a series of dramatic legal changes instituted by the Ministry of Agriculture. These changes both rewrote the direction of agricultural development and recast its leadership. It removed the final remaining legal bases for the position of landlords as the officially backed shapers of farming improvement and the development of the countryside in Japan.

Legal revision came fast and furious in the closing years of the first decade of the twentieth century. One after another, the Industrial Union Law (Sangyō Kumiaihō), the Land Consolidation Law (Kōchi Seirihō), and the Agricultural Association Law (Nōkaihō) were revised between 1909 and 1910. In each case the revisions served to bring the activities concerned under the more direct control of the central government and to make participation in them compulsory.[83] The specific changes made to the laws revealed the new orientation of the Ministry of Agriculture and Commerce and marked a transformation to its approach to agricultural development. The 1909 revision of the Land Consolidation Law moved the focus of the work from the improvement of individual paddies, work of a scale within the means of landlords, to more fundamental improvements of the land relating to waterways and irrigation.[84] It also made available new loan money for the work through the Home Ministry and the Hypothec Bank soon after. The changes to the Agricultural Association Law were intended to deal with the problems of rural hardship and discontent that persisted from the Russo-Japanese War. It too imposed government control over a formerly autonomous group, grafting the Teikoku Nōkai (Imperial Agricultural Association) above the local groups formerly loosely collected under the umbrella of the Zenkoku Nōjikai.[85] More significantly, it made membership in the organizations universal and compulsory, bringing tenant farmers and smallholders into groups formerly monopolized by landlords and extending a degree of government support and protection over them.

New tenancy contracts, new village organizations and leaders, and new agricultural laws and policy directions marked the passing of an era for landlords in northern Miyagi. For nearly a decade, their vision of agricultural development and the improvement of farming villages had been supreme, backed by official support that gave it nearly dictatorial force. Production rose and progress was made in improving the stability of farming in the treacherous Miyagi climate, and these accomplishments were done in a way that directed profits to landlords while deflecting costs to tenants and smallholders. Even famine at mid-decade had failed to bring any significant adversity to the landlords of the countryside. The mass flight of tenants during the crisis had caused inconvenience, even panic, but the return to full harvests and the implementation of rice quality inspections left landlords stronger and with more profits than ever. They had looked forward to another decade or more of agricultural growth on their own terms and in their own interests with a feeling of security.

This prospect was illusory. The costs of landlord-led improvement were too much for villagers and officials alike and drove both groups against them. Tenant farmers and smallholders, combining lessons learned from the famine with desperation over the prospect of strict quality inspections, struck first and forced a rewriting of the productive relations of agriculture. The Home and Agriculture Ministries followed with their own assaults. Through ideological campaigns and legal revisions, they asserted government control over village improvement and agricultural development. The accompanying search for new local leaders did not necessarily disqualify the landlords who had monopolized the positions earlier, but no longer was it to be their exclusive and officially supported domain. Nor would agriculture depend so completely on landlords and follow the path they dictated. While local agents and resources remained central to development, the extension of government authority over agricultural improvement moved the locus of control over its direction and goals. Gone forever, for Saitō and landlords everywhere, were the peculiar conditions that dedicated government and law to the support of a vision of agriculture designed by and working for them. In their place opened up a period of new possibilities for farming now backed directly by a national government ready to apply its financial resources, administrative expertise, and technological assets to agricultural improvement.

CHAPTER SIX

Coming Full Circle

The Future History of Miyagi Meibōka

> In order that the imperial Japanese government shall remove economic obstacles to the revival and strengthening of democratic tendencies, establish respect for the dignity of man, and destroy the economic bondage which has enslaved the Japanese farmer to centuries of feudal oppression, the Japanese Imperial Government is directed to take measures to insure that those who till the soil of Japan shall have a more equal opportunity to enjoy the fruits of their labor.
>
> —SCAPIN 411, December 9, 1945

When American Occupation officials set about assessing the state of agriculture in Japan in the autumn and winter of 1945, they found little to praise. Spurred both by an ideological imperative to correct the deficiencies in villages seen as having failed to properly ignite democratic fires in Japanese souls and a more immediate need to feed a defeated nation on the brink of starvation, newly arrived American administrators wasted little time in beginning their assessment of the condition of Japanese farming. Displeased at what they saw, the leaders deputized by the Supreme Commander for the Allied Powers (SCAP) issued a series of directives to the Japanese government between September and December of 1945. These aimed at maximizing production, expanding agricultural lands, and ensuring an adequate food supply for the following year, displaying little respect for what should have been more than a half century of agricultural improvement and calling for revolutionary changes to the established agricultural order.

In describing the future course for agricultural development, SCAP officials outlined a litany of weaknesses to be overcome in Japanese farming. Some of these shortcomings came directly from the damage and disorder wrought by the war. The urgency behind the Occupation's call for reform was a response to the physical destruction inflicted by the Allied bombing campaign of the half year prior to the surrender, which had reduced the nation "to a point where starvation was imminent."[1] Adding to the pressures placed upon the food supply by the devastated cities was the increased burden imposed by soldiers, emigrants, and other personnel returning from the battlefields and now-lost empire. Such returnees drove the pressure on farmland from 4.8 to 5.8 people per cultivating acre. Farms needed to produce food for a larger population in more desperate need than ever before.

While the fallout of the war imposed its own pressures, more fundamental and disturbing to Occupation analysts were problems posed by a score of weaknesses inherent to agriculture in Japan. In enumerating these failings, SCAP officials unwittingly recreated a half century of criticisms voiced by the various actors concerned with farming in prewar Japan. Most naturally, given the democratizing mission pursued by the Occupation, their complaints echoed many of the dissatisfactions that had long been voiced by tenant farmers. The lack of a material government commitment to agriculture was singled out as a contributing factor to a pervasive "hopelessness and restlessness" among neglected farmers nationwide.[2] The systematic inequalities inherent to tenant farming, an issue that had been central to the Senboku Tenant Union movement thirty-five years prior, were assigned similar blame, particularly "the very small, uneconomical farm units, widespread tenancy practices and the low standard of living and inferior social status of those who tilled the soil."[3] Farming could neither reach its productive potential nor lay down the roots for popular democracy within a system that allowed for the immiseration of those responsible for bringing forth the agricultural bounty of the nation.

A different set of SCAP criticisms reflected those of Japanese officials and ideologues of earlier times. As late Meiji agricultural technicians had done, American analysts bemoaned the insufficient use of chemical fertilizers, required to tease the necessary production from Japan's "inherently infertile" soil.[4] A separate coterie of familiar artificial vulnerabilities continued to complicate these natural deficiencies. SCAPIN 411, issued in December of 1945, identified farm indebtedness and the high interest payments it extracted as one of three "pernicious ills" of Japanese agriculture.[5] Similar disdain was directed at official institutions dedicated to agricultural improvement, evoking the critiques of Maeda Masana and the mid-Meiji *rōno* in the late nineteenth century. While Occupation investigators were impressed with the scale of the agricultural research system overseen by the prewar and wartime governments, they condemned a "lack, on the part of the scientists, of familiarity or sympathy with or interest in the problems faced by farmers," which resulted in research that was "not sufficiently responsive to farmers' needs."[6]

To account for these problems, and for the unsatisfactory state of agriculture in general, SCAP officials identified a set of root causes that needed to be resolved if farming was to be made feasible. On the most basic level, many of Japan's problems stemmed from problematic natural conditions. Reports again cited the weakness of the soil, which rendered the country "unable to attain food self-sufficiency even in the years of abundant crops" and forced it to "rely on imports to make up the deficit."[7] More intensive use of chemical fertilizer and improved means of cultivation were needed to overcome this natural disadvantage. The social and economic organization of farming made this bad situation even worse. The tenancy system, particularly in the nature of the relationship between the majority population of tenant farmers and the small minority of landlords from whom they rented their lands, exercised a baleful influence. This relationship was characterized by an ambiguous and pervasive granting of advantage to landlords, in which such few written contracts as existed enshrined tenant disadvantage and "many abuses . . . multiplied the difficulties of the Japanese farmer in attaining a level of economic security and political and social status comparable to the remainder of the population."[8] While these conditions plagued farming throughout the country, Occupation analysts located some of the worst excesses in Tōhoku. Of the seven prefectures reported to have the highest tenancy rates in the country, three, including Miyagi, were from the northeast.[9] Concerns over the irredeemable nature of the landlord-tenant order in farming villages became central to SCAP planning, and would shape the most significant of its policies for rural Japan.

In the meantime, however, Occupation officials had hit upon the same issues that had been motivating both public agricultural policy and private efforts at improvement and reform since the late nineteenth century. Bureaucrats like Yanagita Kunio and the architects of the Local Improvement Campaign, agricultural ideologues like Tamari Kizō and Yokoi Tokiyoshi, and landlord and tenant farmers had all a half century earlier identified land, farming practices, and the social and economic organization of villages as the key problems facing farming. Many of these earlier figures, much like their mid-century SCAP counterparts, saw these latter socioeconomic realities, even more than the vagaries of climate and soil, as the true stumbling blocks to achieving a mode of agriculture that was productive, sustainable, and profitable. This understanding, however, was at odds with a central tenet of agricultural policy from the Meiji period onward. The government approach to agricultural administration and support was constructed around the idea of the self-motivated local leader, be it *gōnō,* landlord, *meibōka, tokushika,* agricultural association leader, or another iteration. SCAP's complaints in the 1940s, like those of late Meiji critics, were an indictment of the failure of these local leaders. The situation described by Occupation officials was not simply the result of local leaders falling short of the goals they had been assigned, it was the outcome of a continuing, and more profound, rejection of the *meibōka* ideal by landlords and village officials over the three decades since the national government's first moves to more direct involvement in agricultural improvement.

Despite the failing grades that SCAP officials gave Japanese farming, agriculture in Miyagi, as well as in most of the country, had in fact experienced significant progress toward the goals of increased production, improved efficiency, and greater stability pursued by farmers, landlords, and officials alike in the Taishō and early Shōwa periods. The improvements that landlords had pursued and implemented earlier provided the seeds for these successes, but the harvest was reaped only after the late Meiji legal changes in which government planners withdrew the carte blanche they had provided to landlords. Traditional landlord strongholds like agricultural associations and *kōchi seiri* organizations were placed under official control and the various initiatives undertaken in connection with the Local Improvement Campaign sought out new local leaders to correct the excesses of self-interested landlords.

While landlords' unchecked exploitation of tenant farmers was no longer as comprehensively underwritten by the state, village elites continued to occupy a position of privilege. The fact that the backlash they faced at the end of the first decade of the century challenged neither their ownership of farmland nor the rights this ownership bestowed upon them vis-à-vis the tenant farmers that worked it meant that the benefits produced by increased production fell disproportionately to them. They no longer enjoyed a monopoly over control of *kōchi seiri* associations, but lands reclaimed and commons seized in the process of consolidation work continued to expand the landholdings of the most adroit among them. Although the tenant action in Miyagi had forced some concessions into tenancy contracts, these agreements still largely favored landlords and the fact that legal authorities continued to come down on the side of landlords increasingly suggested that the events of 1908 had been a one-time chastisement. The absolute monopoly over farming profits that landlords enjoyed may have been gone, but they were still far and away the largest beneficiaries of agriculture.

The changes wrought by the legal and other reshufflings of 1908–1910 were not limited to the economic; they also altered the character of local leadership. Landlords and local elites continued to be well represented in both village administrative offices and in positions of responsibility in *nōkai* and other official and semi-official associations. A significant result of the Local Improvement Campaign, however, was the increasing presence of individuals from outside the landlord class alongside them in these posts. On the one hand, the soliciting and recruiting of new leaders from the independent farming and tenant-landowner classes represented an explicit criticism on the part of Home Ministry officials of the failure of landlords to live up to the *meibōka* ideal, but at the same time it eased the responsibilities placed upon them. With *nōkai* and *kōchi seiri* unions placed more directly under the control of central officials and their offices peopled, at least in part, by middling farmers, landlords were presented with more time to devote to their economic and other activities. These changes, which otherwise appeared to be of an evolutionary character, exerted a dramatic effect on the idea of *meibōka* that had been central to the development of agriculture and farming villages. The Taishō and early Shōwa years saw landlords retreat more completely from the responsibilities this abandoned ideal had imposed upon them and alter their relationships with their communities in profound ways. In Senboku, many of the figures and institutions that had played key parts in the story of late Meiji agricultural development turned away from the activities that defined *meibōka* and the mode of local leadership that had hitherto been formative in the development of villages in Senboku and throughout the country.

For all that mid-century would bring disaster to farming communities, agriculture flourished from the 1910s forward in Miyagi in general—and in Senboku in particular. Much of this developing prosperity came directly or indirectly from the efforts that landlords had spearheaded in introducing improved varieties of crops, promoting or enforcing the use of chemical fertilizers, small-scale projects of drainage and flood control, and consolidating and rationalizing paddyland and farm plots. Although undertaken primarily in pursuit of individual profit, these measures had diffuse effects and helped to stabilize agricultural production and raise yields more generally. Put simply, farming grew more and more productive in the years after Meiji, and much of the credit for this improvement was owed to the multifarious works led by landlords over the preceding two decades.

An important area of notable improvement in Senboku agriculture was the taming of the natural challenges that had placed such strict limitations on production and prosperity. The work in flood control, prevention, and preparation and in introducing and promoting products and practices that could survive the challenges of the Miyagi climate begun in the 1890s and 1900s reduced the region's vulnerability to natural threats and acted as a break against crop failures. The results were tangible. Although cold weather battered yields in 1913, undoubtedly prodding still-raw memories among beleaguered farmers of the crop failures of 1905 and 1906, this marked the last time the natural environment would impose a significant disruption on agricultural production in Senboku until the 1930s. Generalized increases in production took hold in the years that followed, providing a buffer that ameliorated future losses due to climate, flooding, or other natural misfortunes. While in other parts of the country the 1920s featured instability in the form of "roller-coaster years of record-setting rice yields followed by harvests smaller than any in recent memory," Senboku experienced steady growth.[10] The stability bestowed by high and consistent harvests spilled over into village life more generally in the 1910s and 1920s. Agricultural rent collection achieved a previously unknown regularity, a reflection of both new prosperity and a resultant pacification of the productive and other relations between large landowners, small farmers, and tenants.[11]

With farmers safely ensconced in favorable circumstances at least partly of their own making, Miyagi posted steady increases in its levels of rice production beginning at the end of the Meiji period. Prefectural production levels stabilized after bad harvests in 1910 and 1913 and grew steadily thereafter. Compared to 975,835 *koku* produced in the first year back at full production after the 1905–1906 crop failures, 1914 rice harvests rang in at 1,557,699 *koku,* 1924 at 1,733,620 *koku,* and 1930 at 1,837,434 *koku,* representing nearly a doubling of production in 23 years.[12] These advances also changed the position of Miyagi among the rice-producing prefectures of the country. Ranked at 13th place in terms of rice production nationally in 1922, Miyagi rose to 8th in 1929, expanding its paddyland and increasing its yields per *tan* to match national averages in developments that dispelled its characterization as an undeveloped prefecture.[13]

Senboku was the engine propelling increased yields and production totals. Outshone by more productive paddies in the south of the prefecture in late Meiji, Senboku rice farms continued to increase their yields throughout the prewar period while southern rice production plateaued in the 1920s. The southern districts of Katta, Shibata, and Igu demonstrated impressive gains in yields between 1911 and 1915 and 1926 and 1930, increasing rice per *tan* by 1.41, 1.62, and 1.34 times respectively (based on average yields over 5 years), but fell into stagnation in the intervening and subsequent years with 1936–1940 production decreasing slightly in Katta and Shibata and increasingly only marginally in Igu. Shida, Tōda, and Monō yields, in contrast, continued to grow over the entire period, with Shida and Tōda meeting and then surpassing yields in the south. This translated into even more dramatic differences in production totals, as the Senboku districts devoted a significantly larger share of their lands to rice production and added to these over the same period. These yields and the farming that produced them even impressed the otherwise critical SCAP analysts, helping prompt Occupation observers to state in 1948 that Japanese farmers' "methods furnish an enormous return: yields per acre in Japan are among the highest in the world. The Japanese farmer grows twice as much rice per acre as do farmers in any of the other rice-growing countries of Asia; his rice yields are 50 percent above those in the United States, while his wheat and barley yields are twice as high."[14]

Demographic trends provided further evidence of the increasing prosperity of Miyagi villages. Although it was not until 1913 that the prefecture again reached the population levels it had seen before the 1905–1906 crop failures, it enjoyed steady growth from that point forward. Staying consistently ahead of national growth statistics, Miyagi recorded an increase in households of 3.98 percent between 1905 and 1913, against a national increase of only 0.07 percent between 1871 and 1913, and 10.58 percent growth from 1923 to 1933, compared to just 1.49 percent nationwide from 1921 to 1933.[15] Post-Meiji-era demographic change in the prefecture went through two distinct periods. While there was mild growth during the remainder of the 1910s punctuated by instability at the end of the First World War, this was mainly a reflection of the booming industrial and commercial sectors of Sendai at the time. Postwar population expansion, however, was concentrated in the countryside, as farming villages experienced natural growth while at the same time acting as catchments for new migration into the prefecture and the bleed of underemployed workers from a recession-wracked Sendai. The years between 1913 and 1925 saw the prefecture gain 77,748 new residents, a moderate increase of 8.45 percent. The following decade saw a much more dramatic shift, however, and population grew between 1925 and 1935 at a rate more than quadrupling that of the preceding years.[16] These were notable numbers even in the context of a general population boom in Tōhoku in the middle decades of the century, and they reflected the growing prosperity of farming villages both in the economic stability that allowed and encouraged existing residents to have larger families and in the attractiveness of rural Miyagi for agricultural migrants from outside the prefecture.[17]

The means by which this agricultural prosperity was achieved were already familiar to Senboku farmers by the end of the Meiji period. The Miyagi prefectural *nōkai* summarized these in 1914 in a laundry list of directives for improved agricultural techniques issued by the prefecture in 1908.[18] These included more efficient methods of threshing, earlier

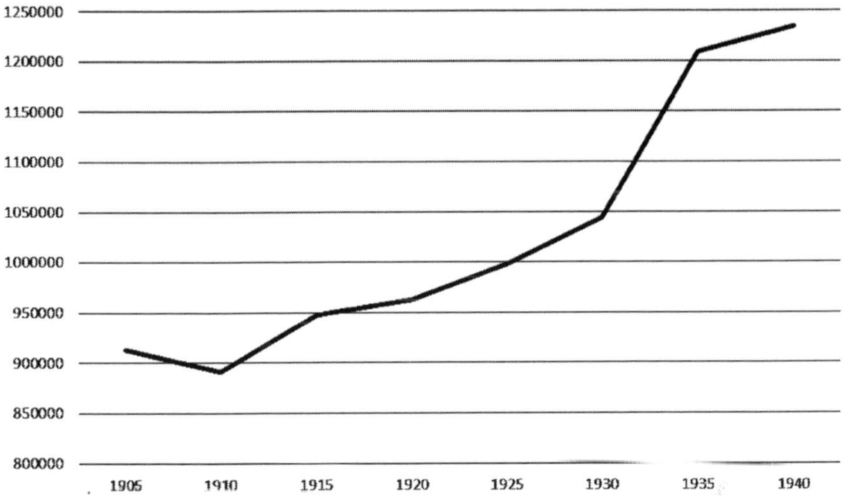

Graph 6.1. Population Growth in Miyagi

planting times, regular line planting, deep plowing, and the increased use of commercial fertilizer, and the *nōkai* proudly stated that these had been successfully put into practice across Miyagi. In the most direct sense, it was the widespread adoption of these methods, whether voluntary or coerced, that made farms more efficient, more resistant to natural adversity, and more productive. Their spread represented the accomplishment of a set of goals that had been central to the efforts of *rōnō,* farmers' societies of all types, and agricultural officials since the 1870s.

Behind these concrete means of increasing production were a set of contextual factors that made the adoption of improved techniques possible, enabled them to operate at maximum efficiency, and ensured that farmers employed them. One of these factors was the very group that reported the successful implementation of the prefecture's agricultural directives. *Nōkai* continued to be a crucial element in agricultural development, made all the more effective in the 1910s and 1920s by the commitment of the central and prefectural governments to support their activities. *Nōkai* in Miyagi enjoyed new attention from the prefecture after the tenant union movement in 1907 and 1908. Understanding crop failures to have been a primary cause of the conflict, officials launched a host of initiatives designed to prevent further problems of this type. Along with the organization of working groups to plan for increasing production, the creation of production expansion councils in each district, and the gathering of expert farmers (*rōnō*) and technicians to devise improved means of production, administrators assigned production expansion technicians to every local *nōkai.*[19]

These local efforts were bolstered by a new commitment to *nōkai* on the part of the national government. In response to the spread of discontent following the Russo-Japanese War and the increased tax burdens it imposed upon the citizenry, officials turned to a more active support of *nōkai* as a countermeasure.[20] Annual spending by the Ministry of Agriculture and Commerce on *nōkai* and related activities exploded between 1905 and 1908, jumping from 212,191 to 438,469 yen.[21] Along with this largesse came the desire for more centralized control over the associations and their activities. The Agricultural Association Law (Nōkaihō) was revised in 1910, establishing the Teikoku Nōkai (Imperial Agricultural Association) as a new central agency and binding prefectural and local branches to it in a tightened hierarchical structure.[22] A Zenkoku Nōjikai–drafted bill calling for a substantial increase in funding having been defeated in the Upper House, the revised law that passed showed clear evidence of official dissatisfaction with the accomplishments of the associations under landlord leadership. While the membership in the various new committees that were established above the prefectural level was to be determined both by elections in the local *nōkai* and appointment by Agriculture and Commerce officials, the organization's central committee included two appointees for every elected member.[23] In 1911, the organization this council oversaw stretched downward into 46 prefectural *nōkai,* 561 district branches, 34 city branches, and over 10,000 town and village branches, enabling central administrators to direct newly available government funds to all corners of the country.[24]

Armed with expanded funding and overseen by central officials, Miyagi *nōkai* activities retained much the same character they had under the previous order, scaled upward to make appropriate use of their new resources. In 1912, the prefectural *nōkai* sat atop a structure that included 16 district and 203 town and village *nōkai.* The prefectural budget of 16,976 yen that year was applied to efforts to continue to build—and to build upon—such familiar endeavors as the promotion of compost production, support and training for horse plowing, product fairs and awards, seed distribution, and the publication of the association journal.[25] Membership dues were bolstered by support from both the prefectural and the national governments, which dictated how the funds would be used. In 1914, funding from each amounted to 3,400 yen and 4,000 yen respectively, providing for 46 percent of the annual operating budget, and was intended to support the hiring and payment of technical advisors, the promotion of composting, and product fairs, in addition to expenses related to administrative and general operating costs.[26]

The continual progress being made in Miyagi in *kōchi seiri* was the key factor in ensuring that these efforts could reap success. The promotion of plowing with draft animals and instruction in planting techniques and seed selection provided by technical instructors had been featured activities of *nōkai* since their earliest forms, but it was only in the 1920s, when the consolidation of paddyland had started to reach a critical mass, that they began to open the doors to the promises of increased production and efficiency that had always been attached to them. *Kōchi seiri* redrew the boundaries of rice paddies, creating plots of regular shape and reasonable size and rationalizing the arcane arrangements of usage rights that had seen tenant farmers working several small plots often separated from one another by inconvenient distances. While the results of this process allowed farmers to make better use of their time, its more important effect was to allow for the meaningful application of improved means of agriculture. Large rectangular plots made animal plowing possible, which in turn allowed for a combination of deep planting and heavy fertilization that offered protection against the cold temperatures and temperamental climate of Miyagi. The consolidation of farmland also presented a more coercive argument for the adoption of advanced methods of farming. As discussed in chapter 4, the landlords who led *kōchi seiri* efforts used the rewriting of land boundaries to seize common lands that had been the property of the defunct *buraku*. The enclosure of these areas eliminated the primary source of natural fertilizer to tenant farmers and smallholders alike, forcing them to purchase the chemical alternatives that were demanded by new seed varieties and weatherproof cultivation.

Kōchi seiri proceeded in Miyagi at a breakneck pace that placed the prefecture at the forefront of the country. Here again, foundational work had already been accomplished before 1910. Bolstered by a new commitment on the part of the prefecture, consolidated land in Senboku increased from 2,683 *chō* in 1905 to 16,373 *chō* 5 years later.[27] Planned and led by landlords, work of this type generally covered areas no larger than a *buraku*, a characteristic that continued to predominate until 1915. The small scale of these projects did not blunt their efficacy, however, and by 1916 half of the paddyland in Miyagi was plowed by horses, with district totals reaching as high as 60.5 percent in Tōda and 70.7 percent in Shida.[28] The locus of initiative shifted after 1915, with larger trans-*buraku kōchi seiri* unions based on projects of drainage and reclamation taking the lead in reordering on a larger scale.[29] These efforts kept Miyagi at the top of paddyland consolidation, and it led the nation in 1939 with work completed on 45,538 *chō* and underway on another 73,209.[30]

The Taishō-era change in the scope of *kōchi seiri* was born of the same brand of legal change that affected *nōkai.* The Land Consolidation Law (Kōchi Seirihō) passed in 1899 was revised in 1909, placing a stronger emphasis on irrigation and drainage work and altering the locus of leadership. Consolidation was taken out of the villages and relocated to the level of the district (*gun*), immediately opening the possibility for *kōchi seiri* on a scale beyond what could be accomplished in its earlier parochial form. This shift shook up the nature of leadership in consolidation activities, but unlike the Nōkai Law revision, it did not replace landlords with government officials. Rather the move to the district, whose offices and assemblies were most often under the control of the top rank of *ōjinushi,* meant that the work came to be planned and overseen by the largest landowners in the area, whose property interests crossed the boundaries that enclosed smaller village-bound landlords.[31] As the authors of the legal revision hoped, *kōchi seiri* projects, under the new leaders and with the new focus on water control, became more ambitious in scale.[32] Paired with a strong new commitment on the part of the prefecture to major riparian and reclamation projects beginning in the 1920s, the revised *kōchi seiri* order made possible an expansion of arable land and consolidation of paddyland beyond the hopes of earlier years.

Smaller-scale consolidation efforts in Senboku resulted in remarkable gains in the aggregate over the first two decades of the twentieth century, but by the late 1910s, the landlords planning and leading the work had all but exhausted their potential for *kōchi seiri.* Standing in the way of further progress was the Kitakami River, whose size and propensity for flooding fractured landowners in its environs into atomized self-interest, and the network of water provision and flood control of which it lay at the center, which diverted flooding along tributaries and buried vast fields of potentially arable land under flood pools and reservoirs. Changing this status quo was no small endeavor. The system of reservoirs and flood pools, whose distribution of disadvantage caused discord as in the Entō conflict in the 1890s, was itself the result of the most extensive and ambitious terraforming project ever undertaken in the region, and the small degree of protection against flooding and drought that it offered—as well as its shielding of the port town of Ishinomaki against the rage of the Kitakami—represented the best that could be done until the arrival of modern earthmoving machinery and a modern administrative apparatus to put it into motion.

The progress of *kōchi seiri* in Senboku gives concrete testimony to the limitations that the Kitakami River imposed on the region. As graph 6.2 illustrates, consolidation work proceeded briskly from the beginning of the century in Shida and Tōda, both situated at a safe remove from the unruly

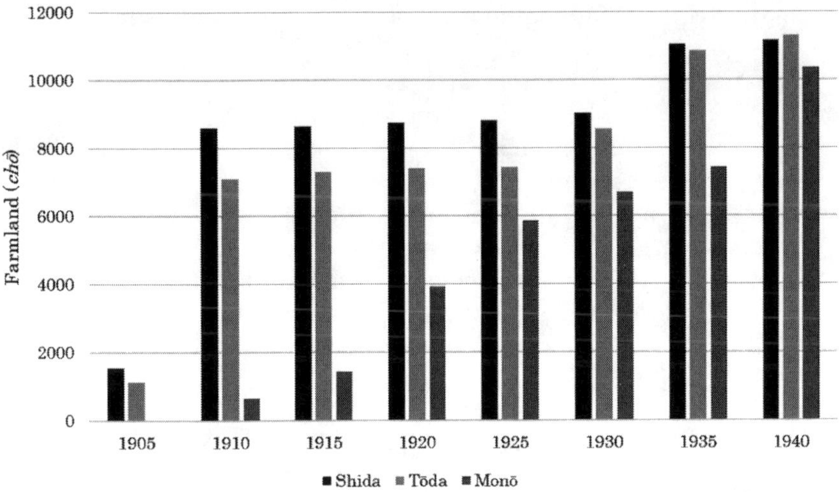

Graph 6.2. *Kōchi Seiri* in Senboku

river and either containing lands ripe for reordering or newly reclaimed arable land ready to be made into paddies. Buoyed particularly by the drainage and reclamation of Shinainuma, in the case of Shida, and the extensive work cooperatively undertaken by the landlords of Nangō, each of the districts had consolidated lands in excess of 7,000 *chō* by 1915. Monō, however, faced the full wrath of the Kitakami. The resources and energy of its landlords were taxed to their limits by efforts to keep their own lands dry, when there were floods, and irrigated, when there was drought, and individual works of limited consolidation were all that could be accomplished.[33] Having only reordered an area less than one-fiftieth that of its Senboku neighbors in 1905, by 1915 *kōchi seiri* in Monō still lingered at only 20 percent of Shida and Tōda. This lack of progress imposed strict limitations on the spread of improved farming techniques. While Tōda and Shida plowed 60.5 percent and 70.7 percent of their paddies with oxen or horses in 1916, only 21.3 percent of cultivated land in Monō was plowed by animals.[34]

Tōda and Shida did achieve significant gains during the Taishō years, but even in these more successful districts the system built around the Kitakami exerted an influence. Ingrained vulnerability had fractured the solidarity of landlords throughout the region, making collective efforts at *kōchi seiri* on a large scale rare. In Nangō itself, whose local landlords found success in a number of cooperative endeavors, their efforts still produced consolidated plots of 50 *chō* or smaller, a far cry from larger works in other parts of the country.[35] The fearsome power of the Kitakami meant that local landlords and officials could not improve the situation on their own; they required the commitment of significant resources from higher levels of government.

The importance of improvements on the Kitakami River to the development of agriculture in Senboku was recognized early by Miyagi officials. While work was done at the end of the nineteenth century to improve the navigability of the waterway, however, the changes necessary to remove the impediments to agricultural improvements in irrigation, flood control, and *kochi seiri* involved costs that went beyond what the prefectural and the central governments were willing and/or able to commit.[36] Promise emerged in the form of a new Rivers Law in 1906 that gave the national government control over water control efforts on major rivers, but the Kitakami still failed to attract the official attention necessary for significant improvements. Extensive flooding in eastern Japan in 1910 proved enough to break this impasse. Plans for major work on the river were unveiled the following year in the form of a 12-year project with a budget of over 14 million yen and the goals of increasing protection against flooding, eliminating reverse flow inundations on tributary rivers, and the further improvement of navigability.[37] These plans ground to a halt only a few years later with the outbreak of the First World War, and delayed by recession, inflation, and spending cuts in the years that followed, the project was only completed in 1929, nearly twenty years after it was launched.

The riparian work on the Kitakami set off a series of connected projects of irrigation, flood control, and reclamation made possible by its progressing taming. With irrigation directly from the great river now possible, landlords and local officials moved quickly to drain the reservoirs that supplied dry villages and reclaim the rich lands that lay buried beneath them. The Hasama River in Tōda was rerouted in 1923, allowing for the drainage of Nabire Lake and the Hirobuchi Reservoir and the dismantling of the water system that had set Tōda and Monō farmers at each other's throats in the early 1890s. As Tōda farmers had anticipated thirty years earlier, the erasure of the water system not only meant an end to the regular flooding of Nangō and neighboring areas, it also opened up vast tracts of land for cultivation. In a single stroke, the danger of flooding on Nabire Lake was replaced with lush new fields ready to be plowed into paddyland. With irrigation water now supplied by a mechanical pump on the defanged Kitakami near Wakuya, Monō farmers no longer had need of land-wasting reservoirs, and they too were able to expand farmland through the reclamation of the Hirobuchi Reservoir and similar artificial wetlands downstream like the Yanaizu.[38] This initiated the second wave of Senboku *kōchi seiri,* now propelled by work done in Monō. A new day dawned in the 1920s, and the bodies of water dotting the landscape that had thwarted improvement efforts in Monō for so long evaporated into broad swaths of drylands, rich with potential for cultivation and *kōchi seiri*. Twelve percent of consolidated lands came from reservoir reclamation, with another 32 percent coming from the opening of new arable land, often a direct result of the new availability of stable irrigation water supplies from the Kitakami.[39] Their irreconcilable water interests finally reconciled, Tōda and Monō moved toward greater cooperation, eventually joining forces in a water use union alliance with Oshika in 1933. The prefecture finished its remaining projects connected to the Kitakami in 1932, from that point on assuming a key role in irrigation, drainage, and *kōchi seiri* in the region.[40]

The opening of new paddyland increased productive capacity, the consolidation of farm plots made farming more efficient and opened the doors to new varieties of rice and types of production, and riparian works offered reliable water supplies and protection from flooding, all working to ensure stable levels of output. Improvements begat improvements; *kōchi seiri* made land suitable for animal plowing, deep plowing required heavy fertilization and spurred the widespread use of phosphate fertilizers, and rice varietals offering protection from weather that required heavy fertilization and deep planting displaced more vulnerable types of rice.[41] Expanded and stable production, along with the weakened, but still effective, quality inspection system, changed the position of Senboku rice on the national market. At last the fears of 1905–1908, when Miyagi rice nearly lost its place on the Tokyo Rice Exchange, were dispelled. The qualitative and quantitative improvements to rice production enabled Miyagi grain to build a nationwide reputation for quality and consistency. By 1926, 46 percent of the 1.6 million *koku* of rice produced in Miyagi was sold outside of the prefecture, the majority being Senboku rice bound for Tokyo.[42] The rate of outside sales had climbed steadily over the previous decade, rising by nearly 20 percent since 1912. Miyagi now stood at the forefront of rice-producing prefectures, with the quality of its products having allowed it to carve out a significant segment of the national market as sales from the southwest went into decline.[43]

A major factor in the marketing success of Miyagi rice was the widespread adoption of improved varieties of rice. As discussed in chapter 4, landlords and the *nōkai* they controlled had attempted to leverage their economic and political influence to enforce the cultivation of the climate-resistant rice strain, Kame no O, early in the twentieth century. First grown in Miyagi in 1902, Kame no O had proven its resilience during the crop failures in 1905 and 1906, but it wasn't until *kōchi seiri* and related improvements had progressed to the point where it was possible to meet its demands for deep planting and heavy fertilizing that it could spread widely. By 1921, it was the most cultivated rice in the prefecture. This growth was almost exclusively due to efforts in Senboku, where its adoption neared 100 percent, while the continuing production of the early harvest and lower quality Aikoku rice in southern Miyagi gave rice production in the prefecture a dual character. In contrast with the upscale urban markets that Senboku Kame no O served, Aikoku rice from Sennan found a place in the cooking pots of mine and factory dormitories in Iwate and Aomori.[44]

The shift to more productive and resilient forms of rice in the north showed further signs of the newly active leadership of official actors in agricultural development. In addition to providing the conditions that made *kōchi seiri* and its resulting improvements possible, the Miyagi government devoted itself in new ways to the promotion of improved varieties of rice. A prefecture-run experimentation station was set up in the northern district of Tamatsukuri where novel varieties of rice were tested, then distributed to farmers through the centrally administered *nōkai*.[45] By the mid-1920s, new grains introduced through the station had begun to displace even Kame no O, and Miyagi came to supply a variety of quality rices to the national market.[46]

Improvements to land, irrigation, and flood control thus enabled Senboku to produce quality grain in unprecedented quantities and sell it on the national market. Natural barriers to production like the Kitakami and the unforgiving northern climate, however, were not the only things standing in the way of the kind of general village prosperity that Yanagita Kunio, Yokoi Tokiyoshi, and other late Meiji critics had hoped for. While the gains made in production and sales were undeniable and gave every indication of continuing, deep problems remained in Senboku. The industrial structure of northern Miyagi, and its place in the larger national economy, continued to mark the region as backwards and underdeveloped. Within these economic circumstances, prosperity remained outside the grasp of large segments of the population. Dissatisfaction with the failure of landlords to convert increased agricultural profits into broad-based prosperity had driven officials to take a more active role in the oversight of farming development at the end of the Meiji period, but they had achieved little in the way of correcting the gross inequalities in economic and political power that existed in villages, the growing rate of tenancy in agriculture, and the ongoing economic difficulties of the most vulnerable parts of village society. Conflicts between landlords and tenants broke out with increasing frequency from the mid-1920s onward, testifying to the deep dissatisfactions that lurked in villages. SCAP critics at mid-century may have given the progress made in agricultural production and efficiency short shrift, but their condemnation of the social and economic realities of farming villages, which was the heart of their critique, rang true.

Senboku's place as a late-developing locality in the larger, but equally backward, Tōhoku region continued to impose limitations on agricultural production and development. In the Meiji period, Miyagi was, along with Tōhoku as a whole, an underperformer in terms of economic and industrial development, but it was not so far off the pace of an entire country that was struggling to meet government and ideologue visions of modernity. Significant progress in industrialization on a broad scale in the years surrounding the First World War, however, transformed agriculture "from the nation's dominant economic and social force into a problem sector of an industrial economy."[47] As this industrial progress had passed over most of Tōhoku, including Senboku, it became a region marked by its backwardness in a country that was relegating agricultural areas to the furthest reaches of marginality.

Still, farming continued to be the only viable means of making a living in Senboku in Taishō and Shōwa. In Tōhoku as a whole, agriculture still represented nearly half of all production and was the chief occupation of more than half of all residents in 1929, when it had dropped to less than a quarter of production in the country as a whole.[48] This discrepancy took on even greater immediacy within Miyagi. The south of the prefecture, already enjoying the benefits of a diversified market economy based on farm produce and sericulture, experienced industrial growth along with the rest of Japan, although this growth was largely disconnected from local capital and profits tended to be siphoned off by the central owners of and investors in the new industrial ventures.[49] Senboku, on the other hand, went decidedly against the national trends. Sericulture had found a limited foothold in the region in the context of the spate of crop failures in the first decade of the twentieth century, but it declined beginning in the second, fading and then all but disappearing as agricultural production stabilized.[50] In the years that followed, secondary production of all types were abandoned wholesale, resulting in survey results in 1948 reporting that the production for the market of anything other than rice was "virtually unseen."[51]

Even within the increasingly marginalized sphere of agriculture, Senboku farmers were moving in directions counter to diversity and the benefits it offered in protections against the vicissitudes of climate and market. The vast tracks of land that were opened to cultivation through reclamation and *kōchi seiri,* endeavors that were undertaken in the first place because land represented the only profitable investment in the backward north, were virtually without exception converted to paddies and planted with rice. Even where other crops had been cultivated earlier, the collapse of vegetable prices in the mid-1930s led farmers to devote their lands entirely to rice production.[52]

While the continual expanding of paddyland and the monomaniacal pursuit of rice farming seemed to Senboku farmers the most secure route to prosperity, the vulnerability inherent in monocrops made itself known in the 1920s and 1930s. Part of this vulnerability came from the proliferating links connecting Japan, and Japanese farming, to the outside world, particularly in the context of the empire being carved out on the Asian continent. Foreign rice first came into Japan in significant quantities at the beginning of the century with imports from Southeast Asia, which were further increased in an effort to quell the massive rice riots that flared across the country at the end of the First World War.[53] With this, the floodgates were opened and, while the acute need for foreign rice receded as postwar inflation came under control in the early 1920s, the tariff on grain from the colonies was permanently reduced and imports, largely from Korea and Taiwan, exploded from 250 thousand tons in 1916–1917 to 1.7 million tons a decade later.[54] The hard-earned successes that farmers had won in rationalizing and increasing production and that had encouraged the abandonment of other kinds of production in northern Miyagi presented another threat to rice farming in general and Senboku villages in particular. The momentum of decades of improvement efforts pushed production totals higher and higher in the late 1920s and early 1930s, posting record national harvests in 1930, 1933, and 1939, and driving rice prices down to as low as half what they had been.[55] Whereas farmers in most areas could at least blunt the sting of smaller returns by means of sericulture and other forms of secondary production, monocrop areas like Senboku had no such recourse. Lower prices meant lower income, reducing the funds available for everything from rent and fertilizer purchases to medical care and food supplies.

While aspects of Senboku's natural environment and the industrial structure that had developed within it impeded the quest to improve agriculture and the lives of farmers, the social patterns of landholding and the economic relationships that grew out of it presented a further threat to village order and prosperity. As notable as Senboku's single-minded pursuit of rice production were its sky-high rates of tenancy, which developed as a natural consequence of the difficulty of rice farming, the fact that it made land ownership the sole means of profitable investment, the vagaries of the market, and the capital-heavy demands made by *kōchi seiri* and land reclamation. In the prefecture generally, tenancy rates grew over the first half of the twentieth century following two distinct patterns. From 1910 to 1925, both farmers who worked their own lands and, to a lesser extent, farmers who worked only rented lands declined, while the number of owner-renter farmers increased.[56] In contrast, 1925 to 1937 saw owners, and especially owner-renters, decline and the number of full tenant farmers swell. Overall, the numbers in the prefecture painted a picture of gradual, but increasing, descent from landowner, to partial renter, to tenant farmer in villages everywhere.

Senboku stood out, within the prefecture and the country, for its expansive populations of tenant farmers and its concentration of large landowners. Tenancy rates in Tōda and Shida plotted a clear course in Taishō and early Shōwa. After showing steady growth in tenant numbers in the first decade of the twentieth century, rates in the two districts stabilized in the 1910s and early 1920s, even declining slightly in Shida (graph 6.3). From 1925, however, Senboku tenancy surged past that in the prefecture as a whole. Mōno, facing its own challenges from the Kitakami River, followed a pattern different from its Senboku neighbors, experiencing above average expansion in 1910–1925, but slowing down somewhat after that point. Still, the district remained lined up with Tōda and Shida at the top of tenancy rates in Miyagi in 1929, contributing to Senboku's status as one of the most heavily tenanted agricultural regions in the country.

Along with outsized rates of tenancy, Senboku also hosted an unusual concentration of large landlords (*ōjinushi*), defined by the ownership of

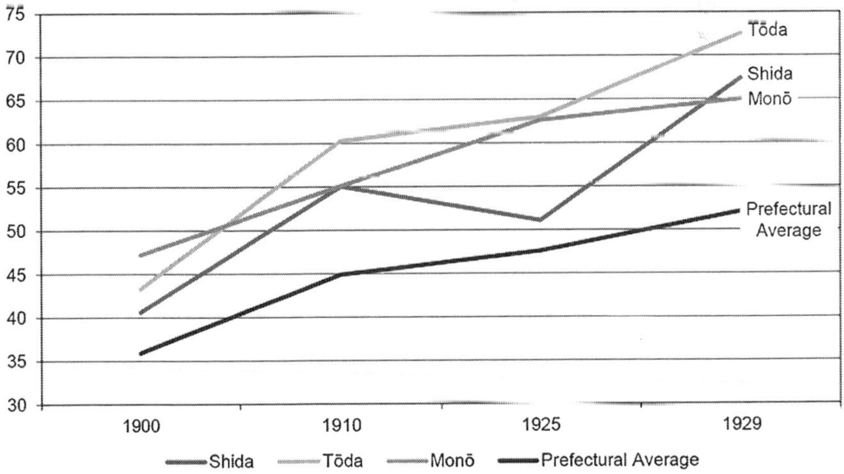

Graph 6.3. Tenancy Rates by Population (%)

50 *chō* or more of farmland. In 1924, Miyagi boasted the third largest population of *ōjinushi* in Japan, with 68 percent of those concentrated in Senboku.[57] Large landowners were not unknown in the south of the prefecture, but Sennan was home to only 18 *ōjinushi* in 1929, compared to the 72 who lived in the north.[58] While tenancy grew on the whole in Taishō and early Shōwa, in contrast with trends elsewhere in the country, this did not result in similar growth in the absolute numbers of *ōjinushi*. Population growth expanded numbers of tenants and tenant-landowners working less than 10 *chō* of paddyland, but *ōjinushi* in both Tōda and Shida declined as a proportion of the total population.[59] This reflected the stability of their positions, rather than instability or decline, their place as an unchanging core amongst a growing population attesting to the barriers preventing upward social mobility in Senboku. After the flooding in 1910 and 1913, many middling landlords with holdings under 50 *chō* fled Senboku for Sendai, and their lands bolstered the holdings of their wealthier former neighbors as they divested themselves of landholdings and moved away from agriculture.[60] An additional feature of Senboku *ōjinushi* was the relatively limited sizes of their landholdings. Many landlords owned enough farmland to put them beyond the 50-*chō* *ōjinushi* threshold, but the majority owned less than 100 *chō* and fell into the bottom rung of this stratum. The Saitō house (discussed in further detail below) in Mōno ranked among the largest landowners in the country, but no others had landholdings greater than 500 *chō*, marking a clear difference from other single crop regions like Niigata, which was home to 10 *ōjinushi* with 500–1,000 *chō* in landholdings and 5 with more than 1,000.[61]

The fact that *ōjinushi* were concentrated in Senboku and were resident in the same villages as many of their tenants influenced social and economic realities and gave the region a particular character. The Taishō period witnessed a general flourishing of cities and industry, both of which drew landlords in most of the country to abandon the countryside as an object of investment and a place of residence. Officials and social critics alike bemoaned the expanding population of absentee landlords and the host of evils their absence visited upon farming villages. While the economically advanced regions of the south and west gnashed their teeth, the backwardness of Tōhoku proved to be a shield against this affliction. The prevalence of resident landlords continued to mark Senboku, as well as the Tōhoku region more generally, as a realm apart and seemed to reveal a blessing hidden in its bleak developmental state.

In actuality, resident *ōjinushi* brought their own set of troubles to Senboku. While those villages that counted outsized landlords among their residents did indeed avoid the hollowing out of local funds that usually occurred when the largest local taxpayers pulled up stakes for the cities and the degradation of agriculture that resulted when landlords were far from the soil, these were not benefits enjoyed throughout Senboku. The fact that so many of the landlords were *ōjinushi* meant that most of them owned at least some land outside of their own villages. Although their lands were rarely at any significant remove from their physical residence, this fact still made them absentee landlords in their relations with these outside farms and tenants. Some villages were composed almost entirely of tenant farmers renting from landlords living elsewhere in Senboku, creating conditions similar to those in the hollowed-out villages in the economically advanced regions. The villages of Monō and Tomisato, both in the district of Monō, were two such cases. A lack of resident landlords, and the leadership and money they might have provided, tended to insulate them both against the improvements that swept through neighboring communities in the 1910s and 1920s. These villages made little progress in flood prevention, saw minimal growth in farm production, and suffered from chronic shortages of local capital as such independent landowners and small-scale landlords who lived in the village were forced to devote their resources to their constant struggle with the Kitakami River.[62] It was not until the prefecture started to make real progress on its riparian projects in the late 1920s and afterward that Mōno, Tomisato, and villages like them began to catch up with the agricultural improvements that had become standard elsewhere in Senboku a decade or more earlier.[63]

The continuing presence of *ōjinushi* created a different set of not-entirely-unproblematic circumstances in the Senboku villages in which they resided. As the critics of non-resident landlords believed, the social ties binding resident landlords to the communities they lived in acted as a check upon some of the worst excesses of the landlord system, at least temporarily. Evictions remained rare in Miyagi through the 1920s, a testament to the success tenant farmers earned in pushing for secure renting rights from their neighbor-landlords. While tenancy contracts generally stipulated at least the possibility of eviction in case of breach of terms, landlords deeply enmeshed in their village communities (with the exception of the Saitō house of Maeyachi), found it better to allow for rent reductions or other temporary accommodations when necessary. What this denied them in immediate profits, it made up for in other ways. The small number of tenant-landlord clashes in the 1920s, when areas outside Tōhoku shook with conflict, was owed at least in part to the flexibility of landlords in enforcing the terms of tenancy contracts.[64] The fact that these landlords lived in the same villages as their tenants seems to have been a contributing factor, as the disputes in other parts of the country erupted in spite of the general readiness of non-resident landlords to offer up rent remissions and their reluctance to evict tenants.[65] In Senboku, with the threat of land seizure unavailable, landlords were forced to seek out alternative means to protect themselves and their profits from the dangers of default and non-payment of rents. One such means was to be wary in choosing their tenants. It became a rule among Senboku landlords to rent land only to tenants who already worked a significant acreage of paddyland, be it land that they owned or rented from others, as it both demonstrated that they could manage funds well enough to have built up lands to work and showed them to have the means to do more than eke out a bare living.[66]

Still, rent defaults in years when weather depressed production or production depressed prices remained a problem, and land ownership became less and less profitable an investment for landlords during the 1920s. With tenancy rights secure, the raising of rents virtually impossible, and the collection of full rents difficult, it was more profitable for farmers to work the land than it was for landlords to purchase it for the purposes of renting it out.[67] Even as this became the norm, the growing population and the shrinking of commons and undeveloped lands drove land prices ever higher. While landlords continued to accumulate land in small-scale or collective reclamation projects, which often received government support and yielded up lands unsaddled with existing contracts and de facto cultivation rights, industrial and other investment avenues in Tokyo and elsewhere became attractive options for those with liquid assets. When such assets were lacking, it could lead vulnerable landlords to make disruptive decisions. Landlords in Yoneyama in Tome district abandoned their plans to reclaim the village-owned Tandai wetlands due to a dearth of funds and chose instead to sell the lands to outsiders from Wakayama and Niigata, who rented out the paddies they reclaimed from the swamp to locals as non-resident landlords.[68] With the threat of eviction off the table, it appeared that the days of landowning as a profitable enterprise in and of itself were limited. It would take generational change and economic shocks in the next decade to reverse this trend.

As ignored as they were, the contracts that bound landlords and tenants were an important determinant in shaping the character of their relations and another element that contributed to the realities that pervaded in Senboku. The trade-off for the easy provision of rent remissions in times of hardship were standard rent rates much higher than those in other parts of the country.[69] This difference was most pronounced in late Meiji, however, and the burden it represented grew lighter as time went on. As production increased in the 1910s, rent levels remained unchanged from the beginning of the twentieth century, correcting the imbalances imposed during the period of landlord ascendency and even allowing for something resembling the profit motive to drive tenants to increase production.[70] The situation became even better for tenants (and even worse for landlords) in the years that followed. Rents fell from mid-Taishō and continued to drop until the early 1930s. The Saitō house, the largest landowner in Senboku and the prefecture as a whole, increased the lands it rented out by 9 percent between 1924 and 1935, while the rent it collected decreased by 9 percent over the same period.[71] Average rents decreased in each of the Senboku districts between 1911 and 1930, dropping from 45 percent of harvests to 41.1 percent in Tōda, 57 percent to 44.7 percent in Shida, 53 percent to 43.2 percent in Tome, and 53.6 percent to 42.2 percent in Monō.[72]

These were the contracts that marked tenancy as different within Tōhoku, where low rents and de facto land rights in perpetuity acted more as constraints on landlords than traps for tenants.[73] We must be cautious, however, about falling into ready-made explanations based on the supposedly feudal character of landlord-tenant relations in Tōhoku. It has been suggested that the pervasive paternalism that defined these relations compelled landlords to offer favorable terms and prevented them from seeking redress through the legal system when the terms of tenancy were not met.[74] In Senboku, at least, advantages that tenants enjoyed in their rental contracts were a direct result of the tenant association conflict in 1908, while the landlords' push for the rice quality inspection system and the fact that Saitō Zen'uemon used the courts as his first recourse in the case of even trivial disputes with tenants suggest that landlords were constrained by no innate sense of paternalism that was keeping the law out of tenancy relations.

But the choices made by landlords vis-à-vis their tenants, whether they were dictated by custom or not, were not the only factors contributing to the improving position of tenant farmers. Legal reform in Miyagi in the 1920s further eased the coercive pressures that had been placed on tenants and rolled back what remained of the legal framework for directing agricultural profits solely to landlords. In 1925, the prefecturally administered quality inspections for rice used as rent payments were made optional and were replaced as a mechanism for promoting the production of improved grain by regulations that compelled landlords to provide compensation for higher quality products.[75] Although still mediated through the landlord, tenants now had the potential for profits to encourage them to produce rice of the caliber that the national market demanded. This change, more than anything else, accounts for the meteoric rise of the reputation of Miyagi rice in the early years of Shōwa.

While the creation of tenant organizations marked the beginning of a self-conscious tenant movement in other parts of the country and set off a flurry of clashes in the 1920s, the same developments were not seen in Senboku. Despite the material gains earned in the 1908 battles—or perhaps because of them—the tenant associations created at that time assumed no enduring form and the groups in Tōda, Monō, and Oshika who had defeated Saitō and his ilk dissolved after achieving their goals. In contrast, the years after the First World War saw tenant organization spread in the west of Japan, the result of a combination of factors including improvements in education, economic crisis and deflation, and landlords made irrelevant by the completion of their improvement work.[76] Much as had been the case in Senboku a decade earlier, these new groups assumed an aggressive stance toward landlords, leading to conflict on a scale not seen before. Alongside the long-held desires for lower rents, stable rights to rented land, and relief measures in bad years, tenants in the west also sought out new places in local adminstrations that landlords had heretofore monopolized.[77] Conflicts of this type reached their highest numbers in the west in 1926, peaking at a total that year of 2,751 incidents involving more than 150,000 tenants and over 40,000 landlords.[78]

Attempts at broad-based organization and a renewal of hostilities with landlords in Senboku took much longer to develop. In 1918, when rice riots swept the country and there were already dozens of landlord-tenant disputes in the west, Tōhoku did not experience a single conflict of this type. Organizations resembling the tenant associations of 1908 only started to appear in the early 1920s in connection with the spread of proletarian political parties and groups. The progress of these groups highlighted the difficulties faced by Senboku villages in which non-resident landlords owned significant landholdings. In 1923, the first two new tenant organizations appeared in the Monō villages of Kanomata and Ōyachi, formed as self-conscious "farmers unions" (*nōmin kumiai*) in connection with the emergent regional Japan Farmers Union Kantō Alliance (Nihon Nōmin Kumiai Kantō Dōmei), organized the previous year.[79] The middle years of the 1920s saw the movement for organization spread, with a spate of groups forming in and around Sendai with the aid of activist students, labor unions, and political parties from the city.[80] Political solidarities continued to play an important part in tenants and farmers unions at the end of the decade. The Rōdōnōmintō (Labor-Farmer Party) represented an amalgamation of the two union movements on the left and provided a political vehicle that led to a seat in the Diet for the party's candidate from Miyagi district. The explicit political orientation of this revived movement soon proved to be a vulnerability. The national government began a crackdown on left-leaning political organizations in 1928, banning the Rōdōnōmintō outright and destroying the foundation for much of the new movement at a stroke.

Carrying the depoliticized tenant organization movement forward into the 1930s were Senboku groups focused on local issues and new challenges leveled by landlords who followed a different logic from their predecessors. These organizations were most often born out of conflict, connected with direct continuity to the mid-1920s revival of the tenant movement. The Kanomata union fired the first shot in what would develop into a longer period of tenant-landlord conflict. Facing a poor harvest in 1923 that promised to leave them in debt, the union's 250 members, representing 60 percent of the farming population of Kanomata, issued a collective demand for a 20 percent reduction in rents for the year to all concerned landlords. Negotiations and local arbitration led to a granting of a 10 percent discount from landlords resident in the village, but the largest landlord was the Saitō house of neighboring Maeyachi, now incorporated as a joint-stock company, and it was steadfast in its refusal to countenance even such moderated demands.[81] Years of hostility followed, punctuated by conflicts, in a pattern that reproduced itself in other villages connected to the Saitō company and eventually spread to Senboku tenants and landlords more generally.

The next significant landlord-tenant conflict in Senboku took place in 1927 in the second center of tenant organization in Senboku, the village of Ōyachi in Monō. Tenants again faced off against recalcitrant landlords, but they were now confronted by a very different kind of threat. Whereas Kanomata farmers had threatened to tear up their tenancy deeds as a means of forcing landlords to back down lest their lands be left fallow, the Ōyachi union mobilized explicitly in defense of their rights to the lands they rented. The conflict began when a number of paddies passed from the hands of one non-resident landlord to another and the new owner attempted to evict a number of his new tenants in order to replace them with waiting renters who were willing to pay higher rates.[82] The evicted tenants created a "cultivators union" (*kōsaku kumiai*) and mobilized with their neighbors in defense of their farming rights, occupying the farms seized from them and planting and cultivating collectively. The conflict moved to the courts, where the national Nihon Nōmin Kumiai (Japan Farmers Union, abbreviated as Nichinō) applied its considerable legal resources in aid of the tenants. Matters came to a close in the summer of 1927 with the first legal confirmation of tenants' rights to the lands they cultivated, the formation of a new Ōyachi branch of the Nichinō, compensation payments from the new landlord to both the (now-restored) evicted tenants and the new renters with whom they were to be replaced, and a framework for new tenant strategies of collective farming and land occupation.[83] The dispute ended in an unqualified victory for Ōyachi tenants, but the issues that fueled the conflict remained points of tension between landlords and tenants across Senboku and went on to spark more expansive and contentious battles in the decade that followed.

The Saitō Company, which sat at the center of many of the disputes of the late 1920s and 1930s, and its links to founder Saitō Zen'uemon, shine a spotlight on one way that Senboku landlords after 1910 moved away from the *meibōka* ideals around which the Meiji agricultural order was built. Saitō, as we have seen, had never been anything like the intermediary figures enshrined in either the Meiji bureaucratic vision of the countryside or the hopes of villagers. His blatantly exploitative approach to landlordism, his early exit from direct involvement in farming, and his ready recourse to courts and legal redress in his dealings with tenant farmers already marked him more nearly as the opposite of these by the beginning of the twentieth century. Still, the changes that Zen'uemon made to his business after the 1908 tenant conflict and the ways in which his household carried it on after his death not only took his earlier approach to its logical extreme, they also exposed the fallacies inherent to the *meibōka* myth.

Forced to accept defeat in the tenant union conflict and bitterly disappointed with the failures of his fellow landlords, Saitō Zen'uemon decided upon a dramatic transformation of his life and business in 1909. In December, he gathered the sum total of his personal assets, amounting to over 2 million yen, and used them to capitalize a new company, the Saitō Corporation (Saitō Kabushikigaisha). Granting himself an overwhelming majority of company stock and limiting ownership of any significant proportion of the remaining shares to members of his immediate family, the change appeared to be little more than an attempt to reduce his tax load, secure his assets, and prepare for the succession of his heirs in the future.[84] The company held the same assets as Zen'uemon had as an individual, it collected the same rents from the same expansive group of tenant farmers, and its day-to-day operations were still overseen by Zen'uemon with the assistance of his family.

Despite the continuities between landlord and landowning company, the establishment of the Saitō Corporation represented a profound shift in the social meaning of the relationship between landowner and tenant and a fatal undermining of the concept and role of *meibōka* in rural communities. It was, in effect, Zen'uemon's rejection of his own individuality and even personhood, at least in connection with his business activities.

Non-resident landlords, separated from those working the lands they owned by distances both physical and cultural, had long been a bugbear in the estimations of bureaucrats, social reformers, and rural activists. But the establishment of the Saitō company replicated all the problems associated with these figures and made them worse. Landlords, however distant their homes might be from their rural landholdings, remained nevertheless people with the inherent potential, small though it might be, of being moved through human contact. Whether they lived in the same village or not, the landlord-tenant relationship was a human relationship. In transferring his lands and business to the Saitō Corporation, Zen'uemon was not becoming a non-resident landlord (something he already was in relation to his extensive holdings outside of Maeyachi). Rather he was creating a non-human landlord, which was even worse for tenants. Whereas the humanity of non-resident landlords could even provide benefits to tenants—as when their unfamiliarity with and disinterest in farming led them to undercharge on rent—the Saitō Corporation put the management of its lands in the hands of its employees who, as employees, had the sole imperative of collecting rents fully and on time and whose decisions were clouded by neither ignorance or boredom.[85]

The transformation in the nature of the Saitō business did not change the family's position as the largest landholder in Miyagi nor the combative approach it took to managing its tenants. In 1911, the company owned property in Hokkaidō, the Kantō and Kansai regions, and across Tōhoku, taking in 20,000 sacks of rent rice from 6,000 tenant farmers.[86] Moneylending was its other principal business, and it lent out a total of 3 million yen the same year, roughly 250 times the total annual budget of its home village of Maeyachi.[87] Business boomed over the years that followed, with loans hitting 3.2 million yen in 1921, 5 million in 1932, and 6 million in 1939 and landholdings reaching a value of 4 million yen in 1942. Ranking high among operating costs each year were legal expenses, a clear indication of tenancy disputes and the company's strategy of addressing them through the court system.

While the day-to-day operations concerning loans and landholding remained unchanged from before the company's creation, Zen'uemon took on the role of urban philanthropist after unmaking himself as a landlord. Donating significant sums for the creation and support of education, libraries, and museums in Sendai, he was awarded the Medal with Dark Blue Ribbon (Konjuhōshō), an honor reserved for those who make financial contributions for public well-being, by the national government in 1919, the first year it was offered.[88] These philanthropic activities reached a zenith in 1923 with the establishment of the Saitō Hōonkai, a still-extant charitable foundation supporting scholarly research and hosting a museum in Sendai. While these works were clearly the efforts of an elderly man attempting to build a legacy in his autumn years, it is hard not to suspect that they were also part and parcel with his abandonment of his personal statuses as a landlord and moneylender and his rebirth as a business owner.

Zen'uemon's children and grandchildren took charge of the corporation after his death in 1925, continuing the hard-nosed and uncompromising tactics that had guided the family since they had been recorded in the Saitō house handbook (*kokoresho*) in the 1890s. This led to near-constant tensions with the company's thousands of tenants and put the house at the center of the new spate of conflicts that produced and was then fueled by the new tenant union movement of the late 1920s. In events like the Kanomata dispute described above, the company remained unshakable in its intransigency and experienced setbacks not entirely dissimilar to those it had suffered in the tenant union dispute of 1908. As the decade neared its close, however, circumstances changed and the non-human landlord that was the Saitō Corporation put the full implications of its deviation from the *meibōka* ideal on clear display.

The tenant success in the Ōyachi dispute and the ongoing rise of combative tenant and farming unions and proletarian political organizations all combined to give hope to tenants and a sense of inflammability to issues related to tenant farming in Senboku at the end of the 1920s. A number of disparate, but ultimately linked, outside developments, however, sent the third major Senboku conflict down a different course in 1927–1928 and set the tone for a new period of contention. What came to be known as the Maeyachi Incident featured the familiar pattern of tenant farmers united in limited solidarity against notably egregious abuses of landlord power. Conflicts of this type had thus far been rare in Senboku, but the track record of tenant victories in the tenant union conflict of 1908 and the recent Ōyachi conflict and the ongoing stalemate in the Kanomata dispute gave hope to the tenant participants that their complaints might find redress.

These hopes were eventually thwarted by three key changes that preceded or happened during the Maeyachi dispute. The first of these were rice prices caught in the financial crisis of 1927.[89] A drop to 30 yen per *koku* added extreme pressures to the expanding numbers of farm households in debt and made 1927 a year in which "rice farmers would not even have *mochi* for New Year's."[90] This also affected the profits of landlords, who still collected rent in rice, and sent them scrambling for ways to ensure that their tenants would bear the burden of changes in price. Just as significant was the political situation. The passage of universal manhood suffrage in 1925 led to the increased activity among socialist and proletarian political parties, and these groups found common cause with the tenant unions that formed and clashed with landlords in western Japan. Apprehension among political elites turned to something like panic after the first election under the new law in February of 1928 brought unprecedented numbers of leftists into the Diet, leading to a crackdown on the already illegal Communist Party and proletarian parties in general at the height of the Maeyachi conflict. In this context, the same connections with the larger national and regional farmer and tenant organizations that had brought victory in Ōyachi now became liabilities. Finally, the nature of the two sides in the conflict differed from those seen earlier. The showdowns connected to the 1908 union movement and the 1927 Ōyachi conflict involved multiple landlords whose inability to create a united front proved decisive in the victories of tenants. The Saitō Corporation, however, stood alone against tenants in the Maeyachi conflict, its status as a landholding company in effect making it peerless. Possessed of vast resources, absolutely unified in its purpose, and invulnerable to the sort of pressure from neighboring landlords that had forced Zen'uemon to capitulate in 1908, the corporation was a kind of opponent that Senboku tenants had never defeated.

The Maeyachi conflict began during the harvest season of 1927 when tenants of the Saitō company in Maeyachi received a "proclamation" (*fure*) stating that Aikoku rice, whose value had fallen on the central rice exchange, would not be accepted for that year's rents. Tenants would have either to pay with another variety or pay a surcharge for each sack of Aikoku they offered. Harvesting was nearly complete and the tenants, virtually all of whom had at least some Aikoku rice set away for rent payment, were left scrambling to find additional rice or cash to make up for it.

Cowed by the power and intransigence of the Saitō Corporation, most of its Maeyachi tenants accepted the demand without complaint, despite the fact that the company had actually promoted the cultivation of Aikoku up until the issuing of the directive.[91] Two tenant farmers, Takahashi Jun, who had a subpar harvest due to fertilizer problems, and Sugawara Kanoei, who balked at the unfairness of the demand, did not. After attempts to negotiate an extended payment period with Saitō representatives failed to make any progress, Takahashi and Sugawara joined forces and approached the recently established branch of the Nichinō in the neighboring village of Tomisato for aid. The Tomisato group helped establish another branch of the organization in Maeyachi under the leadership of Sugawara and enlisted the aid of the prefectural Nichinō to their cause.

Plans proceeded among all three organizations in January of 1928, when the Saitō company announced that it would be evicting the delinquent tenants from their lands and reassigning them to new renters, leading to a series of meetings. The Maeyachi branch announced its establishment in a meeting at Takahashi's house that drew 150 farmers and held a second conference on "the Resolution of the Problems of Farming Villages" in March that featured presentations by the leaders of the prefectural and Tomisato Nichinō groups.[92] The prefectural organization followed this up with another round of speeches in Sendai scheduled for March 15. The government crackdown on Communists and leftists in the March 15 Incident pushed the actual meeting to several days later, when representatives from thirty-one Miyagi branches of the Nichinō and an audience of five hundred, as well as an expansive group of police, turned up to hear about "the power of militant agricultural associations."[93] The size of the audiences at these events demonstrated a wide interest in the Maeyachi dispute and the issues underlying it, but they failed to enlist the other Saitō tenants in the village to participate in a united front, convincing none of them to withhold their rent in opposition to the new rent rules in solidarity with Takahashi and Sugawara.

Facing the imminent threat of the evictions of Takahashi and Sugawara and the seizure of their farms by the Saitō Corporation, the prefectural Nichinō moved into action in late March. It issued an order to all local branches for the "full mobilization of Nichinō branch associates, prepare to be able to freely strike, bring hoes and packed lunches. Those with horses, ride them and gather at the site of the confiscated tenant land. The objective is at the house of the tyrannical Saitō."[94] Over four hundred farmers from all over Senboku and Miyagi arrived at Takahashi's house the next morning and set to work tilling the paddies before moving on to do the same with Sugawara's fields. A substantial contingent of police arrived from Ishinomaki in the afternoon and fighting broke out when they ordered the plowing to stop. Calm was restored after a pitched battle that saw tenant farmers steal the hat and sword of the Ishinomaki police chief and dump him in the mud, and it was agreed that the police chief would meet with the Saitō company and press for the tenant demands. After tense hours in which several hundred tenants and Nichinō members rallied in front of the Saitō house, the police chief emerged and announced that the company had cancelled its plans for eviction, recognized cultivators' rights to the lands they rented in perpetuity, and accepted the proposal for Takahashi and Sugawara to pay their outstanding debts in installments over the next three years. As a bonus, the chief also announced a full amnesty for the tenants and Nichinō members who had been involved in the day's events, promising that no arrests would be pursued.

What looked like a tenant victory and the dawning of a new day for beleaguered Saitō tenants would turn out to be anything but. Displaying the flexibility concerning honesty that its chief applied to his work, the Ishinomaki police headquarters issued warrants for all Nichinō branch leaders who had participated in the collective tilling the next morning and dispatched officers to arrest them. Eight of these men were prosecuted, with the young secretary of the prefectural Nichinō sentenced to six months in prison, where he contracted the tuberculosis that killed him soon after his release.[95] Takahashi and Sugawara did not fare much better. Although both farmers were allowed to remain on the lands they rented and repay their debts to the company in installments, the Saitō Corporation was merely biding its time. When Takahashi and Sugawara discovered inconsistencies in the rent rates in Maeyachi the next year, the company launched a lawsuit against them and sent hired farmers to harvest their paddies and deliver the rice to the company. The police provided support to the company by making preemptory arrests of Nichinō members in the wider area and, after a year in court, the two men found themselves without land and left farming for good. The Saitō Corporation had achieved its original goals, damaging blows had been struck to the local farmers' movement, and the idea of tenant rights to the lands they worked remained a fantasy.

The events of the Maeyachi conflict and the revised status quo it left in its wake would have struck the architects of the Meiji systems of agriculture and local government with horror. One of the primary goals of *meibōka*-based village order was the separation of politics, especially in the form of contentious political parties and movements, from rural society. Yet in both Kanomata and Maeyachi, the Saitō Corporation drove tenants to seek out connections with the explicitly political and proletarian Nichinō and to establish local branches of the organization. *Meibōka* were also supposed to use their wealth and positions to ensure stability and peace within villages, but the conflicts that the Saitō company precipitated led to strife, illegal acts, and even violence. Late Meiji critics had predicted that these sorts of outcomes would become more common with the spread of non resident landlords, but the tenants driven to desperation by Saitō in the Maeyachi conflict lived in the same village as the company headquarters/Saitō family home. It was not a non-resident landlord, but rather a non-human landlord, whose incorporation likely had as much to do with divorcing the landlording business from "moral obligations and humane feelings" as it did with reducing expenses or securing assets.[96] While other Senboku landlords did not go to the extreme of redefining themselves as the Saitō house had done, they demonstrated an affinity with its goals and its approach to tenants in their increasing comfort with eviction as a means of generating greater profits. As their actions provoked nation-leading levels of tenant disputes in the 1930s, the fallacy of the *meibōka* idea became inescapable.

If the limited degree of tenant organization and the restricted scale of tenant-landlord disputes in the 1920s suggested cracks in the seeming tranquility in Senboku villages, the difficulties that came with the onset of the global economic Depression shattered the illusion of rural social stability as new pressures set off a flood of conflicts that dwarfed any that had come before. The Depression hit rural Tōhoku in two waves that struck at central elements of village economies and introduced complications that continued to plague farmers until the outbreak of the Second World War. The worldwide economic shock that followed the crash of the New York Stock Exchange in 1929 struck at the economic and industrial centers of Japan in much the same way that it did those of other countries. The rapid recovery that business and industry achieved in Japan is often cited as demonstrating a canny management of the crisis. What is less often trumpeted, however, is the fact that this recovery was predicated upon maintaining low food prices, essentially shifting the location of economic malaise from the city to the country.[97] Farmers, living from hand to mouth at the best of times, had no choice but to maintain full production even as their efforts brought in less and less money. In Tokyo, the price of rice dropped by 32 percent between August and September 1930, while market conditions in Miyagi were even worse.[98] Compared to an average price of 28.32 yen/*koku* in 1928, the prefecture's average price in 1930 topped out at a paltry 17.68 yen/*koku*. Prices continued to fall in 1931, going as low as 15.20 yen/*koku*, described in the media of the time as a "murderous market price" (*satsujinteki sōba*).[99]

Complicating the problem in Senboku was the region's late development in tenant and productive organizations. In other regions, producers unions (*sangyō kumiai*) made possible such tools as collective purchasing and marketing and cooperative networks that demonstrated their merits best during times of hardship, but Miyagi trailed far behind the rest of the country in the numbers of these groups and their spread. Against national and Tōhoku averages of 322 and 258 unions per prefecture respectively, Miyagi had only 195 in 1933 and the second highest number nationally of towns and villages without any such organization at

28.7 percent.[100] Without recourse to a collective response, the chronic problem of farm debt grew even worse, the average household debt load reaching 1.5 years of income and over 20 percent of farming families falling below the poverty line.

In 1934 a bad situation became worse when freezing Siberian winds brought a summer colder and wetter than any since the beginning of the century. Production totals in Miyagi dropped by more than half compared to the previous year and 86 percent of all crops grown in the prefecture suffered some degree of damage from the cold.[101] The following year was nearly as bad and images and stories from Tōhoku shocked newspaper readers across the nation as Japan's "first modern famine" became a leading preoccupation in the burgeoning mass media.[102] Alongside tenant farmers pushed into desperation by a worsening of their already precarious economic condition, smallholders and smaller landlords lost their lands en masse, intensifying the pattern that periodic flooding had consistently imposed on farming areas surrounding the Kitakami River and concentrating lands even further in the hands of *ōjinushi*.[103]

While the socioeconomic effects of economic recession and crop failures in the 1930s assumed familiar forms, a previously unknown element appeared in the form of aid from the state. The new activist posture that the national government assumed in the last years of Meiji consisted largely of focused infrastructural projects (riparian improvements, transportation infrastructure); the centralization and oversight of *kōchi seiri* unions, *nōkai,* and other local organizations; and moral suasion campaigns such as those that made up the Local Improvement Campaign. Villages remained responsible for planning, funding, and undertaking most projects relating to the improvement of farmland or of village administration and finances. The economic shocks that hit in the early 1930s, introducing new village problems and highlighting existing ones, finally roused officials to action. Takahashi Korekiyo, finance minister in Inukai Tsuyoshi's cabinet, oversaw the launching of a program of emergency aid for trying times (*jikyoku kyōkū*) that included funds for public works as employment and resources for weatherproofing crops, marking the first time the national government had offered direct subsidiary aid to farmers.[104] These funds remained limited in scope during the first year, depending largely on parallel initiatives launched by prefectural governments, but 1932 brought changes that pushed the government into more vigorous action. The May 15th Incident, in which radical agrarianists teamed up with disaffected military officers to assassinate the prime minister, and a dedicated lobbying campaign by farmers and agricultural ideologues that gathered over one hundred thousand signatures in the summer that followed promoted a keener awareness among officials of the acute need in the countryside. The fact that more than a few farmers forwarding their comments to the government issued calls for "a radically transformed, autonomous countryside" undoubtedly startled bureaucrats still reeling after the attempted coup d'état and led them to adopt policy based on the more moderate demands of the Teikoku Nōkai for relief employment, debt restructuring aid, and tighter central coordination.[105]

The response was dramatic and unprecedented. An extraordinary session of the Diet in the summer of 1932 granted a combined total of 86.3 million yen in funds to the Agriculture and Forestry, Home, and Education Ministries for public works as a means of relief aid.[106] While this represented far and away the most substantial commitment of government funds ever for farming villages, the largesse that it signalled was limited by the fact that funds could only be used for projects in which local resources covered a third of the costs. Villages could undertake projects that had been far outside of economic capabilities, but the raising of even this fraction of the costs in such trying times often forced suffering villages deeper into debt. Still, official funds did flow into needy villages, providing desperate farming families with enough to survive the crisis and plan for better days to come. Responding to the calls from *nōkai,* the government provided further aid in the form of loans designed to restructure the household debt that was endemic in the countryside. The two programs ran parallel for three years, until the worst of the economic crisis had passed and the deteriorating situation on the Asian continent directed all available public funds to the military. By that point, between public works projects and debt restructuring loans, 1.6 billion yen had flowed from official coffers into farming villages.[107]

The cold temperatures and crop failures that followed the economic shocks in Tōhoku brought about lobbying of their own and drew additional forms of aid to the region. In addition to the public works and debt aid funds mentioned above, the national government made special provisions of rice, seeds, low-interest loans, and tax exemptions to Tōhoku villages to provide both emergency relief and a foundation for future development in the region as a whole. These measures too fell victim to the aggressive military expansion in Asia, and in 1936 the goal of rural development was abandoned for the promotion of industrial growth in Miyagi.[108]

The other major thrust of official support for farming villages suffering in the 1930s, and the one that proved the most enduring, was the Nōsangyoson Keizai Kōsei Undō (Campaign for Economic Revitalization in Farm, Mountain and Fishing Villages; hereafter Keizai Kōsei Undō). In contrast to the stark novelty of the dedicated funding for public works relief work, the revitalization campaign took on more familiar characteristics. At its heart, it was a program to draw out the productive and economic resources lying dormant in rural communities and mobilize them to eliminate debt and poverty and create self-sufficient farming villages. In place of direct funding, the national government would supply information, instructions, organizational frameworks, and encouragement. If the public works budgets represented radical change, the Keizai Kōsei Undō was a slight modification of the general philosophy that abided prior to 1931 in which "local problems needed to be solved locally."[109]

Launched in October of 1932, the campaign took aim at village economies, societies, education, and lifestyles with the express goal of eliminating the deeply engrained economic problems that afflicted villages by rebuilding society from the ground up. At its launch, the program identified 76 percent of towns and villages throughout the country to be primed for revitalization and issued a call for applications to be included in the program.[110] In order to be designated as a Keizai Kōsei village (*shitei mura*), residents had first to organize a local economic revitalization committee (*Keizai kōsei iin*) composed of local officials and notables, which would draft plans for the village and hold a ceremony in front of the local shrine where every resident of the village pledged their support. The response was immediate and outsized. By 1934, nearly 40 percent of towns and villages in the country had satisfied the conditions and become designated villages, and numbers continued to grow such that the government created a special designated village (*tokubetsu shitei mura*) category that provided limited direct aid from the government for villages demonstrating especially strong potential for improvement.[111] Local governments and official organizations jumped at the chance to take part in the campaign. The Miyagi government formed a Keizai Kōsei committee in October of 1932 and issued its *Economic Outline for Farming Villages* (*Nōson keizai taikō*), which included items concerning the use of producers' unions (*sangyō kumiai*) as savings banks, public works as relief for impoverished farmers, and the formation of local committees to provide loans to help needy villagers either to find work or to relocate to more prosperous environs.[112] Miyagi *nōkai* also sprang into action. A central coordinating committee launched a campaign to form producers' unions and other organizations around local *nōkai* for the purposes of "building a farming spirit" (*nōmin seishin no sakkō*), enabling individual self-sufficiency, and expanding cooperative organizations.[113]

In its goals and the means it proposed to achieve them, the Keizai Kōsei Undō bears a striking resemblance to the Local Improvement

Campaign launched a quarter century earlier. Of the three major goals of the revitalization campaign, the elimination of household debt was largely a novelty and the creation of producers' unions only tangentially related to the earlier movement's organizational imperatives, but the final object of cultivating a solid middle class (*chūken jinbutsu*) of farming villagers who would assume roles of leadership in local administration and organizations seemed like a page straight out of the Local Improvement handbook. While the newer initiative was embarking on the same search for local leaders as its predecessor campaign, there was, however, a pronounced difference in the people it proposed to install in these positions. The Local Improvement Campaign had broken with the established agricultural order, seeking out an alternative to the landlords whose leadership had proven so disappointing to officials. In their place, it put forward an idealized class of skilled farmers and others with proven practical accomplishments. Personal characteristics and individual abilities were thus put front and center, but local improvement planners were explicit in their identification of the independent landowning and minor landlord classes as the fount from whence these leaders would be drawn. The Keizai Kōsei Undō also saw these social strata as a fertile source of local leadership, but they put out an additional call for "younger and more technically skilled individuals," reflecting the belief among bureaucrats that "the traditional sources of leadership were not up to the task at hand."[114] These young worthies also potentially included people from the owner-tenant and even full tenant classes, something rejected outright by the planners of the Meiji-era movement. The revitalization campaign picked up the earlier critique of the landlord-*meibōka* ideal and took it toward its logical conclusion.

A second way that the Keizai Kōsei Undō undermined the conception of *meibōka* that had been so central to agricultural and rural policy decades earlier was in the roles it envisioned for the new leaders it sought. Meiji-era *meibōka* were needed for their crucial role as middlemen bridging the vast distances dividing farming communities from the central government in Tokyo. Their local knowledge and positions within the village represented resources that officials aimed to exploit in one way or another to achieve their goals of self-sufficient and developing farming communities. At the same time, the intermediary position of *meibōka* offered similar benefits in reverse to the residents of their home villages. Their connections with elites in government and the capital opened doors that could direct attention and money to the village to be put to local ends. The *chūken jinbutsu* sought out by the revitalization movement, in contrast, were targeted for preventative intervention as much as for the mobilization of their abilities and positions. Keizai Kōsei planners were preoccupied with steering their solid middle class away from leftist politics, where their capabilities could be turned against the government, and indoctrinating and mobilizing them "in service of what was portrayed as the national interest."[115] They were identifying local talent not to exploit it for local development, but rather to stifle it lest it be used against them. These leaders were not to be middlemen; they were conduits through which officials could transmit their goals to villages.

The Keizai Kōsei Undō intersected with events in Senboku in two ways that showed how completely the *meibōka* idea failed in the decades after 1910. The first of these appeared in Nangō and the plans farmers there formulated for mass emigration to Manchuria. The second can be related to Kamata Sannosuke's activities as mayor of Kashimadai and public figure promoting messages of austerity and self-sacrifice to farmers.

After the Manchurian Incident in September 1931 and the Japanese conquest of much of northeastern China over the following half year, Manchuria came to occupy a central place in the imaginations of both policy makers within the government and the public in general. Foremost in the thoughts of officials and military leaders (now often the same people) was defense. The territories the Japanese empire was seizing from China, whether in the chipping away that characterized the southward progress before the Marco Polo Bridge Incident or the dramatic seizure of the expansive Manchurian region, was targeted in service of security concerns while at the same time raising further concerns relating to the new needs for defense created by the incorporation of new lands into the Japanese empire.

To provide for the defense of the region, which had been renamed Manchukuo under the fiction that it was an independent country liberated by Japanese forces, the Ministry of Colonial Affairs moved quickly to put boots on the ground. It published the *Manshū nōgyō imin keikaku taikō* (Outline of a Plan for Agricultural Colonists to Manchuria) in March of 1932 and selected and dispatched the first group of emigrants to the continent at the year's end. This began the first period of Manchurian emigration, whose participants were known as "armed emigrants" (*busō imin*) as they consisted of soldiers from farming villages who were dispatched to borderlands facing the Soviet Union as a human wall against the threat of invasion. Four more dispatches of armed emigrants were sent out over the next four years before the program was reconfigured in the summer of 1936.

While security-obsessed officials dictated the form of the first period of Manchurian emigration, the thought of the region's vast (and assumed to be empty) fields of arable land also captured the imagination of farmers and agrarian ideologues. Activist Nagano Akira, who had been working to secure relief for farmers hurt by the Depression and by landlord predations, included calls for mass emigration of farmers to Manchuria in petitions for restrictions on tenant evictions he submitted to the Diet in 1932.[116] This was particularly for the sake of farmers in Nagano and Tōhoku, who, Nagano claimed, had told him of their interest in emigration.

The idea of fleeing Miyagi and its problems to break new farmland overseas began to take hold among farmers in the late 1920s. Although total numbers of emigrants were limited, 1929 produced twice as many as the previous year at 353 people, and this number was again doubled in 1930.[117] These were economic migrants and, while Miyagi soldier-farmers later joined each of the five *busō imin* dispatches to Manchuria, others were interested in the region as a site for dedicated agricultural colonies. Popular imagination, bolstered by government propaganda concerning Manchuria after 1931, believed the region to be something akin to a pristine farmer's paradise. Fertile fields spread across the landscape, offering a one-stop solution to the troubles that were endemic to Tōhoku's farming villages. Population growth in the 1920s had led to land shortages in the 1930s, creating a situation in which the sons of tenant farmers and independent farmers alike found no fields or paddies to rent or buy and landlords pursued evictions of existing tenants in order to let the lands out to others willing to pay higher rents. Manchuria seemed to offer farmland to anyone willing to work it.

These ideas were especially attractive in Nangō, where the plans to replace the *busō imin* policy with mass farmer emigration were created. As a village notable for its large number of resident landlords, Nangō experienced the problems of land shortages and landlord machinations in full force. Matsukawa Gorō, principal of the Nangō practical school, was inspired by the stories his students told him of the difficulties their families faced and responded by drafting plans for a farming colony in Brazil.[118] As he prepared to depart for South America with funds he had solicited from local landlords to purchase land for the colony, however, the international situation changed and Brazil closed its doors to Japanese immigrants.[119] Instead, he received a visit soon afterward from prominent agrarian Katō Kanji, who had long been a proponent of agricultural immigration to Manchuria. Katō had been sent by Ishiwara Kanji, then a colonel in charge of the Fourth Infantry Regiment in Sendai and a figure with deep connections to the Kwantung Army in Manchuria. Matsukawa became an instant convert to the idea of Manchurian emigration and set to work recruiting colonists from among his students and making comprehensive plans for a dedicated program of emigration from Nangō.

Gaining a substantial group of supporters from among the tenant farmers of Nangō, Matsukawa formed the Nangō Supporters of Emigration to Manchuria and Mongolia Association (Nangō Man Mō Kōenkai) and composed a plan for the mass emigration of farmers from the village to Manchuria. He documented the plan's purpose in its preface as being "to solve the problems of land availability and fertility, create a grounding for the revitalization of the village, rouse the spirits of the villagers, and to manage the prosperity of the empire by incrementally sending the excess farming population as agricultural emigrants under the Ministry of Colonial Affairs to northern Manchuria and establishing in that land the village of Nangō Mark II (dai-ni Nangō)."[120] This was a *bunson* (village-splitting) plan that proposed relocating 40 percent of Nangō's farming population to the second village on the continent, which would leave at least 3 hectares of farmland for each of those remaining. Cheered on by his backers, Matsukawa took the plan to the village council and asked that they adopt it as village policy. Instead, the landlords who monopolized the positions of administrative authority in Nangō registered their absolute opposition to the plan.[121] Complaining that they did not intend their school to be a site to indoctrinate the young with ideas of emigration to Manchuria, they did Matsukawa a final indignity by telephoning him while he was at a conference in Sendai and requesting that he resign his position at the school.

The antipathy that Nangō's leadership class held toward the mass emigration of farmers to Manchuria was rooted in the particular character of the village and its structure. The concentration of large landlords in the village meant that the population was largely divided between a majority of tenant farmers and a small minority of wealthy landowners. The latter had early on established a monopoly over village offices and they used the power their control over the administration gave them to further their own interests while impeding tenant activities that threatened their profits. Notable among these latter activities in the early 1930s were Nangō's repeated refusals of the attempts of the government to name it a designated village under the Keizai Kōsei Undō, which would have established new organizations outside of their control and allowed for positions of leadership for tenant farmers, and the village leaders' suppression of the producers' union that tenants and smallholders had established in 1929.[122] Regarding the emigration plan, they had two clear objections. The first was that the very problem that the plan was supposed to solve for tenants was a means of profit for landlords. A population that outstripped available lands meant greater demand and made evicting tenants in favor of renters willing to pay higher prices a profitable enterprise. Second, tenants and landlords were often linked by debt, in addition to (and often as the basis of) their rental contracts. Landlords were concerned about what would happen to the money they were owed if the people who owed it to them relocated to Manchuria.[123]

Faced with his censure in Nangō, Matsukawa moved to Tokyo to work directly with Katō and his allies to lobby the government to adopt the *bunson* plan as national policy. Their efforts received a boost in 1936 when, after the February 26th Incident terror attacks, the Kwantung Army's "Plan for the Emigration of One Million Families of Farming Emigrants to Manchuria" was first adopted by the Manchukuo government and then the Ministry of Colonial Affairs. It became official policy and was granted a budget of nearly 5 million yen the following year for the dispatch of a preliminary group of 6,000 settlers as the first step in the plan. Manchurian *bunson* plans were subsequently linked to the Keizai Kōsei Undō and became a cornerstone policy in the central government's efforts to address its twin concerns with the sorry state of farming villages and the security of the expanding empire.

The *bunson* plan's embrace by the national government meant that Nangō landlords could no longer oppose it. Village officials were forced to participate in mass weddings and farewell parties for departing emigrants that national and prefectural officials organized.[124] Nangō leaders were able to keep the *bunson* plan out of village policy until 1937, when the pressure became too much and they were forced to capitulate. This opened the doors for Nangō's designation as a Keizai Kōsei Undō village, which the village's landlords had avoided for so long, resulting in the revival of the moribund producers' union and garnering official support for the establishment of various new organizations designed to address the problems faced by impoverished tenants.

In fact, it appears that these local outcomes were what the tenant farmers who had provided vocal support to Matsukawa in the early stages of his planning had wanted all along.[125] When the time came to dispatch farmers to create the second Nangō in Manchuria, volunteers were scarce. Even the students that Matsukawa had originally recruited from the village school balked when their families refused to back their plans. By the end of the war nearly a decade later, only 164 Nangō families had made the move to Manchuria, a number well short of the plan's call for 800 households. In the end, the attempt to establish Nangō Mark II failed and the population removed to the continent opened only a paltry 1/10 *chō* of land per household for the farmers who remained.[126]

The saga of Nangō's emigration plan, particularly the roles played by the village landlords and by Matsukawa himself, represent a further undermining of the *meibōka* ideal. The landlords, in their quest to maintain their monopoly over political authority in the village, worked in ways that were in direct opposition to the role of middleman that the local government system and agricultural policy had been constructed around. Rather than bridging the gap between village and national government, they actively blocked any links between the two, as in their refusal of the Keizai Kōsei designation. In contrast, Matsukawa did act as an intermediary, soliciting elite allies and mobilizing central authorities in support of his local goals. But the local was also the sight of his deviation from the *meibōka* course. The figures at the heart of agricultural policy were supposed to have their sights set squarely on the local village; making plans to split the village and dispatch half its population overseas was antithetical to the ideal. Either way, there existed in Nangō faint evidence of any survival into the middle years of the century of the kind of middlemen upon whom the development and prosperity of villages was supposed to depend.

In not entirely dissimilar ways, the later career of Kamata Sannosuke as Mayor Straw Sandals featured an evolution in his activity and thought that saw him move away from the role of local middleman he had played so effectively in the drainage of the Shinainuma wetlands and toward something less ambiguously aligned with the goals of central bureaucrats. Presaged in his efforts to establish the Mexican farming colony, as well as his attempts to build a name for himself on the national stage, these developments may not have signaled a complete break in the character that Kamata had displayed in his youth. Still, if they were not completely inconsistent with the person that was Kamata, they stood at odds with the vision of the ideal Meiji local leader that his role in the Shinainuma reclamation had seemed to represent.

Having accepted the position of mayor of Kashimadai in 1909 with the theatrical flourishes of shaving his mustache and trading his suit and shoes for a threadbare *jimbei* and straw sandals, Kamata set to work with his plans to capitalize upon the taming of Shinainuma and introduce a prosperity to Kashimadai that it had never known before. In the speech he made in front of the assembled villagers on the day of his inauguration, Kamata declared that the first priority of the village could be nothing other than improving economic conditions and reclaiming the 70 percent of village farmland that was in the hands of outside landlords.[127] While his return of all the tenanted lands he personally owned to the farmers that worked them and the cancellation of all debts owed to him were dramatic gestures, the concrete means he enacted in pursuit of the dream of a locally owned village were of a more prosaic nature.[128] Alongside standard initiatives like an outline of village production plans (*sonze*), the promotion of education, and the formation of a producers' collective, Kamata spearheaded a project for the village to buy government-owned land to create a community pine forest and worked with the local flood control union to promote settlement on the lands opened by the drainage of Shinainuma.

To the latter end, the union and the village administration offered tenancy terms designed to draw in farmers from impoverished Tōhoku villages. Tenants willing to break the new lands and begin cultivation of them could work the lands rent-free for the first two years and were promised the titles to their farms when their rent payments (which were paid to the village as landlord) had collectively paid off the debts incurred in the drainage of Shinainuma.[129] The program was successful from the start. The first wave of incoming migrants arrived in 1910, while the drainage was still underway, and by 1915, 185 households had taken up residence and begun work breaking the reclaimed lands for cultivation. The early years of the newcomers were spent in extreme poverty, with many surviving hand-to-mouth by means of local charity and day labor on public works, but by 1923 all had food and shelter and most owned farm animals and additional lands.[130] Growing prosperity attracted further waves of migration, eventually expanding to over seven hundred households as the Kamata family's visions of Shinainuma-free prosperity began to take shape.

The reclaimed lands represented only one aspect of Kamata's leadership as mayor. More characteristic of his long career in the office, and standing in some contrast with his work before becoming mayor, were his efforts to consolidate the administration of Kashimadai. In the same inaugural speech in which he called for the repatriation of ownership of the village's farmland, Kamata laid out his plans to wage war on what remained of the hamlets (*buraku*) that had been incorporated into the amalgamated village at the end of the last century. Having made a conspicuous land donation worth more than 2,000 yen to his home hamlet of Kimazuka only two years earlier, Kamata as mayor announced the destruction of the bases of it and the other hamlets that made up Kashimadai as being among his highest priorities. In his sights were schools, shrines, and hamlet-held assets. He called for the shuttering of the first and their replacement with a single village elementary school, a dismantling of the second and their concentration in a solitary village shrine, and a seizure of the last and their reassignment as village assets. Reference was made to the wastefulness of multiple schools and the pernicious dangers inherent in neglected shrines, but Kamata was explicit in declaring the destruction of the hamlets themselves to be the object of his crusade. The harm they did, he warned, went far beyond their financial costs, giving rise to a "hamlet-style thinking" they imposed in "early childhood" that had paralyzed government in the village and threatened so often to derail the Shinainuma reclamation.[131] To eliminate any trace of hamlets from the village administration, Kamata rezoned Kashimadai into sixty new administrative districts and placed each under the supervision of a member of a centralized standing committee who transmitted village policy and oversaw tax payment. Removing the institutions that lay at their hearts and rewriting the administrative map to deny them of any function, Kamata effectively closed the book on the hamlets from which Kashimadai had been assembled.

Although his economic arguments and the fact that the new *chōson* was an administrative reality that none could escape certainly went some distance to justify his assault on hamlets, it was no coincidence that the destruction of these units was also a central part of the Local Improvement Campaign that the Home Ministry was leading at just this time. Through a variety of policies and admonitions, the campaign attempted to use programs of moral reform, administrative rationalization, and exhortations of delinquent local elites to revive the fortunes of ailing villages. Officials involved in campaigns like the Local Improvement Campaign showed their unreserved appreciation for the success of Kamata's efforts, which stood out in contrast to partial or complete failures in most areas. In the brief biography of Kamata written as a part of the mayor's nomination for the national government's Medal with Blue Ribbon in 1927, Miyagi governor Ushizuka Toratarō named Kamata as precisely the type of village leader the Local Improvement Campaign had sought and praised the mayor's concerted efforts to "eliminate the idea of the hamlet" in Kashimadai.[132] This was an idea that both the Home Ministry and the prefectural government had demonstrated a clear interest in eliminating. Officials reviled the continuing existence of hamlets, condemning them for leeching loyalty from official administrative districts, for impeding development through their maintenance of "undeveloped" common lands, and for standing in the way of the rational reorganization of farmland.[133] In granting him the medal, they rewarded Kamata's success and held him up as a model for other local leaders to follow in erasing the traces of their own hamlets.

Kamata's victories against Kashimadai's hamlets and his oversight of the successful cultivation of the lands reclaimed from Shinainuma combined with the mayor's own eccentric asceticism to bring him wider fame from the 1920s forward. Continuing the pattern that began with the visit of the future Taishō emperor to Shinainuma in which official recognition of Kamata's work both reflected his growing celebrity and contributed to its further extension, he was granted an audience with the soon-to-be Shōwa emperor and received an award from the Dai Nihon Nōkai in November of 1925.[134] As word about Kamata spread, the persona he had adopted upon taking up the top office in Kashimadai—that of Mayor Straw Sandals—became an even greater source of fame than the work on Shinainuma. The speaking events he booked across the country invariably billed themselves as talks with Mayor Straw Sandals and the increasing number of newspaper stories about him never failed to employ this sobriquet, often in the headline, and photos and descriptions of his theatrically ascetic manner of dress.

Kamata's growing celebrity as Mayor Straw Sandals represented a canny piece of branding, but it also reflected a more substantial change in his approach to village prosperity. His work on Shinainuma was characterized, above all else, by his efficacy in teasing funding and other forms of support from various levels of government and other elite actors in Tokyo and Kyoto. To the efforts aimed at the center, he paired a vigorous promotion of local cooperation and the discovery and exploitation of such wealth and production that could be derived from the village. Upon assuming the office of mayor, however, Kamata's attentions turned exclusively to this latter pursuit. He signaled what was to be the source of future village development in his inaugural speech as mayor. "Our village is poor, so we can't imitate the people from other villages. If we imitate rich villagers, we can't catch up to others no matter how many years we spend, so we absolutely have to take one step down from others and work."[135] While the chronic difficulty of soliciting government funds, as well as the newly established and structured programs of central support for agricultural and riparian improvements introduced in the previous chapter, might explain Kamata's new approach as mayor, the fact of the change was clear. The capacity for labor in farmers and other villagers, which still held untouched reserves, would be the fuel for all future development and improvement in Kashimadai.

Many of Kamata's signature initiatives in his long career as mayor read like they had been lifted directly from the policies and admonitions of central bureaucrats. They described the problems of the village in ways that associated them with the moral and intellectual failings of villagers and proclaimed that the only way to solve them was through an intensification of labor, the reform of morality, and an abandonment of even the most modest forms of luxury. Among the lifestyle reforms he introduced into village policy upon assuming the role of mayor were restrictions on drinking and parties, bans on New Year's gift giving, the imposition of a curfew, and the prohibition of tea and sweets.[136] To these disciplinary measures, he added continual instruction in correct manners of behavior and household organization. The guidelines he produced yearly and hand-delivered to every house in the village outlined the basics of proper household economics as:

1. Simplicity and Frugality: great growth is untroubled by great economizing; clothes are for protection and ceremony, food is for maintaining bodily strength and should be self-produced by farming families, housing is for shelter from rain and dew, and big houses just make problems for raising good children.
2. Work: each person needs to take on the appropriate work, farming families need to do secondary work.
3. Accounting: calculating your income and controlling your expenses are the fundamental rules of economics.[137]

Life was to be stripped down to bare economic function and the saving of the village would be achieved by the strictest possible regimen of self-denial and hard work.

Unsurprisingly, despite their proscriptive, authoritarian, and dehumanizing nature, Kamata's reforms could make economic sense. As cold as it may have been, logic, after all, had been informing the push for similar measures by bureaucrats since the end of the previous century. Combined with the economic policies enacted on a village-wide basis, they produced rapid and notable results. By 1935, personal debt in the village, which had once been endemic, was all but eliminated. The wide adoption of the raising of chickens and ducks had created new sources of revenue for village households. And Kamata's compulsory program of micropayments from the local elementary school students eventually gathered enough funds to purchase a full-sized rice paddy for use in practical instruction.[138] The growing prosperity of the village also displayed itself in demographic change. The population rose steadily throughout Kamata's mayorhood, growing from 5,198 in the year before he took office to 6,206 in 1916, 8,220 in 1927, and 9,526 in 1935.[139] These gains were accounted for in large measure by the in-migration of farmers who settled on the lands reclaimed from Shinainuma, but that abundance of arable land also allowed Kashimadai to grow without suffering from the same dearth of lands that led to the creation of the plans for mass migration to Manchuria in Nangō.

As the country moved toward war in the 1930s, Kamata took on a more prominent role on the national stage. His personal asceticism, and the village program of self-sacrifice that appeared to be an extension of it, matched the evolving view among central bureaucrats of what the war demanded from farming villages across the country. The compatibility of his approach with the initiatives of the national government was nothing new. In the 1910s, Kamata stumped for the Local Improvement Campaign, giving public lectures at the behest of the Home Ministry and by the time the Keizai Kōsei Undō was gaining a foothold in the 1930s, his orientation had, if anything, fallen into even tighter step with those of bureaucrats. Beginning in 1936, Kamata became a regular attendee at an irregular series of congresses between high officials in the Finance and Agriculture and Forestry Ministries and "expert farmers" (*tokunō*). The resulting newspaper coverage, which focused heavily on his "straw sandals and tattered clothes," cemented his position as a national celebrity.[140] His accomplishments in achieving village *jichi*—the associations with "autonomy" the term had held in the late nineteenth century were now entirely abandoned in favor of "self-sufficiency"—granted him a place of honor among the other participants from across the country. Kamata's contributions at the congresses and in newspaper interviews connected to them made it clear that officials had made no error in inviting him. In a 1941 survey of how the various participants believed villages could help to deal with the challenges of the wartime homefront, Kamata rolled out his familiar strategy of forbearance and discipline, declaring that "Farming villages still have plenty more to give. . . . I believe if villages tighten their belts (*hikishimete*) a little more and provide for themselves (*jikyū jisoku*), they will be able to do their public duty."[141] At a meeting with officials a week later, he expressed his belief that, should farmers nationwide apply themselves fully to secondary work (in addition to rice farming), they could produce an additional 3 million *koku* of barley that could be used in the war effort.[142]

These and similar sentiments that Kamata expressed during the course of the war reveal direct links to the proclamations he made on his first day as mayor in Kashimadai, but they placed him now at an even further remove from his accomplishments as an intermediary during his decades of work on the drainage of Shinainuma. At that time, he sought out friendships with political elites in the capital like Ozaki Yukio and Katō Takaaki and leveraged them in his pursuit of government aid for his quest. Now his associates included such figures as ultranationalist Tōyama Mitsuru and Admiral Yamamoto Eisuke and his efforts seemed geared to maximizing the exploitation of farming villages in service of their goals of military conquest.[143] These activities were not limited to the time he spent on the national stage. At home in Miyagi he was made a special consultant for the prefectural branch of the totalitarian Imperial Rule Assistance Association in December 1940 and went on to hold a variety of posts related to the group over the next three years. A 1942 advertisement for Honma Rakukan's then-recent biography of Kamata (*Waraji sonchō Kamata Sannosuke ō: Yokusan no ijin—Shōwa no Sontoku*) provides a telling indicator of the mayor's public image at the time.[144] Not only had his fame reached the point where a book based on his life could be marketed to the general public in the pages of the nation's largest newspaper, but the character of that fame was such that the publisher chose to advertise the book with the phrase, "Let's move forward in defense of the homeland with his spirit!"[145] In Kashimadai, Kamata gave a final confirmation of the inversion of his earlier *meibōka* ideals. Despite his efforts to build village unity and his success in promoting its prosperity, he lent his support to the adoption of a Manchurian emigration *bunson* plan in 1940 and reported to the national media his delight at seeing the remarkable agricultural production Kashimadai emigrants were achieving after touring their continental settlement in 1942.[146]

Thus, by the height of the war, little trace remained of the qualities that had made Kamata an ideal middleman of modernity a half century earlier. No longer concerned with opening doors in the center for his fellow peripheral villagers—or even mediating between the local and the central—he now transmitted the demands of the government downward and worked to maximize the mobilization of farmers in service of the state. This work also highlighted the abandonment of his former focus on and dedication to the local village. While a laudatory profile of him published at the beginning of his rise to nationwide fame stated that his successes had started when "he hid himself away in Kashimadai," he was anything but hidden in the 1930s and 1940s.[147] The country as a whole was his stage, the goals of the state were his goals, and the village he had once championed, and thousands of others like it, were now the means to achieve ends formulated in the capital.

Thus, with tenant conflicts growing more intense as evictions continued, the Keizai Kōsei Undō reordering villages and daily life, the *bunson* campaign funneling unsatisfactory, but still significant, numbers of villagers into colonial Manchuria, and Kamata and the national government calling for ever greater agricultural production, Miyagi and Senboku moved into full mobilization and the darkness of total war. As the military situation degraded, problems that had been perennial in Senboku found unexpected resolutions. The increasing mobilization of soldiers to the front lines opened urban jobs and village farmland, ending the crisis facing second and subsequent sons with no family land to inherit. The heightened need for food brought various forms of government support for farming and legal changes shifted the balance of power from less- or non-productive landlords to cultivating tenants.

But these were dubious forms of relief. As the course of the war worsened, general conditions on the homefront followed. More and more men, and then boys, were taken from the paddies and the factories and official condolence calls became chillingly familiar sights in villages. Farming production levels, which had been pushed to record-breaking heights early in the war, dropped in the early 1940s, victim to shortages of labor and inputs. Fertilizer purchases in Miyagi dropped by half between 1940 and 1942, then halved again two years later, when total agricultural output fell 14 percent in a single year.[148] As desperation mounted, Nangō and other villages turned their hopes once again to Manchuria. After 4 years without emigration, another group was dispatched from Nangō in 1944. The surprise felt by the earlier emigrants at the new arrivals was compounded by the fact that it included a member of the village's landlord class, prompting one of the settlers to stammer out in bewilderment, "You're a landlord with plenty to eat . . . why?"[149]

While the nuclear destruction of Nagasaki and Hiroshima in August 1945 and the subsequent surrender of the Imperial Japanese government affected the country as a whole, the final weeks of the war brought Miyagi its own set of disasters. Allied strategic bombing campaigns targeted areas in the prefecture for the first time in the summer of 1945, immolating nearly a quarter of Sendai and its population in a mission with the explicit aim of civilian megadeath less than a month before the two atomic bombings. Air raids on Sendai and other targets in Miyagi continued over the weeks that followed, ending only after a final strike on August 10, when fevered surrender negotiations were already underway. Similar catastrophe awaited the Manchurian emigrants from Nangō, Kashimadai, and other villages that had adopted *bunson* plans. The Soviet Union launched its invasion of Manchuria on August 9, quickly cutting through the ragged remnants of the Japanese military that remained. Japanese colonists, cut off from contact with the homeland, were rounded up en masse in the weeks that followed. While the specific fates of the settlers captured varied widely, in the end only 1,380 of the 2,300 farmers who emigrated to Machuria from Miyagi ever made it back.[150]

These then were the developments that led both to the Occupation survey of the farmlands of Japan and the sorry conditions it uncovered. While Occupation officials cast blame for this state in a variety of directions, the idea that Japanese agricultural development had stagnated decades earlier or that it had faced insurmountable natural challenges were simply not accurate. The decades since 1910 had been a period of continual and dramatic growth for farming in Senboku. As the early foundations of agricultural improvement began to produce results, new government commitment to development had enabled riparian and reclamation works that had been impossible earlier. These transformations of the landscape enabled farmers to employ new methods and increased the efficacy of these means, resulting in a diffusion of improved agricultural technology and techniques. A modern revolution in agriculture unfolded over the decades, effecting a transformation that was comparable to the mechanization of industry in the cities. Despite the multifarious damages wrought on farming villages during the war, agriculture had come a long way in the previous thirty-five years.

One area singled out for blame by the Occupation surveyors and analysts, however, was undeniably accurate, as many an early-twentieth-century agricultural official or ideologue would have readily agreed. While the technical and productive advances in farming matched many of the hopes attached to agriculture in the Meiji period, the social circumstances of agriculture did not experience similar development and in fact grew worse over the same decades. At the heart of the problem was the failure of the idea that Meiji-era bureaucrats had placed at the heart of agricultural policy, that ideologues and officials had championed in the new century, and that campaign after campaign from government ministries had attempted to realize: that of self-motivated local leaders who would employ specialized knowledge and personal resources to raise farming yields, bring about generalized prosperity, and ensure happy and peaceful villages. Broadening their search for the local leaders they needed beyond the original vision of village elites and making new commitments for direct government support after being disappointed by landlord-led village development at the beginning of the century, officials nevertheless continued to pursue a course that relied upon local middlemen who would connect guidance and instruction from the center with the local resources needed to implement it in villages.

While the policy changes of 1908–1911 worked to eliminate the rampant exploitation by landlords of the privileged status accorded to them as the designated intermediaries, the still largely decentralized nature of both agricultural development and village administration continued to depend upon local figures possessing economic resources of some significance. In the wake of the tenant association conflicts of 1908, Senboku landlords stood chastised and the mass revision of tenant contracts and the freezing of rent rates suggested a reversal of the most pronounced and ingrained inequalities in village society. These gains proved to be temporary, however, and within a decade and a half landlords were again testing the waters for the possibility of regaining the initiative in their relations with tenants. Changes in the political winds came to their aid, dismantling latent, but potentially powerful, new forms of tenant and proletarian organization. Now the ongoing successes of agricultural development came to work against attempts to reduce the disparity between rich and poor in villages as landlords could once again monopolize the greater profits of farming and use them to exploit the growing population for ever greater returns. As abusive as the saber system had been, it nonetheless represented landlords attempting to increase their profits by improving agricultural output. By the 1930s, the improvement of farming no longer figured into the plans of landlords, who sought to maximize profits instead through evictions, maintaining a scarcity of land, and reducing the access of tenants to aid and relief. Nangō, whose landlords suppressed tenant efforts to create a producers' union and cut the village off from government aid programs, revealed where the avenues to landlord profits now lay. The imbalance of power between tenants and landlords reasserted itself, once again reinforced by the state, and the seizure of a greater share of existing production became the most expedient way to increase landlord profits, while ideas of expanding production disappeared from the consciousness of landlords in general.

War and defeat negated or undid many of the gains made by agriculture in the first half of the twentieth century, but for the first time they presented the promise, and then the realization, of a fix for the vast social inequalities that were endemic in farming villages. Occupation authorities, receiving reports from their agents in the field of the "feudal" conditions of rural tenants like those that opened this chapter, made the decision they were probably always going to make and initiated the land reform that rewrote the social realities of the countryside from the ground up. Limits were placed on the size of landholdings, landlording in the manner seen before the war was made effectively illegal, and most tenants gained some degree of ownership over the lands they worked. Farmers faced a myriad of challenges and an uncertain future in the aftermath of war and defeat, but they would have the chance to prove that agricultural development depended on neither hopelessly stratified village communities nor a privileged class of rural elites.

Conclusion

Today, a bronze statue of Kamata Sannosuke stands in the middle of Kashimadai. It depicts him in his Mayor Straw Sandals persona, an old man in a patchwork suit with an umbrella and a straw mat held in his arms, striding forward with purpose. The actual suit depicted in the statue can itself be found not far away in a small museum dedicated to the mayor in the Kamata Memorial Hall, Kashimadai's community center. Alongside the suit, the famous sandals, and a large collection of the mayor's journals, ledgers, and personal effects, the museum also features a unique informative exhibition. A recreation of a prewar rural school room fills one corner, with wooden chairs arranged before a wall-mounted blackboard. When the audience has been seated, the show begins with the two halves of the blackboard sliding away to reveal a video screen. As a twenty-minute film biography of Kamata plays, the lights flash, fade, and fill the room in concert with the narrative of the mostly animated feature. At one particularly memorable moment, the faux windows on the schoolroom wall blast open and lightning flashes as the shutters swing in and out.

The cumulative effect of the show is striking. The biographical film itself is hagiographic and melodramatic in equal measure. The animatronic window activates itself at a crescendo of emotional tension, when Kamata, torn between the choices of accepting the position of mayor or pursuing his dream of a life of national significance, faces his long, dark night of the soul. The narrative taken as a whole is the story of a man—a man of angelic goodness—whose selfless desire to improve the lot of impoverished farmers approaches obsession and the sacrifices he made to build Kashimadai into the prosperous community it is today.

The contemporary townspeople who produced it have (probably unknowingly) created precisely the type of figure sought so desperately by Meiji bureaucrats from Yamagata Aritomo's first call for men with *meibō* to the idealized imaginings behind Yanagida Kunio's critique of landlords. The Kamata of the film could have been drawn directly from the pages of Yokoi Tokiyoshi's novel, *Mohan chōson.*

And yet, the lush green paddies that surround the memorial hall at the height of summer and the prosperity evident in the neat rows of houses that make up Kashimadai bear mute testimony to the grain of truth that runs through even this torturously contorted tale of Kamata's life. The facts are undeniable. The village did undergo a transformation from poverty to prosperity. The most dramatic aspects of this transformation occurred during the lifetime of Kamata Sannosuke. And he was deeply involved with the processes by which it was accomplished. While the melodramatic narrative that plays out on the pseudo-blackboard takes countless liberties with its subject matter and produces a story that is at least as much fiction as fact, its broad contours are accurate. Kamata Sannosuke played an outsized role in removing the natural impediments that kept the village in destitution and managing the new productive capacity unleashed by their removal. To accomplish these ends, he played a role as middleman, negotiating between rich and poor, between the national government and the local community, between the old Edo order and the new age of Meiji, and between the instability of premodernity and the glowing promise of the modern.

Kamata Sannosuke was in many ways a singular individual, but others in Senboku and in villages across the country were taking on similar roles as intermediaries and shaping the character of agricultural modernity in Japan. They were a diverse group. Some, in both their actions and their words, evinced a humanitarian interest in their villages not entirely different from the Kamata of later collective memory. Far more appeared to be motivated to one degree or another by bald self-interest, often in opposition to the interests of their fellow villagers. Generous or selfish, though, all played important roles in determining the course taken by farming and farming villages in response to the new realities of modernity.

It is tempting to understand the differences between the various *gōnō,* rising landlords, and local reformers as reflecting individual idiosyncrasies, but contextual factors were responsible for placing individuals in the positions from which their personal inclinations could take on greater significance. Changes to the nature of governance, economic developments, and the evolution of society moved various figures to the forefront of village society and agricultural improvement at one time, only to force them aside in favor of others at another. The prevailing circumstances determined what things were perceived as needed and who was perceiving them as such, who could take action to address these needs and what actions they could take, and how advantage and disadvantage would be portioned out among the different parties concerned with agriculture.

Would-be *meibōka,* or those whom others had pegged for the role, had their positions defined at a nexus of needs and in a spectrum of expectations and hopes. The lack of government interest in committing public resources to agriculture in the early Meiji period and the paucity of funds available for the purpose when administrative thought began to change in late Meiji created an empty space where the engine powering agricultural development should have been. The simple fact that someone was needed to fill this space and help to usher agriculture to the greater production and profitability promised and demanded by the new age was as apparent to farmers scratching out a living on marginal Tōhoku lands as it was to bureaucrats chasing the dream of joining the ranks of the rich and powerful nations of Europe and America. The efforts to adopt the various technologies, mechanical and organizational, of these countries could amount to nothing without similar developments enabling agriculture to provide a basis in the provision of food and the sustenance of farming villages with their overwhelming share of the national population.

But the exact nature of what was needed from and for agriculture differed according to the position of the person assessing its character. The perception that increasing production was of critical importance was nearly universal, but how best to accomplish this increase, for what purposes it was pursued, and what effects its accomplishment promised to produce all varied according to the position of the person to whom the questions were posed. Higher agricultural production was connected to the differing—and sometimes mutually exclusive—goals of increasing the food supply, building a base for tax revenue, bringing prosperity to villages, enriching individuals, maintaining order in rural regions, and relieving the workload and the uncertainty of the lives of those engaged in farming. In agricultural villages, as in other parts of Meiji society, social and economic position were connected to vastly different answers to the questions of what the abstractions of modernization, modernity, and improvement meant in reality.

The different ends that the various parties involved in agriculture attached to its improvement also connected directly with a varying set of means envisioned to achieve it. Agricultural planners in the capital sought to locate and exploit sources of detailed local knowledge and to identify and activate triggers that would mobilize the reserves of economic resources and manpower that they believed lay unused in farming villages. For villagers, both those with economic resources and those without, the path to agricultural development lay in prying open the doors to government funding by means of the family and other connections that elite members of village society enjoyed with influential figures in the capital. The new landlords that appeared at the end of the nineteenth century felt that legal force applied downward at tenant farmers and an opening of the official coffers above would enable them to maximize production and profits, while keeping their costs in achieving these minimal. And idealistic bureaucrats believed that a widespread program of leading by example would enable moral elites across the country to mobilize their social capital in service of the modernization of agriculture. Different actors and observers at different points in time mixed and matched the elements of these methodologies into new combinations, but all featured knowledge and/or resources—be they local and/or central—and figures who could bridge the gap between villages and the capital and open the reserves held in one or both for the improvement of farming.

The question of who these figures would be was central to both the problems of why and how. It was in answer to this question that Yamagata Aritomo originally identified "figures possessing *meibō*" as the appropriate agents and built his conception of local order around them. Alongside the amorphous qualities of "notability" cited in this description, these figures had a clear set of further core attributes that were remarkable in their consistency over the years and decades that followed. An interest in farming and skills developed through direct experience were essential in enabling them to identify what was possible and what was needed to maximize agricultural production. Personal wealth was required to put into practice the improvement plans that came from this expertise. Influence was also important, in the forms both of local notability that would enable the mobilization of local residents dreamed of by cost-conscious bureaucrats, and of connections to central elites, which local farmers hoped would bring in government funding.

As for who in the villages could be found with this set of attributes, the thoughts of early Meiji government leaders and villagers alike turned to figures who had emerged as agricultural leaders and innovators in the decades that preceded the Restoration. It was imagined that the village elites who served as the local nodes in the networks established by these farming pioneers—or whatever analogues to these appeared in the new age—would continue their work, using their positions to solicit understanding from higher authorities on behalf of their villages and organizing local resources to solve problems. The earliest farmers to step up and promote agricultural development autonomously seemed to follow these expectations. The *rōnō* of the 1870s and 1880s offered up practical techniques to improve farming production in ways similar to Edo-period reformers, which some of them had been before the Restoration. In response to their calls, local farmers sought out their methods and introduced them to their villages, forming the networks that became the foundation for the earliest developments in the agricultural association movement.

While these aspects of *rōnō*-centered activities met with the expectations held by planners and villagers, wide-ranging and deeply transformative changes to the context in which they operated prevented the simple continuation of Edo-era improvement efforts. The signs of this appeared first in the government's response to the growing fame of *rōnō* in the 1880s. Bureaucrats initially made aggressive attempts to discredit the incremental improvements on existing cultivation techniques that *rōnō* advocated in favor of the revolutionary, but ultimately impractical, move to the crops and agricultural methods of the advanced countries of Europe and America. But when *gōnō* techniques were proven more effective and government policy changed course to follow their lead, central authorities adopted a different approach. Officials worked quickly to coopt prominent *rōnō*, employing them on planning boards and dispatching them as proselytizers of the new age of agriculture, and moved to shape the development of the proto-*nōkai* that had emerged alongside them into forms that the government could influence or direct.

Economic shocks set off seismic changes to village society from the 1880s and, together with the passing of the last of those who had reached maturity before the Restoration, marked a transformative moment in the nature of local agricultural leadership. The devastation wrought by the cumulative effects of the Matsukata Deflation and the economic turbulence that followed it erased the hopes of the first generation of landowning farmers in places like northern Miyagi, consigning the greater part of villagers to tenancy and debt and wiping out the fortunes of established and nascent elites alike. New landlords, agile enough to both survive and prosper during the period of economic distress, rose to economic prominence, but they remained at arm's length from the exalted social positions and local administrative offices monopolized by families whose names survived even when their wealth did not. With the various characteristics and capabilities required by the agricultural leaders that officials and villagers envisioned thus scattered among different strata of village society, the future course of farming and its development became unclear.

The older class of leading villagers no longer had the economic resources necessary to lead in farming improvement and innovation, while the newly risen landlords appeared to lack both the influence and the interest required.

The situation changed at the turn of the twentieth century, when a decade of new landlord movement into village administrative positions and a restructuring of *nōkai* combined with an intensified interest from a government enjoying a financial windfall from the resolution of the Sino-Japanese War in supporting agriculture. Landlords leveraged their positions in local governments, district assemblies, and agricultural associations to attract the attention of newly receptive officials and free up funding for agriculture. They also sought legislation that would force tenants and other farmers to take up improved production techniques that would stabilize and increase farming yields. As important to landlords as the potential profits offered by these increases was ensuring that the additional costs in fertilizer, seeds, and labor that they demanded fall to someone else. The question had not been a lack of means, rather landlords had held back from participating in improvement until they could ensure that they would not have to pay for it.

The confluence of official interest, legal force, and landlord activity propelled a decade's worth of development in farming. New government support prodded landlords to take up the long-hoped-for project of consolidating scattered farmplots into forms suitable for rationalized planting and animal ploughing. In Senboku, this allowed for the cultivation of new varieties of rice that had been engineered to thrive in the challenging climatic conditions of Tōhoku. The employment of legal and coercive force to compel farmers to take up the farming techniques required by these new crops, which demanded extra labor for planting and increased costs in cash for chemical fertilizers, was decisive in ensuring their successful systematic institution. In the so-called saber system of state agricultural management, as well as in the introduction of government-overseen rice quality inspections, landlords outsourced the enforcement of their (frequently revised) contracts with tenants to the government and secured a monopoly over the higher profits generated by the increased production of higher quality crops.

Improved crops and techniques in rice farming thus took hold and began to produce results in the first decade of the twentieth century. Beyond the consolidation of land, the limited availability of new farmlands that could be opened in conjunction with it, and the addition of coercive economic power to the legal sanctions imposed by the government in forcing tenant farmers to adopt improved cultivation practices, there was little more that the scattered and deeply self-interested landlords of Senboku could or would do to push for further agricultural development. The barriers to continuing growth lay in lands submerged under wetlands or reservoirs, unstable or insufficient water supplies, and unruly rivers whose flooding prevented even the first stages of improvement in areas like the lower Kitakami River region. The work necessary to overcome these was only possible through projects demanding a firm and consistent dedication of significant public funds.

The government's decision to make the commitment to directly support the work needed to promote further development coincided with reaching the limits of its patience with the social consequences of landlord-led improvement. The goal of producing peaceful, apolitical villages had been stitched into planning for local government from its beginnings in mid-Meiji. The costs of the major wars before and after 1900, both in taxes and blood, pushed this goal to the forefront of official planning just as the baneful social outcomes of the landlord brand of improvement were becoming undeniable. Revisions of the various laws concerning agriculture that had given legal force to landlord-led improvement followed one after another at the end of the first decade of the century. As tensions boiled over into open landlord-tenant conflict in Senboku, the national government exercised central control over *nōkai, kōchi seiri* groups, and other forms of agricultural organization. At the same time, they launched a search for new village leaders that highlighted the fact that personal wealth was no longer a prerequisite for the positions. This marked the beginning of over three decades of half-hearted calls for new village leadership tied to an interminable series of social improvement campaigns.

Thus, the initial period of decentralized agricultural development under a changing cast of characters who all overlapped in one way or another the initial conception of *meibōka* came to an end. Farming continued to make advances in the years that followed, but the official presence in agriculture became permanent. The new circumstances greatly lessened the potential, or even the possibility, of informal intermediaries as agents to shape the evolution of farming. Government planners now had official structures enabling them to reach into villages, while villagers were left with electoral politics, legal gambits, and collective action as their means of reaching higher authorities.

The activities of Kamata, the landlords of Nangō, and the other figures who served as middlemen came about because of a particular type of need that was unique to agriculture and agricultural villages in the Meiji period. The dedication of the bulk of government resources to the projects of industrialization and military development in early Meiji at the same time greater demands were being placed on farming and farming villages created an extended liminal moment for agriculture. Not yet included in the proactive plans of government to transform society and enter the modern age, farming was nonetheless relied upon to serve its standard functions of producing food and providing a means of living for the rural-dwelling majority, as well as its new role as the source of tax revenue funding the government and its modernization project. These were the conditions that created the need for middlemen between village and capital and then made possible the decades of *meibōka*-led agricultural development.

The devolution of agricultural leadership to *meibōka* eventually resulted in the rationalization of production and increases in yields that Meiji authorities had hoped for, but they came at a cost. The consolidation of village power in the hands of landlords, the impoverishment and marginalization of tenant farmers, and the cementing of a deep economic inequality in farming villages—the conditions for which American Occupation analysts later reserved their harshest scorn—were the other chief product of the *meibōka* liminal moment. When official oversight of agriculture ended that moment at the beginning of the twentieth century, it could not undo the social order that landlord-led agricultural development had baked into farming villages across the country. With official support for agriculture and large-scale public works projects promising to carry agricultural development forward, landlords were freed to concentrate on the consolidation of their gains, the maximization of their profits, and the securing of their advantage. Disinterest in the further promotion of agricultural development could even become opposition to it, as in Nangō where landlords actively prevented the formation of an effective producers' union.

This, then, demonstrated the paradox inherent in prewar agricultural development. The *meibōka*-led push for farming improvement in the extended liminality of the Meiji period accomplished the goals of expanded production and laid the foundation for future agricultural improvement. The agricultural village order that it also produced, however, transformed social and economic conditions in villages and acted as a brake on further development. What had made agricultural development possible created the conditions that imposed upper limits on its scope. The modernity ushered in by its middlemen was abbreviated.

In the end, it would take military defeat, occupation, and a comprehensive land reform to uproot the landlord-controlled village order and open the path to future development for agriculture and farming villages. These processes also brought about the ruin of landlords as a class.

The Occupation Land Reform, passed in a series of laws in November 1946, forced the sale of all lands owned by non-resident landlords and all lands beyond what a landowning family could cultivate themselves for their resident cousins and made provisions for the sale of these excess lands to landless tenants on very favorable terms. The Saitō Corporation, the largest landowner in Miyagi, predictably suffered catastrophic losses, but the landlords of Nangō, Wakuya, and the other villages of Senboku fared no better. By the end of 1948, 87 percent of farmland nationally was cultivated by those who owned it, compared to 46 percent in 1940, and the remainder was rented from cultivating landlords owning no more than 1 *chō* beyond what they farmed themselves.[1]

Although no longer a landlord, Kamata Sannosuke's fate was also decided in November of 1946. The positions he held in the Imperial Rule Assistance Association and other wartime groups exposed him to the Purge of Public Officials instituted at that time and removed him from the office of mayor that he had held for thirty-eight years. He spent the last four years of his life as a simple resident in a village that was changing rapidly around him. He died in 1950, the same year that Kashimadai was redesignated as a town (*machi/chō*). His fame remained undiminished, however, and alongside the various biographies published postwar, his statue also became a fixture of public school field trips in Miyagi. The irony of his life was like a funhouse reflection of the paradox of *meibōka* development. Where landlord stewardship over agricultural development ultimately limited its future potential, Kamata's self-sequestering in the mayor's office of Kashimadai proved the means of achieving the fame and significance that he believed he was sacrificing in accepting the position. Like Kamata, the other landlords and *meibōka* also achieved immortality postwar, albeit to a lesser extent. A boom in local history occasioned by sweeping amalgamations of villages and towns in the last decades of the twentieth century spurred the publication of local histories that granted sainthood to Meiji notables now cast as the founding fathers of their communities. As local residents looked back from the prosperity of postwar Japan, they saw the roots of their present circumstances in the middlemen of modernity.

Notes

Introduction

1. Important exceptions to this trend exist that focus upon the experiences of rural areas and the significant roles that they played in the development of modern Japan, including Ann Waswo, *Japanese Landlords: The Decline of a Rural Elite* (Berkeley: University of California Press, 1977); Edward E. Pratt, *Japan's Protoindustrial Elite: The Economic Foundations of the Gōnō,* Harvard East Asian Monographs 179 (Cambridge, MA: Harvard University Asia Center, distributed by Harvard University Press, 1999); Michael Lewis, *Becoming Apart: National Power and Local Politics in Toyama, 1868–1945,* Harvard East Asian Monographs 192 (Cambridge, MA: Harvard University Asia Center, distributed by Harvard University Press, 2000); and Sayaka Chatani, *Nation-Empire: Ideology and Rural Youth Mobilization in Japan and Its Colonies* (Ithaca, NY: Cornell University Press, 2018).

2. For a discussion of the genesis of the idea of "backwardness" in regards to Japanese villages, see "Chapter 4: The Lure of the Modern: Imagining the Temporal Spaces of City and Countryside," in Jason G. Karlin, *Gender and Nation in Meiji Japan: Modernity, Loss, and the Doing of History* (Honolulu: University of Hawai'i Press, 2014).

3. This is even more true of Fukushima, on Miyagi's southern border.

4. The political activities of *meibōka* in local administration and on the regional and national stage has been the subject of research in Japanese and English. Notable works include Yamanaka Einosuke, *Kindai Nihon no chihō seido to meiboka,* Shohan (Tokyo: Kobundo, 1990); Yamanaka Einosuke, *Kindai shisei to toshi meibōka: Ōsakashi o jirei to suru kōsatsu* (Suita: Ōsaka Daigaku Shuppan, 1995); Itō Yukio, "Meibōka chitsujo no kaizō to seinentō: Saitō Takao o meguru Tanba no hitobito," *Nihonshi Kenkyū,* no. 241 (1982): 39–73; Ishikawa Hisao, *Kindai Nihon no meibōka to jichi: meiyoshoku seido no hōshakaishiteki kenkyū* (Tokyo: Bokutakusha, 1987); Ishikawa Hisao, *Nihonteki jichi no tankyū: meibōka jichiron no keifu,* Shohan (Nagoya: Nagoya Daigaku Shuppankai, 1995); Takaku Reinosuke, *Kindai Nihon no chiiki shakai to meibōka,* Potentia sōsho 45 (Tokyo: Kashiwa Shobō, 1997); Ushiki Yukio, *Chihō meibōka no seichō* (Tokyo: Kashiwa Shobō, 2000); Watanabe Takashi, *Kindai ikōki no meiboka to chiiki kokka* (Tokyo: Meicho Shuppan, 2006); Lewis, *Becoming Apart;* and Simon Partner, *The Mayor of Aihara: A Japanese Villager and His Community, 1865–1925* (Berkeley: University of California Press, 2009).

5. For example, Richard Smethurst claims that the northeast was not subject to the same developments as the rest of the country because it was "poorer, less commercial, and probably more widely inhabited by peasants." Richard J. Smethurst, *Agricultural Development and Tenancy Disputes in Japan, 1870–1940* (Princeton, NJ: Princeton University Press, 1986), 41.

6. Roger W. Bowen, *Rebellion and Democracy in Meiji Japan: A Study of Commoners in the Popular Rights Movement* (Berkeley: University of California Press, 1980); William W. Kelly, *Deference and Defiance in Nineteenth-Century Japan* (Princeton, NJ: Princeton University Press, 1985); Kerry Douglas Smith, *A Time of Crisis: Japan, the Great Depression, and Rural Revitalization* (Cambridge, MA: Harvard University Press, 2001).

7. The works of Penelope Francks are a significant exception. See Penelope Francks, *Technology and Agricultural Development in Pre-War Japan* (New Haven, CT: Yale University Press, 1984); Penelope Francks, Johanna Boestel, and Choo Hyop Kim, *Agriculture and Economic Development in East Asia: From Growth to Protectionism in Japan, Korea, and Taiwan* (London; New York: Routledge, 1999); Penelope Francks, *Rural Economic Development in Japan: From the Nineteenth Century to the Pacific War* (London: Routledge, 2006), and others.

Chapter One: Mayor Straw Sandals

1. The words of the telegram are repeated in nearly every work on Kamata and Shinainuma. For example, see Honma Rakukan, *Waraji sonchō Kamata Sannosuke ō: Yokusan no ijin—Shōwa no Sontoku* (Tokyo: Jidaisha, 1942), 135. Neither the telegrams nor the forms on which the messages were written seem to have survived into the present.

2. Kamata's mother's words to her son are also a fixture of his biographies. Examples can be seen in Ko Kamata Sannosuke Ō Shōtokukai, *Kamata Sannosuke ōden* (Kashimadai: Ko Kamata Sannosuke Ō Shōtokukai, 1953), 58; and Koide Kōzō, *Kamata Sannosuke ō: Waraji sonchō no shōgai* (Tokyo: Nihon Jichikensestu Undō Honbu, 1961), 25.

3. Ko Kamata Sannosuke Ō Shōtokukai, 133; Kashimadai Chōshi Hensan Iinkai, *Kashimadai chōshi* (Kashimadai: Kashimadaichō, 1994), 277.

4. Roger F. Hackett, *Yamagata Aritomo in the Rise of Modern Japan, 1838–1922* (Cambridge, MA: Harvard University Press, 1971), 107.

5. Yamagata referred to the need for *chihō no meibō aru mono* in 1888's "Shiseichōsonsei riyū." See Takamura Kōzō, ed., *Shisei chōsonsei* (Kakegawa: Takamura Kōzō, 1888), 61.

6. More properly, the Kamata house was from the rural samurai class known as *gōshi*, a status made possible by Sendai domain's unusual allowance for samurai to reside outside of the castle town. As landlords, the family brought in the not-insubstantial sum of 900 *koku* in rent rice annually. See Ko Kamata Sannosuke Ō Shōtokukai, 1–2; and Kashimadai Chōshi Hensan Iinkai, 283.

7. Ko Kamata Sannosuke Ō Shōtokukai, 5.

8. Koide, 17.

9. Kamata's episode with the Fukuzawa lecture is recorded in most of the materials dealing with his life. For two examples see Ko Kamata Sannosuke Ō Shōtokukai, 12–13; Koide, 15.

10. Although Kashimadai was not brought into existence until 1889, the administrative jurisdiction of the area's *kochō* corresponded roughly to the shape the village, itself an amalgamation of existing villages, would take.

11. Takahashi Kōichirō, "Kindai, Gendai: Gyōzaisei," in Kashimadai chōshi, ed. Kashimadai Chōshi Hensan Iinkai (Kashimadai: Kashimadaichō, 1994), 261–361 (284).

12. Naikaku, "Miyagiken Shidagun Kashimadai sonchō Kamata Sannosuke ranju hōshō kashi no ken," December 17, 1927 (Kōbun zassan: Shōwa ni-nen: dai hachi ken: Naikaku hachi: Naikaku hachi [shōdōkyoku roku]), National Archives of Japan.

13. Kanno Toshimitsu, *Shinainuma kantaku shōshi: Shinainuma o hiraita hitobito no kunan no rekishi* (Sendai: Hōbundō, 1981), 2.

14. The project was not without its setbacks, including the duty-based suicide of the chief engineer and a number of his laborers in an incident whose details have been lost to time. See Koide, 17.

15. Ko Kamata Sannosuke Ō Shōtokukai, 6; Koide, 18.

16. Shinainuma Suigai Yobō Kumiaishi Hensan Iinkai, *Shinainuma suigai yobō kumiaishi* (Sendai: Shinainuma Suigai Yobō Kumiaishi Hensan Iinkai, 1954), 21.

17. Itō Katsuhide, "Shinainuma no kantaku: Meiji senketsu no kaisaku," in *Kashimadai chōshi,* ed. Kashimadai Chōshi Hensan Iinkai (Kashimadai: Kashimadaichō, 1994), 790–805 (790).

18. On van Doorn's career with the Meiji government, see Muramatsu Teijirō, *Kenchiku, doboku.* Oyatoi gaikokujin, 15 (Tokyo: Kajima Shuppankai, 1976), 152–167.

19. Kanno, 65.

20. Nōrinshō Nōmukyoku, *Kaikonchi ijū keiei jirei* (Tokyo: Nōrinshō Nōmukyoku, 1923), 466.

21. Koide, 7–8.

22. Ko Kamata Sannosuke Ō Shōtokukai, 41.

23. Ko Kamata Sannosuke Ō Shōtokukai, 20.

24. Itō Katsuhide, 794.

25. Koide, 38.

26. Ko Kamata Sannosuke Ō Shōtokukai, 150.

27. Ko Kamata Sannosuke Ō Shōtokukai, 151.

28. Ko Kamata Sannosuke Ō Shōtokukai, 151.

29. Kanno, 71–72.

30. David Anson Titus, *Palace and Politics in Prewar Japan* (New York: Columbia University Press, 1974), 69.

31. Ishikawa Teruo, "Shinainuma no kantaku: kaikon no junbi ga susumerareru," in *Kashimadai chōshi,* ed. Kashimadai Chōshi Hensan Iinkai (Kashimadai: Kashimadaichō, 1994), 811–815 (801).

32. Kanno, 70.

33. A particularly confused biographer of Kamata records him as passing through scenes of devastation resulting from Mexico's recent revolution, which would not occur until nearly a decade later. See Koide, 22.

34. On the 1897 attempted colony, see Jerry Garcia, *Looking Like the Enemy: Japanese Mexicans, the Mexican State, and US Hegemony, 1897–1945* (Tucson: University of Arizona Press, 2014), 14–25; Selfa Chew, *Uprooting Community: Japanese Mexicans, World War II, and the U.S.-Mexico Borderlands* (Tucson: University of Arizona Press, 2015), 33–34; and Ko Kamata Sannosuke Ō Shōtokukai, 22 (which places the colony in 1877).

35. Kamata Sannosuke, *Mekishiko shokumin annai* (Tokyo: Seikō Zasshisha, 1908), 9–42.

36. Ko Kamata Sannosuke Ō Shōtokukai, 47.

37. Ko Kamata Sannosuke Ō Shōtokukai, 49.

38. Ishikawa, 804.

39. Ishikawa, 804.

40. Kanno, 74.

41. Kanno, 76.

42. Ishikawa, 811.

43. Understood this way, Kamata appears to match both the sociological categories of broker and coordinator as described by Hillmann Henning. See Henning, "Localism and the Limits of Political Brokerage: Evidence from Revolutionary Vermont," *American Journal of Sociology* 114, no. 2 (2008): 287–331 (314).

44. Samuel Smiles, *Self-Help: With Illustrations of Character and Conduct* (London: Ward, Lock, 1859).

45. As it was, the stopping of the imperial train in mid-journey was unprecedented and unrepeated. See Kanno, 73.

46. Penelope Francks alludes to this necessity in describing the stalling of the spread of advanced farming techniques from the 1910s to the 1920s, when newly accomplished land improvements made them effective in more areas. See Francks, "Rice for the Masses: Food Policy and the Adoption of Imperial Self-Sufficiency in Early Twentieth-Century Japan," *Japan Forum* 15, no. 1 (2003): 125–146 (136), https://doi.org/10.1080/0955580032000077766.

Chapter Two: The World Turned Upside Down

1. For the story of Suzuki and the sluice locks, see Sasaki Toshi, *Nangō suirishi* (Nangō: Nangōchō, 1972), 89; Yamotochō, *Yamoto chōshi,* vol. 3 (Yamoto: Yamotochō, 1976), 220; and Nangōchō, *Nangō chōshi,* vol. 1 (Nangō: Nangōchō, 1980), 709.

2. Entō is a combination of alternative readings of the first character from each of the two districts, with Tōda's 遠 (*en*) followed by Monō's 桃 (*tō*). The order of the two characters, while established at the time in newspapers and the prefectural records of the conflict, was still controversial enough that local historians from Monō continued to refer to it as the Tōen Incident well into the postwar period.

3. Baba Akira, *Suiri jigyō no tenkai to jinushisei,* Kindai tochi seidoshi kenkyū sōsho 7 (Tokyo: Ochanomizu Shobō, 1965), 105.

4. Maki Takayasu, *Nihon suiri shisetsu no kenkyū* (Tokyo: Doboku Zasshisha, 1958), 347. Planners predicted that the new farmland would yield an additional 60,000 *koku* of production for the domain; see Kumagai Kaneo, "Kantaku," in *Doboku,* Miyagi kenshi 8 (Sendai: Miyagi Kenshi Kankōkai, 1960), 219.

5. Nangōchō, 1:700; Sasaki Toshi, 79.

6. Obata Atsushi, "Meiji chūki ni okeru suiri o chūshin to shita nōmin funsō no ichirei: Iwayuru Entō Jiken ni tsuite," *Chiiki shakai kenkyū,* no. 5 (1953): 45.

7. Miyagiken, "Tōda Monō Oshika sangun funsō chōtei tenmatsusho" (Sendai: Miyagiken, 1894).

8. Wakuyachō, *Wakuya chōshi,* vol. 2 (Wakuya: Wakuyachō, 1968), 208.

9. The original proposal split the costs evenly between the two districts. See Yamotochō, 3:208.

10. Yamotochō, 3:209.

11. Nangōchō, 1:703; Yamotochō, 3:210.

12. Nangōchō, 1:704.

13. Kanan Chōshi Hensan Iinkai, ed., *Kanan chōshi,* vol. 1 (Kanan: Kananchō, 1967), 402.

14. Sasaki Toshi, 78.

15. Yamotochō, 3:210; Kanan Chōshi Hensan Iinkai, 1:401.

16. "Administrative village" (*gyōseison*) is often used to describe the villages created under the new system of local government, in contrast to the "natural villages" (*shizenson*), which were formed in what were widely understood as more organic processes and which were absorbed into the new villages. Rejecting the normative assumptions inherent in this latter term (originally formulated as a criticism of the new administrative boundaries), I favor the use of the term "hamlet" to refer to the pre–Three New Laws villages for the purposes of this study.

17. On the various functions served by irrigation associations in the early Meiji period, see Neil L. Waters, *Japan's Local Pragmatists: The Transition from Bakumatsu to Meiji in the Kawasaki Region,* Harvard East Asian Monographs 105 (Cambridge, MA: Council on East Asian Studies, Harvard University, 1983).

18. Nōgyō Suiri Mondai Kenkyūkai, *Nōgyō suiri chitsujo no kenkyū*, 2nd ed. (Tokyo: Ochanomizu Shobō, 1977), 30.

19. Baba, *Suiri jigyō no tenkai to jinushisei*, 210.

20. The full name of the organization was the Meiji Sluice Kuratsubo Canal Aoki River Tsutsunoyama Siphon Flood Control Association (Meiji Suimon Kuratsubo Senketsu Aokigawa Tsutsunoyama Toi ni Kakaru Suigai Yobō Kumiai), but the overwhelming importance of the Meiji Sluice and Lake Nabire to the group has led most Japanese sources dealing with it to use the shortened name.

21. Both the membership and leadership of the MSSYK reflected the greater importance of the group to Tōda. Nangō and Wakuya contributed 986 and 981 members, respectively, while Ono and Fukaya offered up only 408 and 215. Tōda accordingly dominated the leadership council, with Nangō holding six seats and Wakuya holding four, while Ono and Fukaya held only a single seat each. See Nangōchō, 1:703.

22. This was the Chitsuryūsha, an organization associated with the Freedom and Popular Rights Movement that cemented its reputation in the village by successfully facing off against the smaller district head (*kochō*) over the funding of the local elementary school. See Sugano Shunsaku, "Meiji kōhanki no jinushiteki tochi shoyū no kakudai to sonsei shihai," in *Kindai Nihon no jinushi to nōmin: suitō tansaku nōgyō no keizaiteki kenkyū, Nangō-mura*, ed. Sunaga Shigemitsu (Tōkyō: Ochanomizu Shobō, 1966), 100; and Abiko Rin, *Miyagiken no hyakunen*, Kenmin 100-nenshi 4 (Tokyo: Yamakawa Shuppansha, 1999), 37–38.

23. Sugano, "Meiji kōhanki no jinushiteki tochi shoyū no kakudai to sonsei shihai," 107–115.

24. Sugano, "Meiji kōhanki no jinushiteki tochi shoyū no kakudai to sonsei shihai," 102.

25. Sugano, "Meiji kōhanki no jinushiteki tochi shoyū no kakudai to sonsei shihai," 115.

26. Sugano Shunsaku, "Meiji zenhanki ni okeru jinushi no seisei to sonraku kōzō," in *Kindai Nihon no jinushi to nōmin: suitō tansaku nōgyō no keizaiteki kenkyū, Nangō-mura*, ed. Sunaga Shigemitsu (Tokyo: Ochanomizu Shobō, 1966), 90. This is the same Kubo whose decline is related above. Revealingly, the spurious legal assault at the turn of the century that eradicated the last of the Kubo house's prestige in Nangō was led by none other than Suzuki Naoji, who was then in the process of taking control of the village offices in Nangō.

27. Nagasawa Katsuo, *Noda Shin'ichi ōden* (Sendai: Noda Ken'ichi Okina Kōseki Kenshōkai, 1962), 15.

28. Sugano, "Meiji kōhanki no jinushiteki tochi shoyū no kakudai to sonsei shihai," 101–102.

29. Both the tone of this justification as related in a fawning biography of Saiji's son and the fact that his father Namiji forewent any public service in favor of a retirement spent drinking and commissioning statues of himself suggest that the Noda family may have faced criticism concerning a lack of public spirit. See Nagasawa, 13–15.

30. The right to appropriate local taxes to cover operating expenses was one that government regulations in earlier years had jealously guarded. See Nōgyō Suiri Mondai Kenkyūkai, 28.

31. Nōgyō Suiri Mondai Kenkyūkai, 25–27.

32. Patricia Sippel, "Chisui: Creating a Sacred Domain in Early Modern and Modern Japan," in *Public Spheres, Private Lives in Modern Japan, 1600–1950: Essays in Honor of Albert M. Craig*, ed. Gail Lee Bernstein, Andrew Gordon, and Kate Wildman Nakai (Cambridge, MA: Harvard University Asia Center, 2005), 159. For the development of a contrasting distrust of technological interaction with nature and awareness of its destructive potential beginning in the 1890s, see Robert Stolz, *Bad Water: Nature, Pollution, and Politics in Japan, 1870–1950* (London: Duke University Press, 2014).

33. Abe Kumaji, *Azumi-ō shōden* (Wakuya: Yamamoto Kappanjo, 1940), 50. Van Doorn had given up his position and returned to Europe in 1880. Muramatsu Teijirō, *Kenchiku, doboku,* Oyatoi gaikokujin 15 (Tokyo: Kajima shuppankai, 1976), 165.

34. Nōgyō Suiri Mondai Kenkyūkai, 125.

35. Sippel, 173.

36. Sippel, 176.

37. Nōgyō Suiri Mondai Kenkyūkai, 6.

38. Sippel, 176.

39. Sippel, 177. In 1881, newly appointed Finance Minister Matsukata Masayoshi worked behind the scenes to sabotage the efforts of the Home Ministry to install funding for public works projects, a cause he had championed earlier as Home Minister. See Mikuriya Takashi, *Meiji kokka keisei to chihō keiei: 1881–1890 nen* (Tokyo: Tōkyō daigaku shuppankai, 1980), 30–31.

40. Sippel, 178.

41. Nōgyō Suiri Mondai Kenkyūkai, 8.

42. Sanriku Kahoku Shinpōsha, *Kitakamigawa monogatari* (Ishinomaki: Sanriku Kahoku Shinpōsha, 1989), 25.

43. The other two were in Toyama in 1868 and Shizuoka in 1885. See Maki, 342.

44. Yamotochō, 3:217.

45. Yamotochō, 3:217.

46. Nangōchō, 1:704.

47. Sasaki Toshi, 84. Both Imagorō and Ryōkichi had married into and taken the surname of Fukaya's wealthy Endō family, making them adoptive brothers of a sort.

48. Kären Wigen, "Constructing Shinano: The Invention of a Neo-Traditional Region," in *Mirror of Modernity: Invented Traditions of Modern Japan,* ed. Stephen Vlastos, Twentieth-Century Japan 9 (Berkeley: University of California Press, 1998), 231.

49. Wigen, 231. It should be noted that Wigen's larger point concerns the ways in which the "benign" regionalism short-circuited conflicts between the prefectures and the central government, while allowing for the continuation of conflicts between local areas.

50. Sasaki Toshi, 85; Nangōchō, 1:705.

51. Saitō Jintarō and Endō Ryōkichi held official positions as a village clerk and a village educator, respectively. See Sasa Hisashi, "Danseihen," in *Jinbutsushi,* Miyagi kenshi 29 (Sendai: Miyagi Kenshi Kankōkai, 1986), 212–214.

52. Those arrested included Endō and Saitō, on the Monō side, and Kusakari Shinmei and Hiratsuka Kinsaku, Tōda farmers without significant positions in their village administrations. See "Entō jiken no kōhan iyoiyo kaitei," *Ōu nichinichi shinbun,* June 18, 1893.

53. Yamotochō, 3:219.

54. In answer to the Tōda dredging of the long-unused Sangenyashiki drainage channel to the north of Lake Nabire, the HOFSK had one of its members purchase land adjacent to the channel and charge them with trespassing. Endō and Saitō were arrested soon afterward for leading Monō farmers past a police cordon to refill the channel. See Kanan Chōshi Hensan Iinkai, 1:403.

55. *Nangō suirishi* reports that the farmers acted spontaneously and without a leader (*dare no shiki to ui koto naku*); however, most other sources agree that Mayor Noda headed up the work at this time and the charges filed in relation to it named him as the defendant. See Sasaki Toshi, 88.

56. Baba Akira, "Nangōmura no suiri to chisui o meguru chiiki tairitsu," in *Kindai Nihon no jinushi to nōmin: suitō tansaku nōgyō no keizaiteki kenkyū, Nangō-mura,* ed. Sunaga Shigemitsu (Tokyo: Ochanomizu Shobō, 1966), 151. Significantly, the offense against customary practice was considered a more compelling charge than the fact that the Tōda side had

completely broken the agreement made between the two districts at the time of the construction of the Meiji sluice.

57. Sasaki Toshi, 90; Yamotochō, 3:221.

58. Nangōchō, 1:710.

59. Sasaki Toshi, 90.

60. Sasaki Toshi, 92.

61. Both documents can be found in Miyagiken, "Tōda Monō Oshika sangun funsō chōtei tenmatsusho."

62. *Kanan chōshi* is an example of a source that credits the mediators and their reputations with breaking the deadlock between the districts. See Kanan Chōshi Hensan Iinkai, 1:404.

63. Miyagiken, "Tōda Monō Oshika sangun funsō chōtei tenmatsusho."

64. Yamotochō, 3:221.

65. Sasaki Toshi, 95.

66. At a projected cost of 300,000 yen (a total that would almost certainly have risen during construction), it is doubtful that even the prefecture would have been able to accomplish all that had been outlined in the conciliation agreement. See Nangōchō, 1:714.

67. Miyagiken, "Tōda Monō Oshika sangun funsō chōtei tenmatsusho."

68. Kumagai, 222.

Chapter Three: A Harvest of Knowledge and Ambition

1. Information on the meeting here is drawn from Nishimura Eijūrō, *Zenkoku Nōjikaishi* (Tokyo: n.p., 1911), http://dl.ndl.go.jp/info:ndljp/pid/802339.

2. Non-affiliated *yūshisha* were also present at the 1897 meeting, but in small numbers and they were both segregated from the official *nōkai* representatives and had their participation strictly limited. See Nishimura Eijūrō, 62–63.

3. Yasuda Ken, "Meijiki ni okeru kanfu no inasaku shidō," in *Nihon nōgyō hattatsushi: Meiji ikō ni okeru*, vol. 5 (Tokyo: Chūō Kōronsha, 1978), 24.

4. On the "technologists" who fueled developments in farming technology in early modern Japan, see Thomas C. Smith, "Ōkura Nagatsune and the Technologists," in *Native Sources of Japanese Industrialization, 1750–1920*, by Thomas C. Smith (Berkeley: University of California Press, 1988), 173–198.

5. Masakatsu Akino and Yujiro Hayami, "Sources of Agricultural Growth in Japan, 1880–1965," *Quarterly Journal of Economics* 88, no. 3 (1974): 477–478.

6. Historians of Meiji Japan have long seen the legal changes of the 1890s as signaling an important shift in the national government's involvement in villages, but there is no clear consensus on their meaning. Japanese scholars in the 1960s and 1970s tended to see them as an attempt to strengthen government authority in rural areas in a betrayal of the stated ideals of local self-government (*chihō jichi*). See Sasaki Yutaka, "Chihō kairyō undō to chōsonze chōsa," in *Chihō kairyō undōshi shiryō shūsei*, vol. 1 (Tokyo: Kashiwa Shobō, 1986). In the 1980s, Sasaki Yutaka and others rejected this view, finding evidence of the substantial agency possessed by villagers in the influence that the village plans (*chōsonze*) they drafted in early 1890s exerted on the laws enacted at the decade's end. See Sasaki Yutaka, 3–4. Both views share the problem of seeing village populations as undifferentiated wholes that either pushed through changes that served their shared interests or fell victim collectively to the expansion of government authority. The different effects that the legal changes had on different strata of village society fade into obscurity and landlords, smallholders, and tenant farmers are subsumed under the categories of farmer or villager.

7. Penelope Francks, *Rural Economic Development in Japan: From the Nineteenth Century to the Pacific War* (London: Routledge, 2006), 4–5.

8. The land tax still accounted for over 80 percent of all taxes collected as late as 1885. See Kozaburo Kato, "The Agrarian Origins of Modern Japan," in *Agriculture in the Modernization of Japan, 1850–2000,* ed. Shuzo Teruoka, trans. Sarah Ham Akamine (New Delhi: Manohar, 2008), 49.

9. Ogura Sōichi, "Meiji zenki nōsei no dōkō to nōkai no seiritsu," in *Nihon nōgyō hattatsushi: Meiji ikō ni okeru,* vol. 3 (Tokyo: Chūō Kōronsha, 1978), 241.

10. Harry D. Harootunian, "The Economic Rehabilitation of the Samurai in the Early Meiji Period," *The Journal of Asian Studies* 19, no. 4 (1960): 433–444.

11. The Miyagi government intended for its factory to serve as another relief measure for local samurai. See Itō Seijirō and Konishi Rihee, *Sendai mukashigatari Den Tanuki-ō yawa* (Sendai: Konishi Rihee, 1925), 395–409. The invitation of the key players in the Miyagi enterprise to participate in an officially organized discussion of matters concerning mechanized reeling in 1885 further attests to the depth of government interest in the industry's development. See Kenshi Orimono Tōshikki Kyōshūkai, ed., *Menshi shūdankai kiji* (Tokyo: Yūrindō, 1885).

12. Sidney Devere Brown, "Ōkubo Toshimichi: His Political and Economic Policies in Early Meiji Japan," *The Journal of Asian Studies* 21, no. 2 (1962): 195.

13. Ogawa Makoto, "Chisui, suiri, tochi kairyō no taikeiteki seibi," in *Nihon nōgyō hattatsushi: Meiji ikō ni okeru,* vol. 4 (Tokyo: Chūō Kōronsha, 1978), 198.

14. Ogura, "Meiji zenki nōsei no dōkō to nōkai no seiritsu," 237–241.

15. Ogura, "Meiji zenki nōsei no dōkō to nōkai no seiritsu," 310.

16. Murakami Tetsuichi, "Meiji-Taishō ni okeru Miyagiken nōgyō no shinten," in *Sangyō 1,* Miyagi kenshi 9 (Sendai: Miyagi Kenshi Kankōkai, 1968), 104; Ogura, "Meiji zenki nōsei no dōkō to nōkai no seiritsu," 239.

17. Tamari Kizō, "Nōkai konjakudan (shōzen)," *Dai Nihon Nōkaihō,* no. 214 (1899): 1.

18. Takahashi Tansui, *Kashokuden: Nōkai godai ijin* (Tokyo: Rakuyōdō, 1917), 20–23, http://kindai.ndl.go.jp/info:ndljp/pid/948504.

19. Takahashi Tansui, 27.

20. Takahashi Tansui, 25.

21. See Nōshōmushō Nōmukyoku, *Fuken rōnō meibo* (Tokyo: Nōshōmushō Nōmukyoku, 1882), http://kindai.ndl.go.jp/info:ndljp/pid/900159; and Nōshōmushō Nōmukyoku, *Kaku chihō rōnōka oyobi shubyōko meibo* (Tokyo: Nōmukyoku Hōkokuka, 1882), http://kindai.ndl.go.jp/info:ndljp/pid/780373.

22. See Ishikawaken and Fukushimaken, *Ishikawaken Hayashi Enri beisaku kairyō seisekihyō; Fukushimaken shikenden tsubogari seiseki* (Utsunomiya: Tochigiken Naimubu, 1891), http://kindai.ndl.go.jp/info:ndljp/pid/838010. Hayashi's work was also subject to intense criticism from supporters of *rōnō,* whose doubts stemmed from his late entry into farming. See Egami Toshio, "Hayashi Enri to kannōsha," in *Nihon nōgyō hattatsushi: Meiji ikō ni okeru,* vol. 2 (Tokyo: Chūō Kōronsha, 1978), 602.

23. *Meiji hōshōroku,* vol. 1 (Osaka: Naniwa Shoin, 1897), 275–277, http://kindai.ndl.go.jp/info:ndljp/pid/778838.

24. Ogura, "Meiji zenki nōsei no dōkō to nōkai no seiritsu," 328.

25. Yasuda Ken, "Nakamura Naozō no nōji kairyō jiseki," in *Nihon nōgyō hattatsushi: Meiji ikō ni okeru,* vol. 2 (Tokyo: Chūō Kōronsha, 1978), 713–714.

26. Takahashi Tansui, 32–35.

27. Egami, 615–616.

28. Ogura, "Meiji zenki nōsei no dōkō to nōkai no seiritsu," 310.

29. Takahashi Tansui, 107; Aichiken Nōkai, *Zenkoku tokunōka retsuden* (Nagoya: Aichiken Nōkai, 1910), 263, http://kindai.ndl.go.jp/info:ndljp/pid/778253.

30. Hida Namishige, "Hida Roichi shōden," *Ōitaken chihōshi,* no. 50 (1968): 30; *Ōitaken jinshiroku* (Ōita: Ōitaken Jinshiroku Hakkōjo, 1914), 24, http://kindai.ndl.go.jp/info:ndljp/pid/908965.

31. Both Agriculture and Commerce Ministry agricultural chief Sakō Tsuneaki and influential researcher Yokoi Tokiyoshi were noted critics of Hayashi Enri and his stripped-down method of rice seed selection, despite the evidence of its value from scientific tests conducted in Ishikawa, Fukushima, and elsewhere. See Takahashi Tansui, 60.

32. Nōrinshō Nōmukyoku, ed., "Nōsei keikaku zuhyō kaidoku," in *Meiji zenki kannō jiseki shūroku*, vol. 2 (Tokyo: Dai Nihon Nōkai, 1939), 1720. See also Ogura, "Meiji zenki nōsei no dōkō to nōkai no seiritsu," 244.

33. Ichirou Inukai and Arlon R. Tussing, "'Kōgyō Iken': Japan's Ten Year Plan, 1884," *Economic Development and Cultural Change* 16, no. 1 (October 1, 1967): 54, https://doi.org/10.2307/1152507.

34. Ariizumi Sadao, "Kōgyō iken no seiritsu," *Shigaku zasshi* 78, no. 10 (1969): 1–30; Inukai and Tussing; Sydney Crawcour, "Kōgyō Iken: Maeda Masana and His View of Meiji Economic Development," *Journal of Japanese Studies* 23, no. 1 (January 1, 1997): 69–104, https://doi.org/10.2307/133124. The original 1884 thirty-volume series is available online at the National Archives of Japan Digital Archive, http://www.digital.archives.go.jp/index_e.html.

35. The critique of Matsukata's financial policies was more forceful in the initial, uncirculated version of the work, appearing in only a greatly watered-down form in the final version. See Ariizumi Sadao; and Crawcour. Steven Ericson notes, however, that the accusations by Maeda and his subsequent biographers that Matsukata was single-minded in his pursuit of industrial development were overblown, and that the minister in fact displayed flexibility and pragmatism in his attempts to manage economic recovery. See Steven J. Ericson, "The 'Matsukata Deflation' Reconsidered: Financial Stabilization and Japanese Exports in a Global Depression, 1881–1885," *Journal of Japanese Studies* 40, no. 1 (2014): 2.

36. Crawcour, 93.

37. Inukai and Tussing, 55.

38. Crawcour, 96.

39. Iwakura Tomomi, *Iwakura-kō jikki*, vol. 3 (Tokyo: Iwakura-kō Kyūseki Hozonkai, 1927), 934–935.

40. Crawcour, 81.

41. See Ariizumi; and Crawcour.

42. Nishimura Kōichi, *Meiji nōsei to nōkai: Nōkai no hassei kara Teikoku Nōkai no seiritsu made*, Shiryō 3 (N.p.: Nihon Nōgyō Kenkyūjō, 1951), 1; Murakami, 102.

43. Ogura, "Meiji zenki nōsei no dōkō to nōkai no seiritsu," 264.

44. Tōhashi Shiritsu Shōgyō Gakkō, *Kaikō nijū shūnen kinen Higashimikawa sangyō kōrōshaden* (Tōhashi: Tōhashi Shiritsu Shōgyō Gakkō, 1943), 210–211; Ogura, "Meiji zenki nōsei no dōkō to nōkai no seiritsu," 266.

45. Egami, 616.

46. Sasaki Yutaka, 4.

47. Nishimura Kōichi, 1.

48. Tsutsui Masao, "The Impact of the Local Improvement Movement on Farmers and Rural Communities," in *Farmers and Village Life in Twentieth-Century Japan*, ed. Ann Waswo and Yoshiaki Nishida (New York: RoutledgeCurzon, 2003), 69.

49. While the change of land taxes from payment in kind to payment in cash did not dramatically alter the amount of tax most farmers paid, it placed them in more direct competition with one another and drove prices down, which worked against poorer farmers while giving an advantage to their wealthier neighbors. See Yamaguchi Kazuo, *Nihon keizaishi* (Tokyo: Chikuma Shobō, 1968), 149.

50. Murakami, 136.

51. Ogura Sōichi, "Nōsei oyobi nōkai: Meiji kōki, Taishō shoki," in *Nihon nōgyō hattatsushi: Meiji ikō ni okeru*, vol. 5 (Tokyo: Chūō Kōronsha, 1978), 317; Murakami, 137.

52. Ogura, "Nōsei oyobi nōkai: Meiji kōki, Taishō shoki," 319.

53. Ogura, "Meiji zenki nōsei no dōkō to nōkai no seiritsu," 328.

54. Tomoda Kiyohiko, "Meiji shoki no nōkai kessha to Dai Nihon Nōkai no sōsetu (1): Tōyō Nōkai to Tōkyō Dannōkai," *Nōson kenkyū,* no. 102 (2006): 3. Miyagi governor Matsudaira, then putting into practice his rice regulations, was also a member of the group. See Tomoda, "Meiji shoki no nōkai kessha to Dai Nihon Nōkai no sōsetu (1)," 5.

55. Tomoda, "Meiji shoki no nōkai kessha to Dai Nihon Nōkai no sōsetu (1)," 6, 11.

56. Tomoda, "Meiji shoki no nōkai kessha to Dai Nihon Nōkai no sōsetu (1)," 3.

57. Tomoda, "Meiji shoki no nōkai kessha to Dai Nihon Nōkai no sōsetu (1)," 6–7.

58. Dai Nihon Nōkai, *Dai Nihon Nōkai seisekisho* (Tokyo: Dai Nihon Nōkai, 1895), 1, http://dl.ndl.go.jp/info:ndljp/pid/901081.

59. Ogura, "Meiji zenki nōsei no dōkō to nōkai no seiritsu," 270.

60. Tomoda Kiyohiko, "Meiji shoki no nōkai kessha to Dai Nihon Nōkai no sōsetu (2): Tōyō Nōkai to Tōkyō Dannōkai," *Nōson kenkyū,* no. 103 (2006): 26.

61. Dai Nihon Nōkai, *Dai Nihon Nōkai seisekisho,* 1.

62. Dai Nihon Nōkai, Dai Nihon Sanrinkai, and Dai Nihon Suisankai, "Dai Nihon Nōkai ryakushi," in *Dai Nihon Nōkai—Dai Nihon Sanrinkai—Dai Nihon Suisankai sōritsu shichijūgonen kinen* (Tokyo: Dai Nihon Nōkai, 1955), 1.

63. Dai Nihon Nōkai, *Dai Nihon Nōkai seisekisho,* 2–5.

64. Ogura, "Meiji zenki nōsei no dōkō to nōkai no seiritsu," 284.

65. These two landlords were Jūmonji Hideo, who also appeared in the Agriculture and Commerce Ministry's 1882 listing of local *rōnō,* and Kikuchi Hiroshi, who went on to take an active role in the Entō conflict described in chapter 2. See Murakami, 102; and Nōshōmushō Nōmukyoku, *Kaku chihō rōnōka oyobi shubyōko meibo,* 79.

66. Ogura, "Meiji zenki nōsei no dōkō to nōkai no seiritsu," 300.

67. Ogura, "Meiji zenki nōsei no dōkō to nōkai no seiritsu," 327.

68. Murakami, 138–139.

69. Dai Nihon Nōkai, *Dai Nihon Nōkai seisekisho,* 2.

70. Murakami, 103.

71. The groups appear to have built themselves from the ground up, with village groups in Tōda forming first and then sending representatives to plan for the founding of the district *nōkai.* See Tōda Kyōikukai, *Tōda Gunshi* (Tokyo: Meicho Shuppan, 1972), 539.

72. Nishimura Kōichi, 10.

73. Dai Nihon Nōkai, *Dai Nihon Nōkai Seisekisho,* 2–3.

74. "Nōshōmushō no beikoku ni kansuru shitsumon ni taishi Tōkyō kaimai ton'ya no tōshin," *Dai Nihon Nōkai hōkoku,* no. 120 (1891): 44. Shibusawa was the cousin of famed Meiji industrialist Shibusawa Eiichi and the five prefectures he was speaking about were Fukui, Toyama, Yamaguchi, Mie, and Shiga.

75. Tamari, "Nōkai konjakudan (shōzen)," 5.

76. By the second half of the decade, the retrenchment policies for which the Matsukata Deflation is known had been abandoned in a change of strategy, but difficulties continued to plague farmers in the forms of low rice prices, poor harvests, and global financial panics. See Ericson, 12–13.

77. While tenancy rates increased only marginally nationwide in the last decade of the twentieth century, this was not true in Miyagi, which experienced significant expansion in tenanted lands, with very limited acreage of newly cultivated lands to account for it. See Takafusa Nakamura, *Economic Growth in Prewar Japan,* trans. Robert A. Feldman (New Haven, CT: Yale University Press, 1983), 56; Araki Mikio, *Nōgyōshi: kindai Nihon jinushisei shiron* (Tokyo: Bunmei Shobō, 1985), 94; and Araki Mikio, "Nōgyō keiei no hattatsu to kisei jinushiteki tochi shoyū," in *Keizaishi keieishi ronshū* (Osaka: Ōsaka Keizai Daigaku, 1984), 615–651.

78. Ogura, "Meiji zenki nōsei no dōkō to nōkai no seiritsu," 276.

79. Abiko Rin, "Jinushisei no saihensei to teitai," in *Miyagiken nōmin undōshi,* ed. Nakamura Kichiji (Tokyo: Nihon Hyōronsha, 1968), 211–212.

80. Ogura, "Meiji zenki nōsei no dōkō to nōkai no seiritsu," 344. A *chō* is equivalent to 0.99 hectares.

81. Tōhashi Shiritsu Shōgyō Gakkō, 139; Abiko Rin, *Miyagiken no hyakunen,* Kenmin 100-nenshi 4 (Tokyo: Yamakawa Shuppansha, 1999), 88.

82. Murakami, 139–140.

83. Ogura, "Meiji zenki nōsei no dōkō to nōkai no seiritsu," 346.

84. Ogura, "Meiji zenki nōsei no dōkō to nōkai no seiritsu," 360.

85. Carol Gluck, *Japan's Modern Myths: Ideology in the Late Meiji Period* (Princeton, NJ: Princeton University Press, 1985), 179.

86. Nishimura Kōichi, 16.

87. Dai Nihon Nōkai, *Dai Nihon Nōkai seisekisho,* 3.

88. Nishimura Kōichi, 11.

89. Sakō Tsuneaki, "Nihon no nōgyō ha nōka no kyōdōgokoro ni yorazareba shinpo sezu soku nōgyō shokumiai no hitsuyō kyō no taikan ha nōka kinyū no heisoku nari soku sonraku yūtsū no hitsuyō (daijūkai daishūkai enjutsu)," *Dai Nihon Nōkai hōkoku,* no. 119 (1891): 3.

90. On the Freedom and Popular Rights Movement, see Roger W. Bowen, *Rebellion and Democracy in Meiji Japan: A Study of Commoners in the Popular Rights Movement* (Berkeley: University of California Press, 1980).

91. Nishimura Kōichi, 10.

92. Ogura, "Meiji zenki nōsei no dōkō to nōkai no seiritsu," 352.

93. Ogura, "Meiji zenki nōsei no dōkō to nōkai no seiritsu," 355. See also Arima Manabu, "Mura no naka no mintō to ritō: kindai Nihon no chiiki, senkyo, seitō," in *Chiikishi no kanosei: chiiki, Nihon, sekai,* ed. Kindai Nihon Kenkyūkai (Tokyo: Yamakawa Shuppansha, 1997); and Peter Duus, *Party Rivalry and Political Change in Taishō Japan.,* Harvard East Asian Series, 35 (Cambridge, MA: Harvard University Press, 1968), chap. 1: The Growth of Party Respectability.

94. Dai Nihon Nōkai, Dai Nihon Sanrinkai, and Dai Nihon Suisankai, "Dai Nihon Nōkai ryakushi," 44–45.

95. Ogura, "Meiji zenki nōsei no dōkō to nōkai no seiritsu," 366.

96. Ogura, "Meiji zenki nōsei no dōkō to nōkai no seiritsu," 372.

97. Nishimura Kōichi, 18–21.

98. Nishimura Kōichi, 23.

99. Nishimura Kōichi, 24.

100. Ishikawa Rono Jiseki Chōsakai, *Tenka no rōnō Ishikawa Rikinosuke: denki Ishikawa Rikinosuke* (Tokyo: Ōzorasha, 2000), 350–351; Nishimura Kōichi, 57.

101. Ishikawa Rono Jiseki Chōsakai, 343.

102. Maeda Masana, "Kyō no kyūmu ha kokuze kenze gunze sonze o sadamuru ni ari (1892)," in *Kōgyō iken, Shoken,* Meiji Taishō nōsei keizai meichoshū 1 (Tokyo: Nōsangyoson Bunka Kyōkai, 1976), 416.

103. Concerns about tenants' groups also influenced the 1899 Public Order and Police Law, which ordered penalties of one to six months in jail for the use of violence, coercion, or slander in rent negotiations. See Ogura, "Nōsei oyobi nōkai: Meiji kōki, Taishō shoki," 320.

104. Nishimura Kōichi, 64.

105. Sendai Shishi Hensan Iinkai, *Sendai shishi: Shimin seikatsu,* Sendai shishi: Tokubetsuhen 4 (Sendai: Sendaishi, 1997), 492.

106. Sasaki Yutaka, 5–9.

107. Murakami Tetsuichi, 58.

108. Abiko, "Jinushisei no saihensei to teitai," 212.

109. Ogawa, 109–110.

110. These drafts were actually proposed by sympathetic bureaucrats in the Agriculture and Commerce Ministry. See Ogura, "Meiji zenki nōsei no dōkō to nōkai no seiritsu," 345.

111. The revised proposals instead assigned responsibility for the experimentation stations to prefectural governments. See Ogura, "Meiji zenki nōsei no dōkō to nōkai no seiritsu," 356.

112. Ogura, "Meiji zenki nōsei no dōkō to nōkai no seiritsu," 375.

113. Ogawa, 104.

114. Ogawa, 104.

Chapter Four: Fighting the Farmers for National Wealth

1. "Jinushi to kosakunin," *Heimin Shinbun 13,* February 1, 1907.

2. "Kyūsai ihō," *Miyagiken kyōikukai zasshi,* no. 113 (1906): 45.

3. Sawayanagi Masatarō, "Kyōsakuchi kyōiku," *Miyagiken Kyōikukai zasshi,* no. 111 (1905): 66.

4. Abiko Rin, "Jinushisei no saihensei to teitai," in *Miyagiken nōmin undōshi,* ed. Nakamura Kichiji (Tokyo: Nihon Hyōronsha, 1968), 216.

5. Yamotochō, *Yamoto chōshi,* vol. 3 (Yamoto: Yamotochō, 1976), 339.

6. Satō Tadashi, "Tōhoku chihō Meiji makki no nōmin undō no kōzō: Miyagiken Senboku heiya no bunseki (2)," *Iwate shigaku kenkyū,* no. 45 (1964): 69.

7. Ogura Sōichi, "Meiji zenki nōsei no dōkō to nōkai no seiritsu," in *Nihon nōgyō hattatsushi: Meiji ikō ni okeru,* vol. 3 (Tokyo: Chūō Kōronsha, 1978), 338–339.

8. Ogura, "Meiji zenki nōsei no dōkō to nōkai no seiritsu," 348.

9. Satō, "Tōhoku chihō Meiji makki no nōmin undō no kōzō: Miyagiken Senboku heiya no bunseki (2)," 69.

10. Ogura Sōichi, "Nōsei oyobi nōkai: Meiji kōki, Taishō shoki," in *Nihon nōgyō hattatsushi: Meiji ikō ni okeru,* vol. 5 (Tokyo: Chūō Kōronsha, 1978), 352.

11. Hida Rōichi, "Jinushikai setchi no hitsuyō," *Chūō nōjihō,* no. 5 (1900): 3–6.

12. Hida, 3–4.

13. Nōjikai, *Zenkoku nōji taikai hōkoku: Dai hakkai* (Tokyo: Nōjikai Honbu, 1901), 58, http://kindai.ndl.go.jp/info:ndljp/pid/802341.

14. Yamotochō, 3:184; Miyagiken Nōkai, *Kōchi seiri jisshi benran* (Sendai: Miyagiken Nōkai, 1903), http://dl.ndl.go.jp/info:ndljp/pid/900566.

15. Ogawa Makoto, "Chisui, suiri, tochi kairyō no taikeiteki seibi," in *Nihon nōgyō hattatsushi: Meiji ikō ni okeru,* vol. 4 (Tokyo: Chūō Kōronsha, 1978), 203.

16. Ogawa, 199; Udo Eggert, *Land Reform in Japan, Specially Based on the Development of Credit Associations* (Tokyo: Tokyo Tsukiji Kwappan Seizosho, 1890; published in Japanese as *Nihon shinnōsaku* [Tokyo: Hakubunkan, 1891], http://kindai.ndl.go.jp/info:ndljp/pid/802414).

17. Naikaku, "Kōchi seirihō o sadamu," March 20, 1899, Administrative Records: Cabinet/Prime Minister's Office: Records concerning Dajokan/Cabinet: Category No. 6 Kobun Ruishu Various Offices: Kobun Ruishu Vol. 23, 1899: Kōbun ruiju dai-23hen Meiji 32nen dai 33kan chiri tochi shinrin kanshō, National Archives of Japan, http://www.digital.archives.go.jp/DAS/meta/MetSearch.cgi.

18. Naikaku, "Kōchi seirihō o sadamu," 5–6; Ogawa, 113.

19. Miyagiken Nōkai, 5–8.

20. Miyagiken Nōkai, 1–2.

21. Ogura, "Nōsei oyobi nōkai: Meiji kōki, Taishō shoki," 309–310.

22. Dai Nihon Nōkai, Dai Nihon Sanrinkai, and Dai Nihon Suisankai, "Dai Nihon Nōkai ryakushi," in *Dai Nihon Nōkai—Dai Nihon Sanrinkai—Dai Nihon Suisankai sōritsu shichijūgonen kinen* (Tokyo: Dai Nihon Nōkai, 1955), 8.

23. Ogura, "Nōsei oyobi nōkai: Meiji kōki, Taishō shoki," 311–312. Before 1906, the ministry offered only minimal funding for the training of technicians.

24. Nishimura Kōichi, *Meiji nōsei to nōkai: Nōkai no hassei kara Teikoku Nōkai no seiritsu made,* Shiryō 3 (N.p.: Nihon Nōgyō Kenkyūjō, 1951), 34.

25. Abiko Rin, "Meiji kōki no nōgyō," in *Miyagiken nōmin undōshi,* ed. Nakamura Kichiji (Tokyo: Nihon Hyōronsha, 1968), 189.

26. "Kōchi seiri jigyō gaikyō: Nōshōmushō chōsa," *Kobe shinbun,* March 1, 1913, http://www.lib.kobe-u.ac.jp/das/jsp/ja/ContentViewM.jsp?METAID=10074058&TYPE=IMAGE_FILE&POS=1; Ogawa, 228.

27. The lion's share of this work was completed by 1915, when 29.7 percent of the arable land in the prefecture had been consolidated. See Ogawa, 228.

28. Abiko Rin, *Miyagiken no hyakunen,* Kenmin 100-nenshi 4 (Tokyo: Yamakawa Shuppansha, 1999), 94. On the *Meiji nōhō,* see Yujiro Hayami, "Rice Policy in Japan's Economic Development," *American Journal of Agricultural Economics* 54, no. 1 (1972): 23; and Penelope Francks, "Rice for the Masses: Food Policy and the Adoption of Imperial Self-Sufficiency in Early Twentieth-Century Japan," *Japan Forum* 15, no. 1 (2003): 129, https://doi.org/10.1080/0955580032000077766.

29. Sendai Shishi Hensan Iinkai, *Sendai shishi: Shimin seikatsu,* Sendai shishi: Tokubetsuhen 4 (Sendai: Sendaishi, 1997), 448; Inoue Kunio, "Hatasakumotsu no suitai to kōryū," in *Nihon nōgyō hattatsushi: Meiji ikō ni okeru,* vol. 3 (Tokyo: Chūō Kōronsha, 1978), 215.

30. Miyagiken Nōkai, 13–14.

31. Baba Akira, "Suitō tansaku nōgyō no kakuritsu katei," in *Kindai Nihon no jinushi to nōmin: suitō tansaku nōgyō no keizaiteki kenkyū, Nangō-mura,* ed. Sunaga Shigemitsu (Tokyo: Ochanomizu Shobō, 1966), 200–201.

32. Baba, "Suitō tansaku nōgyō no kakuritsu katei," 205.

33. Abiko, *Miyagiken no hyakunen,* 90.

34. Abiko, "Meiji kōki no nōgyō," 190; Abiko, *Miyagiken no hyakunen,* 94.

35. Abiko, "Meiji kōki no nōgyō," 191.

36. Yamotochō, 3:348.

37. Baba, "Suitō tansaku nōgyō no kakuritsu katei," 204–205.

38. Yamotochō, 3:195.

39. Yamotochō, 3:382.

40. Abiko, "Jinushisei no saihensei to teitai," 191. Here again Nangō proved exceptionally successful, consolidating plots of 202, 71, and 83 hectares in 1903, 1905, and 1907, respectively. See Baba, "Suitō tansaku nōgyō no kakuritsu katei," 206.

41. Baba, "Suitō tansaku nōgyō no kakuritsu katei," 202.

42. Baba, "Suitō tansaku nōgyō no kakuritsu katei," 200.

43. This work is described in chapter 6.

44. Baba, "Suitō tansaku nōgyō no kakuritsu katei," 200.

45. Baba, "Suitō tansaku nōgyō no kakuritsu katei," 205.

46. Baba, "Suitō tansaku nōgyō no kakuritsu katei," 202.

47. Abiko, *Miyagiken no hyakunen,* 90.

48. Miyagiken, *Meiji sanjūgonen Miyagiken kyōkanshi* (Sendai: Miyagiken, 1904), 130.

49. Of the seventeen Kurihara villages reporting *kōchi seiri* relief work, fifteen note that it was "private relief work," with only Kannari and Omatsu reporting that relief was conducted by the village government. See Miyagiken, *Meiji sanjūgonen Miyagiken kyōkanshi,* 198–238.

50. Miyagiken, *Meiji sanjūgonen Miyagiken kyōkanshi,* 187–188.

51. Miyagiken, *Meiji sanjūgonen Miyagiken kyōkanshi,* 256.
52. Miyagiken, *Meiji sanjūhachinen Miyagiken kyōkōshi* (Sendai: Miyagiken, 1916), 377.
53. For an example, see Miyagiken, *Meiji sanjūgonen Miyagiken kyōkanshi,* 216.
54. Miyagiken, *Meiji sanjūhachinen Miyagiken kyōkōshi,* 40, 307; Satō Tadashi, "Taishō-Shōwa shoki no nōgyō," in *Miyagiken nōmin undōshi,* ed. Nakamura Kichiji (Tokyo: Nihon Hyōronsha, 1968), 377.
55. Miyagiken, *Meiji sanjūhachinen Miyagiken kyōkōshi,* 311.
56. Baba, "Suitō tansaku nōgyō no kakuritsu katei," 203.
57. Baba, "Suitō tansaku nōgyō no kakuritsu katei," 203.
58. Abiko, *Miyagiken no hyakunen,* 94.
59. Tōhoku custom held that plowing by horse or ox in rice farming invited divine punishment. See Murakami Tetsuichi, "Meiji-Taishō ni okeru Miyagiken nōgyō no shinten," in *Sangyō 1,* Miyagi kenshi 9 (Sendai: Miyagi Kenshi Kankōkai, 1968), 109.
60. Ogura, "Meiji zenki nōsei no dōkō to nōkai no seiritsu," 221.
61. Tamari, *Tōhoku shinkōsaku: Yamato minzoku no kankoku ni okeru hattensaku* (Tokyo: Zenkoku Nōjikai, 1904), 6, http://dl.ndl.go.jp/info:ndljp/pid/802390.
62. Abiko, "Meiji kōki no nōgyō," 190.
63. Sven Beckert, *Empire of Cotton: A Global History* (New York: Alfred A. Knopf, 2014), 181.
64. Sumitomo Akifumi, "Kindai chihō jichisei kakuritsuki no chihō gyōsei: Chihō kairyō undō to chiiki un'ei chitsujo," *Nihonshi kenkyū,* no. 368 (1992): 94.
65. Kenneth B. Pyle, "The Technology of Japanese Nationalism: The Local Improvement Movement, 1900–1918," *Journal of Asian Studies* 33, no. 1 (1973): 59.
66. Pyle, 59; Miyagiken Naimubu Daiyonka, *Miyagiken Natorigun Oidemura Sonze Chōsasho* (Oide [Miyagi]: Miyagiken Natorigun Oidemura, 1902).
67. Pyle, 60; Abiko Rin, "Nōchi kaikaku to buraku: Buraku no tochi kanri kinō o chūshin ni," *Rekishi hyōron,* no. 435 (1986): 33. Landlords and local officials like Kamata Sannosuke often engaged in similar actions of their own. See chapter 1.
68. Abiko, "Jinushisei no saihensei to teitai," 221.
69. Sumitomo, 97–98.
70. Nishimura Kōichi, 42–43.
71. Tamari, *Tōhoku shinkōsaku: Yamato minzoku no kankoku ni okeru hattensaku,* 3.
72. Abiko, *Miyagiken no hyakunen,* 88.
73. Ogura, "Nōsei oyobi nōkai: Meiji kōki, Taishō shoki," 315; Yamotochō, 3:179; Yasuda Ken, "Meijiki ni okeru kanfu no inasaku shidō," in *Nihon nōgyō hattatsushi: Meiji ikō ni okeru,* vol. 5 (Tokyo: Chūō Kōronsha, 1978), 107–108.
74. Yamotochō, 3:179.
75. Yamotochō, 3:196.
76. Murakami, 143.
77. Criticisms of the Tohoku practice of leaving seedbeds fallow for most of the year stemmed from the then-new practice in western Japan of replanting them with rice after the transfer of the seedlings. Little attention was paid to the dramatically different climactic conditions that made this possible, and a *nōkai* official claimed in 1899 that test results finding that fallow seedbeds created conditions for higher yields in Akita and Miyagi had resulted from flawed experimentation. See Katō Shigemoto, "Ōu chihō no nawashiro to kikō to no kankei," *Dai Nihon nōkaihō,* no. 210 (1899): 19–22.
78. Yamotochō, 3:354.
79. Ogawa, 112.
80. Murakami, 114.
81. Abiko, *Miyagiken no hyakunen,* 90.
82. Ogura, "Nōsei oyobi nōkai: Meiji kōki, Taishō shoki," 316.

83. Murakami, "Meiji-Taishō ni okeru Miyagiken nōgyō no shinten," 141.
84. Ogura, "Nōsei oyobi nōkai: Meiji kōki, Taishō shoki," 316.
85. Nōshōmushō, *Beisaku ni kansuru fukenrei* (Tokyo: Nōshōmushō, 1904), 3, http://dl.ndl.go.jp/info:ndljp/pid/796421.
86. Yamotochō, 3:196; Abiko, *Miyagiken no hyakunen*, 89.
87. Ogura, "Nōsei oyobi nōkai: Meiji kōki, Taishō shoki," 316.
88. Abiko, "Meiji kōki no nōgyō," 194.
89. Similar government interference in work contracts was a characteristic feature of industrial labor in factories in Western Europe and North America in the nineteenth century and was a crucial element in the processes of the proletarianization of labor. See Beckert, 181–182.
90. The explicit labeling of these landlords as "parasite landlords" (*kisei jinushi*) did not appear until Marxist historians took up the subject later in the century.
91. Abiko Rin, "Jinushi keiei no henka to jinushisei no igi," in *Kindai Nihon no jinushi to nōmin: suitō tansaku nōgyō no keizaiteki kenkyū, Nangō-mura*, ed. Sunaga Shigemitsu (Tokyo: Ochanomizu Shobō, 1966), 259.
92. Murakami, 150.
93. The institution of similar regulations in Ōita, Okayama, and Toyama in the years leading up to the new system in Miyagi attests to the new permissiveness of central officials to government intervention in farming villages. See Murakami, 149.
94. Abiko, "Meiji kōki no nōgyō," 197.
95. Abiko, "Meiji kōki no nōgyō," 197.
96. Satō Tadashi, "Meiji makki no nōmin undō," in *Miyagiken nōmin undōshi*, ed. Nakamura Kichiji (Tokyo: Nihon Hyōronsha, 1968), 317.
97. Ogura, "Meiji zenki nōsei no dōkō to nōkai no seiritsu," 320.
98. Ogura, "Meiji zenki nōsei no dōkō to nōkai no seiritsu," 321.
99. Abiko, "Jinushisei no saihensei to teitai," 226.
100. Abiko, "Jinushisei no saihensei to teitai," 226.
101. Abiko, *Miyagiken no hyakunen*, 134. Local rice dealers did no favors to their public image by declaring their dissatisfaction in this intrusion upon their business interests.
102. Miyagiken, *Meiji sanjūgonen Miyagiken kyōkanshi*, 226.
103. Abiko, "Jinushisei no saihensei to teitai," 218.
104. This was in comparison to the 1,900 Miyagi residents who moved to Hokkaidō in 1902. See Nōshōmushō Nōmukyoku, ed., *Jinushi to Kosakunin* (Tokyo: Sangyō Kumiai Chūōkai, 1909), 192; and Miyagiken, *Meiji sanjūgonen Miyagiken kyōkanshi*, 225.
105. Abiko, "Jinushisei no saihensei to teitai," 212.
106. Baba, "Suitō tansaku nōgyō no kakuritsu katei," 203.
107. Abiko, "Jinushisei no saihensei to teitai," 218.
108. Yamotochō, 3:488.
109. Nōshōmushō Nōmukyoku, *Jinushi to Kosakunin*, 194–195.
110. Ōshō Shigeru, "Kyōsaku zakkan," *Miyagiken Kyōikukai zasshi*, no. 112 (1905): 25.
111. Abiko, "Jinushisei no saihensei to teitai," 231.
112. Abiko, "Jinushisei no saihensei to teitai," 217.
113. Miyagiken, *Meiji sanjūhachinen Miyagiken kyōkōshi*, 1.

Chapter Five: The Spirit of the Times Has Changed

1. "Kosakunin mondai to Saitō gōnō," *Kahoku shinpō*, March 10, 1903. See also Satō Tadashi, "Meiji makki no nōmin undō," in *Miyagiken nōmin undōshi*, ed. Nakamura Kichiji (Tokyo: Nihon Hyōronsha, 1968), 324.

2. Miyagiken chiji kanbō bunshogakari, "Miyagiken furei ruisan, Meiji 40 nen 1 gatsu—Meiji 40 nen 12 gatsu" (Miyagiken Chiji Kanbō Bunshogakari, 1907), 109–110, Miyagiken Kōbunshokan.

3. Tanaka Kazuo, "Kindai Nihon no 'meibōka' zō: Chihō Kairyō Undō de no 'tokushika' to minshū," *Shakai kagaku,* no. 37 (1986): 265. Tamari divides the figures he criticizes into two groups: *ōjinushi,* by whom he appears to mean absentee landlords, and *gōnō,* referring to landlords still involved with farming and still resident in villages. This is something of an idiosyncratic division. *Ōjinushi* in Tōhoku were overwhelmingly of the latter type and the word as used in official documents and scholarship refers to landlords resident in villages, if not necessarily in all the same villages in which they owned land.

4. Nōjikai, *Zenkoku nōji taikai hōkoku: Dai hakkai* (Tokyo: Nōjikai Honbu, 1901), 72, http://kindai.ndl.go.jp/info:ndljp/pid/802341.

5. Sasaki Yutaka, "Chihō Kairyō Undō to chōsonze chōsa," in *Chihō Kairyō Undōshi shiryō shūsei,* vol. 1 (Tokyo: Kashiwa Shobō, 1986), 11.

6. Ogura Sōichi, "Nōsei oyobi nōkai: Meiji kōki, Taishō shoki," in *Nihon nōgyō hattatsushi: Meiji ikō ni okeru,* vol. 5 (Tokyo: Chūō Kōronsha, 1978), 319.

7. Nishimura Kōichi, *Meiji nōsei to nōkai: Nōkai no hassei kara Teikoku Nōkai no seiritsu made,* Shiryō 3 (N.p.: Nihon Nōgyō Kenkyūjō, 1951), 41.

8. Yamagata Aritomo, "Meiji sanjūninen nigatsu nijūyonnichi: shisei hōshin enzetsu," in *Yamagata Aritomo ikensho,* ed. Ōyama Azusa, Meiji hyakunenshi sōsho 16 (Tokyo: Hara Shobō, 1966), 250.

9. Yanagita Kunio, "Chūnō yōseisaku," in *Nōsei ronshū: Yanagita Kunio,* ed. Fujii Takashi (Tokyo: Hōsei Daigaku Shuppankyoku, 1975), 30.

10. *Ōjinushi* were generally defined as landlords with landholdings over 50 *chō.*

11. Miyagiken Keisatsushi Hensan Iinkai, ed., *Miyagiken keisatsushi,* vol. 1, 3 vols. (Sendai: Miyagiken Keisatsu Honbu, 1980), seems to be alone in classifying Senboku landlords as absentee, presumably based on their ownership of land in neighboring villages. See p. 526.

12. Abiko Rin, *Miyagiken no hyakunen,* Kenmin 100-nenshi 4 (Tokyo: Yamakawa Shuppansha, 1999), 97.

13. Abiko Rin, "Jinushisei no saihensei to teitai," in *Miyagiken nōmin undōshi,* ed. Nakamura Kichiji (Tokyo: Nihon Hyōronsha, 1968), 206.

14. For the twisted history of the ownership of the land Saitō purchased, much of which had itself fallen to the bank when the district chief who owned it went bankrupt in 1885, see Saitō Hōonkai, *Saitō Zen'uemon ōden* (Tokyo: Saitō Hōonkai, 1928), 61–62; and Yamotochō, *Yamoto chōshi,* vol. 3 (Yamoto: Yamotochō, 1976), 358.

15. The text of the manual is reprinted in its entirety in Saitō Hōonkai, 145–179.

16. This is very nearly opposite in conception to the social role played by patrons, whose connections through honor-based provision of credit work to strengthen "bonds of friendship, loyalty, and mutual trust" that are the basis of community solidarity. See Hillmann Henning, "Localism and the Limits of Political Brokerage: Evidence from Revolutionary Vermont," *American Journal of Sociology* 114, no. 2 (2008): 300.

17. Saitō Hōonkai, 162.

18. Saitō Hōonkai, 152.

19. Abiko, "Jinushisei no saihensei to teitai," 211.

20. Miyachi Masato, *Nichiro sengo seijishi no kenkyū: teikokushugi keiseiki no toshi to nōson* (Tokyo: Tokyo Daigaku Shuppankai, 1973), 1.

21. Nishimura Yasukichi, "Kangyō hōshin ni kansuru enzetsu hikki," in *Sangyō hōshin,* ed. Seisan Chōsakai, vol. 1 (Tokyo: Seisan Chōsakai, 1911), 630; see also Miyachi, 5–6.

22. Tanaka Norio, "'Chihō kairyō' rinen no ichidanmen: Kansei 'chihō kairyō' undō no shūhen," *Dōshisha hōgaku* 30, no. 1 (1978): 115.

23. Tanaka Norio, 117.

24. Penelope Francks, *Rural Economic Development in Japan: From the Nineteenth Century to the Pacific War* (London: Routledge, 2006), 87.

25. Ogura, "Nōsei oyobi nōkai: Meiji kōki, Taishō shoki," 322.

26. Yokoi Tokiyoshi, *Mohan chōson* (Tokyo: Yomiuri Shinbunsha, 1907), http://dl.ndl.go.jp/info:ndljp/pid/888488.

27. Yokoi, *Mohan chōson,* 14.

28. Yokoi Tokiyoshi, "Jinushi ni taisuru keikoku," in *Daiichi nōgyō jiron: Nōson angya sanjūnen,* Meiji Taishō nōsei keizai meichoshū 17 (Tokyo: Nōsangyoson Bunka Kyōkai, 1976), 153.

29. Wada Seima, *Kindaishi,* Miyagi kenshi 3 (Sendai: Miyagi Kenshi Kankōkai, 1964), 649–654.

30. These accusations, and the jail time he served while waiting for a verdict, did not prevent him from being elected to five more terms in the Diet. See Wada, 213, 726–729.

31. Tamari, "Nōgyō dantai ni tsuite," *Dai Nihon nōkaihō,* no. 157 (1894): 24.

32. Tamari Kizō, *Tōhoku shinkōsaku: Yamato minzoku no kankoku ni okeru hattensaku* (Tokyo: Zenkoku Nōjikai, 1904), 2, http://dl.ndl.go.jp/info:ndljp/pid/802390. He followed up on these comments by relating a story about how the governor of Kagoshima "bravely" dissolved a district assembly that opposed the prefecture's ban on charcoal fertilizer five times before the voters stopped electing the same group and gave in to the inevitable. The scientific reasoning behind the ban on charcoal was later proven false. See Ogura Sōichi, "Beisaku ni kansuru fukenrei," in *Nihon nōgyō hattatsushi: Meiji ikō ni okeru,* vol. 4 (Tokyo: Chūō Kōronsha, 1978), 743.

33. Miyachi, 14.

34. Sumitomo Akifumi, "Kindai chihō jichisei kakuritsuki no chihō gyōsei: Chihō kairyō undō to chiiki un'ei chitsujo," *Nihonshi kenkyū,* no. 368 (1992): 100–102.

35. Tanaka Kazuo, 270.

36. Yanagita Kunio, "Inaka tai tokai no mondai," in *Jidai to nōsei* (Tokyo: Shūseidō, 1910), 64–68.

37. Nakagawa Nozomu, "Nōson no kairyō," in *Kanka kyūsai jigyō kōenshū* (Tokyo: Naimushō Chihōkyoku, 1909), 998, http://kindai.ndl.go.jp/info:ndljp/pid/995169.

38. Yokoi, "Jinushi ni taisuru keikoku," 154. See also Tanaka Kazuo, 265.

39. Tanaka Kazuo, 265–266.

40. Nishikawa Tadashi, "Yuzei nikki," *Shūkan shakai shinbun 29,* December 15, 1907.

41. "Miyagiken ōjinushikai," *Dai Nihon Nōkaihō,* no. 311 (May 1907): 42. Insensitivity was not monopolized by Miyagi landlords. The following article in the journal relates a proposal from landlords in the neighboring prefecture of Fukushima for product exhibitions as a means of supporting tenant farmers.

42. Nishikawa.

43. Hirata Ichirō, "Miyagiken no kosaku sōdō," *Tōkyō shakai shinbun 11,* June 25, 1908.

44. Abiko, "Jinushisei no saihensei to teitai," 222.

45. Miyagiken, *Meiji sanjūgonen Miyagiken kyōkanshi* (Sendai: Miyagiken, 1904), 49.

46. Miyagiken, *Meiji sanjūhachinen Miyagiken kyōkōshi* (Sendai: Miyagiken, 1916), 225.

47. This was out of a total of only forty-nine tenant unions in the country. See Abiko, *Miyagiken no hyakunen,* 101–102. Abiko argues that the term *"kosakunin dōmei"* is particular to Miyagi, but a 1907 article in the *Shūkan shakai shinbun* uses it in reference to a tenant organization in Tochigi. See "Kosaku dōmei," *Shūkan shakai shinbun 22,* October 27, 1907.

48. Abiko, *Miyagiken no hyakunen,* 103.

49. Satō Tadashi, "Tōhoku chihō Meiji makki no nōmin undō no kōzō: Miyagiken Senboku heiya no bunseki (2)," *Iwate shigaku kenkyū,* no. 45 (1964): 69.

50. Tamari, *Tōhoku shinkōsaku: Yamato minzoku no kankoku ni okeru hattensaku,* 4.

51. Satō, "Tōhoku chihō Meiji makki no nōmin undō no kōzō: Miyagiken Senboku heiya no bunseki (2)," 63–64; Satō, "Meiji makki no nōmin undō," 331.

52. Some leaders also showed evidence of more traditional sentiments of sympathy and philanthropy. Abe Yamahira, the mayor of Sue and Monō district assembly member who assumed the headship of the cross-district Allied Tenants League, demonstrated his passion for the cause of tenants (*kosakunin*) by naming the grandson born to him during the conflict "Kosaku." See Satō, "Tōhoku chihō Meiji makki no nōmin undō no kōzō: Miyagiken Senboku heiya no bunseki (2)," 63.

53. Satō, "Meiji makki no nōmin undō," 313–314.

54. The trauma of landlords' experiences with tenant flight actually bore some of the blame for the rice testing system that set off the conflicts of 1907 and 1908. Floating the specter of abandoned lands, the landlords pushing for quality standards were able to brush aside resistance to the idea and push it through to prefectural law. See Satō, "Meiji makki no nōmin undō," 314.

55. Abiko, *Miyagiken no hyakunen,* 103–104.

56. Satō, "Meiji makki no nōmin undō," 314.

57. Satō, "Meiji makki no nōmin undō," 318.

58. Abiko, *Miyagiken no hyakunen,* 103–104; Satō, "Meiji makki no nōmin undō," 314.

59. Satō, "Meiji makki no nōmin undō," 318–319.

60. Saitō's contention that landlords had no duty beyond what was written in contracts had roots back to his house rules of 1892, but his own history of tenant management put the lie to his righteous indignation. A 1907 issue of the *Miyagi Nōkaihō* (Miyagi Agricultural Association Report) reported on the concessions he had made to his tenants in the face of the continuing crop failures, including support money to purchase fertilizer and the temporary deferral of rents. See Satō, "Meiji makki no nōmin undō," 325. While these acts hardly represented unbounded kindness, they were a far cry from the absolute adherence to contracts that Saitō trumpeted at the height of the 1908 conflict.

61. Nōshōmushō Nōmukyoku, ed., *Jinushi to kosakunin* (Tokyo: Sangyō Kumiai Chūōkai, 1909), 194. The prefectural report on the conflict assigned landlords even more credit for bringing the conflict to a peaceful conclusion, arguing that the efforts of the prefectural *nōkai* "finally brought about a movement toward reconciliation and friendship between landlords and tenants" (*jinushi tai kosakunin kankei mo mata yōyaku yūwa shinzen no katamuki o shōjitaru*). See Miyagiken, *Meiji sanjūhachinen Miyagiken kyōkōshi,* 225–226.

62. Miyagi rents dropped to the lowest in Tōhoku, well below the national average, and remained there for a decade. See Satō, "Tōhoku chihō Meiji makki no nōmin undō no kōzō: Miyagiken Senboku heiya no bunseki (2)," 64.

63. Miyachi, 18.

64. Miyachi, 20.

65. Kenneth B. Pyle, "The Technology of Japanese Nationalism: The Local Improvement Movement, 1900–1918," *Journal of Asian Studies* 33, no. 1 (1973): 53.

66. Yokoi, *Mohan chōson,* i.

67. Yokoi, *Mohan chōson,* 17.

68. Tanaka Kazuo, 255–256.

69. Pyle, 59–61.

70. Miyachi, 24.

71. Tanaka Norio, 127.

72. Tanaka Norio, 129; Tomita Kōji, *Inatori bidan: Shinkyōiku ikimohan* (Inatori: Tomita Kōji, 1907), 44–45, http://kindai.ndl.go.jp/info:ndljp/pid/784536.

73. Tanaka Norio, 129, 134.

74. Sumitomo, 84.

75. Yamazaki Enkichi, *Chihō kairyō no hanashi* (Tokyo: Shōkabō, 1915), 144–145, http://dl.ndl.go.jp/info:ndljp/pid/954881.

76. Pyle, 64.

77. Yamazaki Enkichi, "Chihō kairyōdan," in *Chihō kairyō jigyō koenshū (ge)*, ed. Naimushō Chihōkyoku (Tokyo: Naimushō Chihōkyoku, 1909), 517–525.

78. Yamazaki, "Chihō kairyōdan," 522. Yamazaki was apparently untroubled by the fact that the most celebrated leader he presented was a large landlord.

79. Sumitomo, 103. For more on these organizations, see Richard J. Smethurst, *Agricultural Development and Tenancy Disputes in Japan, 1870–1940* (Princeton, NJ: Princeton University Press, 1986).

80. Uchida Tsukasa, "Nichiro Sengo keieishita ni okeru chōson shinkō to shizen mura: Miyagiken de no Chihō Kairyō Undō no tenkai o jirei to shite (2)," *Shakaigaku nenpō* 7 (1979): 24.

81. Uchida, 28.

82. Miyagiken Shida Gunyakusho, ed., *Shidagun enkakushi* (Furukawa: Miyagiken Shida Gunyakusho, 1912), 304–305. It must be noted that membership to the *rōnō* council was limited to those who were educated and had a mayoral recommendation.

83. Ogawa Makoto, "Chisui, suiri, tochi kairyō no taikeiteki seibi," in *Nihon nōgyō hattatsushi: Meiji ikō ni okeru*, vol. 4 (Tokyo: Chūō Kōronsha, 1978), 104.

84. Ogawa, 113–114.

85. Ogura Sōichi, "Meiji zenki nōsei no dōkō to nōkai no seiritsu," in *Nihon nōgyō hattatsushi: Meiji ikō ni okeru*, vol. 3 (Tokyo: Chūō Kōronsha, 1978), 384–385.

Chapter Six: Coming Full Circle

Epigraph: General Headquarters Supreme Commander for the Allied Powers, *The Rural Land Reform*, vol. 33, History of the Nonmilitary Activities of the Occupation of Japan, 1945–1951 (Tokyo: Nihon Tosho Sentaa, 1990), 35.

1. General Headquarters Supreme Commander for the Allied Powers, *Agriculture*, vol. 41, History of the Nonmilitary Activities of the Occupation of Japan, 1945–1951 (Tokyo: Nihon Tosho Sentaa, 1990), 2.

2. General Headquarters Supreme Commander for the Allied Powers, *Agriculture*, 41:2.

3. General Headquarters Supreme Commander for the Allied Powers, *Agriculture*, 41:3.

4. General Headquarters Supreme Commander for the Allied Powers, *Agriculture*, 41:5.

5. General Headquarters Supreme Commander for the Allied Powers, *The Rural Land Reform*, 33:35.

6. General Headquarters Supreme Commander for the Allied Powers, *Agriculture*, 41:91–92.

7. General Headquarters Supreme Commander for the Allied Powers, *Agriculture*, 41:1.

8. Arthur Franklin Raper, *The Japanese Village in Transition*, Report (Supreme Commander for the Allied Powers. Natural Resources Section) 136 (Tokyo: General Headquarters, Supreme Commander for the Allied Powers, 1950), 11; General Headquarters Supreme Commander for the Allied Powers, *Agriculture*, 41:1–2.

9. The other prefectures from Tōhoku were Akita and Yamagata, along with Ibaraki, Toyama, Osaka, and Kanagawa from elsewhere in the country. See General Headquarters Supreme Commander for the Allied Powers, *The Rural Land Reform*, 33:5.

10. Kerry Douglas Smith, *A Time of Crisis: Japan, the Great Depression, and Rural Revitalization* (Cambridge, MA: Harvard University Press, 2001), 43.

11. Abiko Rin, "Jinushisei no saihensei to teitai," in *Miyagiken nōmin undōshi*, ed. Nakamura Kichiji (Tokyo: Nihon Hyōronsha, 1968), 218.

12. Baba Akira, "Suitō tansaku nōgyō no kakuritsu katei," in *Kindai Nihon no jinushi to nōmin: suitō tansaku nōgyō no keizaiteki kenkyū, Nangō-mura*, ed. Sunaga Shigemitsu (Tokyo: Ochanomizu Shobō, 1966), 192.

13. Satō Tadashi, "Taishō-Shōwa shoki no nōgyō," in *Miyagiken nōmin undōshi*, ed. Nakamura Kichiji (Tokyo: Nihon Hyōronsha, 1968), 372–373.

14. William M. Gilmartin and W. I. Ladejinsky, "The Promise of Agrarian Reform in Japan," *Foreign Affairs* 26, no. 2 (1948): 321.

15. Miyagi Kenritsu Nōgyō Shikenjō, *Miyagi Kenritsu Nōgyō Shikenjōshi: sōritsu 50 shūnen kinen* (Sendai: Miyagi Kenritsu Nōgyō Shikenjō, 1953), 3.

16. Miyagiken Sōmubu Chōsaka, *Shōwa nijūrokunen Miyagiken tōkei sōran*, Chōsaka shiryō 57 (Sendai: Miyagiken Sōmubu Chōsaka, 1951), 15.

17. Fabian Franz Drixler, *Mabiki: Infanticide and Population Growth in Eastern Japan, 1660–1950* (Berkeley: University of California Press, 2013), 9.

18. Ōmori Ken, *Ōu Hokkaidō jitsugyō shisatsu hōkoku* (Mito: Ibarakiken Jitsugyō Shisatsudan, 1914), 101.

19. Wada Seima, *Kindaishi*, Miyagi kenshi 3 (Sendai: Miyagi Kenshi Kankōkai, 1964), 494.

20. Ogura Sōichi, "Nōsei oyobi nōkai: Meiji kōki, Taishō shoki," in *Nihon nōgyō hattatsushi: Meiji ikō ni okeru*, vol. 5 (Tokyo: Chūō Kōronsha, 1978), 314.

21. Ogura, "Nōsei oyobi nōkai: Meiji kōki, Taishō shoki," 311.

22. Ogura Sōichi, "Meiji zenki nōsei no dōkō to nōkai no seiritsu," in *Nihon nōgyō hattatsushi: Meiji ikō ni okeru*, vol. 3 (Tokyo: Chūō Kōronsha, 1978), 384–385. On the foundation of the Teikoku nokai, see Keitō Nōkaishi Hensankai, *Keitō Nōkai no enkaku* (Keitō Nōkaishi Hensankai, 20th century, 150–151.

23. Ogura, "Nōsei oyobi nōkai: Meiji kōki, Taishō shoki," 328.

24. Sendai Shishi Hensan Iinkai, *Sendai shishi: Shimin seikatsu*, Sendai shishi: Tokubetsuhen 4 (Sendai: Sendaishi, 1997), 487.

25. Ōmori, 101.

26. Ōmori, 102–103.

27. Uehara Nobuhiro, *Miyagken Senboku nōgyō chitai no kōsei* (Tokyo: Tochi Seido Shiryō Hozonkai, 1958), 31.

28. Satō, "Taishō-Shōwa shoki no nōgyō," 380.

29. Baba Akira, *Suiri jigyō no tenkai to jinushisei*, Kindai tochi seidoshi kenkyū sōsho 7 (Tokyo: Ochanomizu Shobō, 1965), 148.

30. Baba, *Suiri jigyō no tenkai to jinushisei*, 145.

31. Baba, *Suiri jigyō no tenkai to jinushisei*, 143.

32. Wada, 494.

33. Baba, *Suiri jigyō no tenkai to jinushisei*, 107.

34. Satō, "Taishō-Shōwa shoki no nōgyō," 380.

35. Abiko Rin, "Meiji kōki no nōgyō," in *Miyagiken nōmin undōshi*, ed. Nakamura Kichiji (Tokyo: Nihon Hyōronsha, 1968), 191.

36. Abiko, "Meiji kōki no nōgyō," 188.

37. Wada, 493.

38. Satō, "Taishō-Shōwa shoki no nōgyō," 382; Wada, 513.

39. Baba, *Suiri jigyō no tenkai to jinushisei*, 146.

40. Yamao Michio, "Miyagiken no nōgyō kaikaku," in *Sangyō 1*, Miyagi kenshi 9 (Sendai: Miyagi Kenshi Kankōkai, 1968), 208.

41. Yamotochō, *Yamoto chōshi*, vol. 3 (Yamoto: Yamotochō, 1976), 347.

42. Satō, "Taishō-Shōwa shoki no nōgyō," 380.

43. Baba, "Suitō tansaku nōgyō no kakuritsu katei," 194.

44. Murakami Tetsuichi, "Meiji-Taishō ni okeru Miyagiken nōgyō no shinten," in *Sangyō 1*, Miyagi kenshi 9 (Sendai: Miyagi Kenshi Kankōkai, 1968), 158; Satō, "Taishō-Shōwa shoki no nōgyō," 380.

45. Murakami, 155.

46. Murakami, 159.

47. Penelope Francks, Johanna Boestel, and Choo Hyop Kim, *Agriculture and Economic Development in East Asia: From Growth to Protectionism in Japan, Korea, and Taiwan* (London; New York: Routledge, 1999), 47.

48. Smith, *A Time of Crisis*, 20–22.

49. Iwamoto Yoshiteru, "Shōkōgyō to kinyū," in *Miyagiken nōmin undōshi*, ed. Nakamura Kichiji (Tokyo: Nihon Hyōronsha, 1968), 343–344.

50. Baba, *Suiri jigyō no tenkai to jinushisei*, 120.

51. While the effects of the war and Occupation may have played a role in disrupting market production, the fact that the same survey found extensive production of non-rice products for the market in other parts of Miyagi demonstrates the dominance of rice in Senboku. See Wada, 483.

52. Wada, 490–491.

53. Ōmameuda Minoru, *Kindai Nihon no shokuryō seisaku: taigai izon beikoku kyōkyū kōzō no henyō* (Kyoto: Minerva Shobō, 1993), 166, 174–175.

54. Smith, *A Time of Crisis*, 48.

55. Smith, *A Time of Crisis*, 52–53.

56. Miyagi Kenritsu Nōgyō Shikenjō, 3.

57. Baba, *Suiri jigyō no tenkai to jinushisei*, 129.

58. Wada, 485–486.

59. Abiko, "Meiji kōki no nōgyō," 187.

60. Abiko, "Jinushisei no saihensei to teitai," 228–229.

61. Baba, *Suiri jigyō no tenkai to jinushisei*, 130–131.

62. Wada, 496–497.

63. Baba, *Suiri jigyō no tenkai to jinushisei*, 154.

64. Michael Lewis, *Rioters and Citizens: Mass Protest in Imperial Japan* (Berkeley: University of California Press, 1990), 178.

65. Ann Waswo, *Japanese Landlords: The Decline of a Rural Elite* (Berkeley: University of California Press, 1977), 88–89.

66. Wada, 506–507.

67. Wada, 500, 505.

68. Wada, 514.

69. Waswo, 31, 63.

70. Satō, "Taishō-Shōwa shoki no nōgyō," 387–388.

71. Asahi Shinbunsha, *Saitōke—Shūhen monogatari: Miyagi no nōchi kaihō* (Sendai: Hōbundō Shuppan Hanbai, 1979), 28.

72. Satō, "Taishō-Shōwa shoki no nōgyō," 390.

73. Lewis, *Rioters and Citizens*, 180.

74. Lewis, *Rioters and Citizens*, 180.

75. Murakami, 152–153.

76. Waswo, 33–34; Smith, *A Time of Crisis*, 75. On the deflationary years of the early 1920s, see chapter 7 of Mark Metzler, *Lever of Empire: The International Gold Standard and the Crisis of Liberalism in Prewar Japan* (Berkeley: University of California Press, 2006).

77. Smith, *A Time of Crisis*, 75.

78. Smith, *A Time of Crisis,* 74.

79. Yonekura Tatsujirō, *Miyagi kusanone undō no gunzō* (Sendai: Shakai Undō Kenkyūkai, 1984), 24–36.

80. Abiko Rin, *Miyagiken no hyakunen,* Kenmin 100-nenshi 4 (Tokyo: Yamakawa Shuppansha, 1999), 159.

81. Yonekura, 28. For more on the Saitō company, see below.

82. Yonekura, 73–76.

83. Kanan Chōshi Hensan Iinkai, ed., *Kanan chōshi,* vol. 2 (Kanan: Kananchō, 1971), 17; Yamao, 204; Yonekura, 76.

84. Sunaga Shigemitsu, *Sen chōbu jinushi Saitōke no tochi shūseki katei to sono kyoson Maeyachimura no nōchi kaikaku* (Tokyo: Nōsei Chōsakai, 1952), 16–17.

85. Waswo, 88–89.

86. Saitō Hōonkai, *Saitō Zen'uemon ōden* (Tokyo: Saitō Hōonkai, 1928), 89.

87. Sunaga, 17.

88. Saitō Hōonkai, 95–97.

89. On the 1927 crisis, see Metzler, 175–180.

90. Kanan Chōshi Hensan Iinkai, *Kanan chōshi,* 2:17.

91. Asahi Shinbunsha, 45.

92. It also attracted twenty police officers, whose anticipated attendance led the organizers to remove all the tatami mats from the house, as police were infamous for refusing to remove their boots when on duty. See Asahi Shinbunsha, 47–48; Kanan Chōshi Hensan Iinkai, *Kanan chōshi,* 2:19.

93. Asahi Shinbunsha, 48.

94. Asahi Shinbunsha, 43.

95. Abiko, *Miyagiken no hyakunen,* 162.

96. Yonekura, 28.

97. Kerry Smith, "Building the Model Village: Rural Revitalization and the Great Depression," in *Farmers and Village Life in Twentieth-Century Japan,* ed. Ann Waswo and Nishida Yoshiaki (New York: RoutledgeCurzon, 2003), 131.

98. Abiko, *Miyagiken no hyakunen,* 168–169.

99. Abiko, *Miyagiken no hyakunen,* 168.

100. Teikoku Nōkai, *Tōhoku chihō nōson ni kansuru chōsa* (Tokyo: Teikoku Nōkai, 1933), 253.

101. Abiko, *Miyagiken no hyakunen,* 171.

102. Smith, *A Time of Crisis,* 252.

103. Abiko, *Miyagiken no hyakunen,* 170.

104. Abiko, *Miyagiken no hyakunen,* 175–177.

105. Smith, *A Time of Crisis,* 86–87.

106. Wasaki Kōzō and Yamazaki Harushige, "Nōgyō kyōkō kara sensō keizaika no nōgyō e," in *Nihon nōgyō hattatsushi: Meiji ikō ni okeru,* vol. 8 (Tokyo: Chūō Kōronsha, 1978), 35–36.

107. Smith, *A Time of Crisis,* 12.

108. Abiko, *Miyagiken no hyakunen,* 181.

109. Abiko, *Miyagiken no hyakunen,* 170.

110. Mori Takemaro, "Colonies and Countryside in Wartime Japan," in *Farmers and Village Life in Twentieth-Century Japan,* ed. Ann Waswo and Nishida Yoshiaki (New York: RoutledgeCurzon, 2003), 176.

111. Wasaki Kōzō and Yamazaki Harushige, 44.

112. Takahashi Kōichirō, "Kindai, Gendai: Gyōzaisei," in *Kashimadai chōshi,* ed. Kashimadai Chōshi Hensan Iinkai (Kashimadai: Kashimadaichō, 1994), 315.

113. Abiko, *Miyagiken no hyakunen,* 177–178.

114. Smith, *A Time of Crisis,* 145.

115. Mori, 177.

116. Smith, *A Time of Crisis*, 108–111.

117. Miyagi Kengikaishi Hensan Iinkai, ed., *Miyagi kengikaishi*, vol. 4 (Sendai: Miyagi Kengikaishi Hensan Iinkai, 1979), 274.

118. Abiko Rin, "Manshū bunson imin no tenkai," in *Nangō chōshi*, ed. Nangō Chōshi Hensan Iinkai, vol. 2 (Nangō: Nangōchō, 1985), 339–340.

119. Abiko Rin, "'Manshū' bunson imin to sonraku no henshitsu: Miyagiken Tōdagun Nangōmura no jirei," in *Kindai Nihon shakai hatten shiron: Kidota Shirō kyōju taikan kinen ronbunshū*, ed. Higashi Toshio and Tanno Seishū (Tokyo: Perikansha, 1988), 330.

120. Nōson Kōsei Kyōkai, "Bunson keikaku jirei: keizai kōsei mura ni okeru Manshū imin bunson keikaku jirei (1937)," in *Dai-nihen: Bunson bungō imin keikaku, imin mura chōsa shiryō 1–7*, Manshū imin kankei shiryō shūsei 7 (Tokyo: Fuji Shuppan, 1990), 3.

121. Reminiscing later about his difficulties in Nangō, Matsukawa recalled that landlords and technicians, the same types who opposed *bunson* plans in the *nōkai*, were his most obstinate opponents. See Nōrinshō Keizai Kōseibu, ed., *Shinnōson no kensetsu: tairiku e bunson daiidō* (Tokyo: Tokyō Asahi Shinbunsha, 1939), 106.

122. Abiko, "Manshū bunson imin no tenkai," 327.

123. This marks Nangō's landlords as different from the Tōhoku landlords described by Louise Young, who supported mass emigration plans because they saved them the trouble of evicting their tenants. See Louise Young, *Japan's Total Empire: Manchuria and the Culture of Wartime Imperialism* (Berkeley: University of California Press, 1998), 331, 334.

124. Abiko, "'Manshū' bunson imin to sonraku no henshitsu: Miyagiken Tōdagun Nangōmura no jirei," 347.

125. See Christopher Craig, "Nihon no Tōhoku chihō ni okeru nōmin to Manshū imin: Miyagiken no jinushi, kosakunin o chūshin ni," *Harurimu Nihongaku*, no. 31 (2017): 55–72.

126. Abiko, "'Manshū' bunson imin to sonraku no henshitsu: Miyagiken Tōdagun Nangōmura no jirei," 343–345.

127. Takahashi, 290.

128. Koide Kōzō, *Kamata Sannosuke ō: Waraji sonchō no shōgai* (Tokyo: Nihon Jichi Kensetsu Undō Honbu, 1961), 29–30.

129. Ishikawa Teruo, "Shinainuma no kantaku: kaikon no junbi ga susumerareru," in *Kashimadai chōshi*, ed. Kashimadai Chōshi Hensan Iinkai (Kashimadai: Kashimadaichō, 1994), 811–812.

130. Nōrinshō Nōmukyoku, *Kaikonchi ijū keiei jirei* (Tokyo: Nōrinshō Nōmukyoku, 1923), 470.

131. Kashimadai Shōgakkō, *Wa ga sonshi* (Kashimadai: Kashimadai Shōgakkō, 1936), 37.

132. Naikaku, "Miyagiken Shidagun Kashimadai sonchō Kamada Sannosuke ranju hōshō kashi no ken," December 17, 1927, Kōbun zassan: Shōwa ni-nen: dai hachi ken: Naikaku hachi: Naikaku hachi (shōdōkyoku roku), National Archives of Japan.

133. Abiko, "Meiji kōki no nōgyō," 190.

134. Takahashi, 310.

135. Takahashi, 290.

136. Takahashi, 296.

137. Koide, 34.

138. Koide, 30.

139. Koide, 55–56.

140. "Waraji sonchō," *Tōkyō Asahi shinbun*, December 1, 1936, 11.

141. "Retsuretsu, hodobashiru tsuchi no koe: jūninin tokunōka ni kiku," *Tōkyō Asahi shinbun*, June 6, 1941, 2.

142. "Nōson no yūchiku kikaika kokusaku ni saiyō o kibō tokunōka, jitsujō o kaichin," *Tōkyō Asahi shinbun*, June 15, 1941, 1.

143. Ko Kamata Sannosuke Ō Shōtokukai, *Kamata Sannosuke ōden* (Kashimadai: Ko Kamata Sannosuke Ō Shōtokukai, 1953), 131–132.

144. Honma Rakukan, *Waraji sonchō Kamata Sannosuke ō: Yokusan no ijin—Shōwa no Sontoku* (Tokyo: Jidaisha, 1942). Other biographies of Kamata were published in the same and the following year, attesting to his national prominence during the war. See Matsuda Takeshirō, *Waraji sonchō* (Tokyo: Naka Shoten, 1942) and Kōdō Shinbunsha, ed., *Ima Sontoku Kamata Sannosuke* (Okayama: Kōdō Shinbunsha, 1943).

145. "Advertisement for Waraji sonchō Kamata Sannosuke ō: Yokusan no ijin—Shōwa no Sontoku," *Tōkyō Asahi shinbun*, March 3, 1942, 1.

146. "'Hōsaku ni youna' Manshū no bunson o imon ni dekakeru 'Waraji sonchō' Kamata Sannosuke," *Tōkyō Asahi shinbun*, September 15, 1942, 3.

147. "Waraji sonchō," 11.

148. Abiko, *Miyagiken no hyakunen*, 213–215.

149. Abiko, "'Manshū' bunson imin to sonraku no henshitsu: Miyagiken Tōdagun Nangōmura no jirei," 351.

150. Miyagi Kengikaishi Hensan Iinkai, 4:285.

Conclusion

1. Arthur Franklin Raper, *The Japanese Village in Transition*, Report (Supreme Commander for the Allied Powers. Natural Resources Section) 136 (Tokyo: General Headquarters, Supreme Commander for the Allied Powers, 1950), 161.

Bibliography

Abe Kumaji. *Azumi-ō shōden.* Wakuya: Yamamoto Kappanjo, 1940.

Abiko Rin. "Jinushi keiei no henka to jinushisei no igi." In *Kindai Nihon no jinushi to nōmin: suitō tansaku nōgyō no keizaiteki kenkyū, Nangō-mura,* edited by Sunaga Shigemitsu, 246–282. Tokyo: Ochanomizu Shobō, 1966.

———. "Jinushisei no saihensei to teitai." In *Miyagiken nōmin undōshi,* edited by Nakamura Kichiji, 203–243. Tokyo: Nihon Hyōronsha, 1968.

———. "Manshū bunson imin no tenkai." In *Nangō chōshi,* edited by Nangō Chōshi Hensan Iinkai, 2:336–383. Nangō: Nangōchō, 1985.

———. "'Manshū' bunson imin to sonraku no henshitsu: Miyagiken Tōdagun Nangōmura no jirei." In *Kindai Nihon shakai hatten shiron: Kidota Shirō kyōju taikan kinen ronbunshū,* edited by Higashi Toshio and Tanno Seishū, 321–351. Tokyo: Perikansha, 1988.

———. "Meiji kōki no nōgyō." In *Miyagiken nōmin undōshi,* edited by Nakamura Kichiji, 179–202. Tokyo: Nihon Hyōronsha, 1968.

———. *Miyagiken no hyakunen.* Kenmin 100-nenshi 4. Tokyo: Yamakawa Shuppansha, 1999.

———. "Nōchi kaikaku to buraku: Buraku no tochi kanri kinō o chūshin ni." *Rekishi hyōron,* no. 435 (1986): 32–45.

"Advertisement for Waraji sonchō Kamata Sannosuke ō: Yokusan no ijin—Shōwa no Sontoku." *Tōkyō Asahi shinbun,* March 3, 1942.

Aichiken Nōkai. *Zenkoku tokunōka retsuden.* Nagoya: Aichiken Nōkai, 1910. http://kindai.ndl.go.jp/info:ndljp/pid/778253.

Akino, Masakatsu, and Yujiro Hayami. "Efficiency and Equity in Public Research: Rice Breeding in Japan's Economic Development." *American Journal of Agricultural Economics* 57, no. 1 (1975): 1–10.

———. "Sources of Agricultural Growth in Japan, 1880–1965." *Quarterly Journal of Economics* 88, no. 3 (1974): 454–479.

Araki Mikio. "Nōgyō keiei no hattatsu to kisei jinushiteki tochi shoyū." In *Keizaishi keieishi ronshū,* 615–651. Osaka: Ōsaka Keizai Daigaku, 1984.

———. *Nōgyōshi: kindai Nihon jinushisei shiron*. Tokyo: Bunmei Shobō, 1985.

Ariizumi Sadao. "Kōgyō iken no seiritsu." *Shigaku zasshi* 78, no. 10 (1969): 1–30.

Arima Manabu. "Mura no naka no mintō to ritō: kindai Nihon no chiiki, senkyo, seitō." In *Chiikishi no kanosei: chiiki, Nihon, sekai*, edited by Kindai Nihon Kenkyūkai. Tokyo: Yamakawa Shuppansha, 1997.

Asahi Shinbunsha. *Saitōke—Shūhen monogatari: Miyagi no nōchi kaihō*. Sendai: Hōbundō Shuppan Hanbai, 1979.

Baba Akira. "Nangōmura no suiri to chisui o meguru chiiki tairitsu." In *Kindai Nihon no jinushi to nōmin: suitō tansaku nōgyō no keizaiteki kenkyū, Nangō-mura*, edited by Sunaga Shigemitsu, 139–158. Tokyo: Ochanomizu Shobō, 1966.

———. *Suiri jigyō no tenkai to jinushisei*. Kindai tochi seidoshi kenkyū sōsho 7. Tokyo: Ochanomizu Shobō, 1965.

———. "Suitō tansaku nōgyō no kakuritsu katei." In *Kindai Nihon no jinushi to nōmin: suitō tansaku nōgyō no keizaiteki kenkyū, Nangō-mura*, edited by Sunaga Shigemitsu, 185–213. Tokyo: Ochanomizu Shobō, 1966.

Beckert, Sven. *Empire of Cotton: A Global History*. New York: Alfred A. Knopf, 2104.

Bowen, Roger W. *Rebellion and Democracy in Meiji Japan: A Study of Commoners in the Popular Rights Movement*. Berkeley: University of California Press, 1980.

Brown, Sidney Devere. "Ōkubo Toshimichi: His Political and Economic Policies in Early Meiji Japan." *The Journal of Asian Studies* 21, no. 2 (1962): 183–197.

Chatani, Sayaka. *Nation-Empire: Ideology and Rural Youth Mobilization in Japan and Its Colonies*. Ithaca, NY: Cornell University Press, 2018.

Chew, Selfa. *Uprooting Community: Japanese Mexicans, World War II, and the U.S.-Mexico Borderlands*. Tuscon: University of Arizona Press, 2015.

Craig, Christopher. "Nihon no Tōhoku chihō ni okeru nōmin to Manshū imin: Miyagiken no jinushi, kosakunin o chūshin ni." *Harurimu Nihongaku*, no. 31 (2017): 55–72.

Crawcour, Sydney. "Kōgyō Iken: Maeda Masana and His View of Meiji Economic Development." *Journal of Japanese Studies* 23, no. 1 (January 1, 1997): 69–104. https://doi.org/10.2307/133124.

Dai Nihon Nōkai. *Dai Nihon Nōkai seisekisho*. Tokyo: Dai Nihon Nōkai, 1895. http://dl.ndl.go.jp/info:ndljp/pid/901081.

Dai Nihon Nōkai, Dai Nihon Sanrinkai, and Dai Nihon Suisankai. "Dai Nihon Nōkai ryakushi." In *Dai Nihon Nōkai—Dai Nihon Sanrinkai—Dai Nihon Suisankai sōritsu shichijūgonen kinen*. Tokyo: Dai Nihon Nōkai, 1955.

Drixler, Fabian Franz. *Mabiki: Infanticide and Population Growth in Eastern Japan, 1660–1950*. Berkeley: University of California Press, 2013.

Duus, Peter. *Party Rivalry and Political Change in Taishō Japan*. Harvard East Asian Series, 35. Cambridge, MA: Harvard University Press, 1968.

Egami Toshio. "Hayashi Enri to kannōsha." In *Nihon nōgyō hattatsushi: Meiji ikō ni okeru*, 2:597–668. Tokyo: Chūō Kōronsha, 1978.

Eggert, Udo. *Land Reform in Japan, Specially Based on the Development of Credit Associations*. Tokyo: Tokyo Tsukiji Kwappan Seizosho, 1890.

———. *Nihon shinnōsaku*. Tokyo: Hakubunkan, 1891. http://kindai.ndl.go.jp/info:ndljp/pid/802414.

"Entō jiken no kōhan iyoiyo kaitei." *Ōu nichinichi shinbun*, June 18, 1893.

Ericson, Steven J. "The 'Matsukata Deflation' Reconsidered: Financial Stabilization and Japanese Exports in a Global Depression, 1881–1885." *Journal of Japanese Studies* 40, no. 1 (2014): 1–28.

Francks, Penelope. "Rice for the Masses: Food Policy and the Adoption of Imperial Self-Sufficiency in Early Twentieth-Century Japan." *Japan Forum* 15, no. 1 (2003): 125–146. https://doi.org/10.1080/0955580032000077766.

———. *Rural Economic Development in Japan: From the Nineteenth Century to the Pacific War.* London: Routledge, 2006.

———. *Technology and Agricultural Development in Pre-War Japan.* New Haven, CT: Yale University Press, 1984.

Francks, Penelope, Johanna Boestel, and Choo Hyop Kim. *Agriculture and Economic Development in East Asia: From Growth to Protectionism in Japan, Korea, and Taiwan.* London; New York: Routledge, 1999.

Garcia, Jerry. *Looking Like the Enemy: Japanese Mexicans, the Mexican State, and US Hegemony, 1897–1945.* Tuscon: University of Arizona Press, 2014.

General Headquarters Supreme Commander for the Allied Powers. *Agriculture.* Vol. 41. History of the Nonmilitary Activities of the Occupation of Japan, 1945–1951. Tokyo: Nihon Tosho Sentaa, 1990.

———. *The Rural Land Reform.* Vol. 33. History of the Nonmilitary Activities of the Occupation of Japan, 1945–1951. Tokyo: Nihon Tosho Sentaa, 1990.

Gilmartin, William M., and W. I. Ladejinsky. "The Promise of Agrarian Reform in Japan." *Foreign Affairs* 26, no. 2 (1948): 312–324.

Gluck, Carol. *Japan's Modern Myths: Ideology in the Late Meiji Period.* Princeton, NJ: Princeton University Press, 1985.

Hackett, Roger F. *Yamagata Aritomo in the Rise of Modern Japan, 1838–1922.* Cambridge, MA: Harvard University Press, 1971.

Harootunian, Harry D. "The Economic Rehabilitation of the Samurai in the Early Meiji Period." *The Journal of Asian Studies* 19, no. 4 (1960): 433–444.

Hayami, Yujiro. "Rice Policy in Japan's Economic Development." *American Journal of Agricultural Economics* 54, no. 1 (1972): 19–31.

Heibonsha chihō shiryō sentaa, ed. *Miyagiken no chimei.* Nihon rekishi chimei taikei 4. Tokyo: Heibonsha, 1987.

Henning, Hillmann. "Localism and the Limits of Political Brokerage: Evidence from Revolutionary Vermont." *American Journal of Sociology* 114, no. 2 (2008): 287–331.

Hida Namishige. "Hida Roichi shōden." *Ōitaken chihōshi,* no. 50 (1968): 27–39.

Hida Rōichi. "Jinushikai setchi no hitsuyō." *Chūō nōjihō,* no. 5 (1900): 3–6.

Hirata Ichirō. "Miyagiken no kosaku sōdō." *Tōkyō shakai shinbun 11,* June 25, 1908.

Honma Rakukan. *Waraji sonchō Kamata Sannosuke ō: Yokusan no ijin—Shōwa no Sontoku.* Tokyo: Jidaisha, 1942.

" 'Hōsaku ni youna' Manshū no bunson o imon ni dekakeru 'Waraji sonchō' Kamata Sannosuke." *Tōkyō Asahi shinbun,* September 15, 1942.

Inoue Kunio. "Hatasakumotsu no suitai to kōryū." In *Nihon nōgyō hattatsushi: Meiji ikō ni okeru,* 3:101–217. Tokyo: Chūō Kōronsha, 1978.

Inukai, Ichirou, and Arlon R. Tussing. " 'Kōgyō Iken': Japan's Ten Year Plan, 1884." *Economic Development and Cultural Change* 16, no. 1 (October 1, 1967): 51–71. https://doi.org/10.2307/1152507.

Ishikawa Hisao. *Kindai Nihon no meibōka to jichi: meiyoshoku seido no hōshakaishiteki kenkyū.* Tokyo: Bokutakusha, 1987.

———. *Nihonteki jichi no tankyū: meibōka jichiron no keifu.* Shohan. Nagoya: Nagoya Daigaku Shuppankai, 1995.

Ishikawa Rono Jiseki Chōsakai. *Tenka no rōnō Ishikawa Rikinosuke: denki Ishikawa Rikinosuke.* Tokyo: Ōzorasha, 2000.

Ishikawa Teruo. "Shinainuma no kantaku: kaikon no junbi ga susumerareru." In *Kashimadai chōshi,* edited by Kashimadai Chōshi Hensan Iinkai, 811–815. Kashimadai: Kashimadaichō, 1994.

Ishikawaken and Fukushimaken. *Ishikawaken Hayashi Enri beisaku kairyō seisekihyō; Fukushimaken shikenden tsubogari seiseki.* Utsunomiya: Tochigiken Naimubu, 1891. http://kindai.ndl.go.jp/info:ndljp/pid/838010.

Itō Katsuhide. "Shinainuma no kantaku: Meiji senketsu no kaisaku." In *Kashimadai chōshi,* edited by Kashimadai Chōshi Hensan Iinkai, 790–805. Kashimadai: Kashimadaichō, 1994.

Itō Seijirō and Konishi Rihee. *Sendai mukashigatari Den Tanuki-ō yawa.* Sendai: Konishi Rihee, 1925.

Itō Yukio. "Meibōka chitsujo no kaizō to seinentō: Saitō Takao o meguru Tanba no hitobito." *Nihonshi kenkyū,* no. 241 (1982): 39–73.

Iwakura Tomomi. *Iwakura-kō jikki.* Vol. 3. Tokyo: Iwakura-kō Kyūseki Hozonkai, 1927.

Iwamoto Yoshiteru. "Shōkōgyō to kinyū." In *Miyagiken nōmin undōshi,* edited by Nakamura Kichiji, 343–371. Tokyo: Nihon Hyōronsha, 1968.

"Jinushi to kosakunin." *Heimin Shinbun 13,* February 1, 1907.

Kamata Sannosuke. *Mekishiko shokumin annai.* Tokyo: Seikō Zasshisha, 1908.

Kanan Chōshi Hensan Iinkai, ed. *Kanan chōshi.* Vol. 1. 2 vols. Kanan: Kananchō, 1967.

———, ed. *Kanan chōshi.* Vol. 2. 2 vols. Kanan: Kananchō, 1971.

Kanno Toshimitsu. *Shinainuma kantaku shōshi: Shinainuma o hiraita hitobito no kunan no rekishi.* Sendai: Hōbundō, 1981.

Karlin, Jason G. *Gender and Nation in Meiji Japan: Modernity, Loss, and the Doing of History.* Honolulu: University of Hawai'i Press, 2014.

Kashimadai Chōshi Hensan Iinkai. *Kashimadai chōshi.* Kashimadai: Kashimadaichō, 1994.

Kashimadai Shōgakkō. *Wa ga sonshi.* Kashimadai: Kashimadai Shōgakkō, 1936.

Kato, Kozaburo. "The Agrarian Origins of Modern Japan." In *Agriculture in the Modernization of Japan, 1850–2000,* edited by Shuzo Teruoka, translated by Sarah Ham Akamine. New Delhi: Manohar, 2008.

Katō Shigemoto. "Ōu chihō no nawashiro to kikō to no kankei." *Dai Nihon Nōkaihō,* no. 210 (1899): 19–26.

Keitō Nōkaishi Hensankai. *Keitō Nōkai no enkaku.* Keitō Nōkaishi Hensankai, 20th century.

Kelly, William W. *Deference and Defiance in Nineteenth-Century Japan.* Princeton, NJ: Princeton University Press, 1985.

Kenshi Orimono Tōshikki Kyōshūkai, ed. *Menshi shūdankai kiji.* Tokyo: Yūrindō, 1885.

Ko Kamata Sannosuke Ō Shōtokukai. *Kamata Sannosuke ōden.* Kashimadai: Ko Kamata Sannosuke Ō Shōtokukai, 1953.

"Kōchi seiri jigyō gaikyō: Nōshōmushō chōsa." *Kobe shinbun,* March 1, 1913. http://www.lib.kobe-u.ac.jp/das/jsp/ja/ContentViewM.jsp?METAID=10074058&TYPE=IMAGE_FILE&POS=1.

Kōdō Shinbunsha, ed. *Ima Sontoku Kamata Sannosuke.* Okayama: Kōdō Shinbunsha, 1943.

Koide Kōzō. *Kamata Sannosuke ō: Waraji sonchō no shōgai.* Tokyo: Nihon Jichikensestu Undō Honbu, 1961.

"Kosaku dōmei." *Shūkan shakai shinbun 22,* October 27, 1907.

"Kosakunin mondai to Saitō gōnō." *Kahoku shinpō,* March 10, 1903.

Kumagai Kaneo. "Kantaku." In *Doboku,* 123–234. Miyagi kenshi 8. Sendai: Miyagi Kenshi Kankōkai, 1960.
"Kyūsai ihō." *Miyagiken Kyōikukai zasshi,* no. 113 (1906).
Lewis, Michael. *Becoming Apart: National Power and Local Politics in Toyama, 1868–1945.* Harvard East Asian Monographs 192. Cambridge, MA: Harvard University Asia Center, 2000.
———. *Rioters and Citizens: Mass Protest in Imperial Japan.* Berkeley: University of California Press, 1990.
Maeda Masana. "Kyō no kyūmu ha kokuze kenze gunze sonze o sadamuru ni ari (1892)." In *Kōgyō iken, Shoken,* 415–420. Meiji Taishō nōsei keizai meichoshū 1. Tokyo: Nōsangyoson Bunka Kyōkai, 1976.
Maki Takayasu. *Nihon suiri shisetsu no kenkyū.* Tokyo: Doboku Zasshisha, 1958.
Matsuda Takeshirō. *Waraji sonchō.* Tokyo: Naka Shoten, 1942.
Matsuzawa Yūsaku. "Daiku shōku sei' no kōzō to chihō minkai: Kumagayaken no baai." *Shigaku zasshi* 112, no. 1 (2003): 1–33.
Meiji hōshōroku. Vol. 1. Osaka: Naniwa Shoin, 1897. http://kindai.ndl.go.jp/info:ndljp/pid/778838.
Metzler, Mark. *Lever of Empire: The International Gold Standard and the Crisis of Liberalism in Prewar Japan.* Berkeley: University of California Press, 2006.
Mikuriya Takashi. *Meiji kokka keisei to chihō keiei: 1881–1890 nen.* Tokyo: Tōkyō Daigaku Shuppankai, 1980.
Miyachi Masato. *Nichiro sengo seijishi no kenkyū: teikokushugi keiseiki no toshi to nōson.* Tokyo: Tokyo Daigaku Shuppankai, 1973.
Miyagi Kengikaishi Hensan Iinkai, ed. *Miyagi kengikaishi.* Vol. 4. Sendai: Miyagi Kengikaishi Hensan Iinkai, 1979.
Miyagi Kenritsu Nōgyō Shikenjō. *Miyagi Kenritsu Nōgyō Shikenjōshi: sōritsu 50 shūnen kinen.* Sendai: Miyagi Kenritsu Nōgyō Shikenjō, 1953.
Miyagiken. *Meiji sanjūgonen Miyagiken kyōkanshi.* Sendai: Miyagiken, 1904.
———. *Meiji sanjūhachinen Miyagiken kyōkōshi.* Sendai: Miyagiken, 1916.
———. "Tōda Monō Oshika sangun funsō chōtei tenmatsusho." Sendai: Miyagiken, 1894.
Miyagiken chiji kanbō bunshogakari. "Miyagiken furei ruisan, Meiji 40 nen 1 gatsu—Meiji 40 nen 12 gatsu." Miyagiken Chiji Kanbō Bunshogakari, 1907. Miyagiken Kōbunshokan.
Miyagiken Keisatsushi Hensan Iinkai, ed. *Miyagiken keisatsushi.* Vol. 1. 3 vols. Sendai: Miyagiken Keisatsu Honbu, 1980.
Miyagiken Naimubu Daiyonka. *Miyagiken Natorigun Oidemura Sonze Chōsasho.* Oide (Miyagi): Miyagiken Natorigun Oidemura, 1902.
Miyagiken Nōkai. *Kōchi seiri jisshi benran.* Sendai: Miyagiken Nōkai, 1903. http://dl.ndl.go.jp/info:ndljp/pid/900566.
"Miyagiken ōjinushikai." *Dai Nihon Nōkaihō,* no. 311 (May 1907): 42.
Miyagiken Shida Gunyakusho, ed. *Shidagun enkakushi.* Furukawa: Miyagiken Shida Gunyakusho, 1912.
Miyagiken sōmubu chōsaka. *Shōwa nijūrokunen Miyagiken tōkei sōran.* Chōsaka shiryō 57. Sendai: Miyagiken Sōmubu Chōsaka, 1951.
Mori Takemaro. "Colonies and Countryside in Wartime Japan." In *Farmers and Village Life in Twentieth-Century Japan,* edited by Ann Waswo and Nishida Yoshiaki, 175–198. New York: RoutledgeCurzon, 2003.

Murakami Tetsuichi. "Meiji-Taishō ni okeru Miyagiken nōgyō no shinten." In *Sangyō 1,* 1–175. Miyagi kenshi 9. Sendai: Miyagi Kenshi Kankōkai, 1968.
Muramatsu Teijirō. *Kenchiku, doboku.* Oyatoi gaikokujin 15. Tokyo: Kajima Shuppankai, 1976.
Nagasawa Katsuo. *Noda Shin'ichi ōden.* Sendai: Noda Ken'ichi Okina Kōseki Kenshōkai, 1962.
Naikaku. "Kōchi seirihō o sadamu," March 20, 1899. Administrative Records: Cabinet/Prime Minister's Office: Records concerning Dajokan/Cabinet: Category No. 6 Kobun Ruishu Various Offices: Kobun Ruishu Vol. 23, 1899: Kōbun ruiju dai-23hen Meiji 32nen dai 33kan chiri tochi shinrin kanshō. National Archives of Japan. http://www.digital.archives.go.jp/DAS/meta/MetSearch.cgi.
———. "Miyagiken Shidagun Kashimadai sonchō Kamata Sannosuke ranju hōshō kashi no ken," December 17, 1927. Kōbun zassan: Shōwa ni-nen: dai hachi ken: Naikaku hachi: Naikaku hachi (shōdōkyoku roku). National Archives of Japan.
Nakagawa Nozomu. "Nōson no kairyō." In *Kanka kyūsai jigyō kōenshū,* 989–1015. Tokyo: Naimushō Chihōkyoku, 1909. http://kindai.ndl.go.jp/info:ndljp/pid/995169.
Nakamura, Takafusa. *Economic Growth in Prewar Japan.* Translated by Robert A. Feldman. New Haven, CT: Yale University Press, 1983.
Nangōchō. *Nangō chōshi.* Vol. 1. 2 vols. Nangō: Nangōchō, 1980.
Nishikawa Tadashi. "Yuzei nikki." *Shūkan shakai shinbun 29,* December 15, 1907.
Nishimura Eijūrō. *Zenkoku Nōjikaishi.* Tokyo: n.p., 1911. http://dl.ndl.go.jp/info:ndljp/pid/802339.
Nishimura Kōichi. *Meiji nōsei to nōkai: Nōkai no hassei kara Teikoku Nōkai no seiritsu made.* Shiryō 3. N.p.: Nihon Nōgyō Kenkyūjō, 1951.
Nishimura Yasukichi. "Kangyō hōshin ni kansuru enzetsu hikki." In *Sangyō hōshin,* edited by Seisan Chōsakai, Vol. 1. Tokyo: Seisan Chōsakai, 1911.
Nōgyō Suiri Mondai Kenkyūkai. *Nōgyō suiri chitsujo no kenkyū.* 2nd ed. Tokyo: Ochanomizu Shobō, 1977.
Nōjikai. *Zenkoku nōji taikai hōkoku: Dai hakkai.* Tokyo: Nōjikai Honbu, 1901. http://kindai.ndl.go.jp/info:ndljp/pid/802341.
Nōrinshō Keizai Kōseibu, ed. *Shinnōson no kensetsu: tairiku e bunson daiidō.* Tokyo: Tōkyō Asahi Shinbunsha, 1939.
Nōrinshō Nōmukyoku. *Kaikonchi ijū keiei jirei.* Tokyo: Nōrinshō Nōmukyoku, 1923.
———, ed. "Nōsei keikaku zuhyō kaidoku." In *Meiji zenki kannō jiseki shūroku,* Vol. 2. Tokyo: Dai Nihon Nōkai, 1939.
Nōshōmushō. *Beisaku ni kansuru fukenrei.* Tokyo: Nōshōmushō, 1904. http://dl.ndl.go.jp/info:ndljp/pid/796421.
"Nōshōmushō no beikoku ni kansuru shitsumon ni taishi Tōkyō kaimai ton'ya no tōshin." *Dai Nihon Nōkai hōkoku,* no. 120 (1891): 43–49.
Nōshōmushō Nōmukyoku. *Fuken rōnō meibo.* Tokyo: Nōshōmushō Nōmukyoku, 1882. http://kindai.ndl.go.jp/info:ndljp/pid/900159.
———, ed. *Jinushi to kosakunin.* Tokyo: Sangyō Kumiai Chūōkai, 1909.
———. *Kaku chihō rōnōka oyobi shubyōko meibo.* Tokyo: Nōmukyoku Hōkokuka, 1882. http://kindai.ndl.go.jp/info:ndljp/pid/780373.
Nōson Kōsei Kyōkai. "Bunson keikaku jirei: keizai kōsei mura ni okeru Manshū imin bunson keikaku jirei (1937)." In *Dai-nihen: Bunson bungō imin keikaku, imin mura chōsa shiryō 1–7.* Manshū imin kankei shiryō shūsei 7. Tokyo: Fuji Shuppan, 1990.
"Nōson no yūchiku kikaika kokusaku ni saiyō o kibō tokunōka, jitsujō o kaichin." *Tōkyō Asahi shinbun,* June 15, 1941.

Obata Atsushi. "Meiji chūki ni okeru suiri o chūshin to shita nōmin funsō no ichirei: Iwayuru Entō Jiken ni tsuite." *Chiiki shakai kenkyū,* no. 5 (1953).

Ogawa Makoto. "Chisui, suiri, tochi kairyō no taikeiteki seibi." In *Nihon nōgyō hattatsushi: Meiji ikō ni okeru,* 4:104–232. Tokyo: Chūō Kōronsha, 1978.

Ogura Sōichi. "Beisaku ni kansuru fukenrei." In *Nihon nōgyō hattatsushi: Meiji ikō ni okeru,* 4:739–794. Tokyo: Chūō Kōronsha, 1978.

———. "Meiji zenki nōsei no dōkō to nōkai no seiritsu." In *Nihon nōgyō hattatsushi: Meiji ikō ni okeru,* 3:219–386. Tokyo: Chūō Kōronsha, 1978.

———. "Nōsei oyobi nōkai: Meiji kōki, Taishō shoki." In *Nihon nōgyō hattatsushi: Meiji ikō ni okeru,* 5:309–415. Tokyo: Chūō Kōronsha, 1978.

Ōitaken jinshiroku. Ōita: Ōitaken Jinshiroku Hakkōjo, 1914. http://kindai.ndl.go.jp /info:ndljp/pid/908965.

Ōmameuda Minoru. *Kindai Nihon no shokuryō seisaku: taigai izon beikoku kyōkyū kōzō no henyō.* Kyoto: Minerva Shobō, 1993.

Ōmori Ken. *Ōu Hokkaidō jitsugyō shisatsu hōkoku.* Mito: Ibarakiken Jitsugyō Shisatsudan, 1914.

Ōshō Shigeru. "Kyōsaku zakkan." *Miyagiken kyoikukai zasshi,* no. 112 (1905): 25–27.

Partner, Simon. *The Mayor of Aihara: A Japanese Villager and His Community, 1865–1925.* Berkeley: University of California Press, 2009.

Pratt, Edward E. *Japan's Protoindustrial Elite: The Economic Foundations of the Gōnō.* Harvard East Asian Monographs 179. Cambridge, MA: Harvard University Asia Center, distributed by Harvard University Press, 1999.

Pyle, Kenneth B. "The Technology of Japanese Nationalism: The Local Improvement Movement, 1900–1918." *Journal of Asian Studies* 33, no. 1 (1973): 51–65.

Raper, Arthur Franklin. *The Japanese Village in Transition.* Report (Supreme Commander for the Allied Powers. Natural Resources Section) 136. Tokyo: General Headquarters, Supreme Commander for the Allied Powers, 1950.

"Retsuretsu, hodobashiru tsuchi no koe: jūninin tokunōka ni kiku." *Tōkyō Asahi shinbun,* June 6, 1941.

Saitō Hōonkai. *Saitō Zen'uemon ōden.* Tokyo: Saitō Hōonkai, 1928.

Sakō Tsuneaki. "Nihon no nōgyō ha nōka no kyōdōgokoro ni yorazareba shinpo sezu soku nōgyō shokumiai no hitsuyō kyō no taikan ha nōka kinyū no heisoku nari soku sonraku yūtsū no hitsuyō (daijūkai daishūkai enjutsu)." *Dai Nihon Nōkai hōkoku,* no. 119 (1891): 1–31.

Sanriku Kahoku Shinpōsha. *Kitakamigawa monogatari.* Ishinomaki: Sanriku Kahoku Shinpōsha, 1989.

Sasa Hisashi. "Danseihen." In *Jinbutsushi,* 3–237. Miyagi kenshi 29. Sendai: Miyagi Kenshi Kankōkai, 1986.

Sasaki Toshi. *Nangō suirishi.* Nangō: Nangōchō, 1972.

Sasaki Yutaka. "Chihō kairyō undō to chōsonze chōsa." In *Chihō kairyō undōshi shiryō shūsei,* Vol. 1. Tokyo: Kashiwa Shobō, 1986.

Satō Tadashi. "Meiji makki no nōmin undō." In *Miyagiken nōmin undōshi,* edited by Nakamura Kichiji, 307–339. Tokyo: Nihon Hyōronsha, 1968.

———. "Taishō-Shōwa shoki no nōgyō." In *Miyagiken nōmin undōshi,* edited by Nakamura Kichiji, 371–404. Tokyo: Nihon Hyōronsha, 1968.

———. "Tōhoku chihō Meiji makki no nōmin undō no kōzō: Miyagiken Senboku heiya no bunseki (2)." *Iwate shigaku kenkyū,* no. 45 (1964): 61–72.

Sawayanagi Masatarō. "Kyōsakuchi kyōiku." *Miyagiken kyōikukai zasshi,* no. 111 (1905): 65–66.

Sendai Shishi Hensan Iinkai. *Sendai shishi: Shimin seikatsu.* Sendai shishi: Tokubetsuhen 4. Sendai: Sendaishi, 1997.

Shinainuma suigai yobō kumiaishi hensan iinkai. *Shinainuma suigai yobō kumiaishi.* Sendai: Shinainuma suigai yobō kumiaishi hensan iinkai, 1954.

Sippel, Patricia. "Chisui: Creating a Sacred Domain in Early Modern and Modern Japan." In *Public Spheres, Private Lives in Modern Japan, 1600–1950: Essays in Honor of Albert M. Craig,* edited by Gail Lee Bernstein, Andrew Gordon, and Kate Wildman Nakai. Cambridge, MA: Harvard University Asia Center, 2005.

Smethurst, Richard J. *Agricultural Development and Tenancy Disputes in Japan, 1870–1940.* Princeton, NJ: Princeton University Press, 1986.

Smiles, Samuel. *Self-Help: With Illustrations of Character and Conduct.* London: Ward, Lock, 1859.

Smith, Kerry. "Building the Model Village: Rural Revitalization and the Great Depression." In *Farmers and Village Life in Twentieth-Century Japan,* edited by Ann Waswo and Nishida Yoshiaki, 126–155. New York: RoutledgeCurzon, 2003.

Smith, Kerry Douglas. *A Time of Crisis: Japan, the Great Depression, and Rural Revitalization.* Cambridge, MA: Harvard University Press, 2001.

Smith, Thomas C. "Ōkura Nagatsune and the Technologists." In *Native Sources of Japanese Industrialization, 1750–1920,* by Thomas C. Smith, 173–198. Berkeley: University of California Press, 1988.

Stolz, Robert. *Bad Water: Nature, Pollution, and Politics in Japan, 1870–1950.* London: Duke University Press, 2014.

Sugano Shunsaku. "Meiji kōhanki no jinushiteki tochi shoyū no kakudai to sonsei shihai." In *Kindai Nihon no jinushi to nōmin: suitō tansaku nōgyō no keizaiteki kenkyū, Nangō-mura,* edited by Sunaga Shigemitsu, 100–139. Tokyo: Ochanomizu Shobō, 1966.

———. "Meiji zenhanki ni okeru jinushi no seisei to sonraku kōzō." In *Kindai Nihon no jinushi to nōmin: suitō tansaku nōgyō no keizaiteki kenkyū, Nangō-mura,* edited by Sunaga Shigemitsu, 39–99. Tokyo: Ochanomizu Shobō, 1966.

Sumitomo Akifumi. "Kindai chihō jichisei kakuritsuki no chihō gyōsei: Chihō Kairyō Undō to chiiki un'ei chitsujo." *Nihonshi kenkyū,* no. 368 (1992): 83–109.

Sunaga Shigemitsu. *Sen chōbu jinushi Saitōke no tochi shūseki katei to sono kyoson Maeyachimura no nōchi kaikaku.* Tokyo: Nōsei Chōsakai, 1952.

Takahashi Kōichirō. "Kindai, Gendai: Gyōzaisei." In *Kashimadai chōshi,* edited by Kashimadai Chōshi Hensan Iinkai, 261–361. Kashimadai: Kashimadaichō, 1994.

Takahashi Tansui. *Kashokuden: Nōkai godai ijin.* Tokyo: Rakuyōdō, 1917. http://kindai.ndl.go.jp/info:ndljp/pid/948504.

Takaku Reinosuke. *Kindai Nihon no chiiki shakai to meibōka.* Potentia sōsho 45. Tokyo: Kashiwa Shobō, 1997.

Takamura Kōzō, ed. *Shisei chōsonsei.* Kakegawa: Takamura Kōzō, 1888.

Tamari Kizō. "Nōgyō dantai ni tsuite." *Dai Nihon Nōkaihō,* no. 157 (1894): 1–38.

———. "Nōkai konjakudan (shōzen)." *Dai Nihon Nōkaihō,* no. 214 (1899): 1–8.

———. *Tōhoku shinkōsaku: Yamato minzoku no kankoku ni okeru hattensaku.* Tokyo: Zenkoku Nōjikai, 1904. http://dl.ndl.go.jp/info:ndljp/pid/802390.

Tanaka Kazuo. "Kindai Nihon no 'meibōka' zō: Chihō Kairyō Undō de no 'tokushika' to minshū." *Shakai kagaku,* no. 37 (1986): 250–282.

Tanaka Norio. "'Chihō kairyō' rinen no ichidanmen: Kansei 'chihō kairyō' undō no shūhen." *Dōshisha hōgaku* 30, no. 1 (1978): 115–160.

Teikoku Nōkai. *Tōhoku chihō nōson ni kansuru chōsa.* Tokyo: Teikoku Nōkai, 1933.

Titus, David Anson. *Palace and Politics in Prewar Japan.* New York: Columbia University Press, 1974.

Tōda Kyōikukai. *Tōda Gunshi.* Tokyo: Meicho Shuppan, 1972.

Tōhashi Shiritsu Shōgyō Gakkō. *Kaikō nijū shūnen kinen Higashimikawa sangyō kōrōshaden.* Tōhashi: Tōhashi Shiritsu Shōgyō Gakkō, 1943.

Tomita Kōji. *Inatori bidan: Shinkyōiku ikimohan.* Inatori: Tomita Kōji, 1907. http://kindai.ndl.go.jp/info:ndljp/pid/784536.

Tomoda Kiyohiko. "Meiji shoki no nōkai kessha to Dai Nihon Nōkai no sōsetu (1): Tōyō Nōkai to Tōkyō Dannōkai." *Nōson kenkyū,* no. 102 (2006): 1–14.

———. "Meiji shoki no nōkai kessha to Dai Nihon Nōkai no sōsetu (2): Tōyō Nōkai to Tōkyō Dannōkai." *Nōson kenkyū,* no. 103 (2006): 25–44.

Tsutsui Masao. "The Impact of the Local Improvement Movement on Farmers and Rural Communities." In *Farmers and Village Life in Twentieth-Century Japan,* edited by Ann Waswo and Yoshiaki Nishida, 60–78. New York: RoutledgeCurzon, 2003.

Uchida Tsukasa. "Nichiro Sengo keieishita ni okeru chōson shinkō to shizen mura: Miyagiken de no Chihō Kairyo Undō no tenkai o jirei to shite (2)." *Shakaigaku nenpō* 7 (1979): 19–33.

Uehara Nobuhiro. *Miyagken Senboku nōgyō chitai no kōsei.* Tokyo: Tochi Seido Shiryō Hozonkai, 1958.

Ushiki Yukio. *Chihō meibōka no seichō.* Tokyo: Kashiwa Shobō, 2000.

Wada Seima. *Kindaishi.* Miyagi kenshi 3. Sendai: Miyagi Kenshi Kankōkai, 1964.

Wakuyachō. *Wakuya chōshi.* Vol. 2. Wakuya: Wakuyachō, 1968.

"Waraji sonchō." *Tōkyō Asahi shinbun,* December 1, 1936.

Wasaki Kōzō and Yamazaki Harushige. "Nōgyō kyōkō kara sensō keizaika no nōgyō e." In *Nihon nōgyō hattatsushi: Meiji ikō ni okeru,* 8:2–72. Tokyo: Chūō Kōronsha, 1978.

Waswo, Ann. *Japanese Landlords: The Decline of a Rural Elite.* Berkeley: University of California Press, 1977.

Waswo, Ann, and Yoshiaki Nishida, eds. *Farmers and Village Life in Twentieth-Century Japan.* New York: RoutledgeCurzon, 2003.

Watanabe Takashi. *Kindai ikōki no meiboka to chiiki kokka.* Tokyo: Meicho Shuppan, 2006.

Waters, Neil L. *Japan's Local Pragmatists: The Transition from Bakumatsu to Meiji in the Kawasaki Region.* Harvard East Asian Monographs 105. Cambridge, MA: Council on East Asian Studies, Harvard University Press, 1983.

Wigen, Kären. "Constructing Shinano: The Invention of a Neo-Traditional Region." In *Mirror of Modernity: Invented Traditions of Modern Japan,* edited by Stephen Vlastos, 229–242. Twentieth-Century Japan 9. Berkeley: University of California Press, 1998.

Yamagata Aritomo. "Meiji sanjūninen nigatsu nijūyonnichi: shisei hōshin enzetsu." In *Yamagata Aritomo ikensho,* edited by Ōyama Azusa, 248–251. Meiji hyakunenshi sōsho 16. Tokyo: Hara Shobō, 1966.

Yamaguchi Kazuo. *Nihon keizaishi.* Tokyo: Chikuma Shobō, 1968.

Yamanaka Einosuke. *Kindai Nihon no chihō seido to meibōka.* Shohan. Tokyo: Kōbundō, 1990.

———. *Kindai shisei to toshi meibōka: Ōsakashi o jirei to suru kōsatsu.* Suita: Ōsaka Daigaku Shuppan, 1995.

Yamao Michio. "Miyagiken no nōgyō kaikaku." In *Sangyō 1,* 179–262. Miyagi kenshi 9. Sendai: Miyagi Kenshi Kankōkai, 1968.

Yamazaki Enkichi. *Chihō kairyō no hanashi.* Tokyo: Shōkabō, 1915. http://dl.ndl.go.jp/info:ndljp/pid/954881.

———. "Chihō kairyōdan." In *Chihō kairyō jigyō koenshū (ge),* edited by Naimushō Chihōkyoku. Tokyo: Naimushō Chihōkyoku, 1909.

Yamotochō. *Yamoto chōshi.* Vol. 3. Yamoto: Yamotochō, 1976.

Yanagita Kunio. "Chūnō yōseisaku." In *Nōsei ronshū: Yanagita Kunio,* edited by Fujii Takashi, 20–52. Tokyo: Hōsei Daigaku Shuppankyoku, 1975.

———. "Inaka tai tokai no mondai." In *Jidai to nōsei,* 39–83. Tokyo: Shūseidō, 1910.

Yasuda Ken. "Meijiki ni okeru kanfu no inasaku shidō." In *Nihon nōgyō hattatsushi: Meiji ikō ni okeru,* 5:9–122. Tokyo: Chūō Kōronsha, 1978.

———. "Nakamura Naozō no nōji kairyō jiseki." In *Nihon nōgyō hattatsushi: Meiji ikō ni okeru,* 2:703–731. Tokyo: Chūō Kōronsha, 1978.

Yokoi Tokiyoshi. "Jinushi ni taisuru keikoku." In *Daiichi nōgyō jiron: Nōson angya sanjūnen,* 153–159. Meiji Taishō nōsei keizai meichoshū 17. Tokyo: Nōsangyoson Bunka Kyōkai, 1976.

———. *Mohan chōson.* Tokyo: Yomiuri Shinbunsha, 1907. http://dl.ndl.go.jp/info:ndljp/pid/888488.

Yonekura Tatsujirō. *Miyagi kusanone undō no gunzō.* Sendai: Shakai Undō Kenkyūkai, 1984.

Young, Louise. *Japan's Total Empire: Manchuria and the Culture of Wartime Imperialism.* Berkeley: University of California Press, 1998.

Index

About the Author

Christopher Craig is associate professor of Japanese history in the Department of Innovative Japanese Studies at Tohoku University. He received a bachelor's degree and a master's degree in history at the University of British Columbia, and a PhD in history from Columbia University. His research interests include modern Japanese agriculture, colonial migration, and the history of disasters. He has published articles and chapters in journals and anthologies and has co-edited the books *Furusato: Home at the Nexus of History, Art, Society, and Self* (2020); *311: Disaster and Trauma in Experience, Understanding, and Imagination* (2019); *Knowledge and Arts on the Move: Transformations of the Self-Aware Image Through East-West Encounters* (2018); and *How to Learn? Nippon/Japan as Object, Nippon/Japan as Method* (2017).

Studies of the Weatherhead East Asian Institute

Columbia University

Selected Titles

(Complete list at: https://weai.columbia.edu/content/publications/)

Recovering Histories: Life and Labor after Heroin in Reform-Era China, by Nicholas Bartlett. University of California Press, 2020.

A Third Way: The Origins of China's Current Economic Development Strategy, by Lawrence Chris Reardon. Harvard University Asia Center, 2020.

Disruptions of Daily Life: Japanese Literary Modernism in the World, by Arthur M. Mitchell. Cornell University Press, 2020.

Figures of the World: The Naturalist Novel and Transnational Form, by Christopher Laing Hill. Northwestern University Press, 2020.

Arbiters of Patriotism: Right-Wing Scholars in Imperial Japan, by John Person. University of Hawai'i Press, 2020.

The Chinese Revolution on the Tibetan Frontier, by Benno Weiner. Cornell University Press, 2020.

Making It Count: Statistics and Statecraft in the Early People's Republic of China, by Arunabh Ghosh. Princeton University Press, 2020.

Tea War: A History of Capitalism in China and India, by Andrew B. Liu. Yale University Press, 2020.

Revolution Goes East: Imperial Japan and Soviet Communism, by Tatiana Linkhoeva. Cornell University Press, 2020.

Vernacular Industrialism in China: Local Innovation and Translated Technologies in the Making of a Cosmetics Empire, 1900–1940, by Eugenia Lean. Columbia University Press, 2020.

Fighting for Virtue: Justice and Politics in Thailand, by Duncan McCargo. Cornell University Press, 2020.

Beyond the Steppe Frontier: A History of the Sino-Russian Border, by Sören Urbansky. Princeton University Press, 2020.

Pirates and Publishers: A Social History of Copyright in Modern China, by Fei-Hsien Wang. Princeton University Press, 2019.

The Typographic Imagination: Reading and Writing in Japan's Age of Modern Print Media, by Nathan Shockey. Columbia University Press, 2019.

Down and Out in Saigon: Stories of the Poor in a Colonial City, by Haydon Cherry. Yale University Press, 2019.

Beauty in the Age of Empire: Japan, Egypt, and the Global History of Aesthetic Education, by Raja Adal. Columbia University Press, 2019.

Mass Vaccination: Citizens' Bodies and State Power in Modern China, by Mary Augusta Brazelton. Cornell University Press, 2019.

Residual Futures: The Urban Ecologies of Literary and Visual Media of 1960s and 1970s Japan, by Franz Prichard. Columbia University Press, 2019.

The Making of Japanese Settler Colonialism: Malthusianism and Trans-Pacific Migration, 1868–1961, by Sidney Xu Lu. Cambridge University Press, 2019.

The Power of Print in Modern China: Intellectuals and Industrial Publishing from the end of Empire to Maoist State Socialism, by Robert Culp. Columbia University Press, 2019.

Beyond the Asylum: Mental Illness in French Colonial Vietnam, by Claire E. Edington. Cornell University Press, 2019.

Borderland Memories: Searching for Historical Identity in Post-Mao China, by Martin Fromm. Cambridge University Press, 2019.

Arc of Containment: Britain, the United States, and Anticommunism in Southeast Asia, by Wen-Qing Ngoei. Cornell University Press, 2019.

Sovereignty Experiments: Korean Migrants and the Building of Borders in Northeast Asia, 1860–1949, by Alyssa M. Park. Cornell University Press, 2019.

The Greater East Asia Co-Prosperity Sphere: When Total Empire Met Total War, by Jeremy A. Yellen. Cornell University Press, 2019.

Thought Crime: Ideology and State Power in Interwar Japan, by Max Ward. Duke University Press, 2019.

Statebuilding by Imposition: Resistance and Control in Colonial Taiwan and the Philippines, by Reo Matsuzaki. Cornell University Press, 2019.

Nation-Empire: Ideology and Rural Youth Mobilization in Japan and Its Colonies, by Sayaka Chatani. Cornell University Press, 2019.

Fixing Landscape: A Techno-Poetic History of China's Three Gorges, by Corey Byrnes. Columbia University Press, 2019.